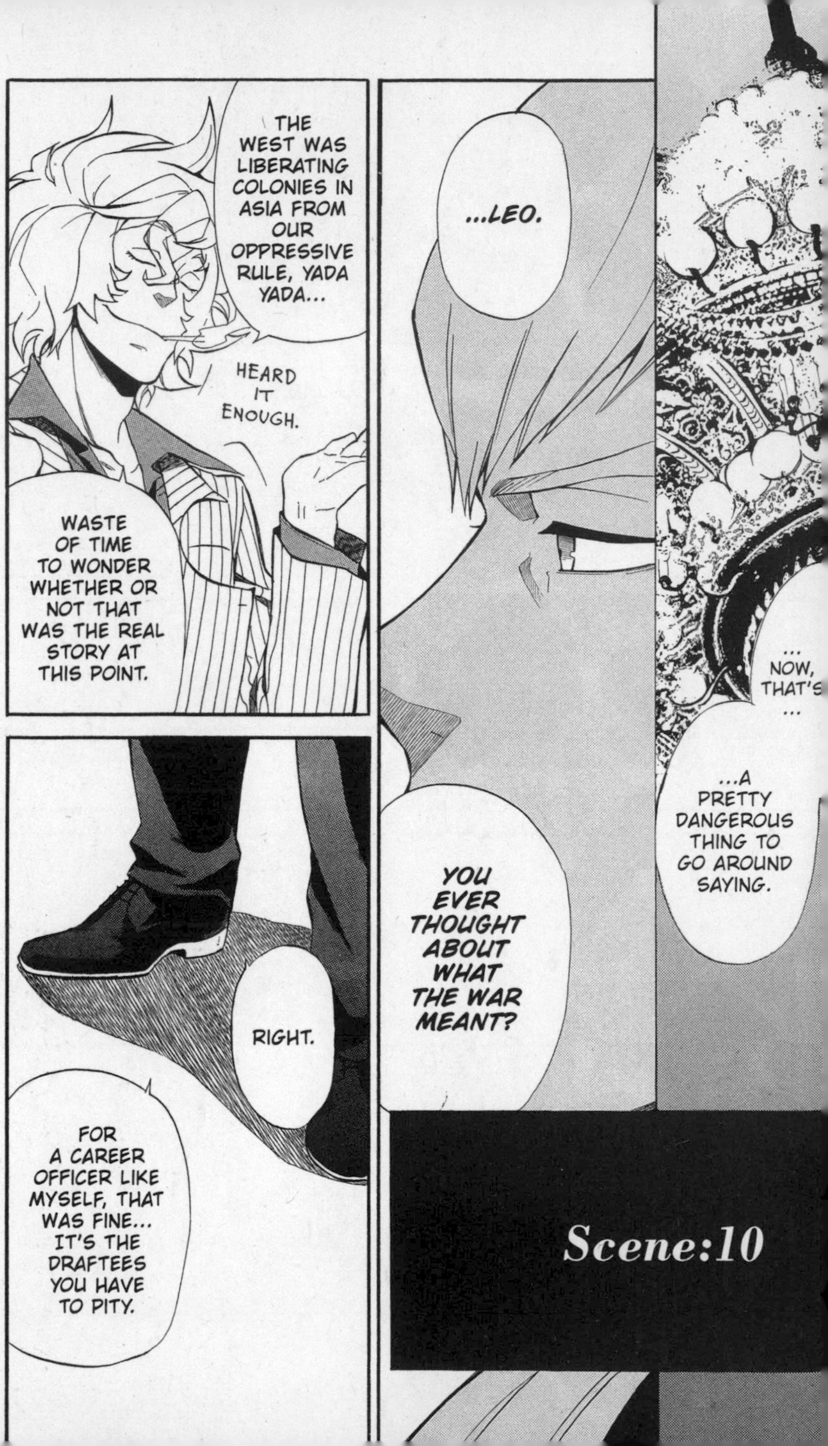

... NOW, THAT'S ...
...A PRETTY DANGEROUS THING TO GO AROUND SAYING.
...LEO.
YOU EVER THOUGHT ABOUT WHAT THE WAR MEANT?
Scene:10
THE WEST WAS LIBERATING COLONIES IN ASIA FROM OUR OPPRESSIVE RULE, YADA YADA...
HEARD IT ENOUGH.
WASTE OF TIME TO WONDER WHETHER OR NOT THAT WAS THE REAL STORY AT THIS POINT.
RIGHT.
FOR A CAREER OFFICER LIKE MYSELF, THAT WAS FINE... IT'S THE DRAFTEES YOU HAVE TO PITY.

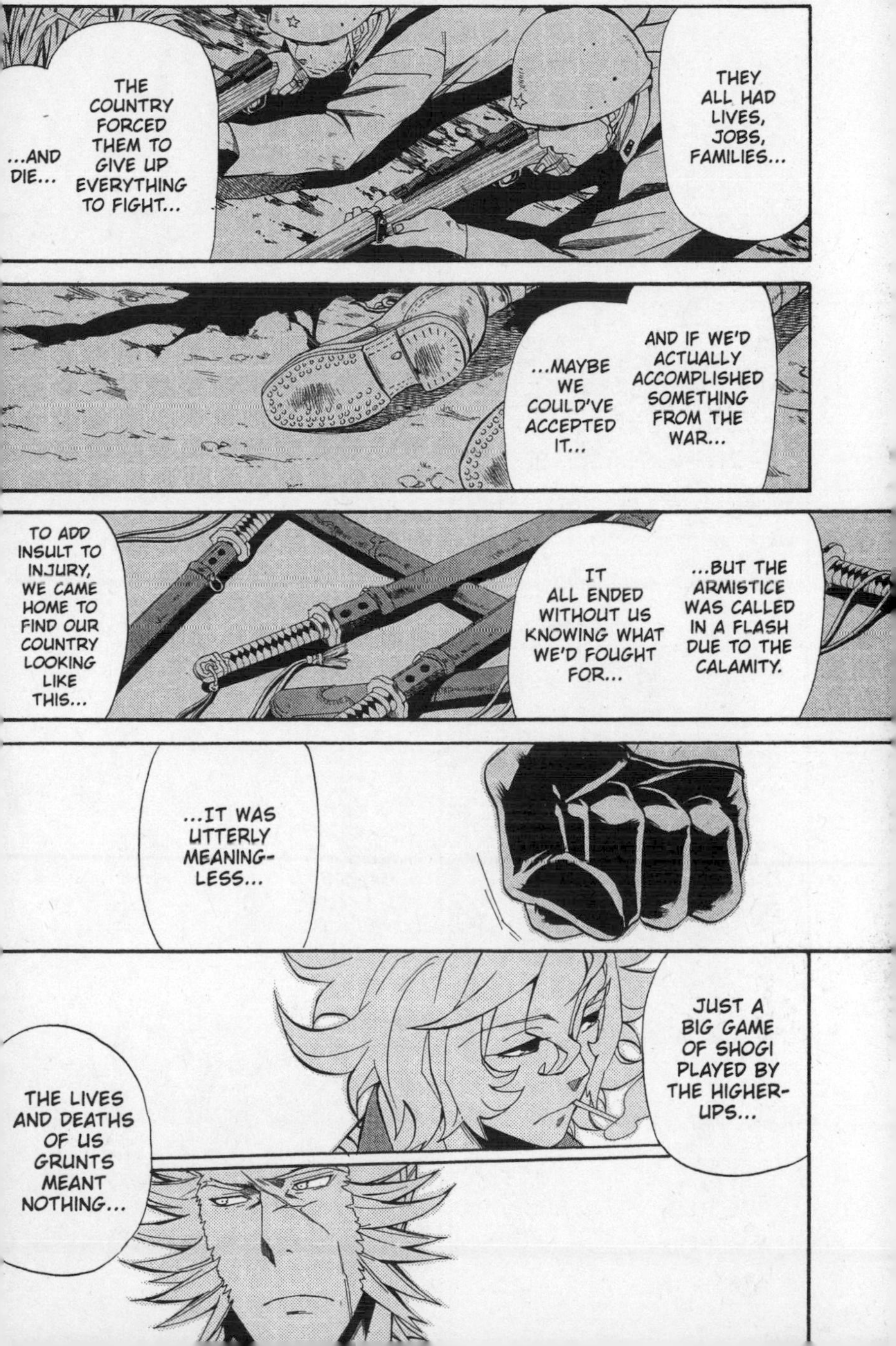
THEY ALL HAD LIVES, JOBS, FAMILIES...
THE COUNTRY FORCED THEM TO GIVE UP EVERYTHING TO FIGHT...
...AND DIE...
AND IF WE'D ACTUALLY ACCOMPLISHED SOMETHING FROM THE WAR...
...MAYBE WE COULD'VE ACCEPTED IT...
...BUT THE ARMISTICE WAS CALLED IN A FLASH DUE TO THE CALAMITY.
IT ALL ENDED WITHOUT US KNOWING WHAT WE'D FOUGHT FOR...
TO ADD INSULT TO INJURY, WE CAME HOME TO FIND OUR COUNTRY LOOKING LIKE THIS...
...IT WAS UTTERLY MEANINGLESS...
JUST A BIG GAME OF SHOGI PLAYED BY THE HIGHER-UPS...
THE LIVES AND DEATHS OF US GRUNTS MEANT NOTHING...

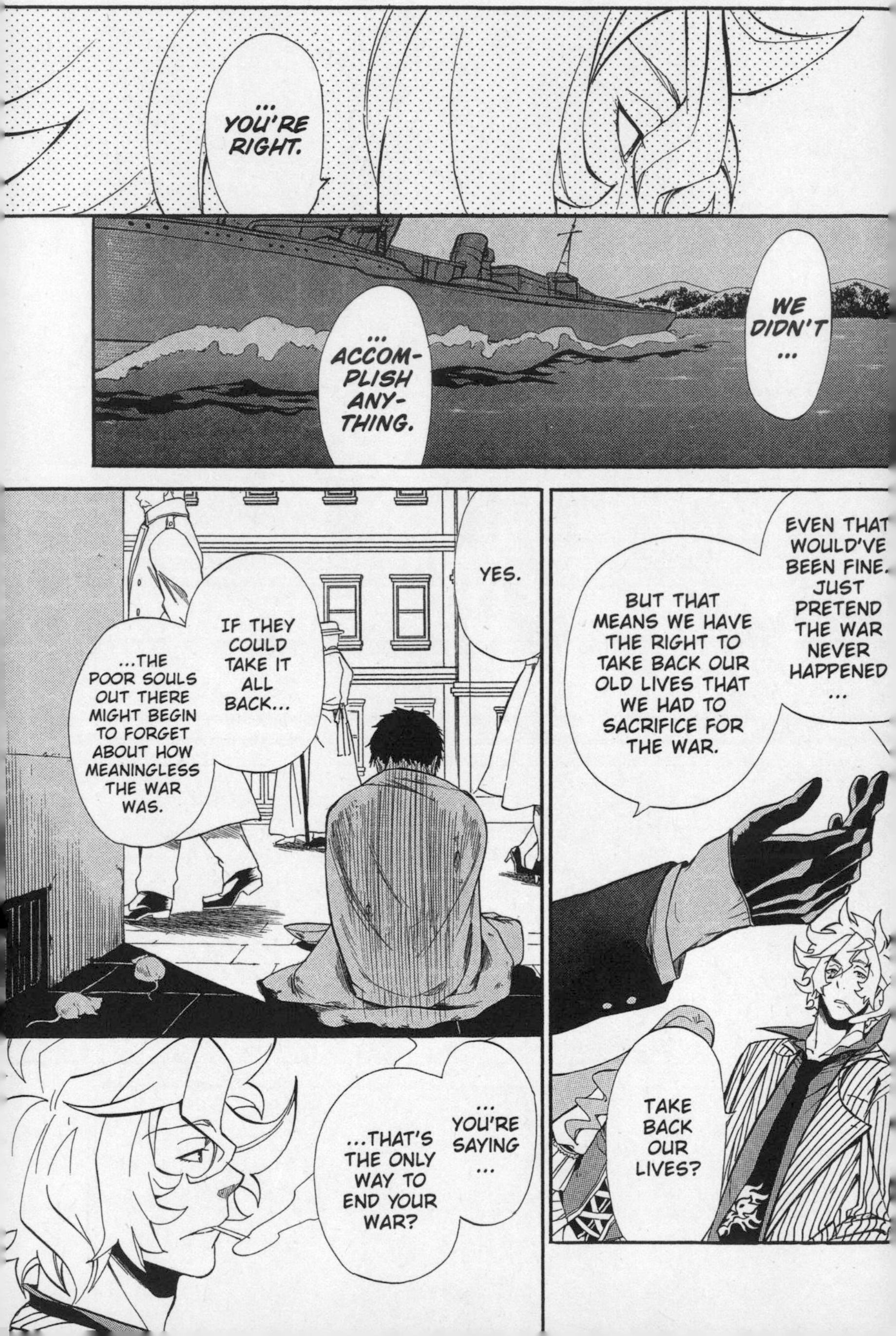
...YOU'RE RIGHT.
WE DIDN'T ...
...ACCOMPLISH ANYTHING.
EVEN THAT WOULD'VE BEEN FINE. JUST PRETEND THE WAR NEVER HAPPENED ...
BUT THAT MEANS WE HAVE THE RIGHT TO TAKE BACK OUR OLD LIVES THAT WE HAD TO SACRIFICE FOR THE WAR.
TAKE BACK OUR LIVES?
YES.
IF THEY COULD TAKE IT ALL BACK...
...THE POOR SOULS OUT THERE MIGHT BEGIN TO FORGET ABOUT HOW MEANINGLESS THE WAR WAS.
...YOU'RE SAYING ...
...THAT'S THE ONLY WAY TO END YOUR WAR?

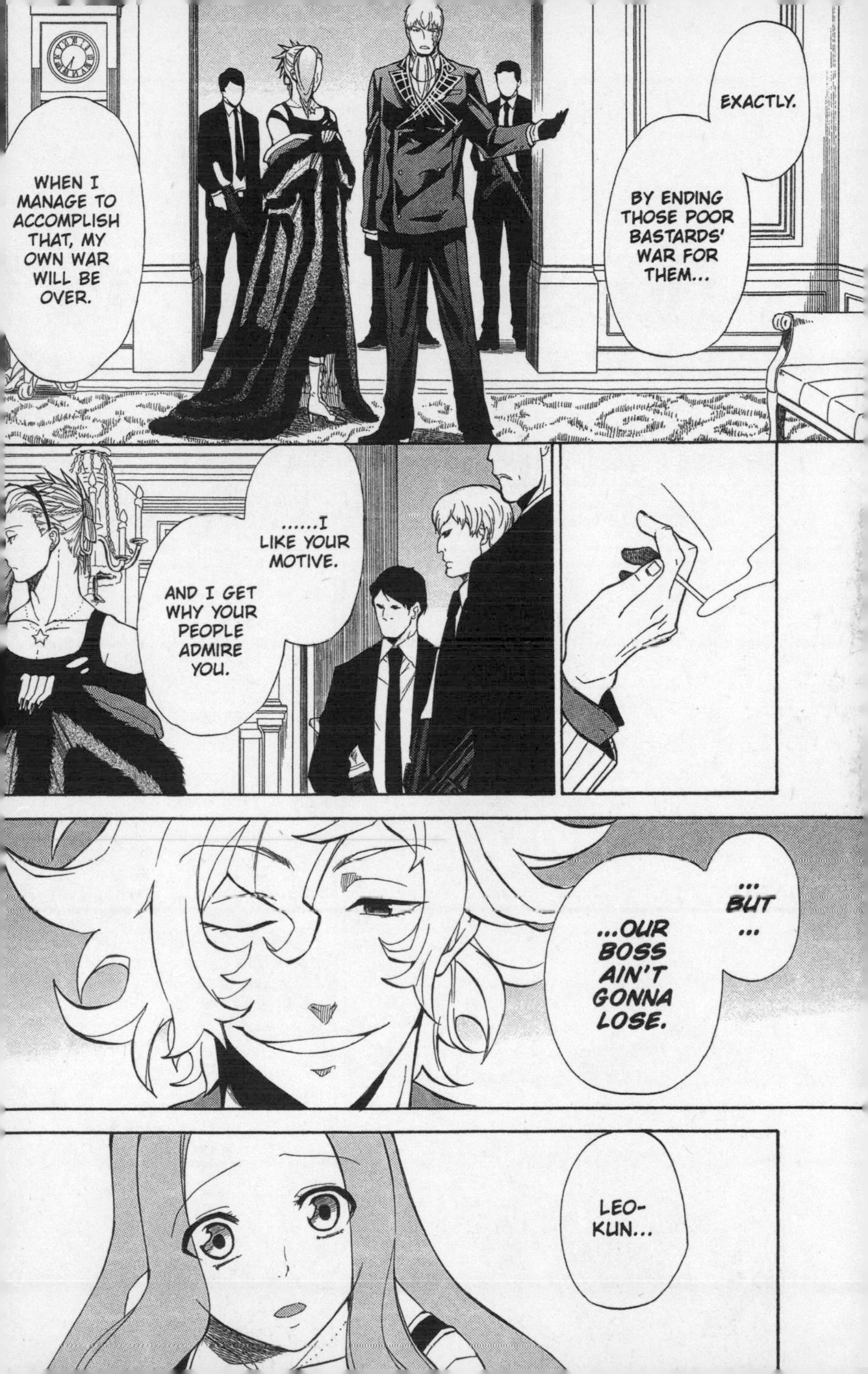
EXACTLY.
BY ENDING THOSE POOR BASTARDS' WAR FOR THEM...
WHEN I MANAGE TO ACCOMPLISH THAT, MY OWN WAR WILL BE OVER.
......I LIKE YOUR MOTIVE.
AND I GET WHY YOUR PEOPLE ADMIRE YOU.
...BUT...
...OUR BOSS AIN'T GONNA LOSE.
LEO-KUN...

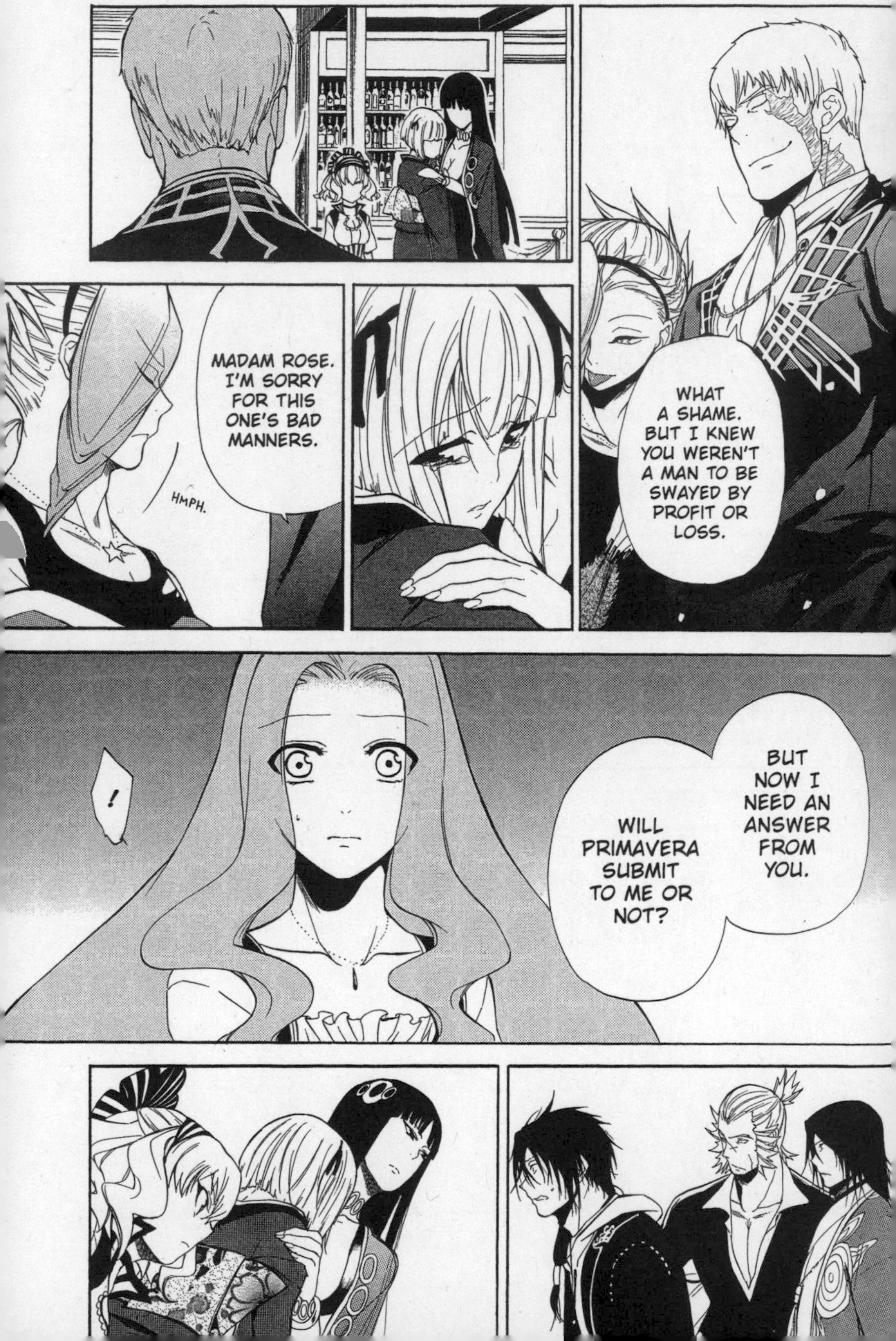
WHAT A SHAME. BUT I KNEW YOU WEREN'T A MAN TO BE SWAYED BY PROFIT OR LOSS.
MADAM ROSE. I'M SORRY FOR THIS ONE'S BAD MANNERS.
HMPH.
BUT NOW I NEED AN ANSWER FROM YOU.
WILL PRIMAVERA SUBMIT TO ME OR NOT?
!

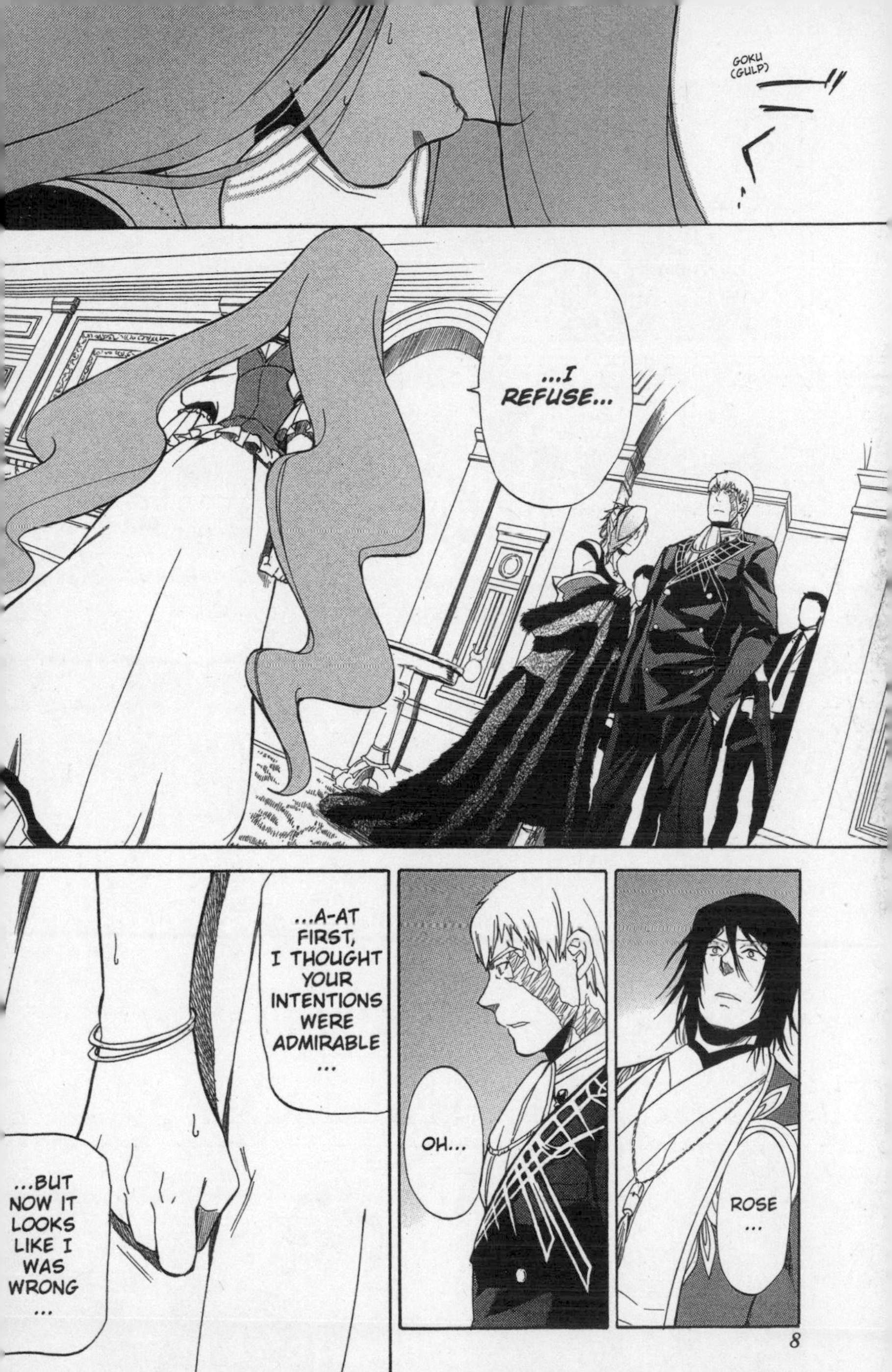

GOKU (GULP)
...I REFUSE...
ROSE ...
OH...
...A-AT FIRST, I THOUGHT YOUR INTENTIONS WERE ADMIRABLE ...
...BUT NOW IT LOOKS LIKE I WAS WRONG ...

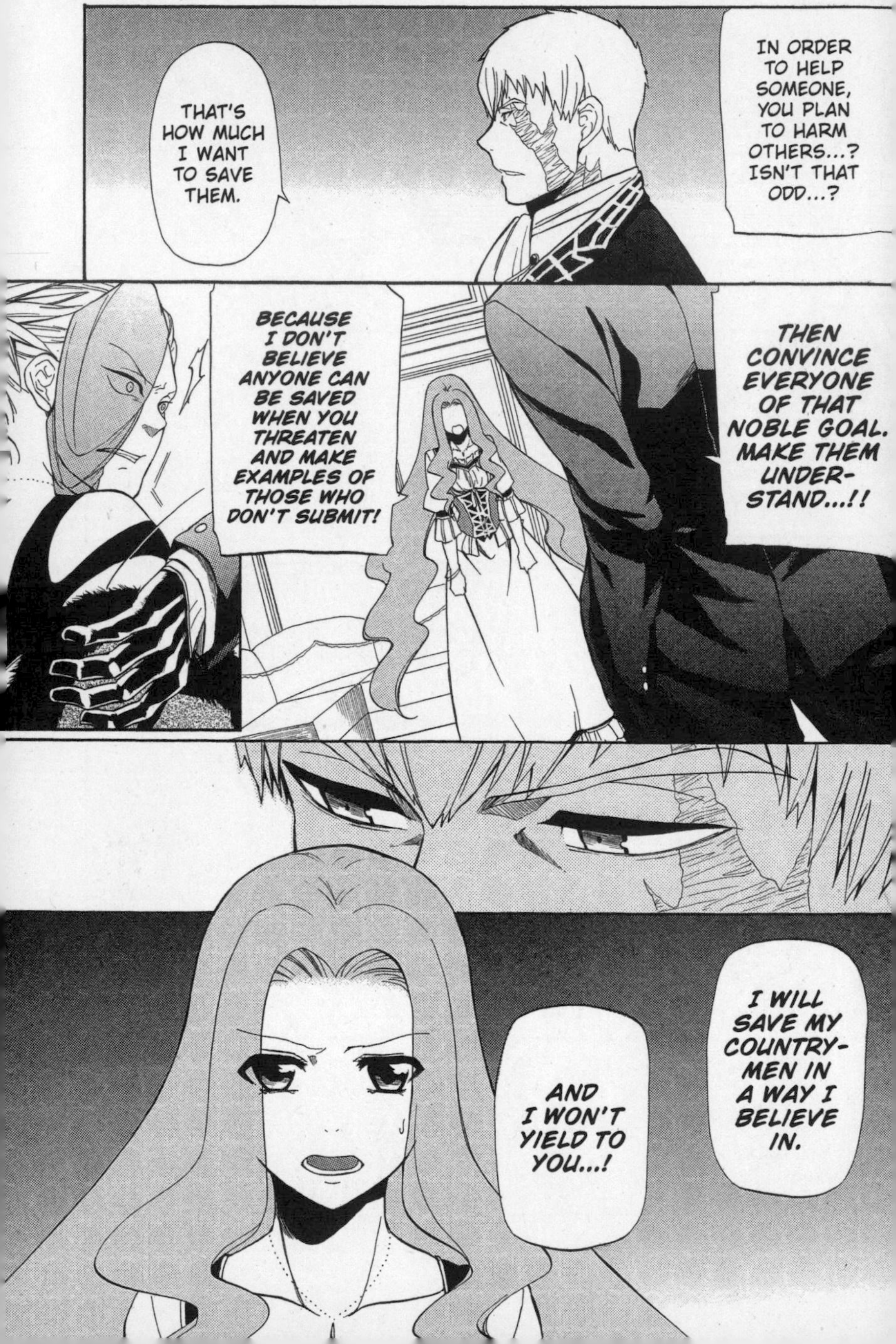
IN ORDER TO HELP SOMEONE, YOU PLAN TO HARM OTHERS...? ISN'T THAT ODD...?
THAT'S HOW MUCH I WANT TO SAVE THEM.
THEN CONVINCE EVERYONE OF THAT NOBLE GOAL. MAKE THEM UNDER-STAND...!!
BECAUSE I DON'T BELIEVE ANYONE CAN BE SAVED WHEN YOU THREATEN AND MAKE EXAMPLES OF THOSE WHO DON'T SUBMIT!
I WILL SAVE MY COUNTRY-MEN IN A WAY I BELIEVE IN.
AND I WON'T YIELD TO YOU...!

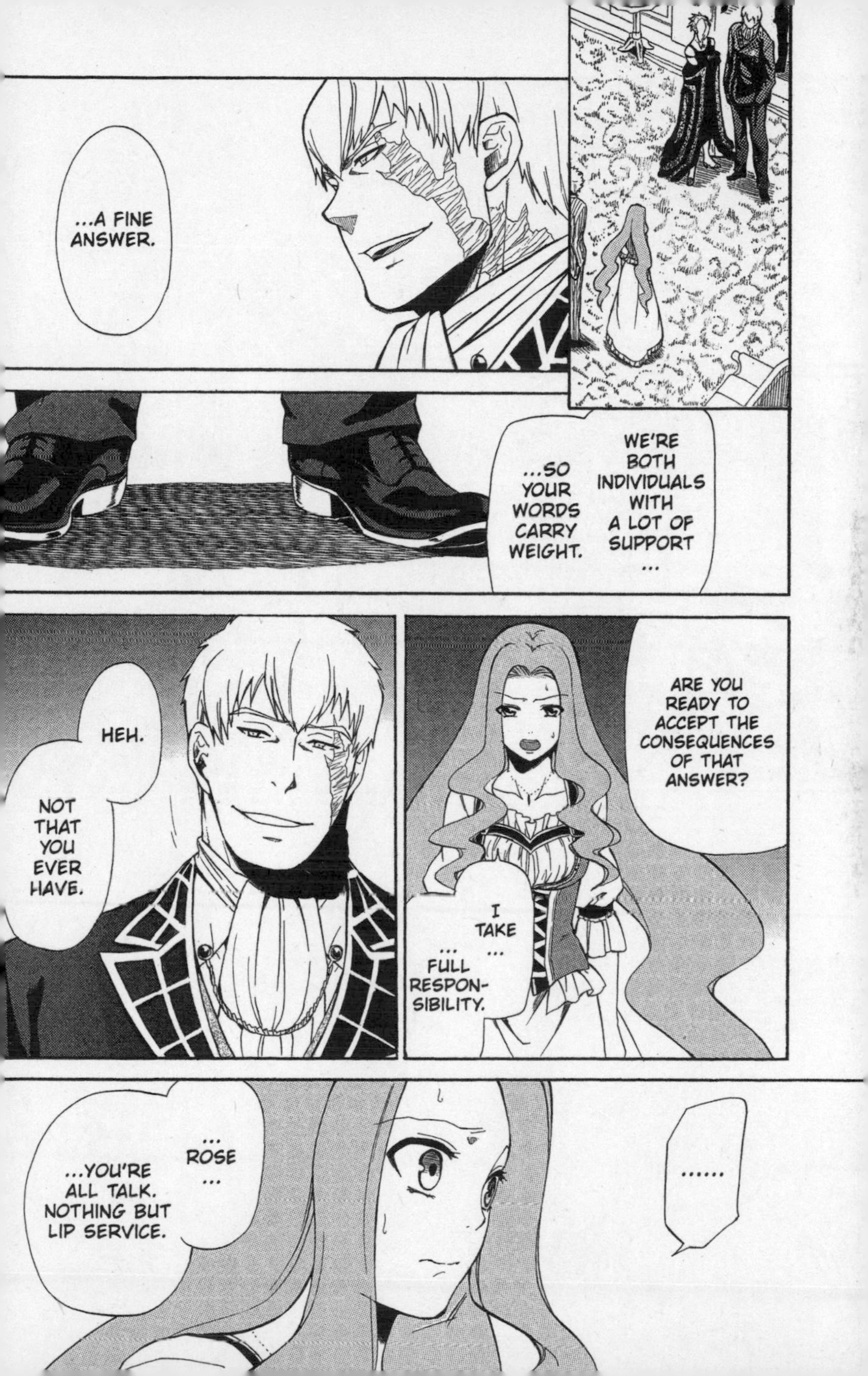
...A FINE ANSWER.
WE'RE BOTH INDIVIDUALS WITH A LOT OF SUPPORT ...
...SO YOUR WORDS CARRY WEIGHT.
ARE YOU READY TO ACCEPT THE CONSEQUENCES OF THAT ANSWER?
I TAKE ... ... FULL RESPONSIBILITY.
HEH.
NOT THAT YOU EVER HAVE.
......
... ROSE ...
...YOU'RE ALL TALK. NOTHING BUT LIP SERVICE.

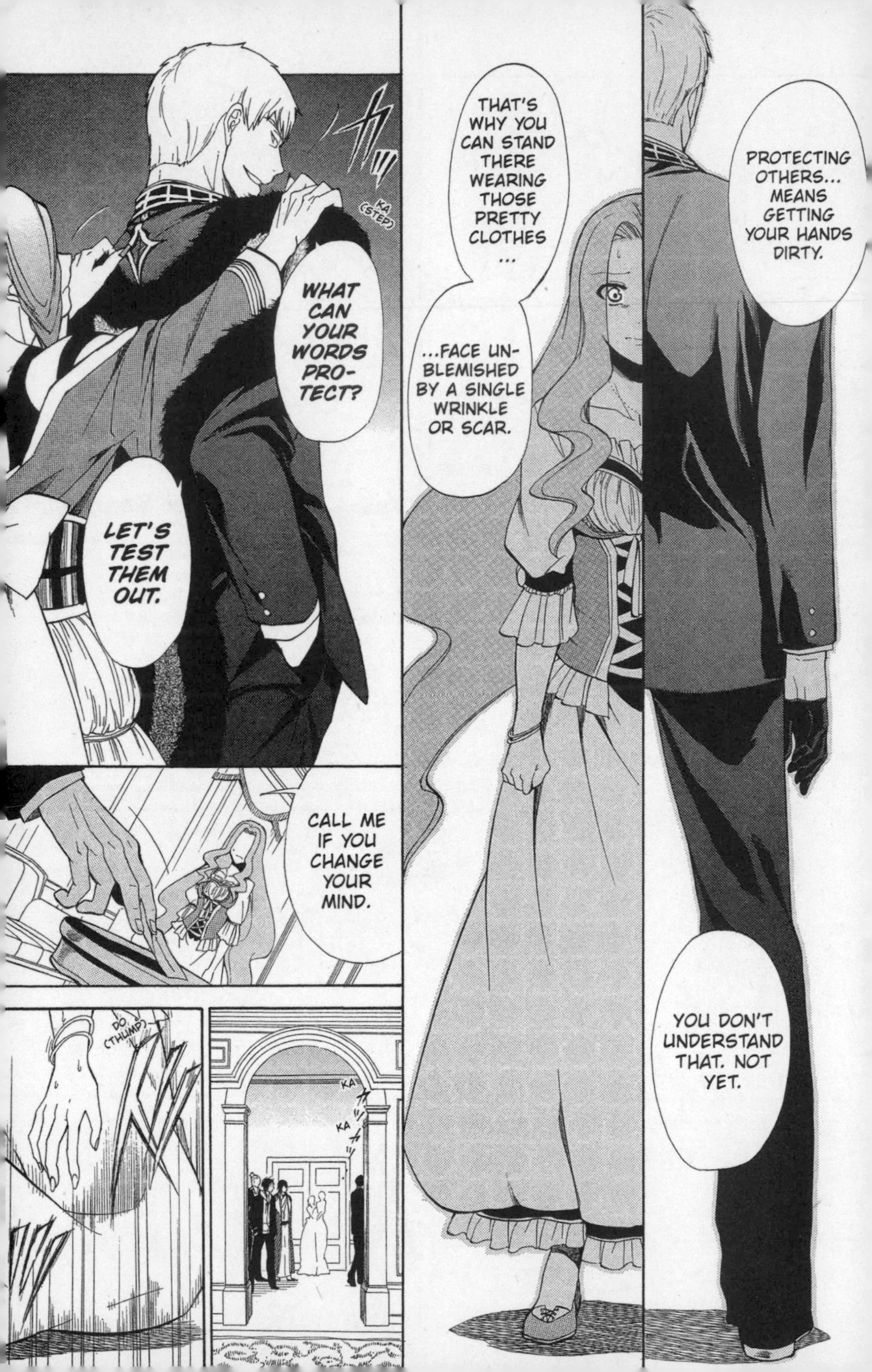
PROTECTING OTHERS... MEANS GETTING YOUR HANDS DIRTY.
YOU DON'T UNDERSTAND THAT. NOT YET.
THAT'S WHY YOU CAN STAND THERE WEARING THOSE PRETTY CLOTHES ...
...FACE UN-BLEMISHED BY A SINGLE WRINKLE OR SCAR.
KA (STEP)
WHAT CAN YOUR WORDS PRO-TECT?
LET'S TEST THEM OUT.
CALL ME IF YOU CHANGE YOUR MIND.
KA
KA
DO (THUMP)

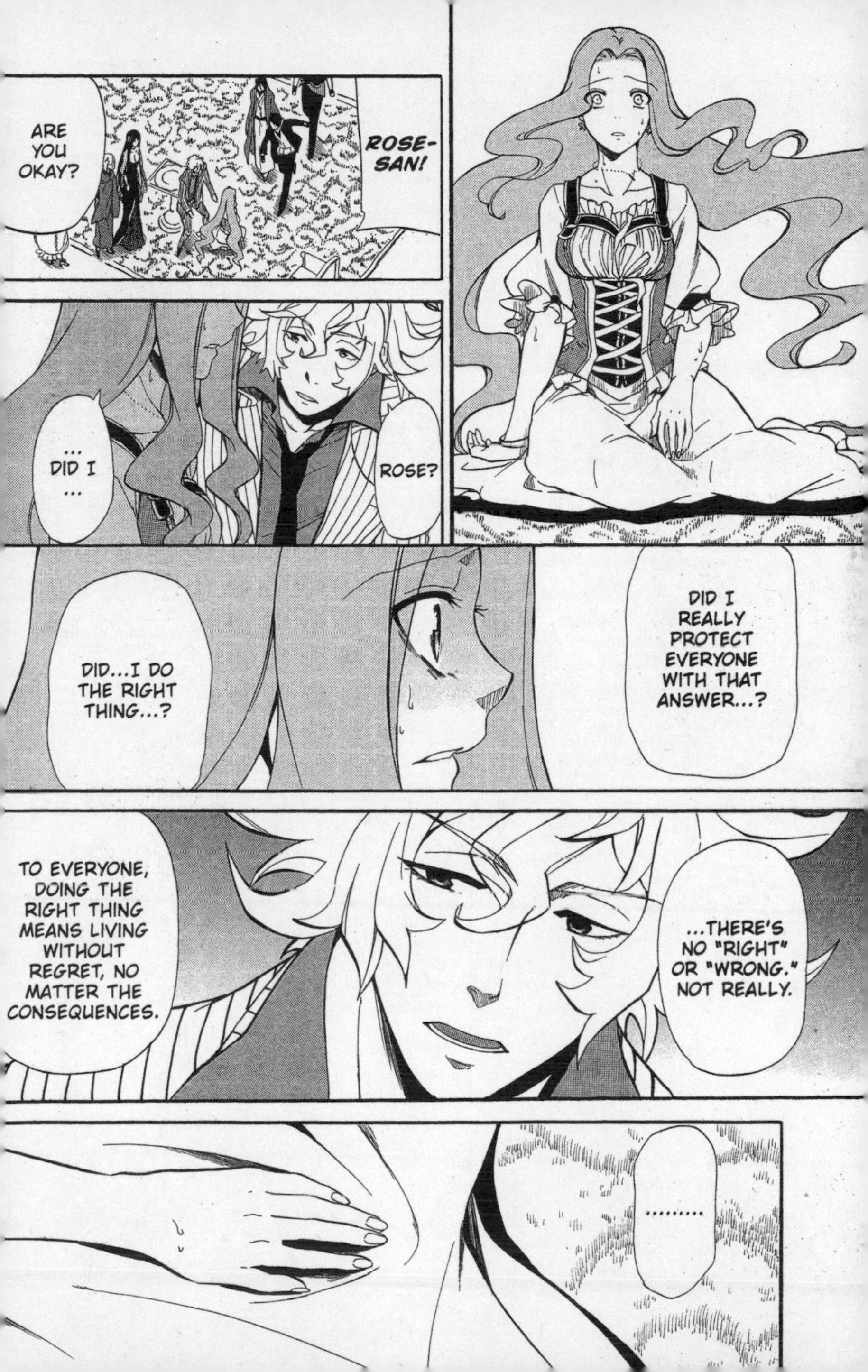
ROSE-SAN!
ARE YOU OKAY?
ROSE?
... DID I ...
DID I REALLY PROTECT EVERYONE WITH THAT ANSWER...?
DID...I DO THE RIGHT THING...?
...THERE'S NO "RIGHT" OR "WRONG." NOT REALLY.
TO EVERYONE, DOING THE RIGHT THING MEANS LIVING WITHOUT REGRET, NO MATTER THE CONSEQUENCES.
....

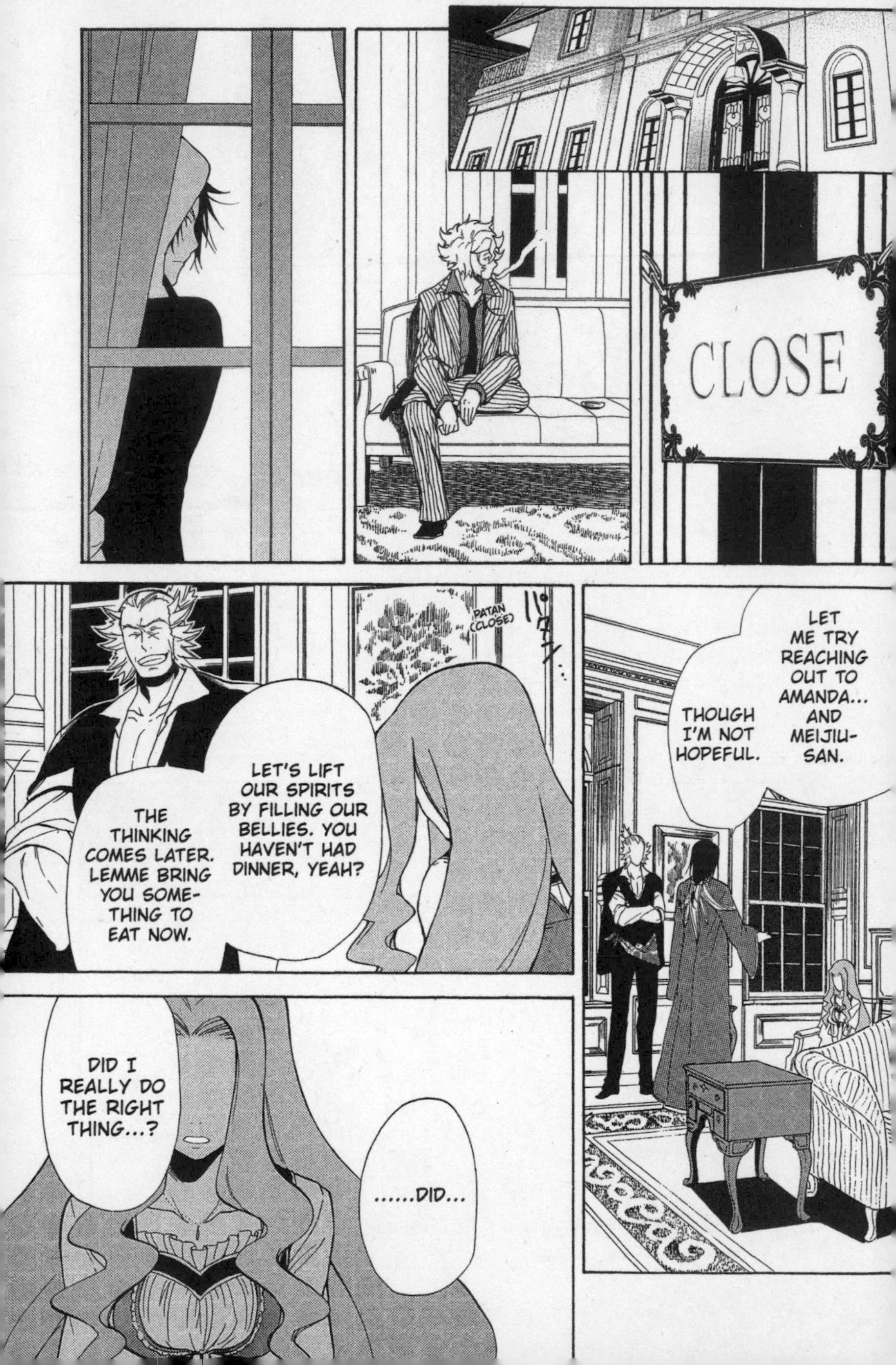
CLOSE
LET ME TRY REACHING OUT TO AMANDA... AND MEIJIU-SAN.
THOUGH I'M NOT HOPEFUL.
PATAN (CLOSE)
LET'S LIFT OUR SPIRITS BY FILLING OUR BELLIES. YOU HAVEN'T HAD DINNER, YEAH?
THE THINKING COMES LATER. LEMME BRING YOU SOME-THING TO EAT NOW.
DID I REALLY DO THE RIGHT THING...?
......DID...

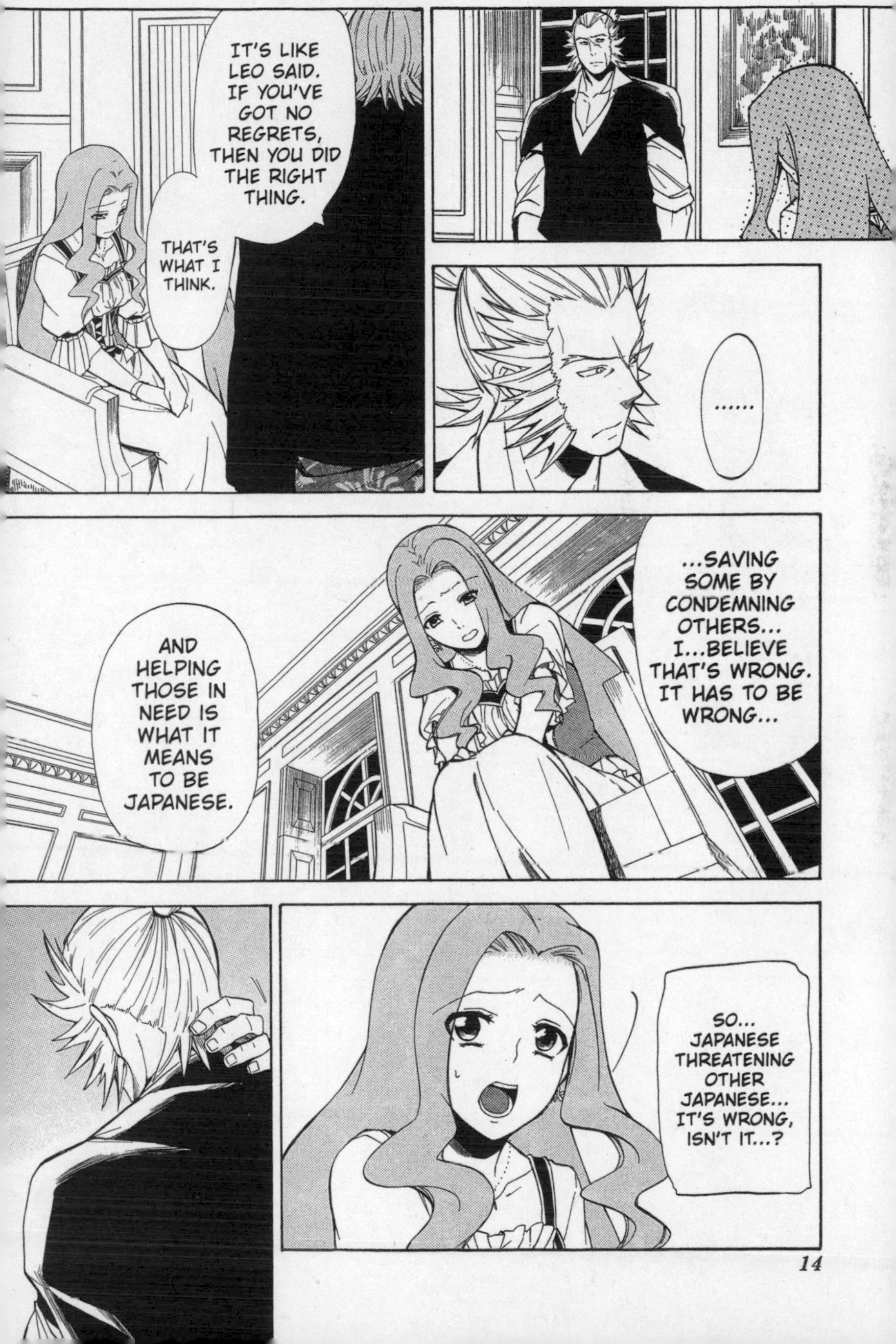
......
IT'S LIKE LEO SAID. IF YOU'VE GOT NO REGRETS, THEN YOU DID THE RIGHT THING.
THAT'S WHAT I THINK.
...SAVING SOME BY CONDEMNING OTHERS... I...BELIEVE THAT'S WRONG. IT HAS TO BE WRONG...
AND HELPING THOSE IN NEED IS WHAT IT MEANS TO BE JAPANESE.
SO... JAPANESE THREATENING OTHER JAPANESE... IT'S WRONG, ISN'T IT...?

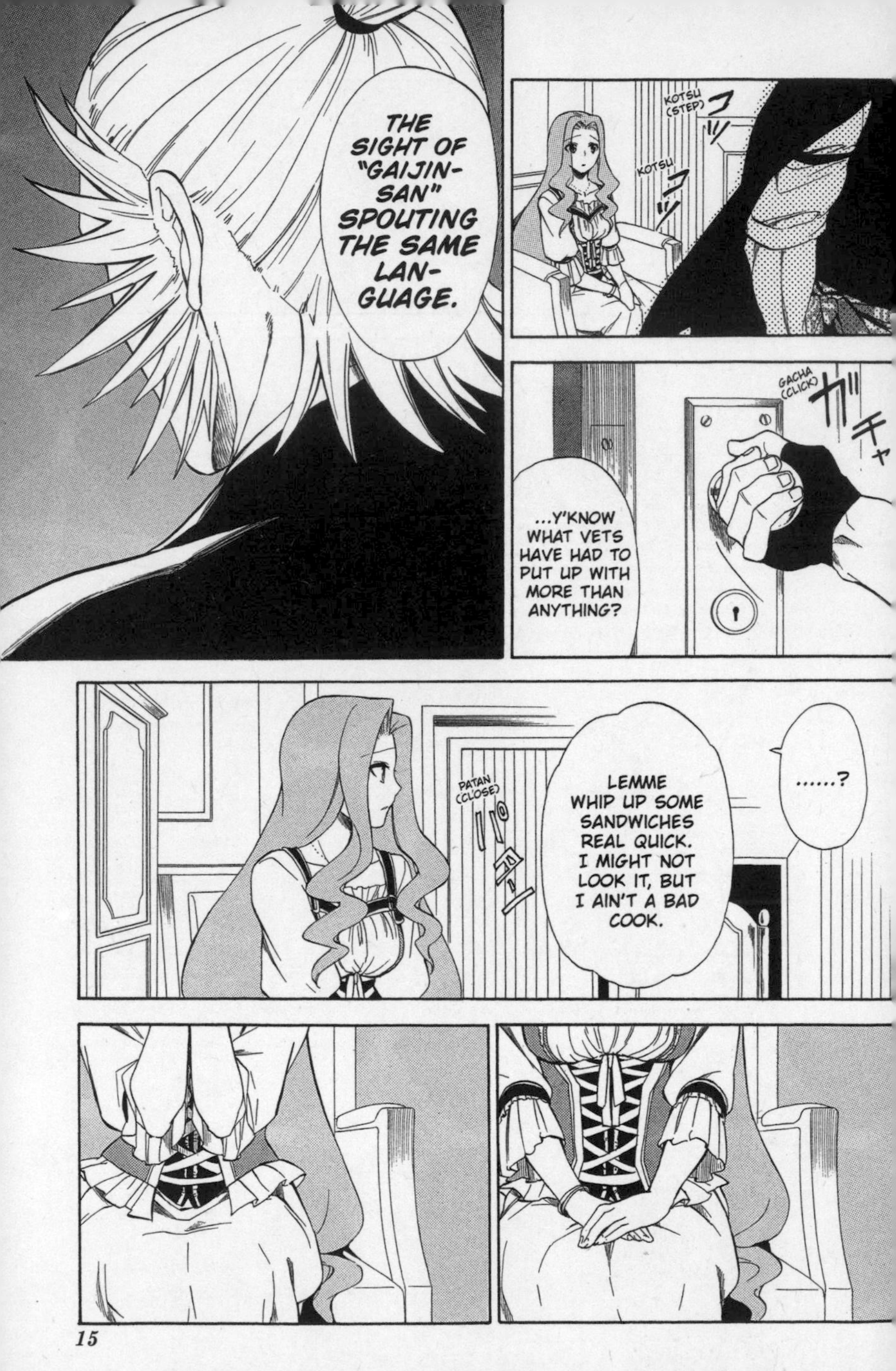
KOTSU (STEP)
KOTSU
GACHA (CLICK)
...Y'KNOW WHAT VETS HAVE HAD TO PUT UP WITH MORE THAN ANYTHING?
THE SIGHT OF "GAIJIN-SAN" SPOUTING THE SAME LAN-GUAGE.
......?
LEMME WHIP UP SOME SANDWICHES REAL QUICK. I MIGHT NOT LOOK IT, BUT I AIN'T A BAD COOK.
PATAN (CLOSE)

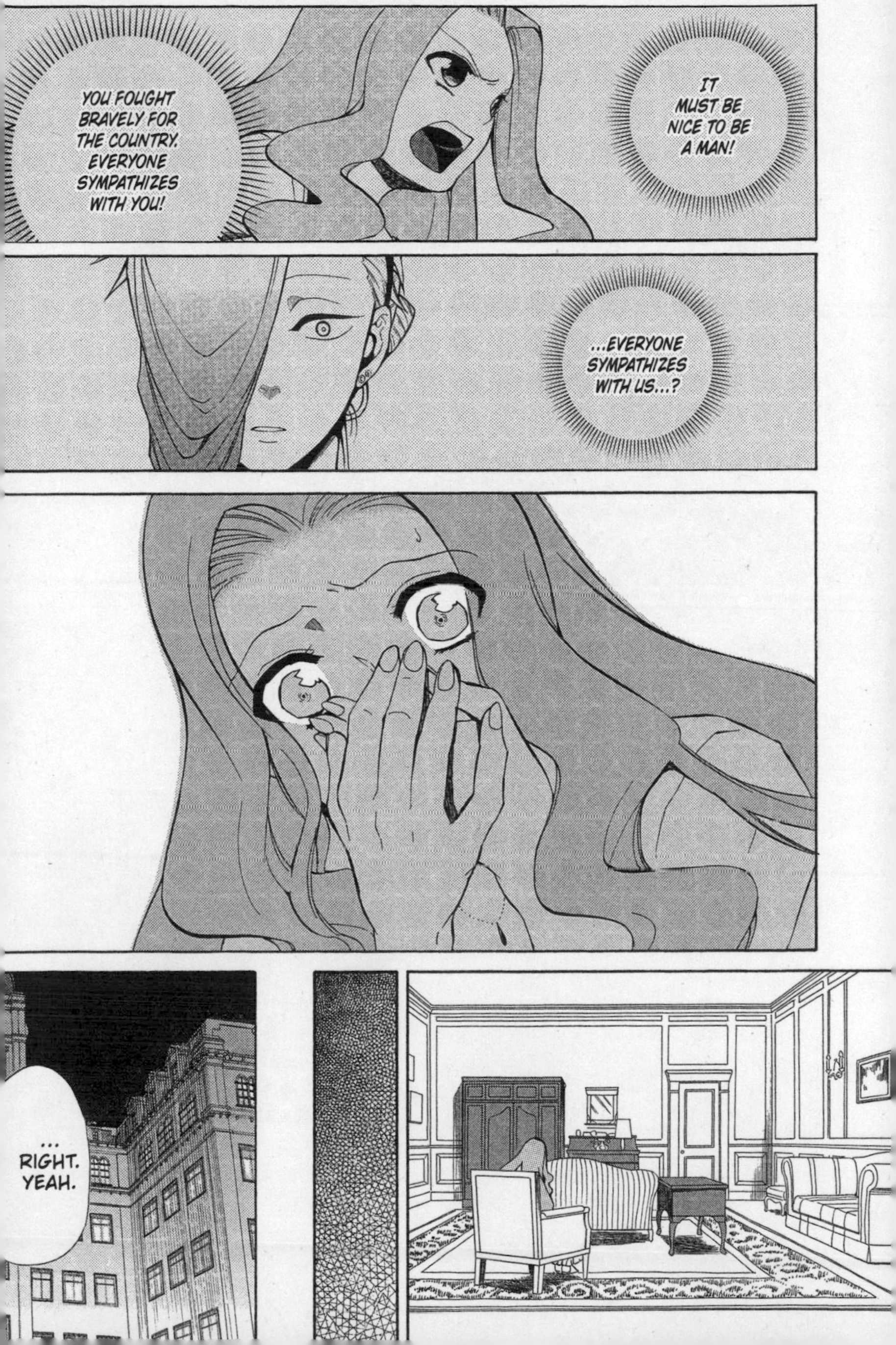
IT MUST BE NICE TO BE A MAN!
YOU FOUGHT BRAVELY FOR THE COUNTRY. EVERYONE SYMPATHIZES WITH YOU!
...EVERYONE SYMPATHIZES WITH US...?
... RIGHT. YEAH.

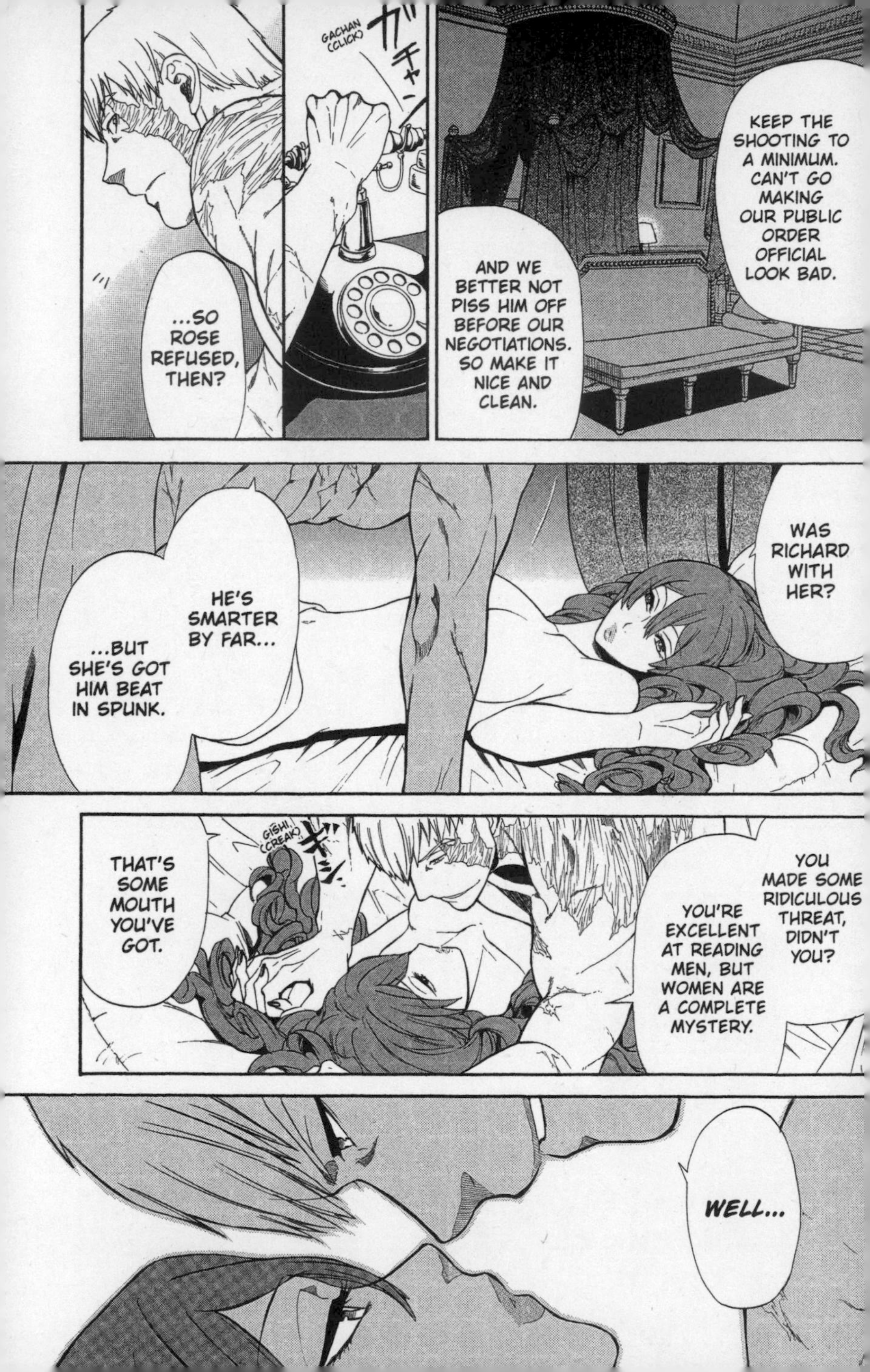
KEEP THE SHOOTING TO A MINIMUM. CAN'T GO MAKING OUR PUBLIC ORDER OFFICIAL LOOK BAD.
AND WE BETTER NOT PISS HIM OFF BEFORE OUR NEGOTIATIONS. SO MAKE IT NICE AND CLEAN.
GACHAN (CLICK)
...SO ROSE REFUSED, THEN?
WAS RICHARD WITH HER?
HE'S SMARTER BY FAR...
...BUT SHE'S GOT HIM BEAT IN SPUNK.
YOU MADE SOME RIDICULOUS THREAT, DIDN'T YOU?
YOU'RE EXCELLENT AT READING MEN, BUT WOMEN ARE A COMPLETE MYSTERY.
GISHI (CREAK)
THAT'S SOME MOUTH YOU'VE GOT.
WELL...

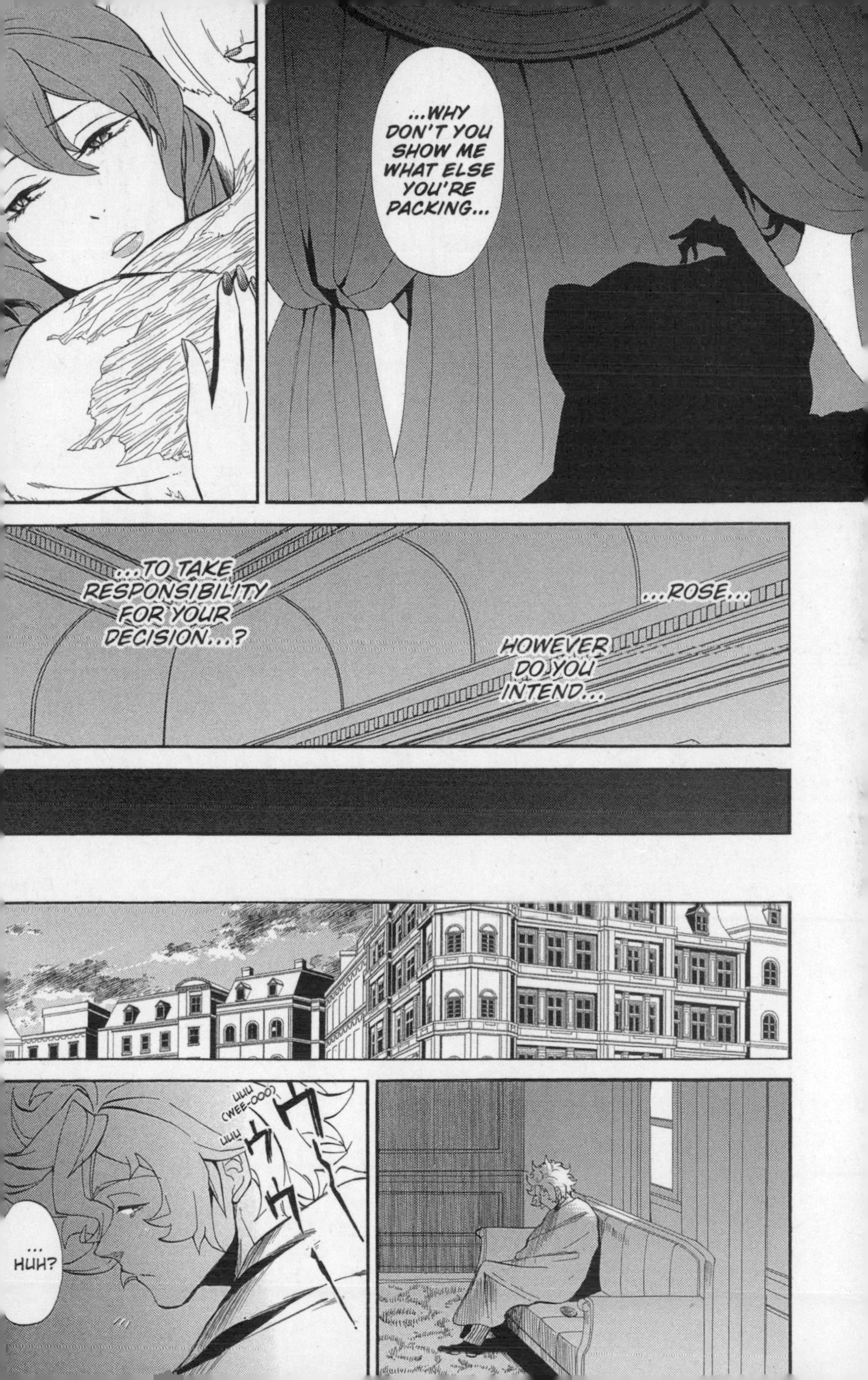
...WHY DON'T YOU SHOW ME WHAT ELSE YOU'RE PACKING...
...ROSE...
HOWEVER DO YOU INTEND...
...TO TAKE RESPONSIBILITY FOR YOUR DECISION...?
UUU (WEE-OOO) UUU
... HUH?

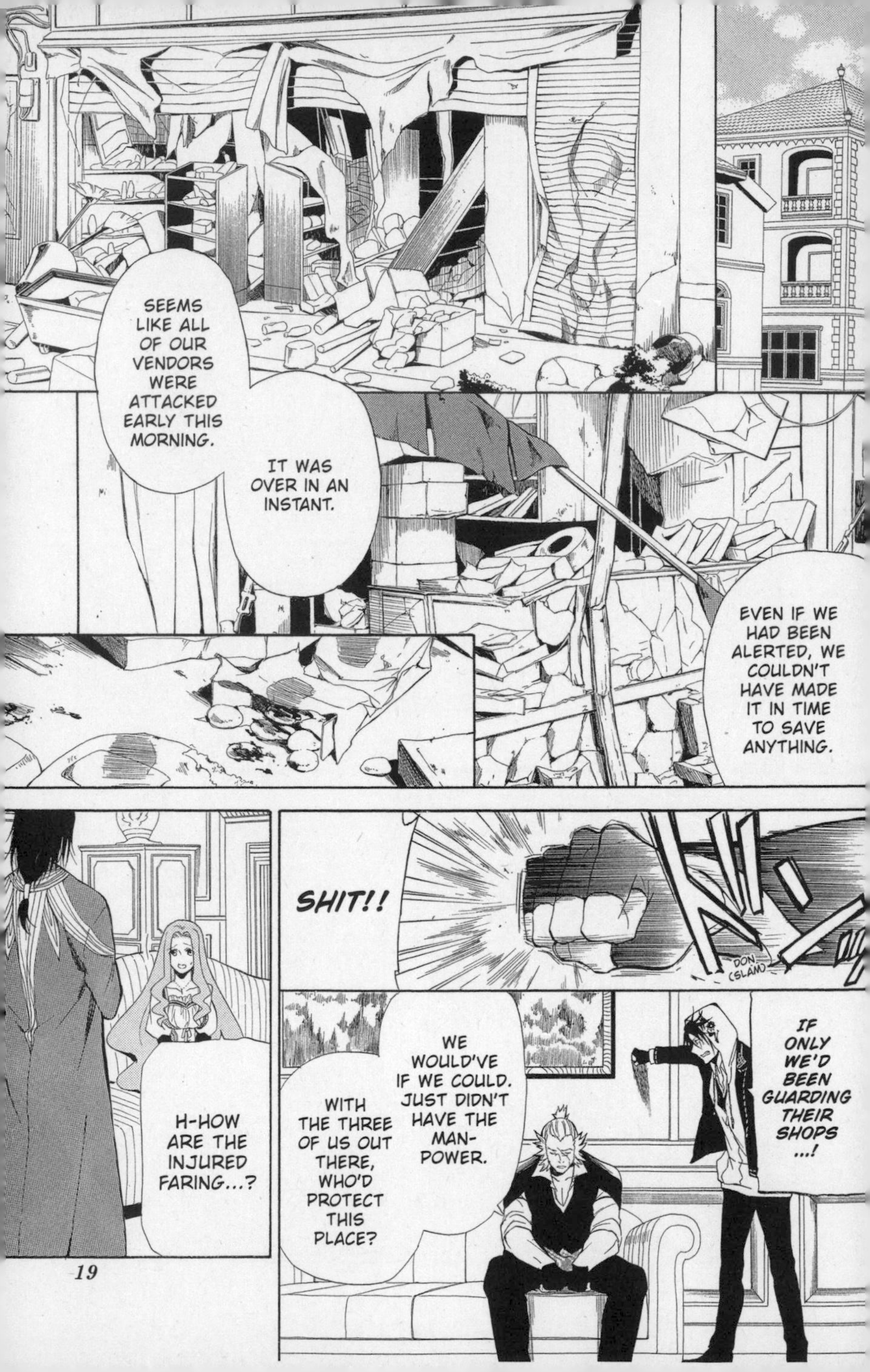
SEEMS LIKE ALL OF OUR VENDORS WERE ATTACKED EARLY THIS MORNING.
IT WAS OVER IN AN INSTANT.
EVEN IF WE HAD BEEN ALERTED, WE COULDN'T HAVE MADE IT IN TIME TO SAVE ANYTHING.
SHIT!!
DON (SLAM)
IF ONLY WE'D BEEN GUARDING THEIR SHOPS ...!
WE WOULD'VE IF WE COULD. JUST DIDN'T HAVE THE MAN-POWER.
WITH THE THREE OF US OUT THERE, WHO'D PROTECT THIS PLACE?
H-HOW ARE THE INJURED FARING...?

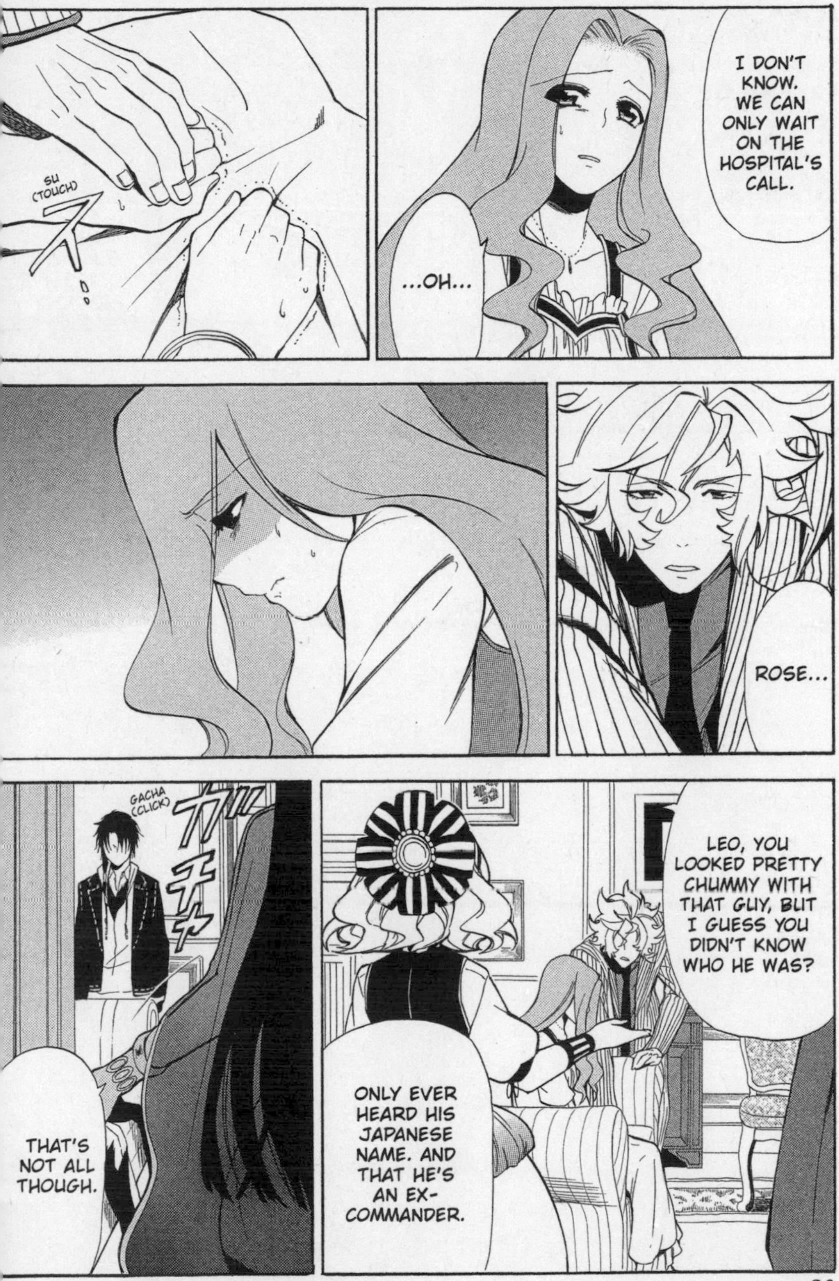
I DON'T KNOW. WE CAN ONLY WAIT ON THE HOSPITAL'S CALL.
...OH...
SU (TOUCH)
ROSE...
LEO, YOU LOOKED PRETTY CHUMMY WITH THAT GUY, BUT I GUESS YOU DIDN'T KNOW WHO HE WAS?
ONLY EVER HEARD HIS JAPANESE NAME. AND THAT HE'S AN EX-COMMANDER.
GACHA (CLICK)
THAT'S NOT ALL THOUGH.

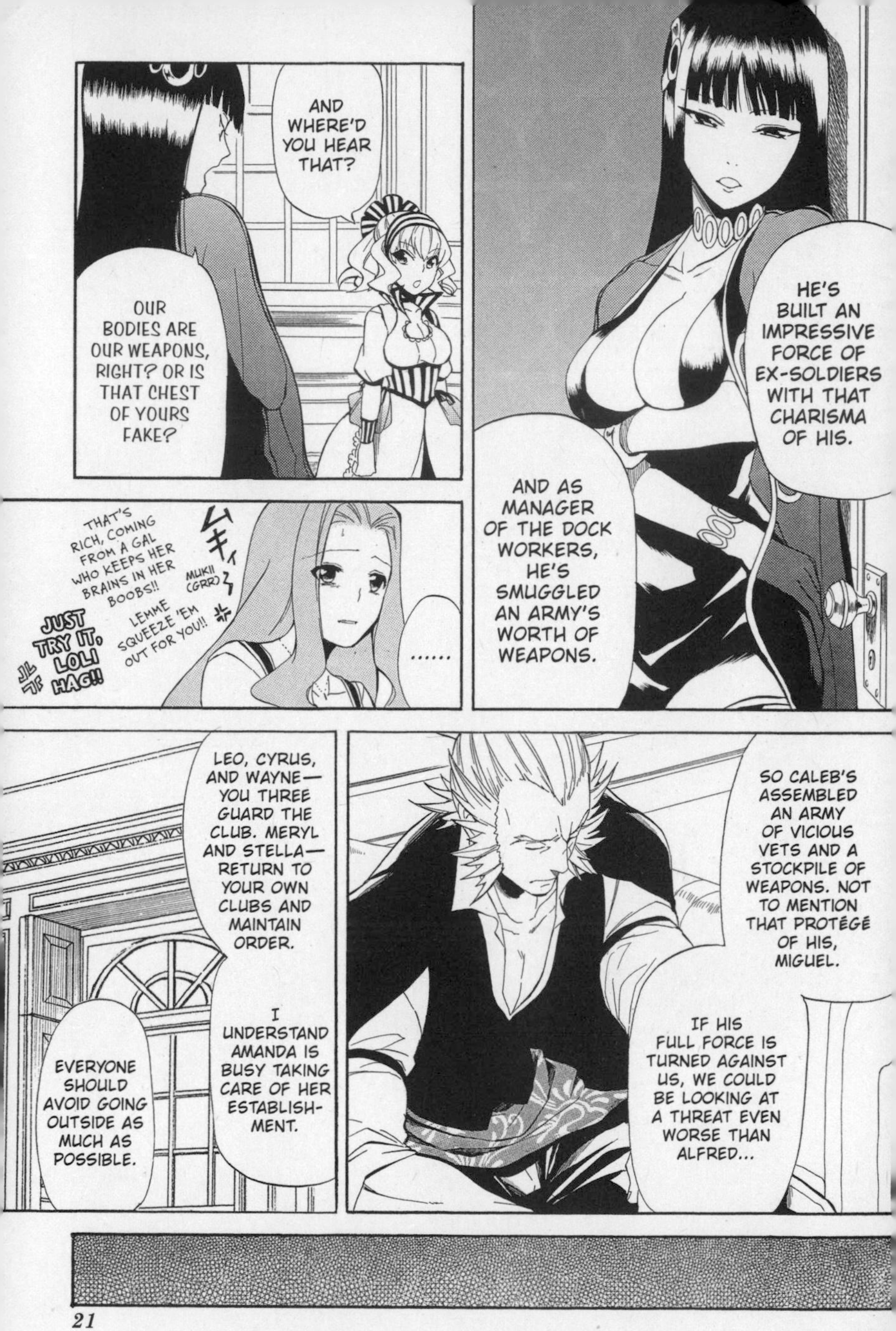
HE'S BUILT AN IMPRESSIVE FORCE OF EX-SOLDIERS WITH THAT CHARISMA OF HIS.
AND AS MANAGER OF THE DOCK WORKERS, HE'S SMUGGLED AN ARMY'S WORTH OF WEAPONS.
AND WHERE'D YOU HEAR THAT?
OUR BODIES ARE OUR WEAPONS, RIGHT? OR IS THAT CHEST OF YOURS FAKE?
......
MUKI! (GRR)
THAT'S RICH, COMING FROM A GAL WHO KEEPS HER BRAINS IN HER BOOBS!!
LEMME SQUEEZE 'EM OUT FOR YOU!!
JUST TRY IT, LOLI HAG!!
SO CALEB'S ASSEMBLED AN ARMY OF VICIOUS VETS AND A STOCKPILE OF WEAPONS. NOT TO MENTION THAT PROTÉGÉ OF HIS, MIGUEL.
IF HIS FULL FORCE IS TURNED AGAINST US, WE COULD BE LOOKING AT A THREAT EVEN WORSE THAN ALFRED...
LEO, CYRUS, AND WAYNE—YOU THREE GUARD THE CLUB. MERYL AND STELLA—RETURN TO YOUR OWN CLUBS AND MAINTAIN ORDER.
I UNDERSTAND AMANDA IS BUSY TAKING CARE OF HER ESTABLISH-MENT.
EVERYONE SHOULD AVOID GOING OUTSIDE AS MUCH AS POSSIBLE.

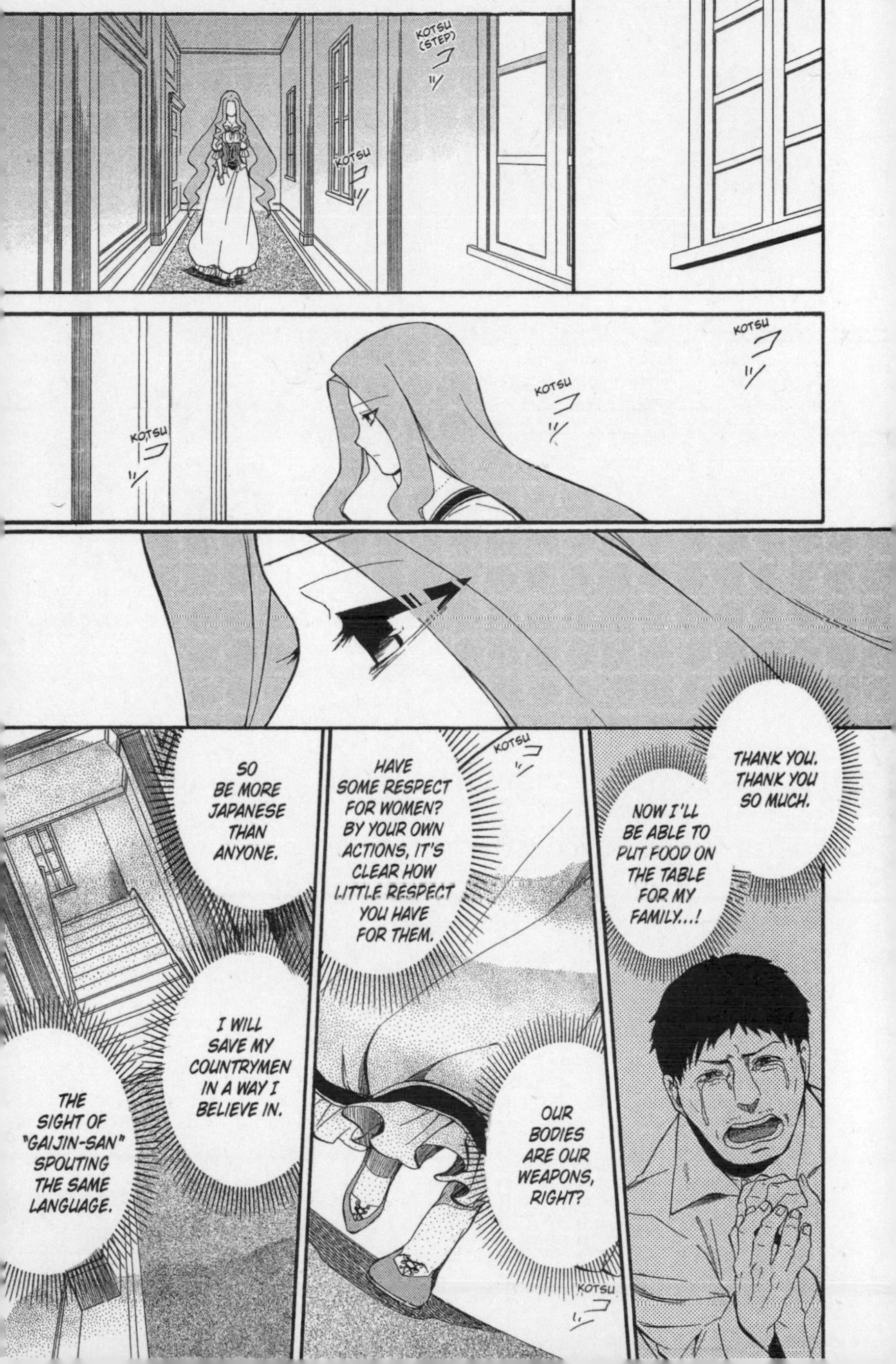
KOTSU (STEP)
KOTSU
KOTSU
KOTSU
KOTSU
THANK YOU. THANK YOU SO MUCH.
NOW I'LL BE ABLE TO PUT FOOD ON THE TABLE FOR MY FAMILY...!
KOTSU
HAVE SOME RESPECT FOR WOMEN? BY YOUR OWN ACTIONS, IT'S CLEAR HOW LITTLE RESPECT YOU HAVE FOR THEM.
OUR BODIES ARE OUR WEAPONS, RIGHT?
KOTSU
SO BE MORE JAPANESE THAN ANYONE.
I WILL SAVE MY COUNTRYMEN IN A WAY I BELIEVE IN.
THE SIGHT OF "GAIJIN-SAN" SPOUTING THE SAME LANGUAGE.

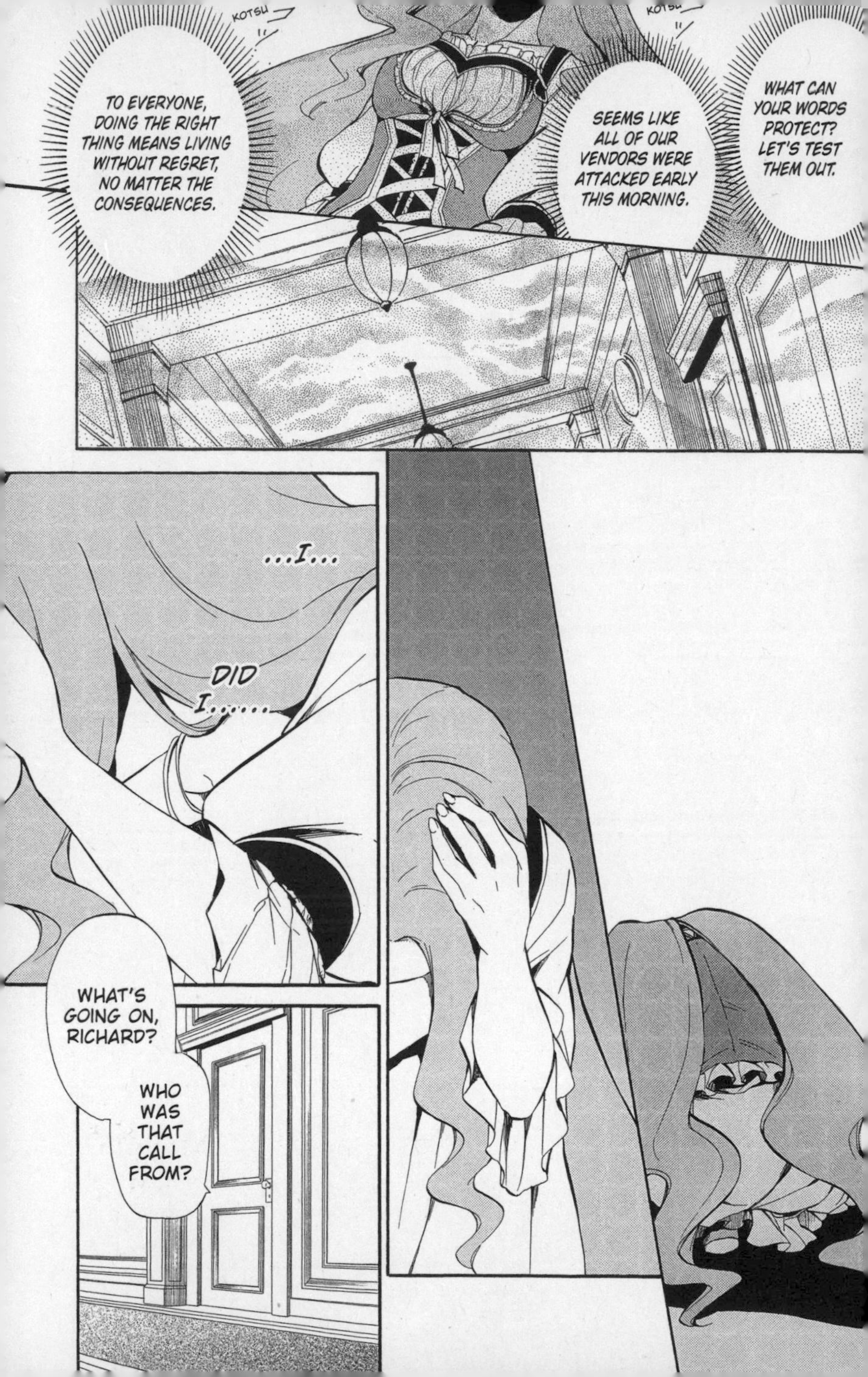
KOTSU
WHAT CAN YOUR WORDS PROTECT? LET'S TEST THEM OUT.
SEEMS LIKE ALL OF OUR VENDORS WERE ATTACKED EARLY THIS MORNING.
KOTSU
TO EVERYONE, DOING THE RIGHT THING MEANS LIVING WITHOUT REGRET, NO MATTER THE CONSEQUENCES.
...I...
DID I......
WHAT'S GOING ON, RICHARD?
WHO WAS THAT CALL FROM?

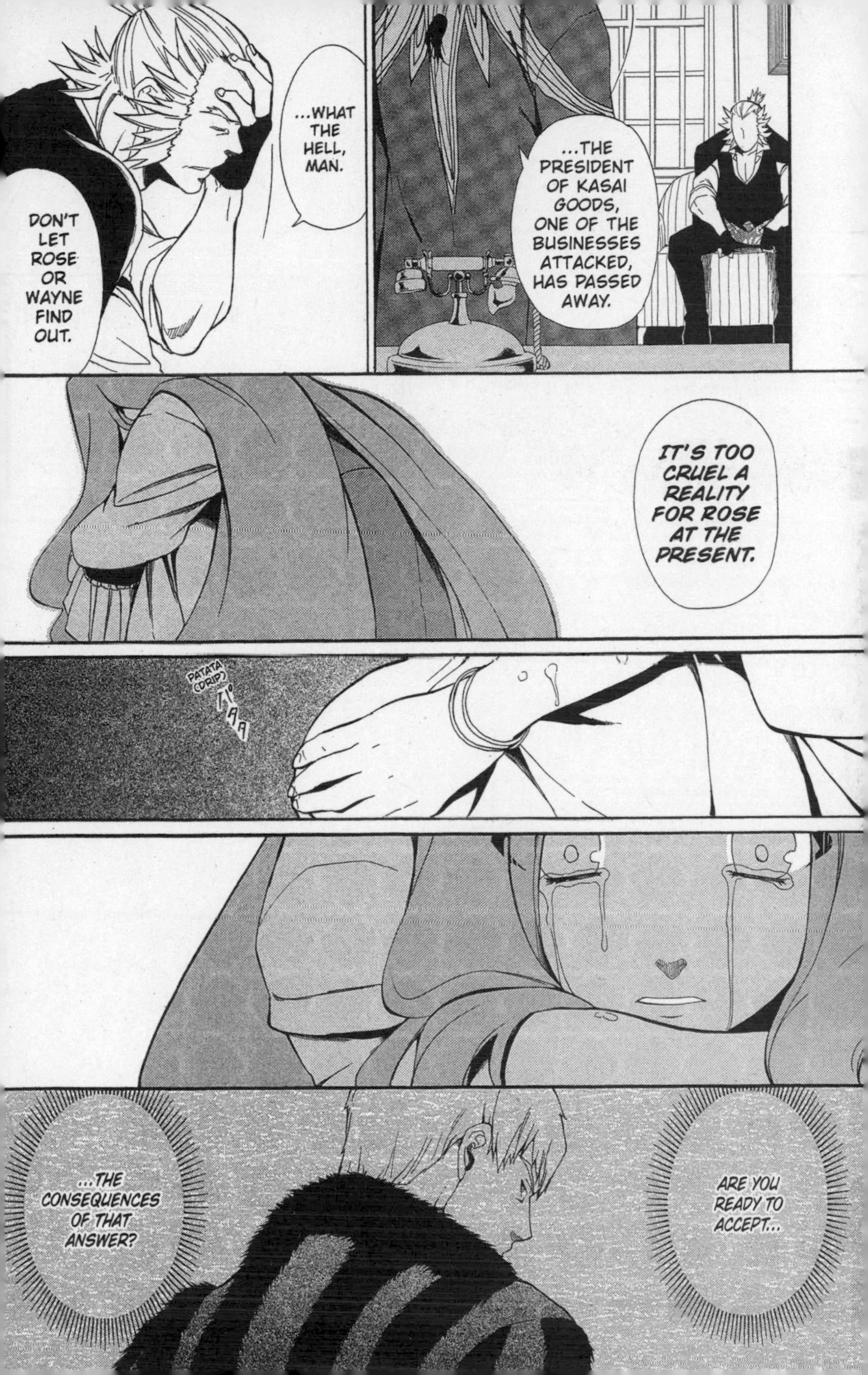
...THE PRESIDENT OF KASAI GOODS, ONE OF THE BUSINESSES ATTACKED, HAS PASSED AWAY.
...WHAT THE HELL, MAN.
DON'T LET ROSE OR WAYNE FIND OUT.
IT'S TOO CRUEL A REALITY FOR ROSE AT THE PRESENT.
PATATA (DRIP)
ARE YOU READY TO ACCEPT...
...THE CONSEQUENCES OF THAT ANSWER?

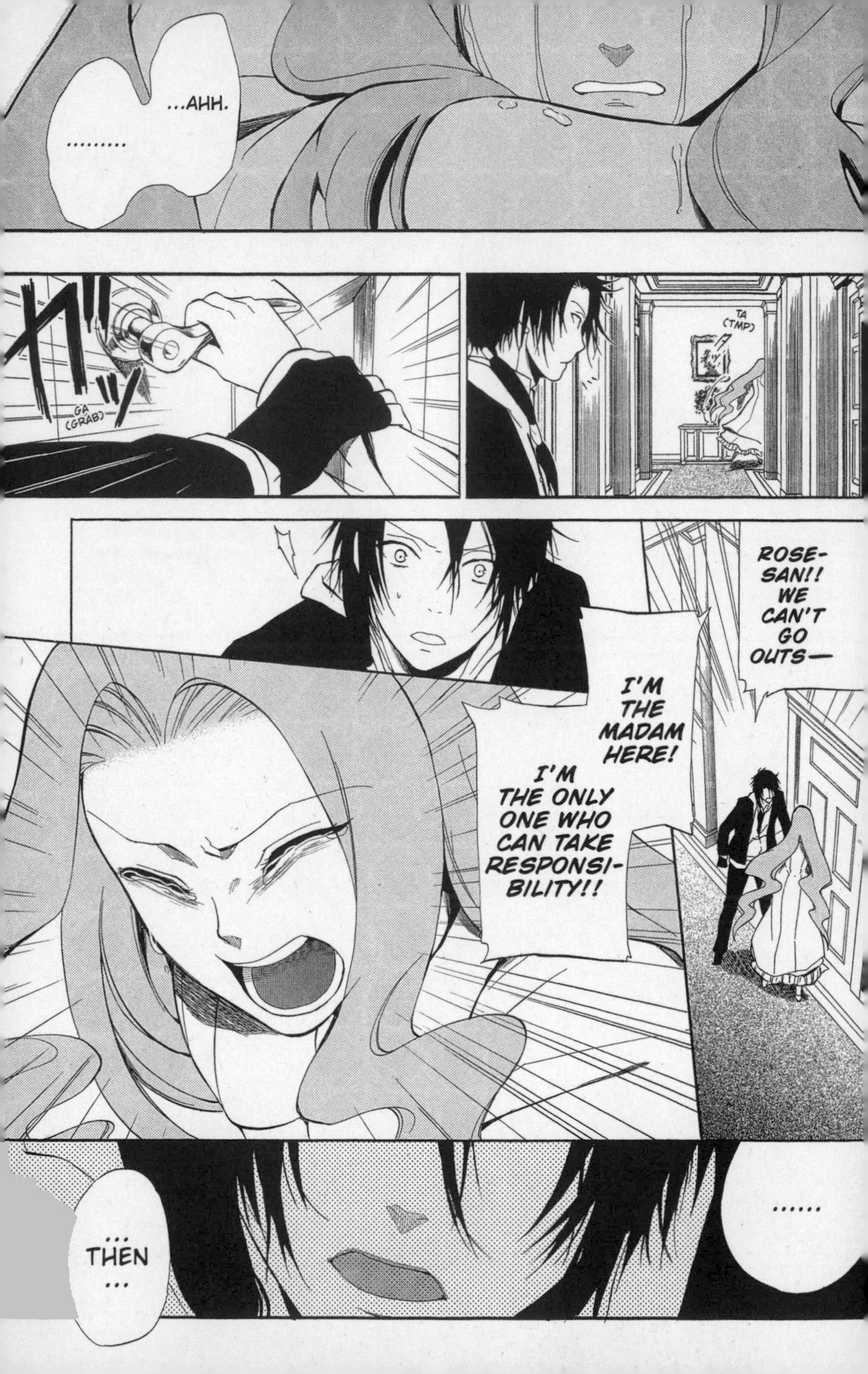
...AHH.
....
TA (TMP)
GA (GRAB)
ROSE-SAN!! WE CAN'T GO OUTS—
I'M THE MADAM HERE!
I'M THE ONLY ONE WHO CAN TAKE RESPONSI-BILITY!!
......
... THEN ...

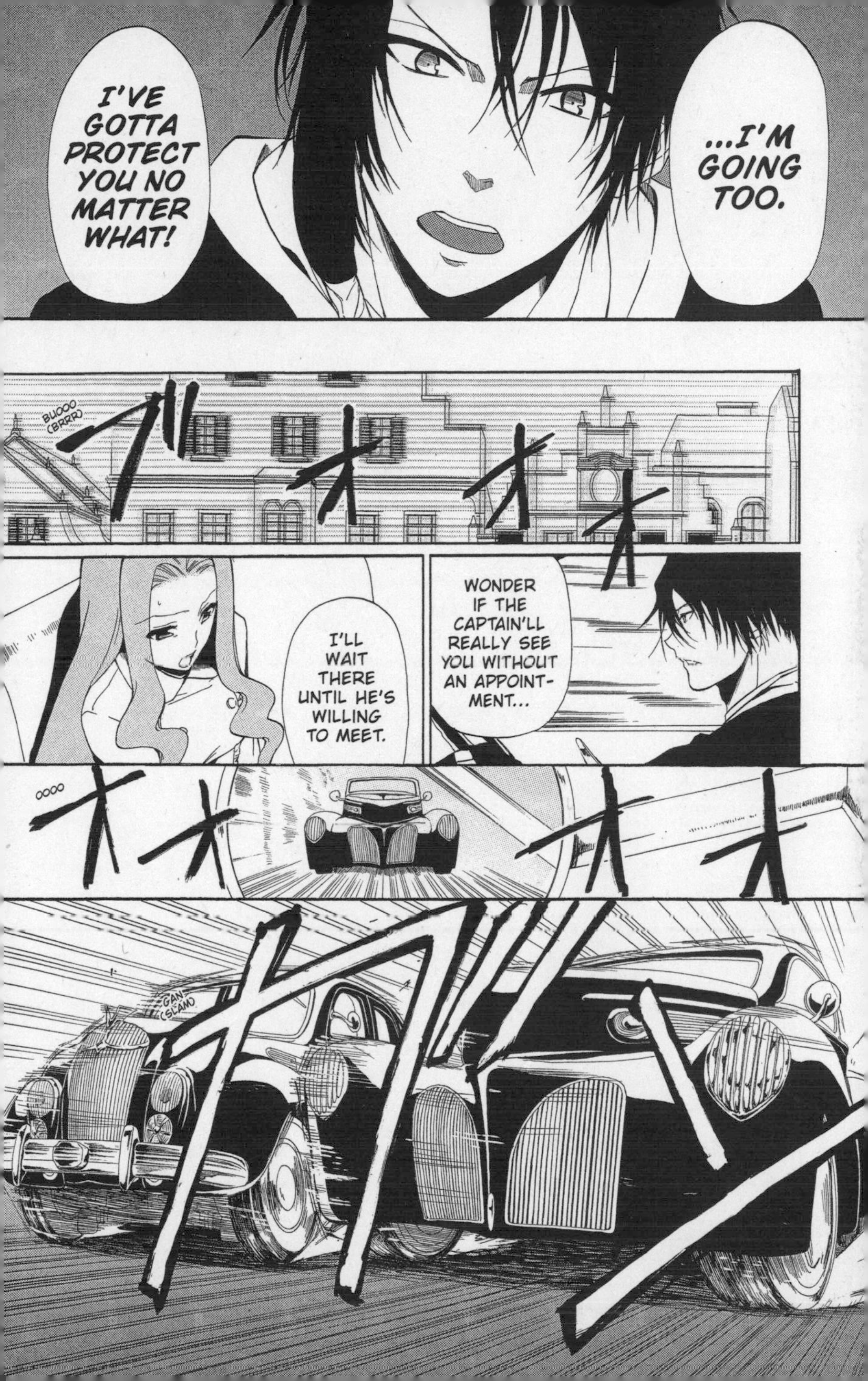
...I'M GOING TOO.
I'VE GOTTA PROTECT YOU NO MATTER WHAT!
BUOOO (BRRR)
WONDER IF THE CAPTAIN'LL REALLY SEE YOU WITHOUT AN APPOINT-MENT...
I'LL WAIT THERE UNTIL HE'S WILLING TO MEET.
OOOO
GAN (SLAM)

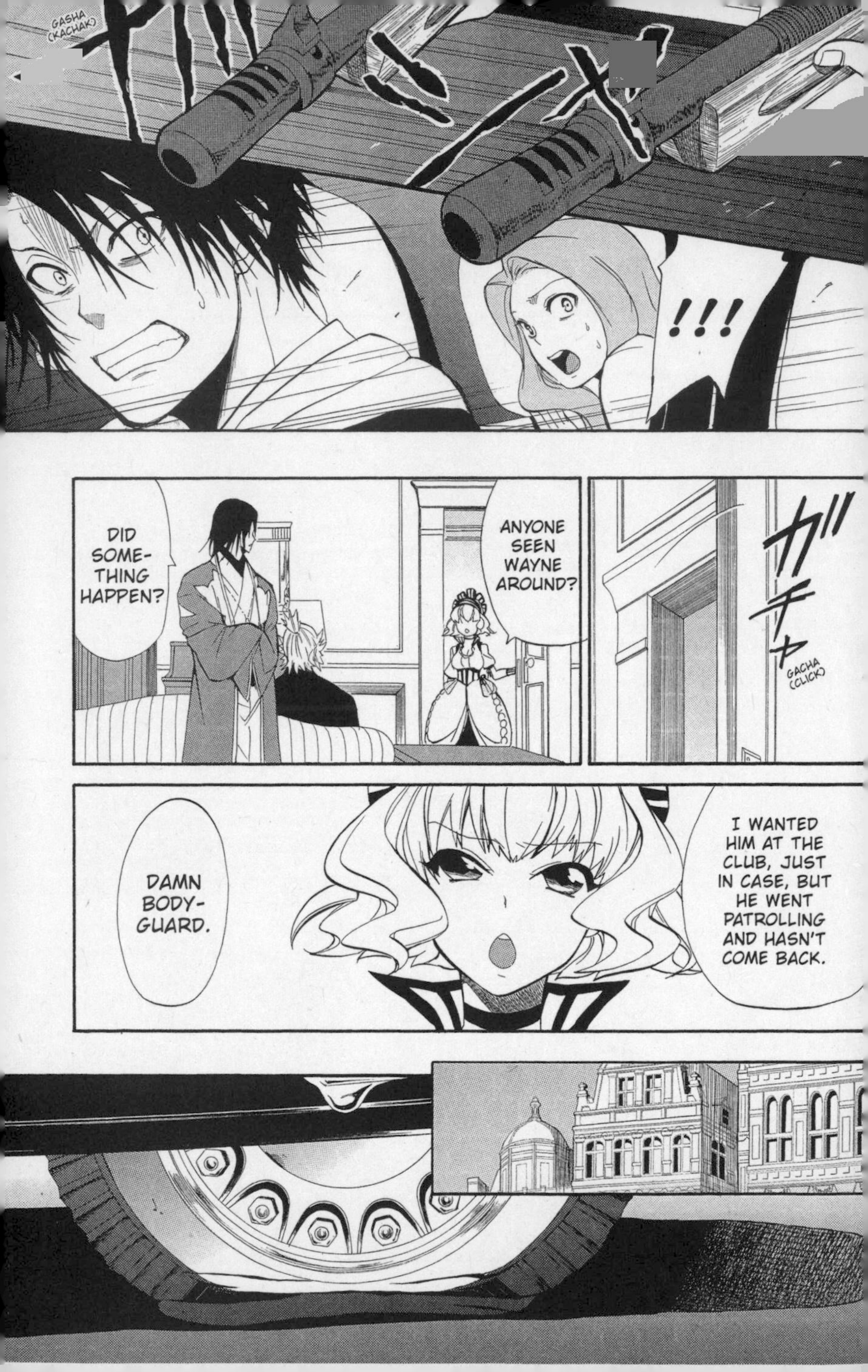
GASHA (KACHAK)
!!!
GACHA (CLICK)
ANYONE SEEN WAYNE AROUND?
DID SOME-THING HAPPEN?
I WANTED HIM AT THE CLUB, JUST IN CASE, BUT HE WENT PATROLLING AND HASN'T COME BACK.
DAMN BODY-GUARD.

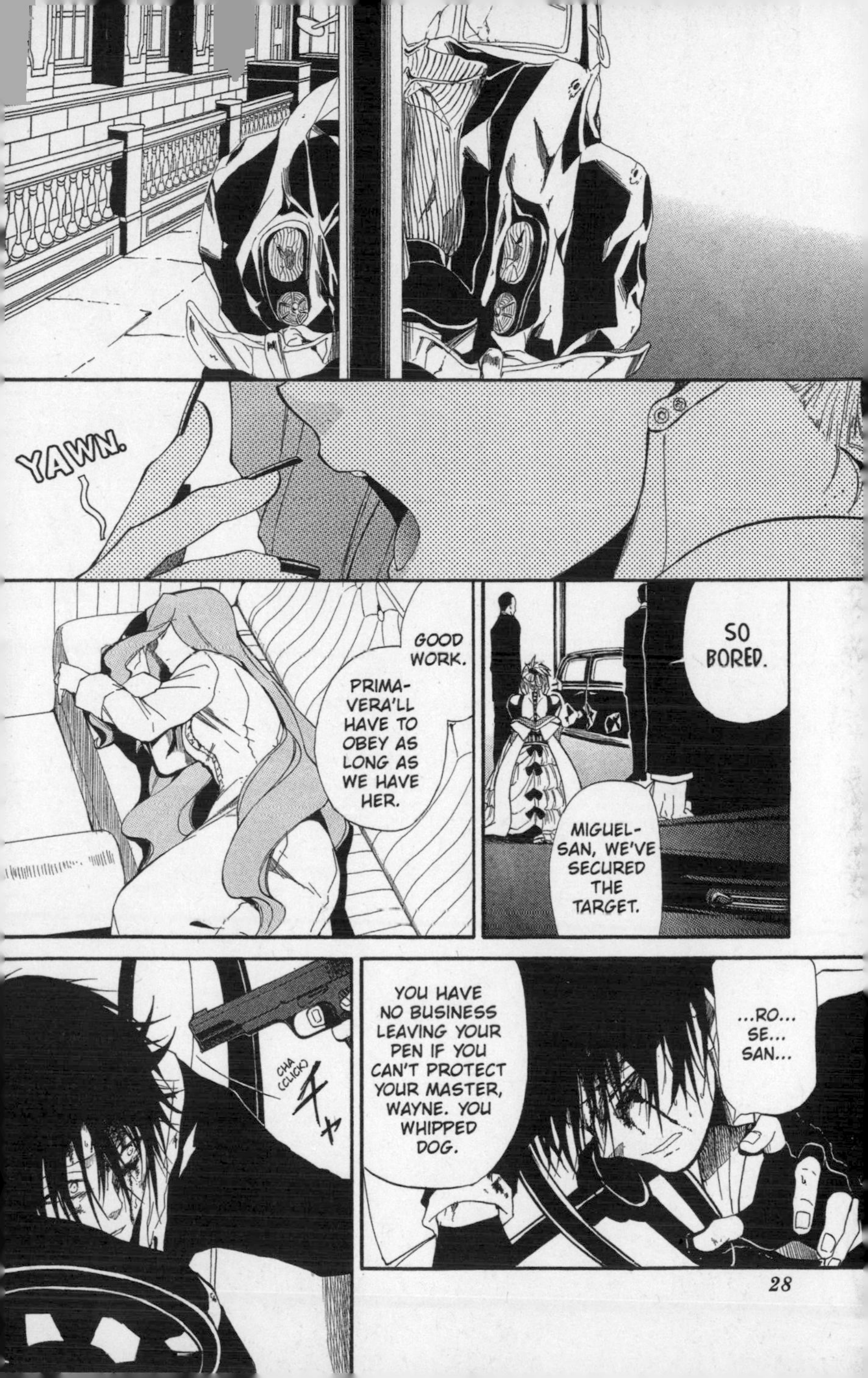
YAWN.
SO BORED.
MIGUEL-SAN, WE'VE SECURED THE TARGET.
GOOD WORK.
PRIMA-VERA'LL HAVE TO OBEY AS LONG AS WE HAVE HER.
...RO... SE... SAN...
YOU HAVE NO BUSINESS LEAVING YOUR PEN IF YOU CAN'T PROTECT YOUR MASTER, WAYNE. YOU WHIPPED DOG.
CHA (CLICK)

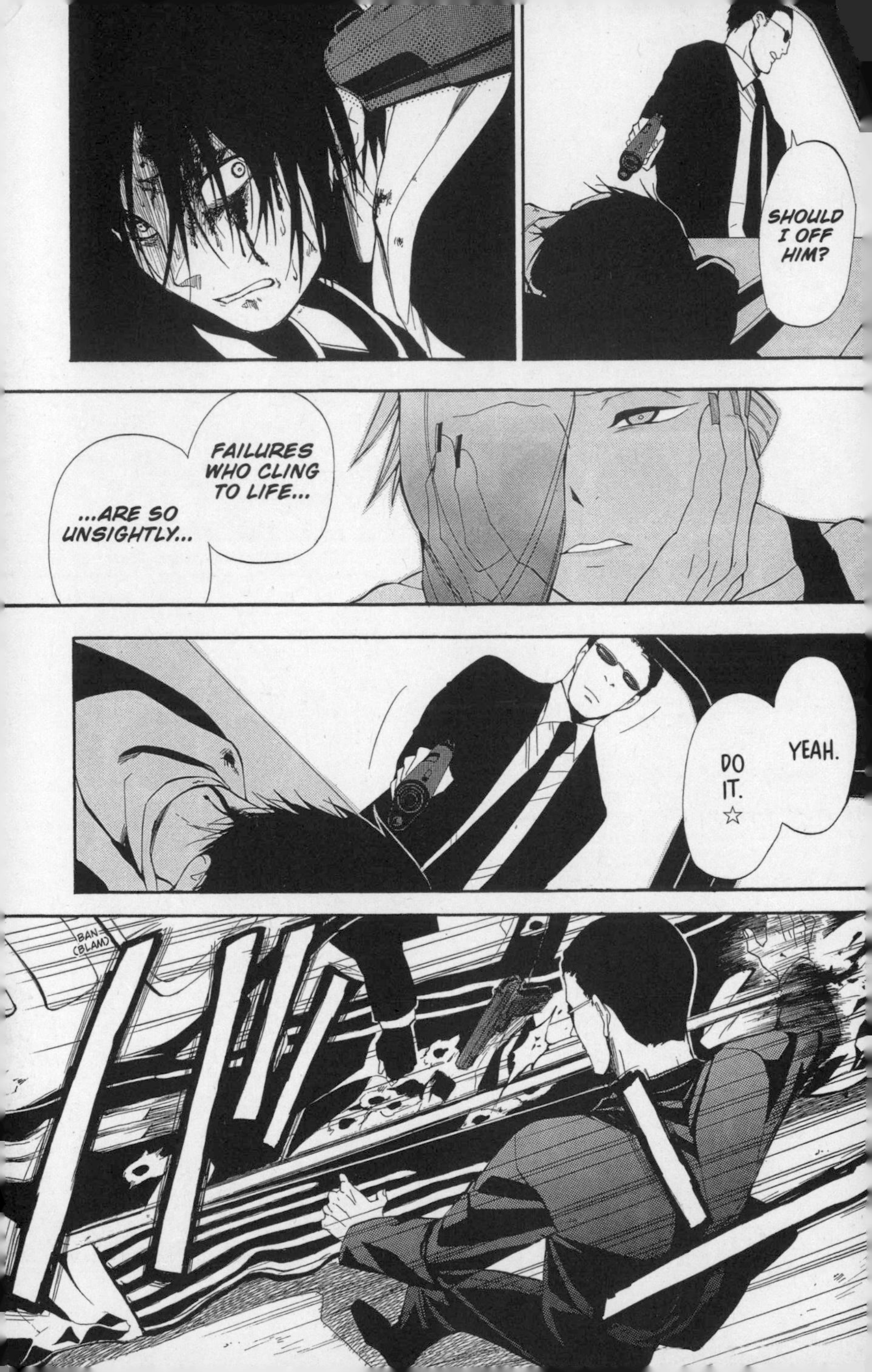
SHOULD I OFF HIM?
FAILURES WHO CLING TO LIFE...
...ARE SO UNSIGHTLY...
YEAH.
DO IT. ☆
BAN (BLAM)

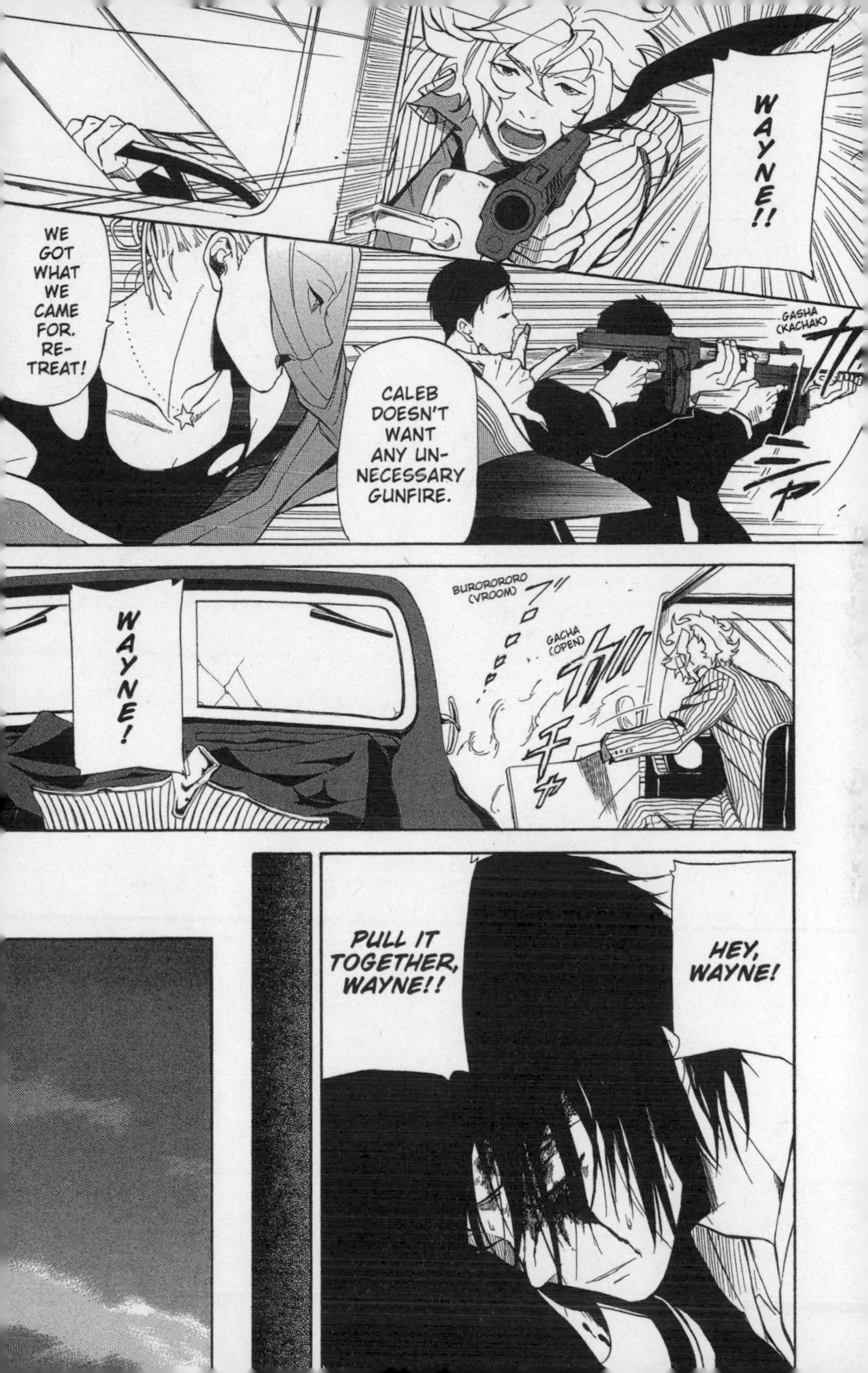
WAYNE!!
GASHA (KACHAK)
CALEB DOESN'T WANT ANY UN-NECESSARY GUNFIRE.
WE GOT WHAT WE CAME FOR. RE-TREAT!
BURORORORO (VROOM)
GACHA (OPEN)
WAYNE!
HEY, WAYNE!
PULL IT TOGETHER, WAYNE!!

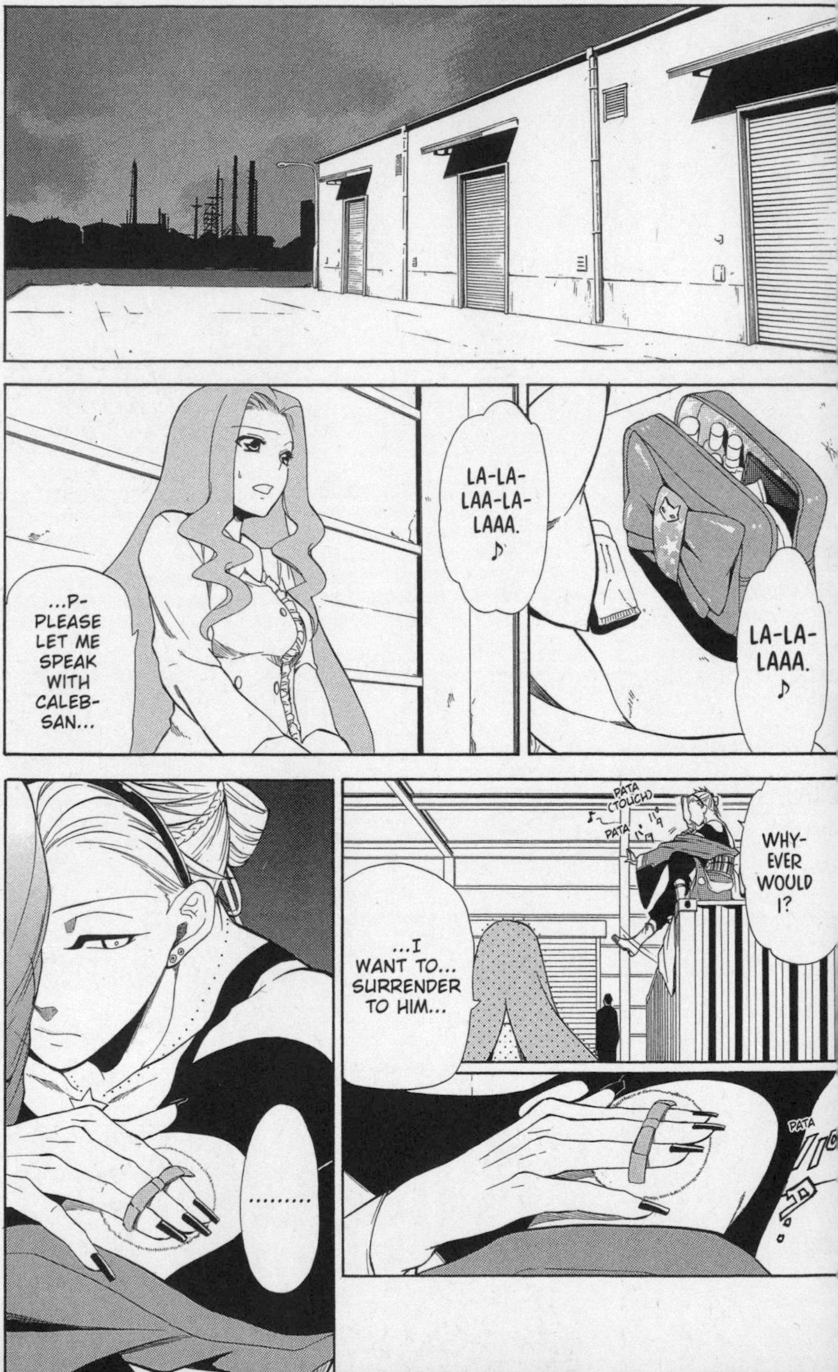
LA-LA-LAAA. ♪
LA-LA-LAA-LA-LAAA. ♪
...P-PLEASE LET ME SPEAK WITH CALEB-SAN...
PATA (TOUCH)
PATA
WHY-EVER WOULD I?
...I WANT TO... SURRENDER TO HIM...
PATA
....

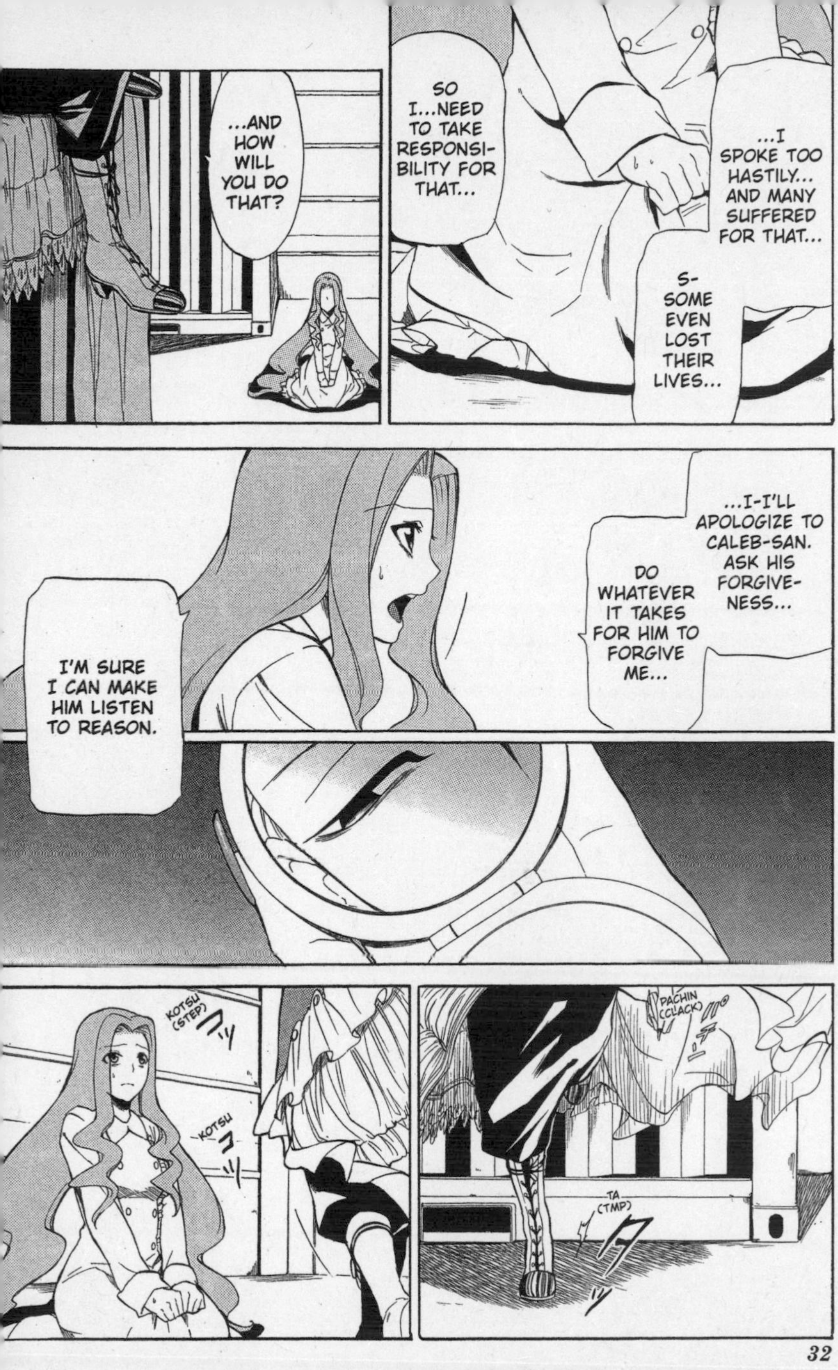
...I SPOKE TOO HASTILY... AND MANY SUFFERED FOR THAT...
S-SOME EVEN LOST THEIR LIVES...
SO I...NEED TO TAKE RESPONSIBILITY FOR THAT...
...AND HOW WILL YOU DO THAT?
...I-I'LL APOLOGIZE TO CALEB-SAN. ASK HIS FORGIVENESS...
DO WHATEVER IT TAKES FOR HIM TO FORGIVE ME...
I'M SURE I CAN MAKE HIM LISTEN TO REASON.
PACHIN (CLACK)
TA (TMP)
KOTSU (STEP)
KOTSU

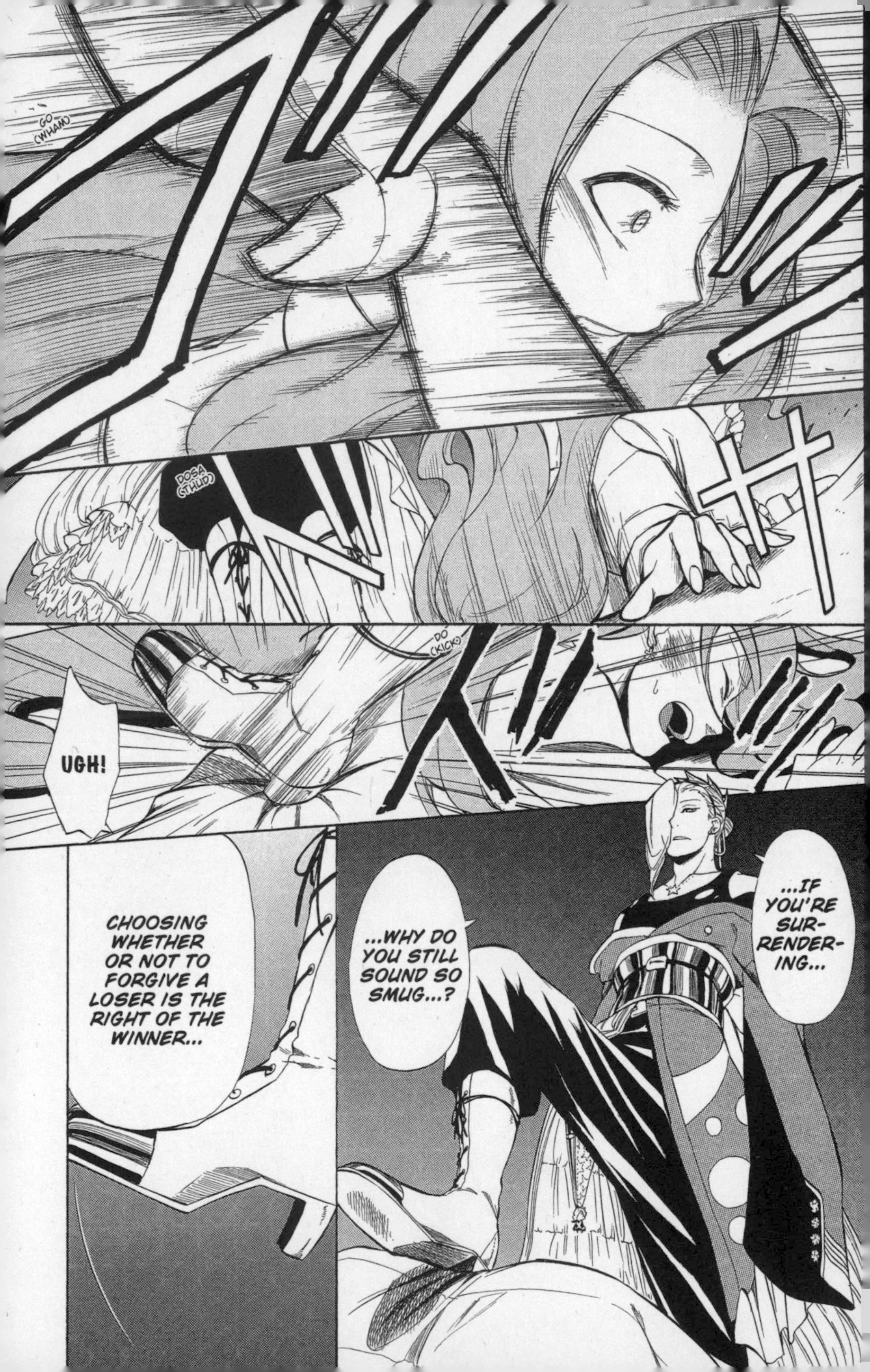
GO (WHAM)
DOSA (THUD)
DO (KICK)
UGH!
...IF YOU'RE SUR-RENDER-ING...
...WHY DO YOU STILL SOUND SO SMUG...?
CHOOSING WHETHER OR NOT TO FORGIVE A LOSER IS THE RIGHT OF THE WINNER...

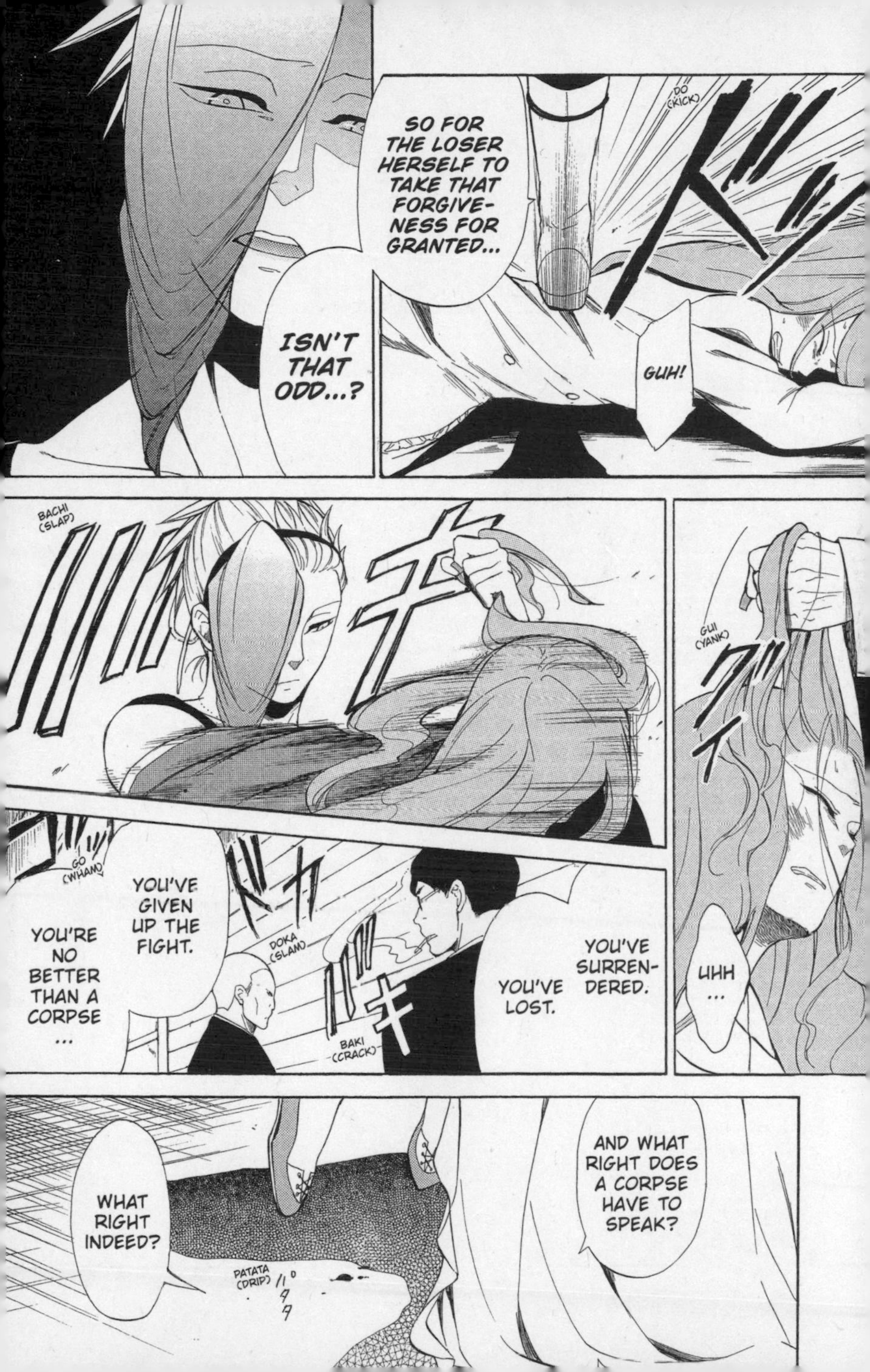
SO FOR THE LOSER HERSELF TO TAKE THAT FORGIVENESS FOR GRANTED...
DO (KICK)
GUH!
ISN'T THAT ODD...?
GUI (YANK)
UHH...
BACHI (SLAP)
YOU'VE SURRENDERED.
YOU'VE LOST.
BAKI (CRACK)
DOKA (SLAM)
GO (WHAM)
YOU'VE GIVEN UP THE FIGHT.
YOU'RE NO BETTER THAN A CORPSE...
AND WHAT RIGHT DOES A CORPSE HAVE TO SPEAK?
PATATA (DRIP)
WHAT RIGHT INDEED?

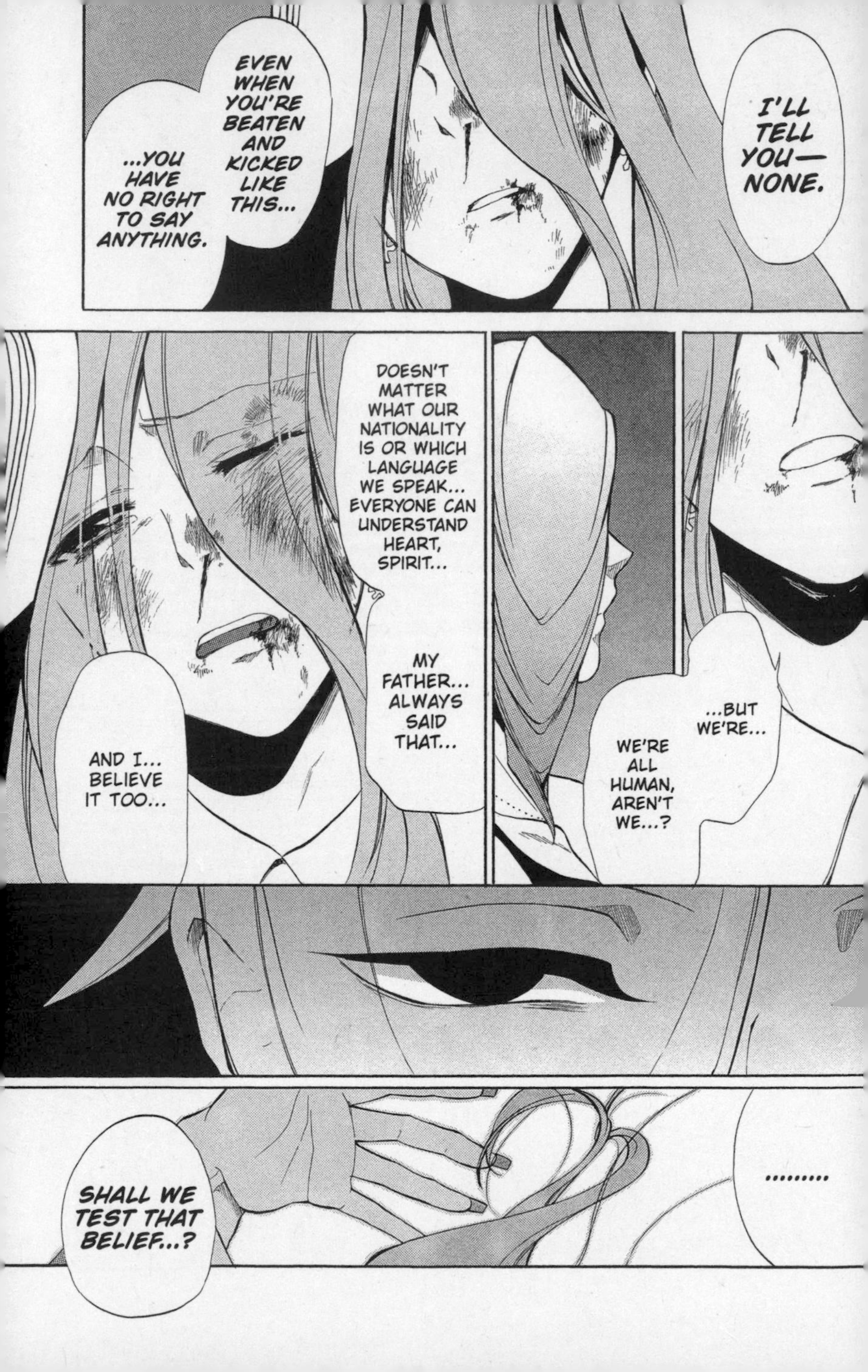
I'LL TELL YOU— NONE.
EVEN WHEN YOU'RE BEATEN AND KICKED LIKE THIS...
...YOU HAVE NO RIGHT TO SAY ANYTHING.
...BUT WE'RE...
WE'RE ALL HUMAN, AREN'T WE...?
DOESN'T MATTER WHAT OUR NATIONALITY IS OR WHICH LANGUAGE WE SPEAK... EVERYONE CAN UNDERSTAND HEART, SPIRIT...
MY FATHER... ALWAYS SAID THAT...
AND I... BELIEVE IT TOO...
....
SHALL WE TEST THAT BELIEF...?

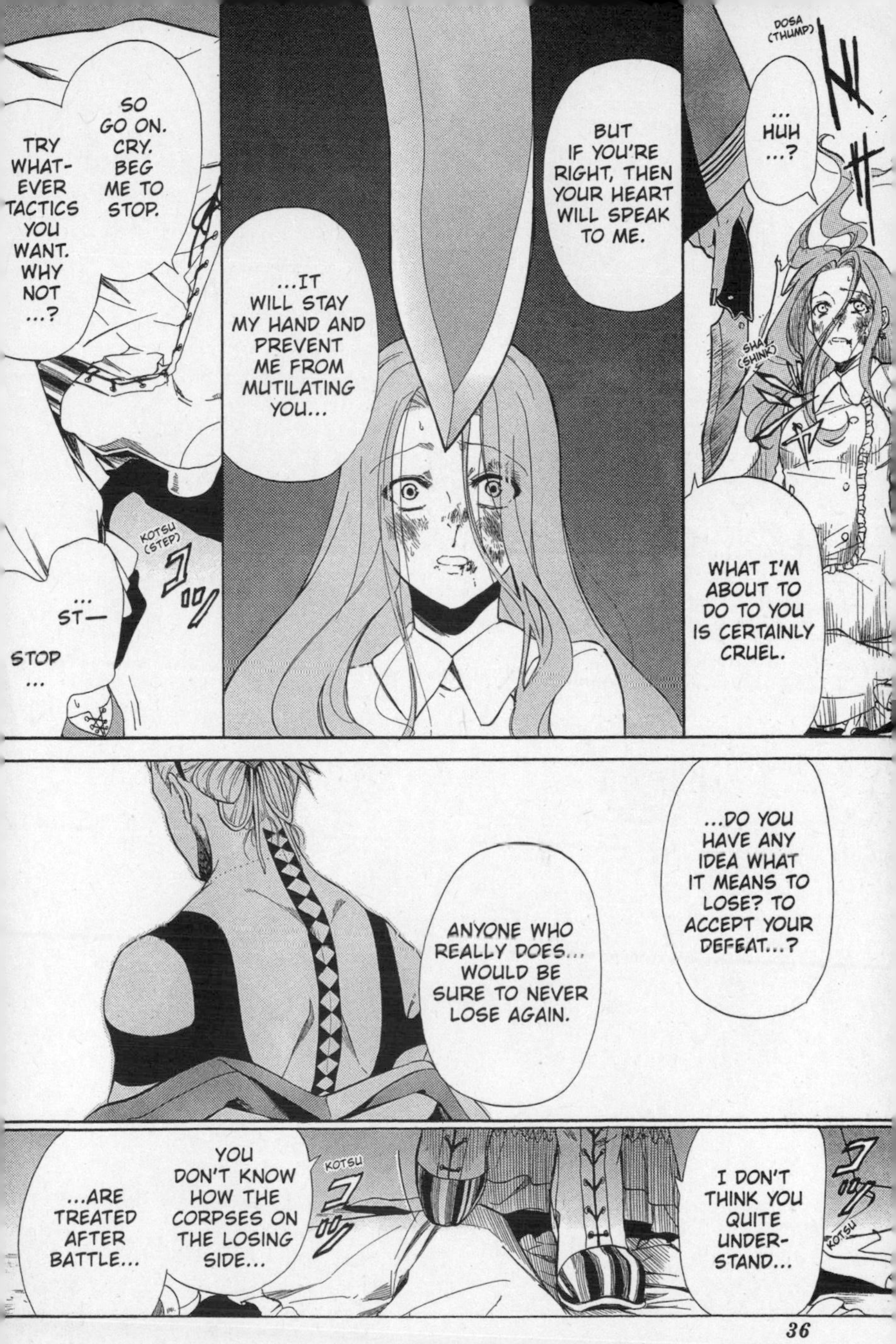
DOSA (THUMP)
...HUH...?
SHA (SHINK)
WHAT I'M ABOUT TO DO TO YOU IS CERTAINLY CRUEL.
BUT IF YOU'RE RIGHT, THEN YOUR HEART WILL SPEAK TO ME.
...IT WILL STAY MY HAND AND PREVENT ME FROM MUTILATING YOU...
SO GO ON. CRY. BEG ME TO STOP.
TRY WHAT-EVER TACTICS YOU WANT. WHY NOT...?
KOTSU (STEP)
...ST—
STOP...
...DO YOU HAVE ANY IDEA WHAT IT MEANS TO LOSE? TO ACCEPT YOUR DEFEAT...?
ANYONE WHO REALLY DOES... WOULD BE SURE TO NEVER LOSE AGAIN.
KOTSU
I DON'T THINK YOU QUITE UNDER-STAND...
KOTSU
YOU DON'T KNOW HOW THE CORPSES ON THE LOSING SIDE...
...ARE TREATED AFTER BATTLE...

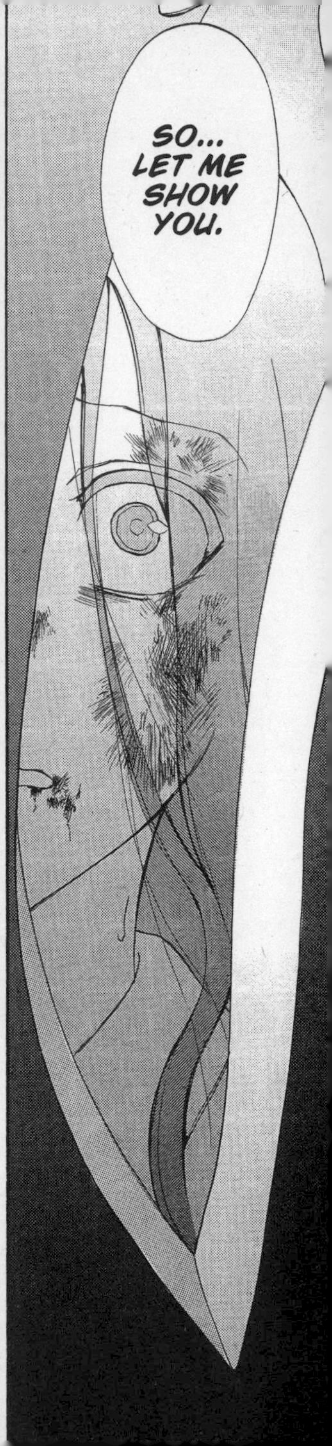
SO... LET ME SHOW YOU.

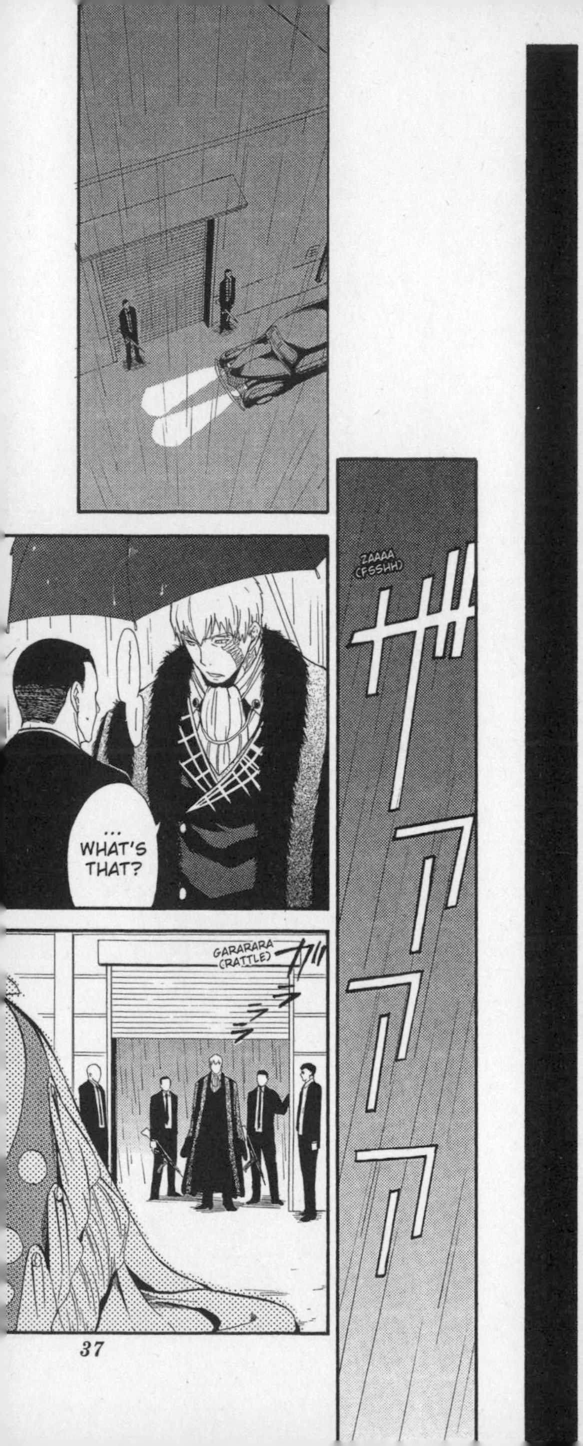
ZAAAA (FSSHH)
... WHAT'S THAT?
GARARARA (RATTLE)

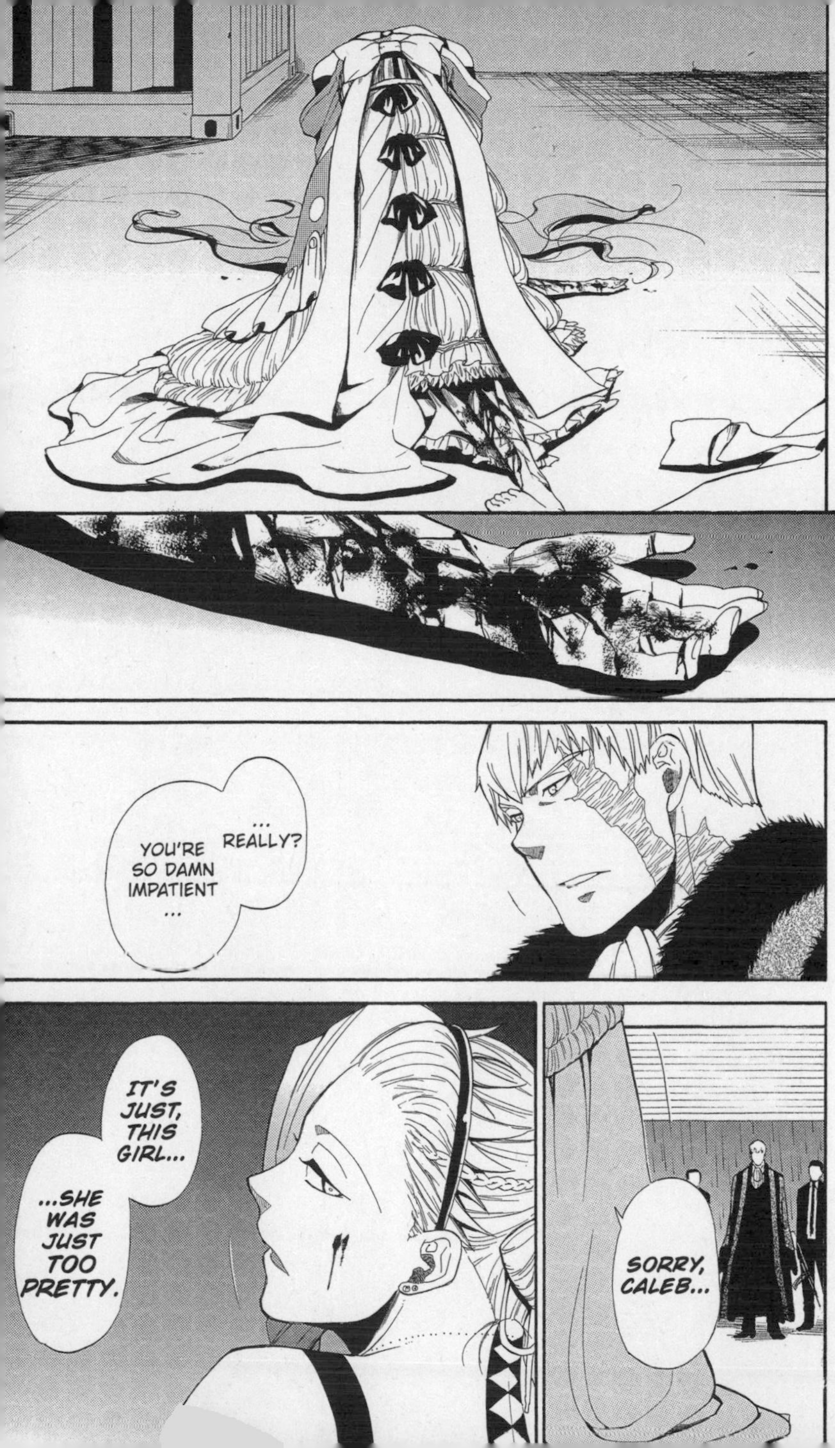
... REALLY?
YOU'RE SO DAMN IMPATIENT ...
SORRY, CALEB...
IT'S JUST, THIS GIRL...
...SHE WAS JUST TOO PRETTY.

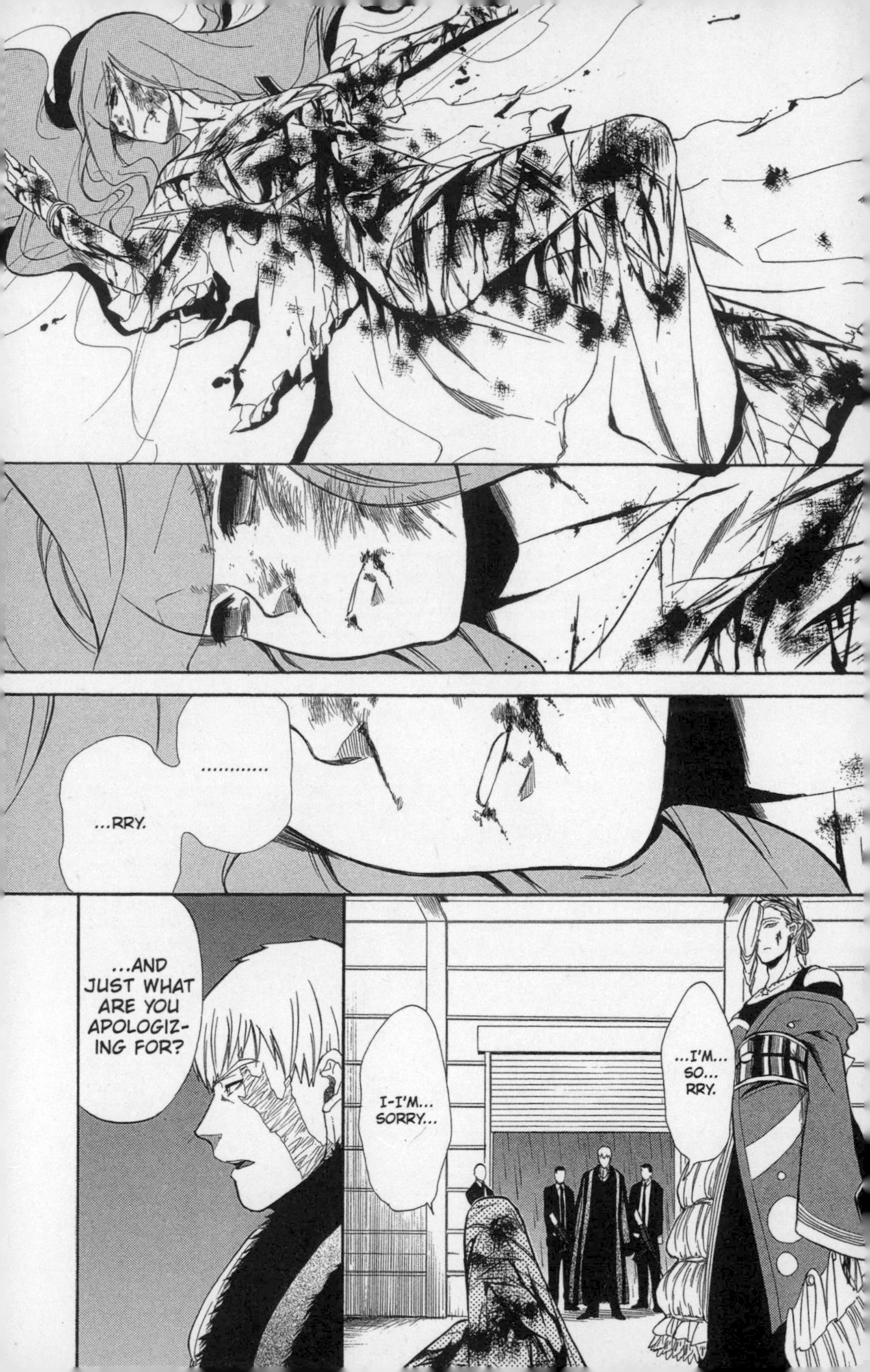
....
...RRY.
...I'M... SO... RRY.
I-I'M... SORRY...
...AND JUST WHAT ARE YOU APOLOGIZING FOR?

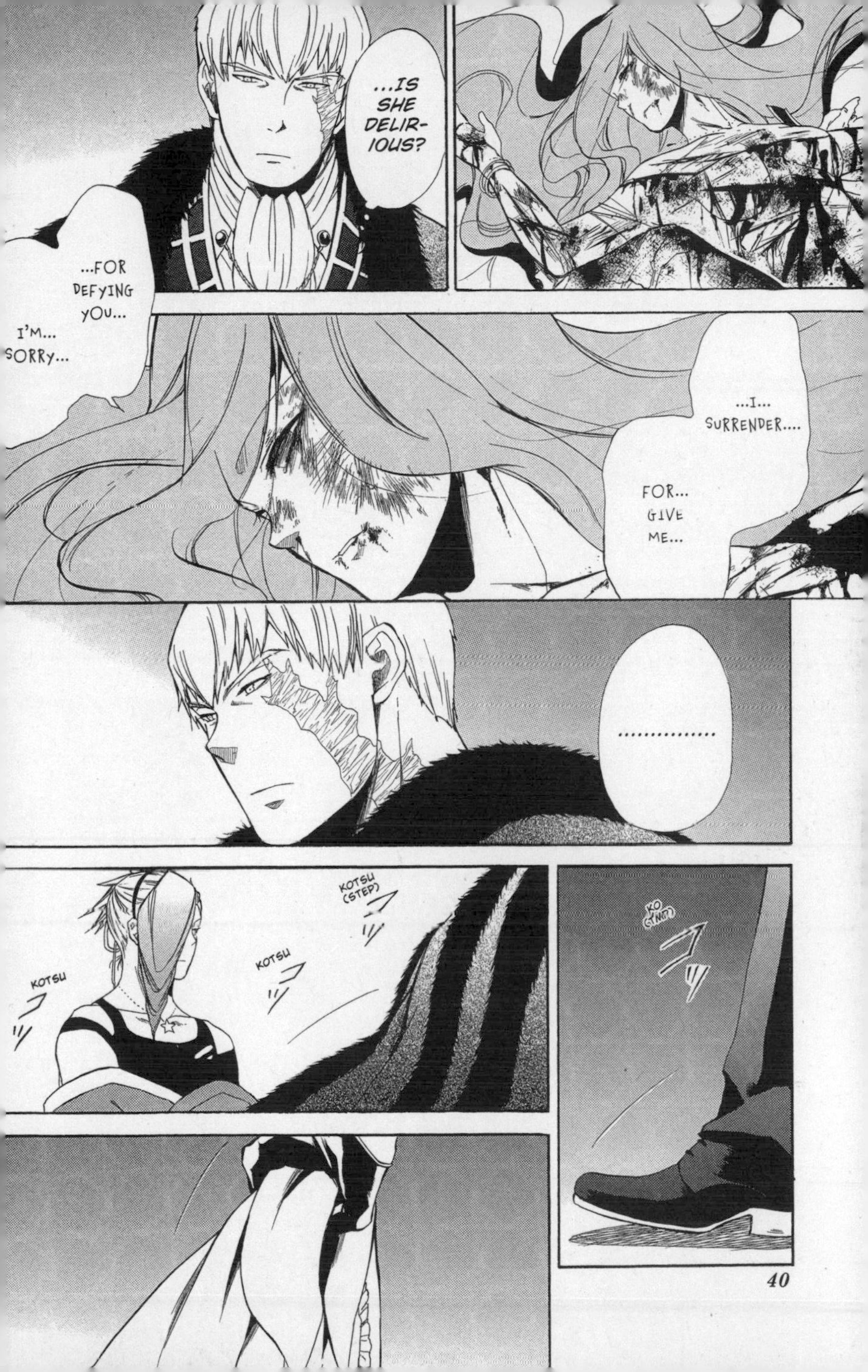
...IS SHE DELIRIOUS?
...I... SURRENDER....
FOR... GIVE ME...
...FOR DEFYING YOU...
I'M... SORRY...
....
KO
KOTSU (STEP)
KOTSU
KOTSU

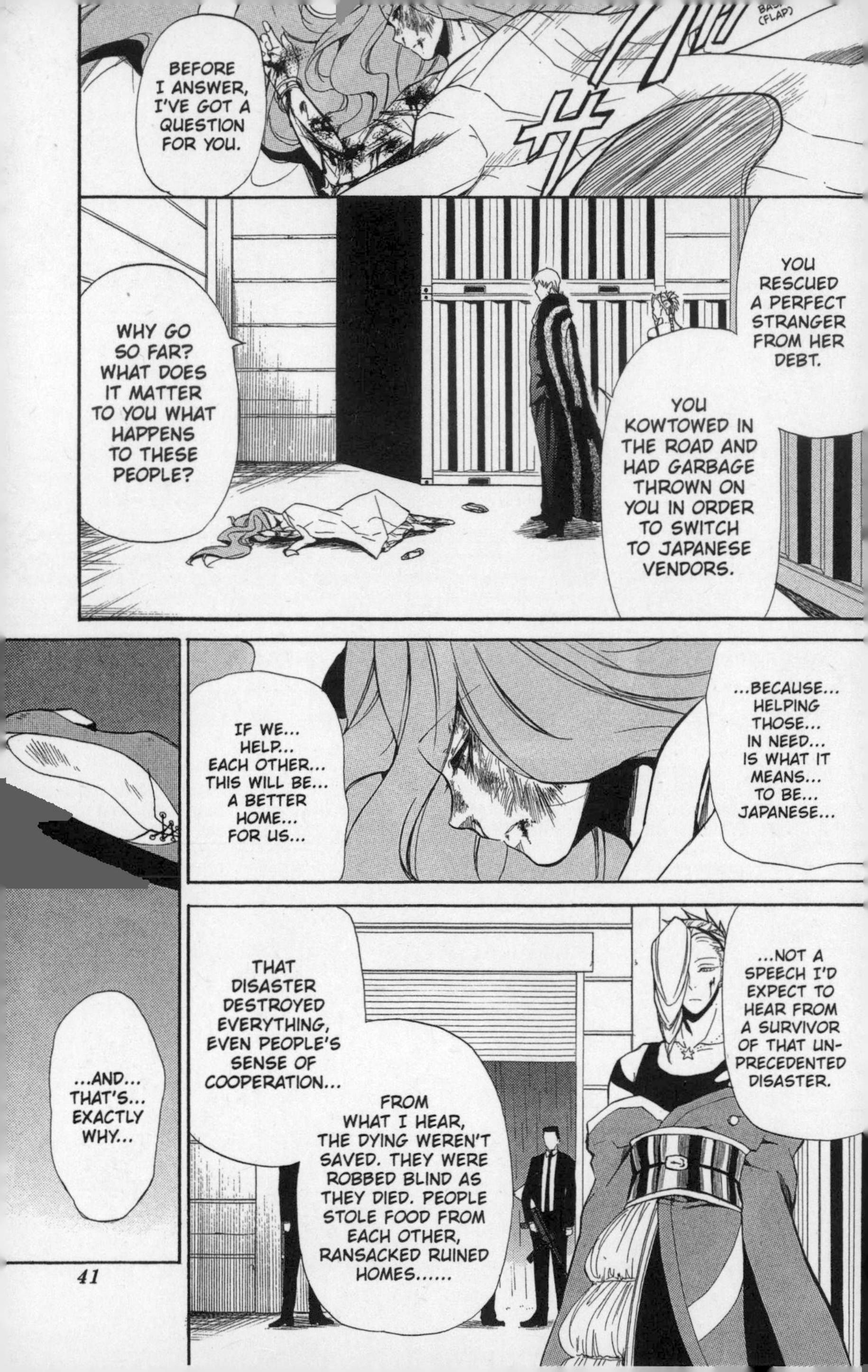
(FLAP)
BEFORE I ANSWER, I'VE GOT A QUESTION FOR YOU.
YOU RESCUED A PERFECT STRANGER FROM HER DEBT.
YOU KOWTOWED IN THE ROAD AND HAD GARBAGE THROWN ON YOU IN ORDER TO SWITCH TO JAPANESE VENDORS.
WHY GO SO FAR? WHAT DOES IT MATTER TO YOU WHAT HAPPENS TO THESE PEOPLE?
...BECAUSE... HELPING THOSE... IN NEED... IS WHAT IT MEANS... TO BE... JAPANESE...
IF WE... HELP... EACH OTHER... THIS WILL BE... A BETTER HOME... FOR US...
...NOT A SPEECH I'D EXPECT TO HEAR FROM A SURVIVOR OF THAT UN-PRECEDENTED DISASTER.
THAT DISASTER DESTROYED EVERYTHING, EVEN PEOPLE'S SENSE OF COOPERATION...
FROM WHAT I HEAR, THE DYING WEREN'T SAVED. THEY WERE ROBBED BLIND AS THEY DIED. PEOPLE STOLE FOOD FROM EACH OTHER, RANSACKED RUINED HOMES......
...AND... THAT'S... EXACTLY WHY...

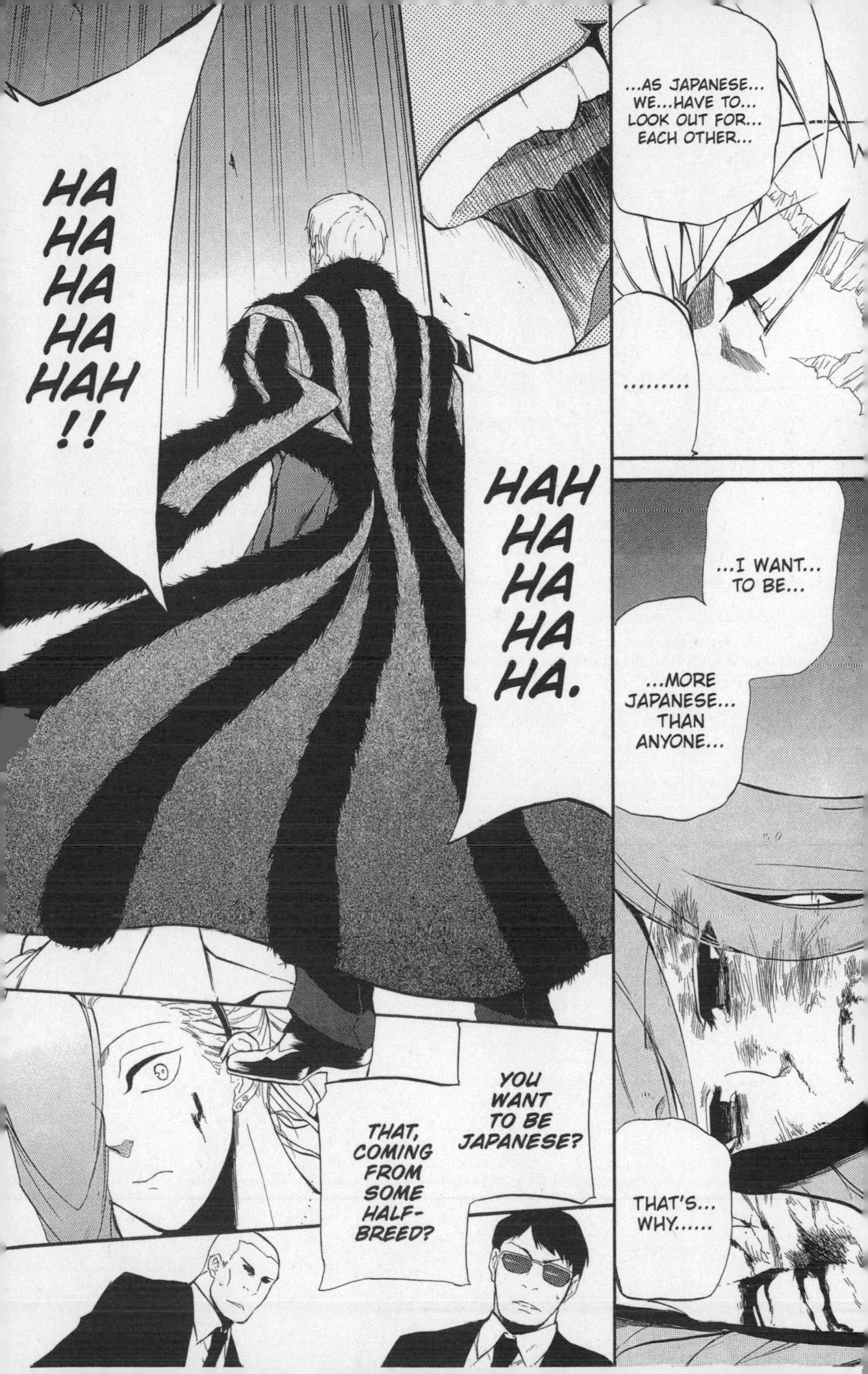
...AS JAPANESE... WE...HAVE TO... LOOK OUT FOR... EACH OTHER...
....
...I WANT... TO BE...
...MORE JAPANESE... THAN ANYONE...
THAT'S... WHY......
HAH HA HA HA HA.
HA HA HA HA HAH!!
YOU WANT TO BE JAPANESE?
THAT, COMING FROM SOME HALF-BREED?

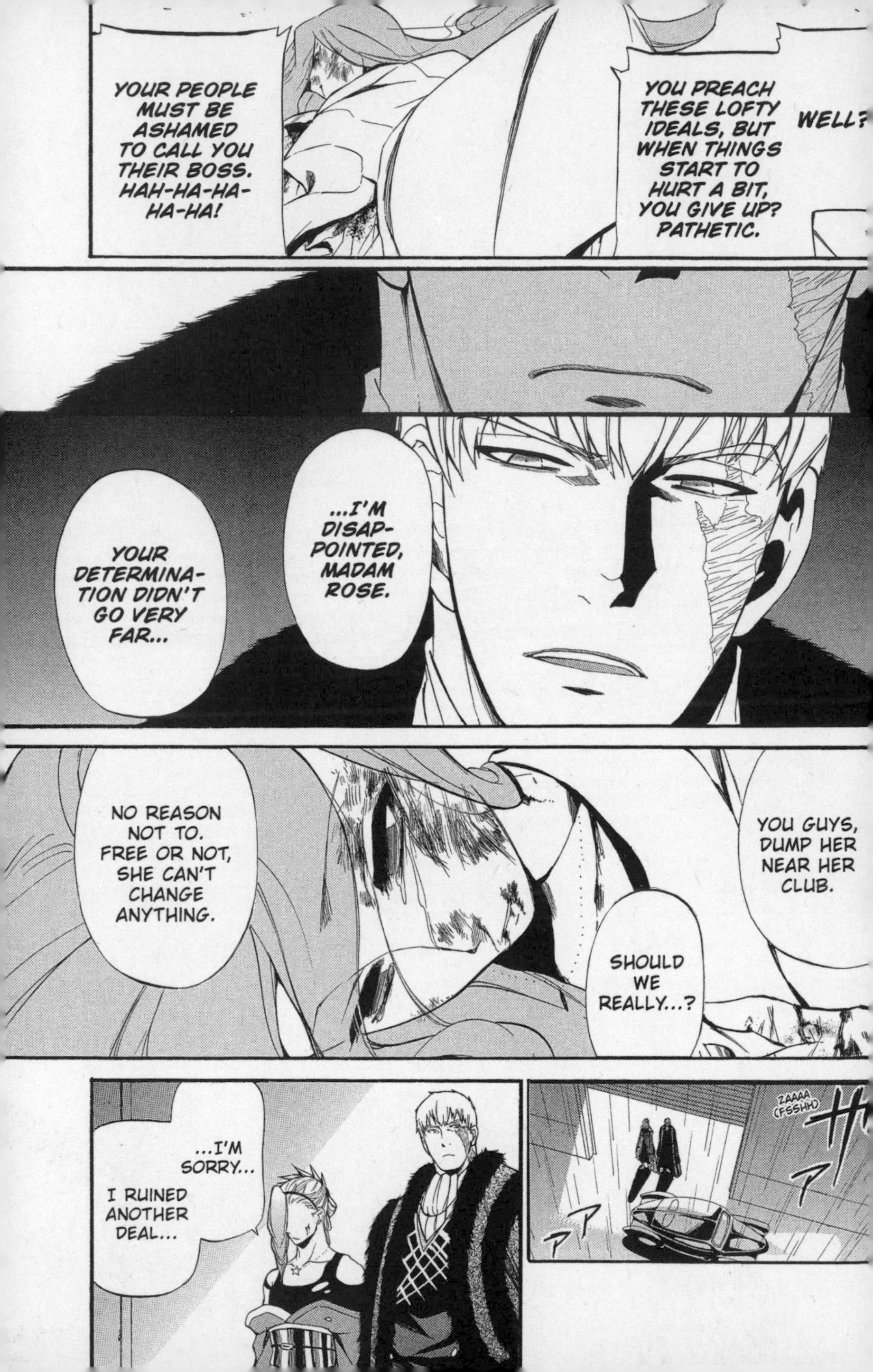
WELL?
YOU PREACH THESE LOFTY IDEALS, BUT WHEN THINGS START TO HURT A BIT, YOU GIVE UP? PATHETIC.
YOUR PEOPLE MUST BE ASHAMED TO CALL YOU THEIR BOSS. HAH-HA-HA-HA-HA!
...I'M DISAP-POINTED, MADAM ROSE.
YOUR DETERMINA-TION DIDN'T GO VERY FAR...
YOU GUYS, DUMP HER NEAR HER CLUB.
SHOULD WE REALLY...?
NO REASON NOT TO. FREE OR NOT, SHE CAN'T CHANGE ANYTHING.
ZAAAA (FSSHH)
...I'M SORRY...
I RUINED ANOTHER DEAL...

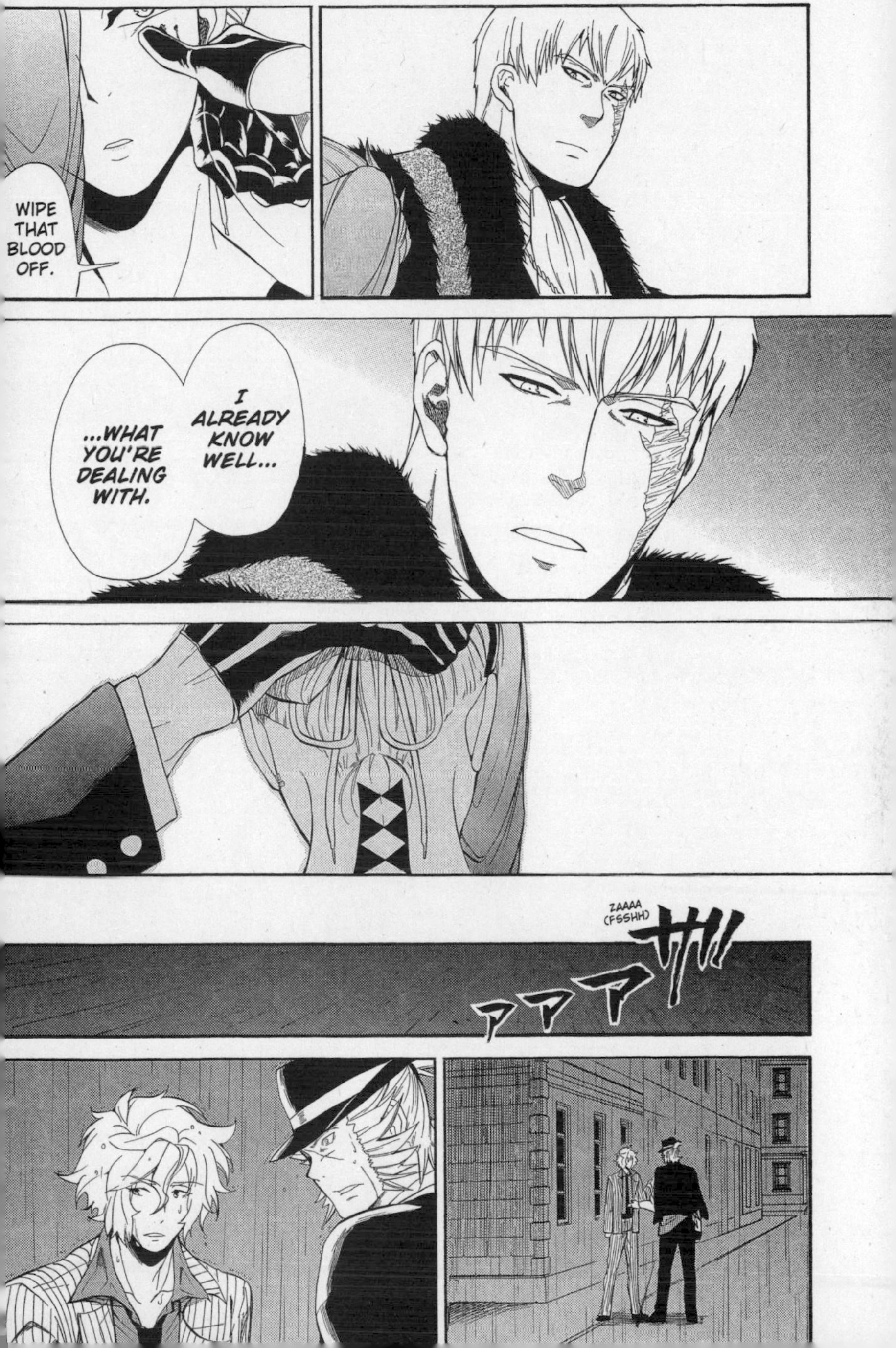
WIPE THAT BLOOD OFF.
I ALREADY KNOW WELL...
...WHAT YOU'RE DEALING WITH.
ザアアア
ZAAAA (FSSHH)

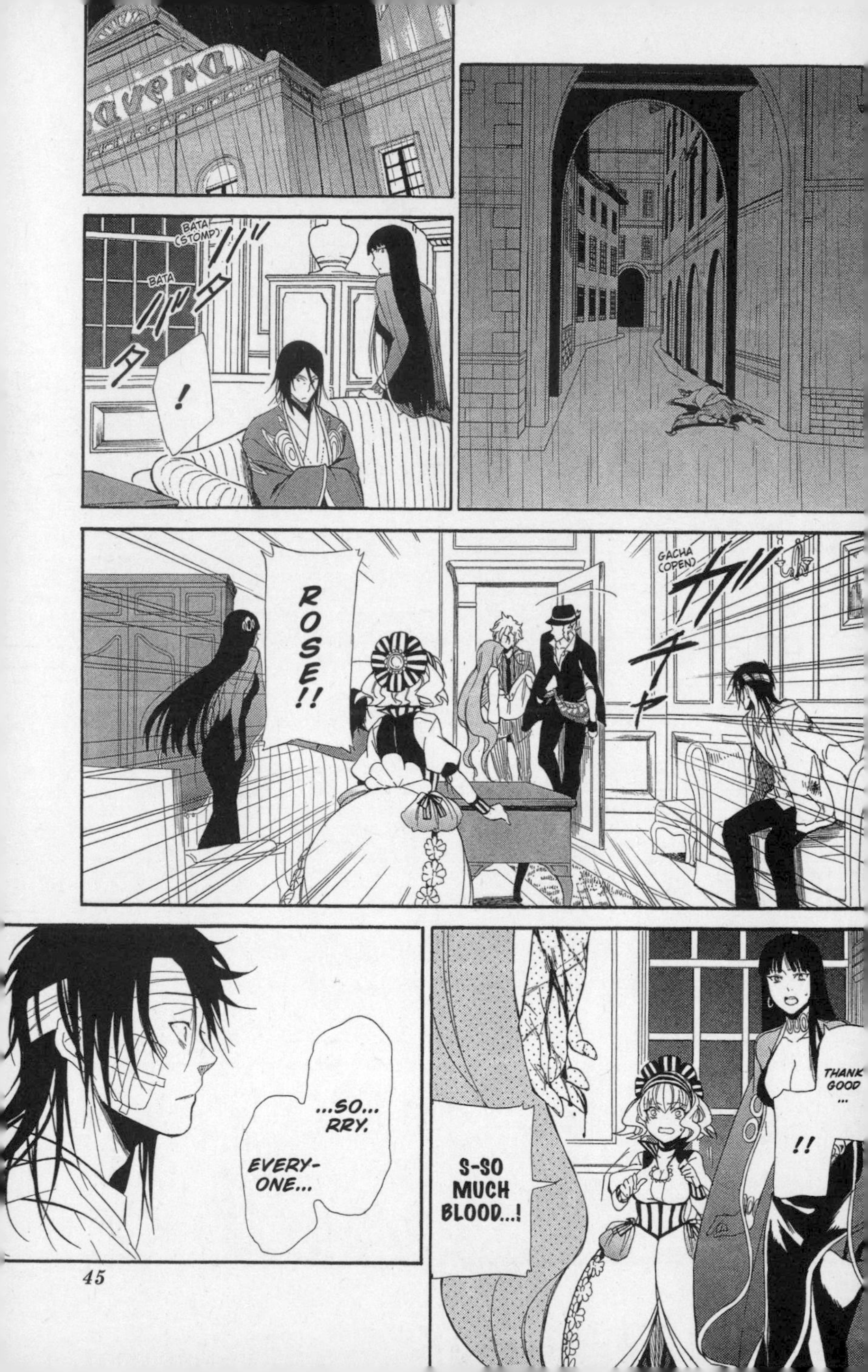

BATA (STOMP)
BATA
!
GACHA (OPEN)
ROSE!!
THANK GOOD ...
!!
S-SO MUCH BLOOD...!
...SO... RRY.
EVERY-ONE...

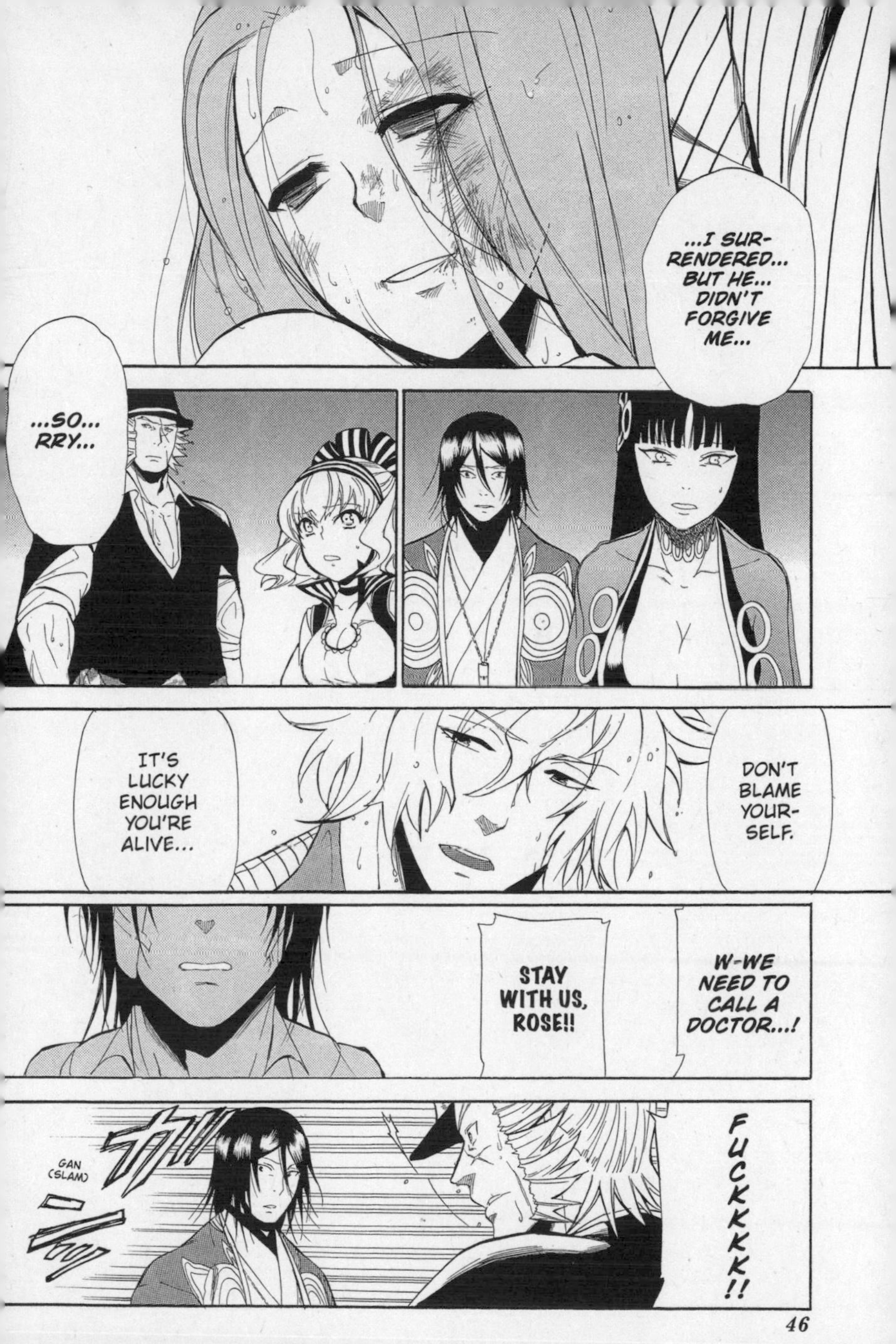
...I SUR-RENDERED... BUT HE... DIDN'T FORGIVE ME...
...SO... RRY...
DON'T BLAME YOUR-SELF.
IT'S LUCKY ENOUGH YOU'RE ALIVE...
W-WE NEED TO CALL A DOCTOR...!
STAY WITH US, ROSE!!
FUCKKKK!!
GAN (SLAM)

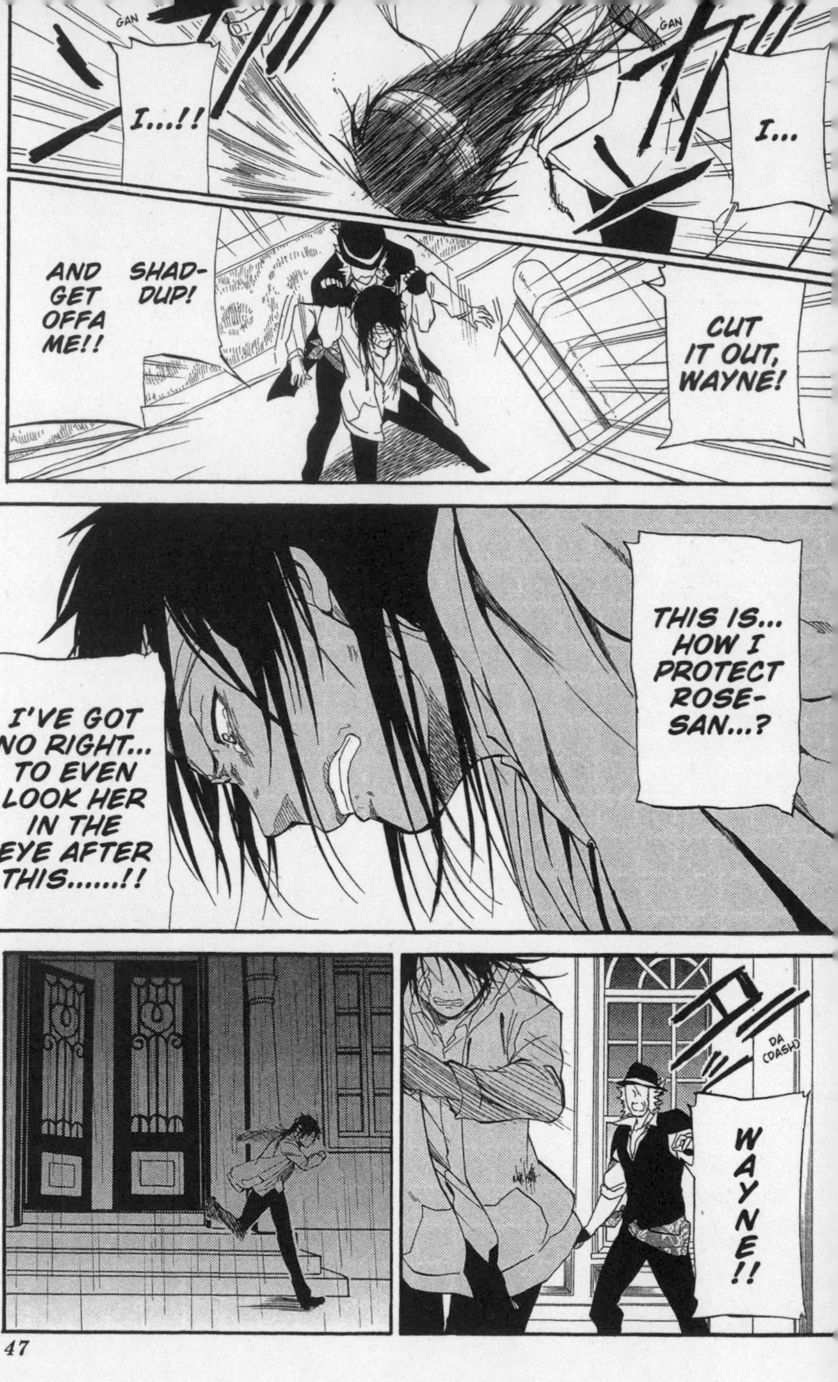
GAN
I...
GAN
I...!!
CUT IT OUT, WAYNE!
SHAD-DUP!
AND GET OFFA ME!!
THIS IS... HOW I PROTECT ROSE-SAN...?
I'VE GOT NO RIGHT... TO EVEN LOOK HER IN THE EYE AFTER THIS......!!
DA (DASH)
WAYNE!!

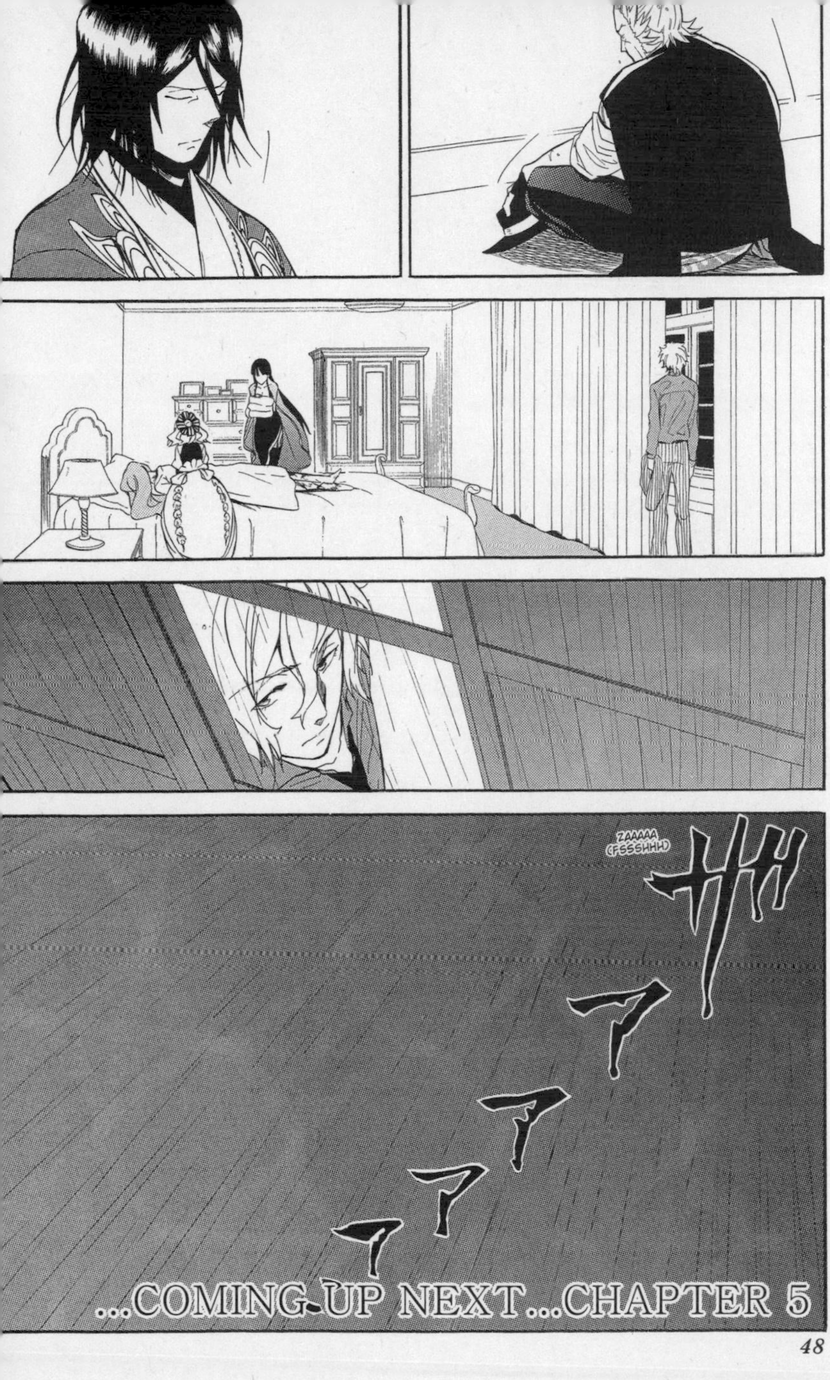
ZAAAAA (FSSSHHH)
ザアアアア
...COMING UP NEXT...CHAPTER 5

Chapter 5

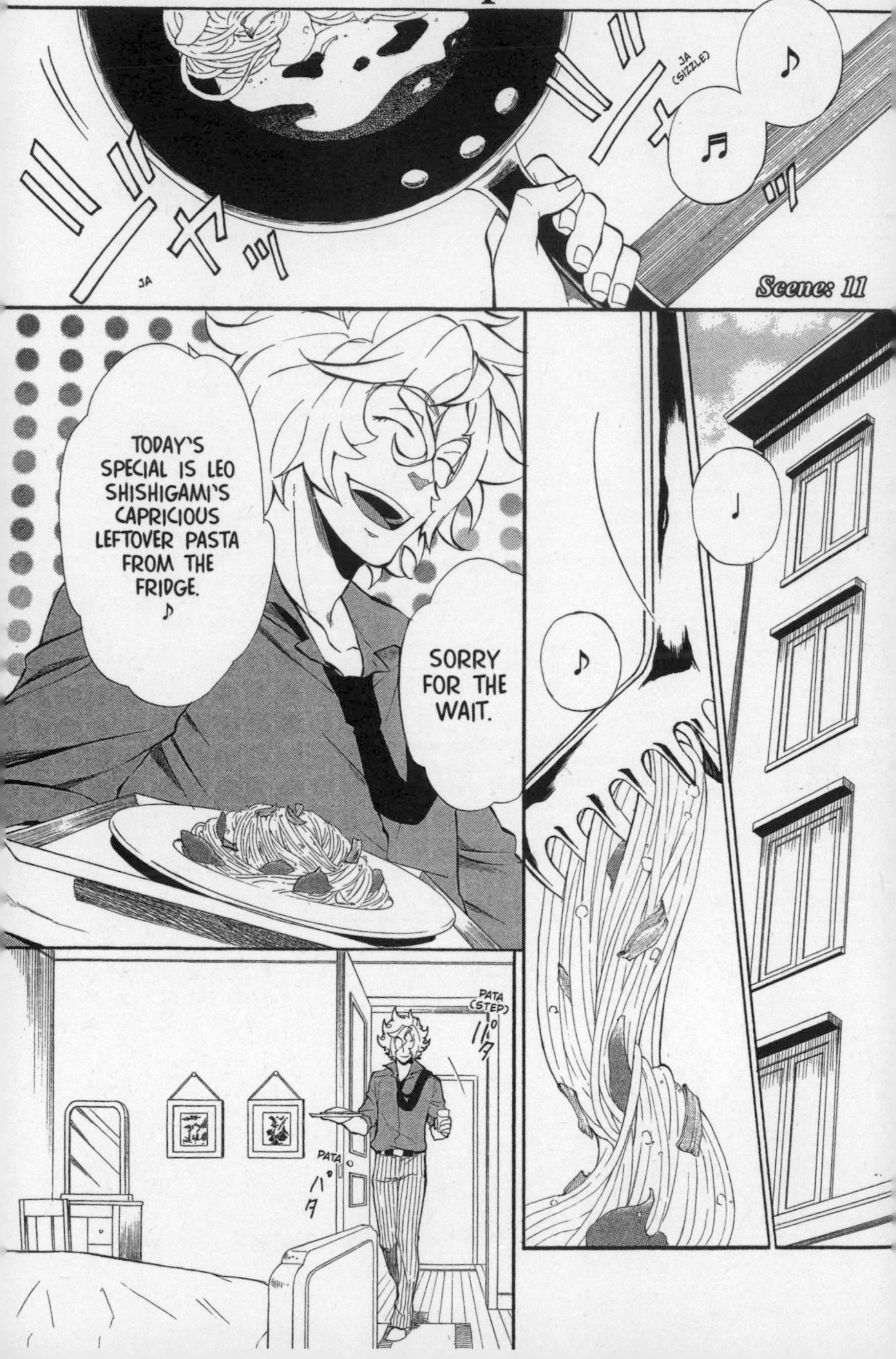
JA (SIZZLE)
JA
Scene: 11
SORRY FOR THE WAIT.
TODAY'S SPECIAL IS LEO SHISHIGAMI'S CAPRICIOUS LEFTOVER PASTA FROM THE FRIDGE. ♪
PATA (STEP)
PATA

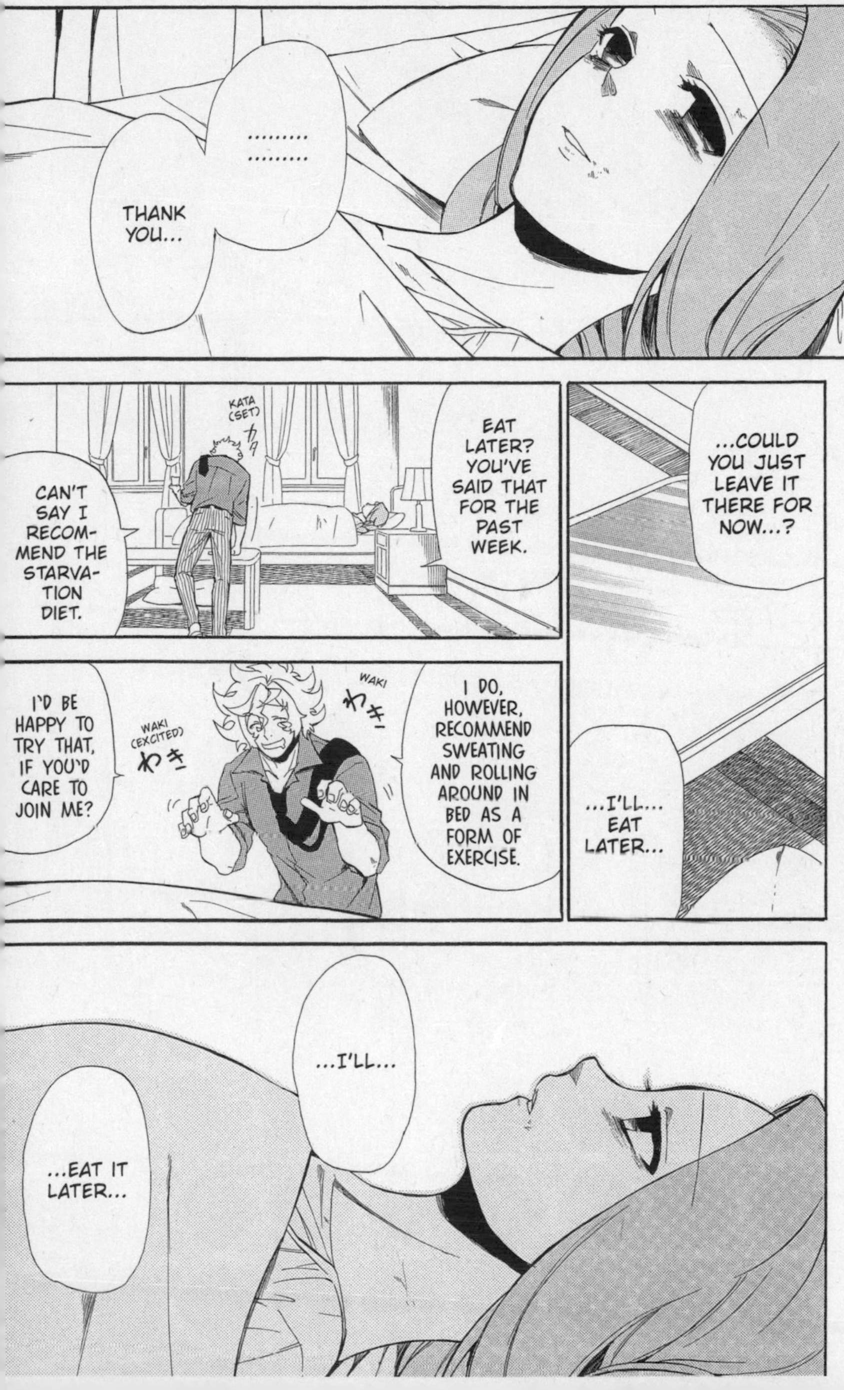
....
....
THANK YOU...
...COULD YOU JUST LEAVE IT THERE FOR NOW...?
...I'LL... EAT LATER...
EAT LATER? YOU'VE SAID THAT FOR THE PAST WEEK.
KATA (SET) カタ
CAN'T SAY I RECOMMEND THE STARVATION DIET.
I DO, HOWEVER, RECOMMEND SWEATING AND ROLLING AROUND IN BED AS A FORM OF EXERCISE.
WAKI わキ
WAKI (EXCITED) わき
I'D BE HAPPY TO TRY THAT, IF YOU'D CARE TO JOIN ME?
...I'LL...
...EAT IT LATER...

Scene: 11

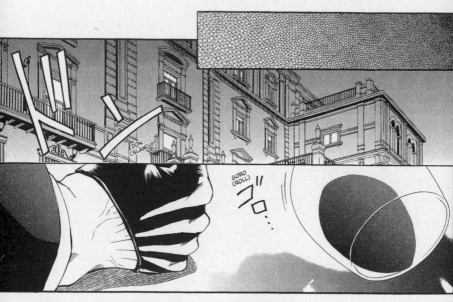

DON (SLAM)

GORO (ROLL)
ゴロ...

OF COURSE NOT.

.... BUTLER.

YOU SURE THAT WASN'T A MISTRANS-LATION...?

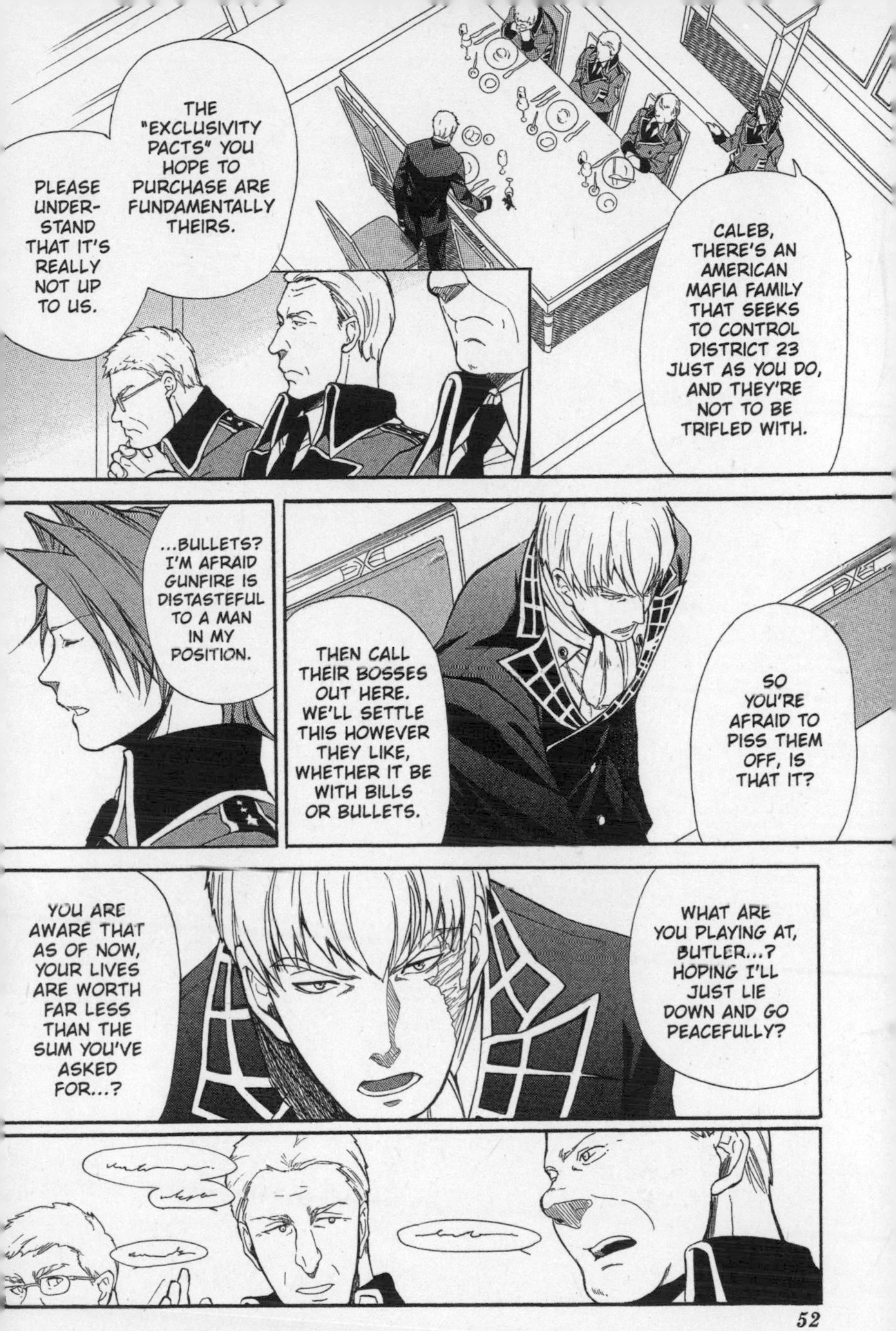
CALEB, THERE'S AN AMERICAN MAFIA FAMILY THAT SEEKS TO CONTROL DISTRICT 23 JUST AS YOU DO, AND THEY'RE NOT TO BE TRIFLED WITH.
THE "EXCLUSIVITY PACTS" YOU HOPE TO PURCHASE ARE FUNDAMENTALLY THEIRS.
PLEASE UNDER-STAND THAT IT'S REALLY NOT UP TO US.
SO YOU'RE AFRAID TO PISS THEM OFF, IS THAT IT?
THEN CALL THEIR BOSSES OUT HERE. WE'LL SETTLE THIS HOWEVER THEY LIKE, WHETHER IT BE WITH BILLS OR BULLETS.
...BULLETS? I'M AFRAID GUNFIRE IS DISTASTEFUL TO A MAN IN MY POSITION.
WHAT ARE YOU PLAYING AT, BUTLER...? HOPING I'LL JUST LIE DOWN AND GO PEACEFULLY?
YOU ARE AWARE THAT AS OF NOW, YOUR LIVES ARE WORTH FAR LESS THAN THE SUM YOU'VE ASKED FOR...?

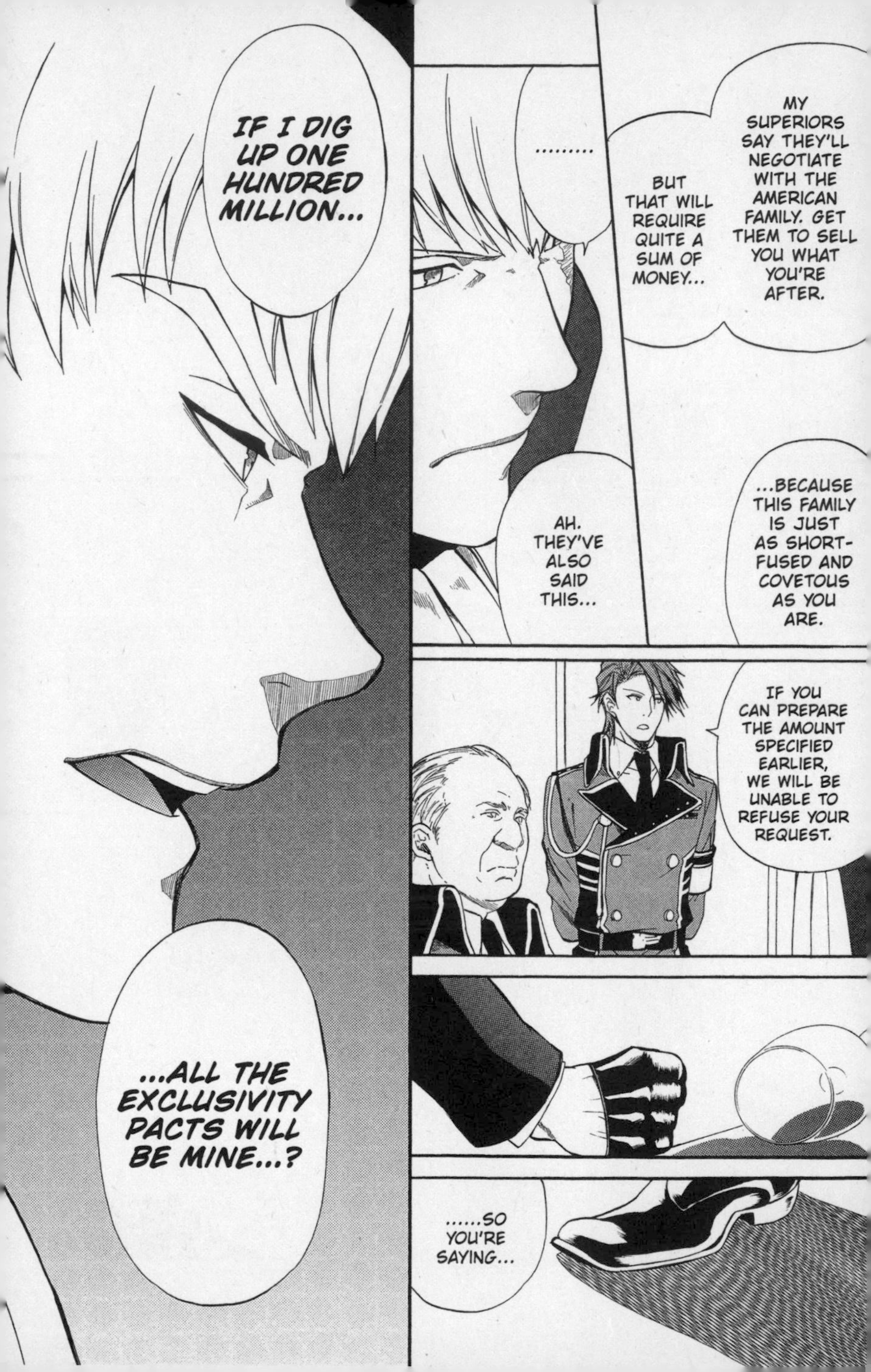
MY SUPERIORS SAY THEY'LL NEGOTIATE WITH THE AMERICAN FAMILY. GET THEM TO SELL YOU WHAT YOU'RE AFTER.
BUT THAT WILL REQUIRE QUITE A SUM OF MONEY...
...BECAUSE THIS FAMILY IS JUST AS SHORT-FUSED AND COVETOUS AS YOU ARE.
....
AH. THEY'VE ALSO SAID THIS...
IF YOU CAN PREPARE THE AMOUNT SPECIFIED EARLIER, WE WILL BE UNABLE TO REFUSE YOUR REQUEST.
......SO YOU'RE SAYING...
IF I DIG UP ONE HUNDRED MILLION...
...ALL THE EXCLUSIVITY PACTS WILL BE MINE...?

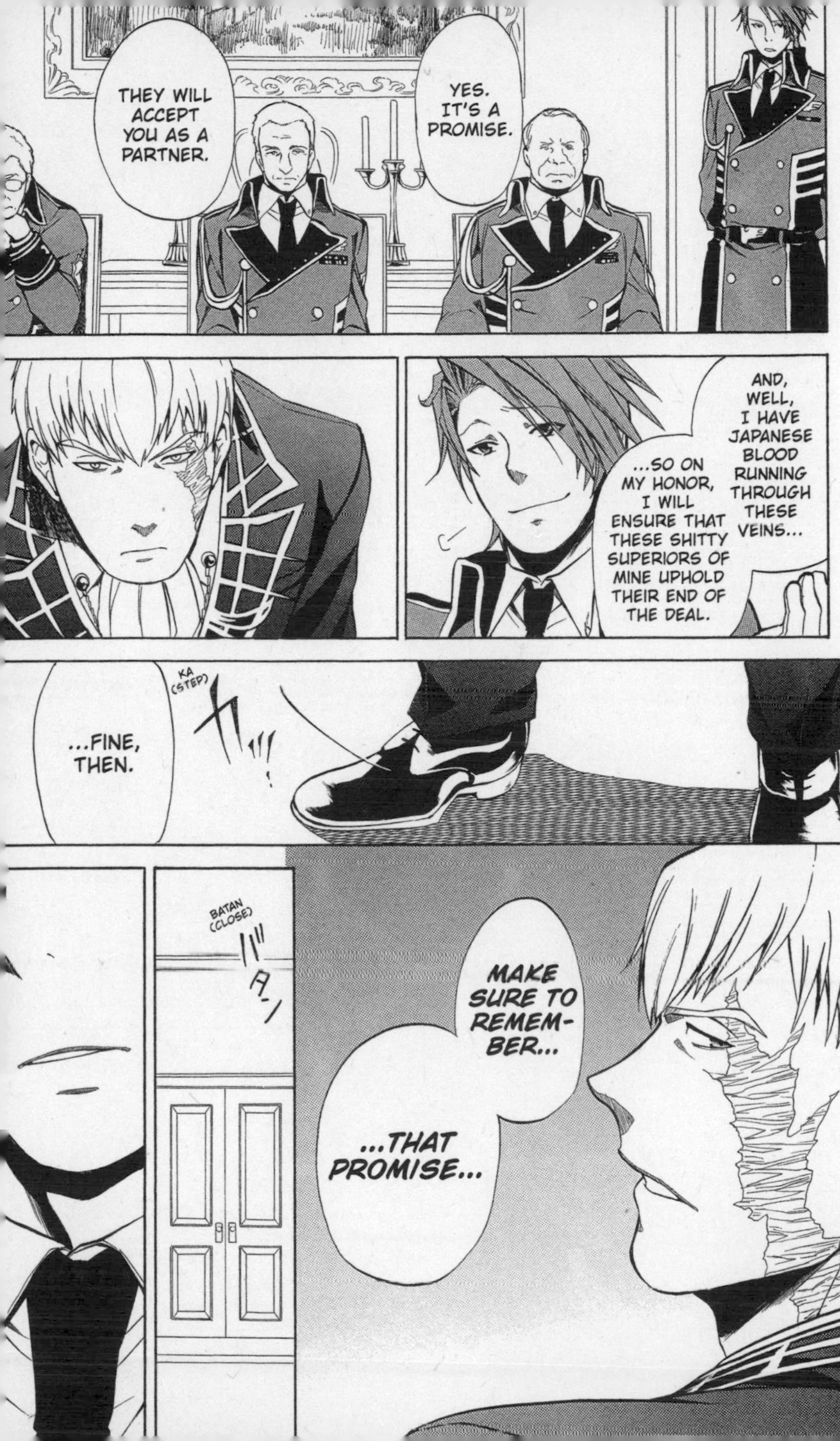
YES. IT'S A PROMISE.
THEY WILL ACCEPT YOU AS A PARTNER.
AND, WELL, I HAVE JAPANESE BLOOD RUNNING THROUGH THESE VEINS...
...SO ON MY HONOR, I WILL ENSURE THAT THESE SHITTY SUPERIORS OF MINE UPHOLD THEIR END OF THE DEAL.
KA (STEP)
...FINE, THEN.
MAKE SURE TO REMEMBER...
...THAT PROMISE...
BATAN (CLOSE)

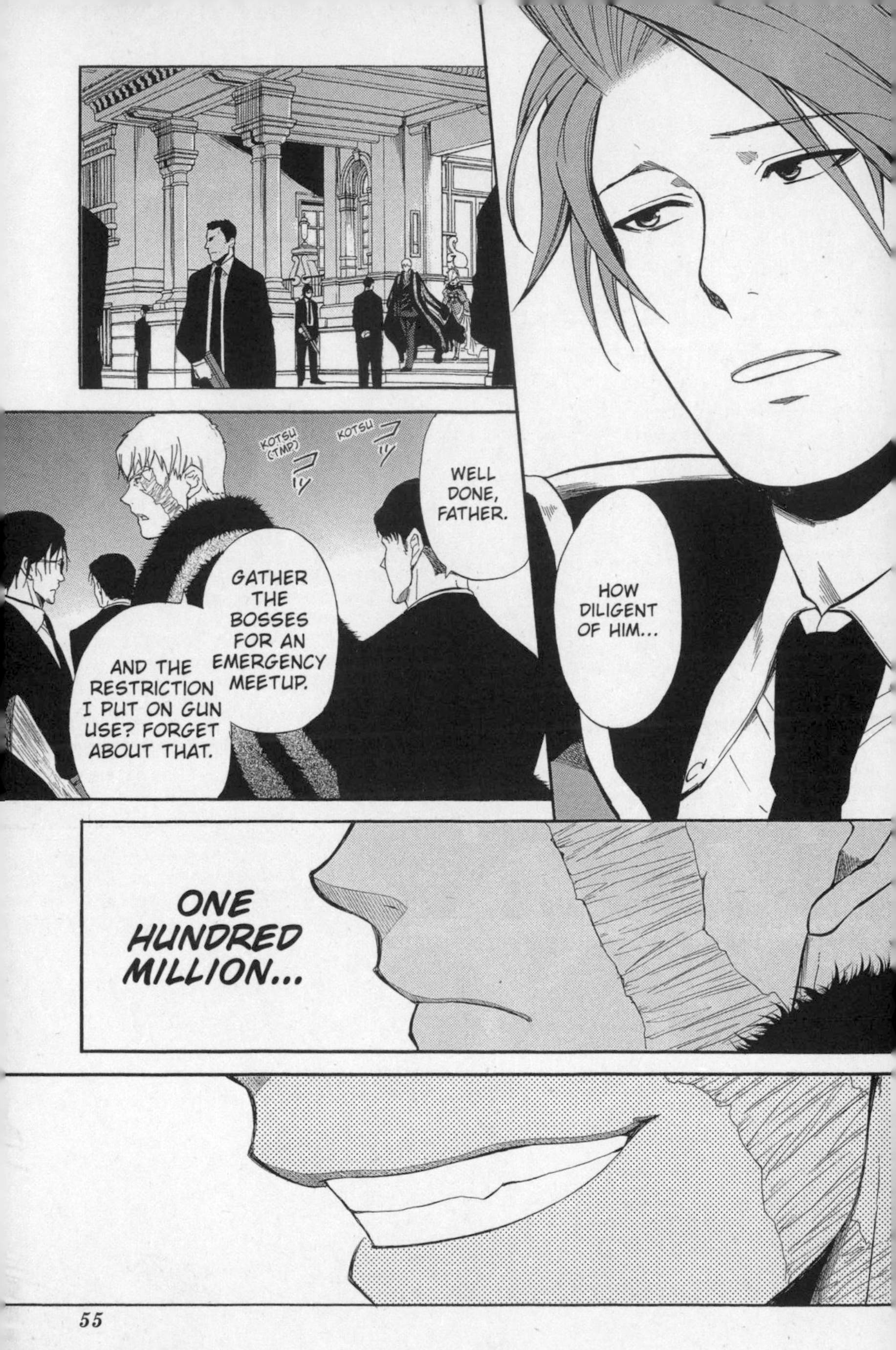
HOW DILIGENT OF HIM...
KOTSU
KOTSU (TMP)
WELL DONE, FATHER.
GATHER THE BOSSES FOR AN EMERGENCY MEETUP.
AND THE RESTRICTION I PUT ON GUN USE? FORGET ABOUT THAT.
ONE HUNDRED MILLION...

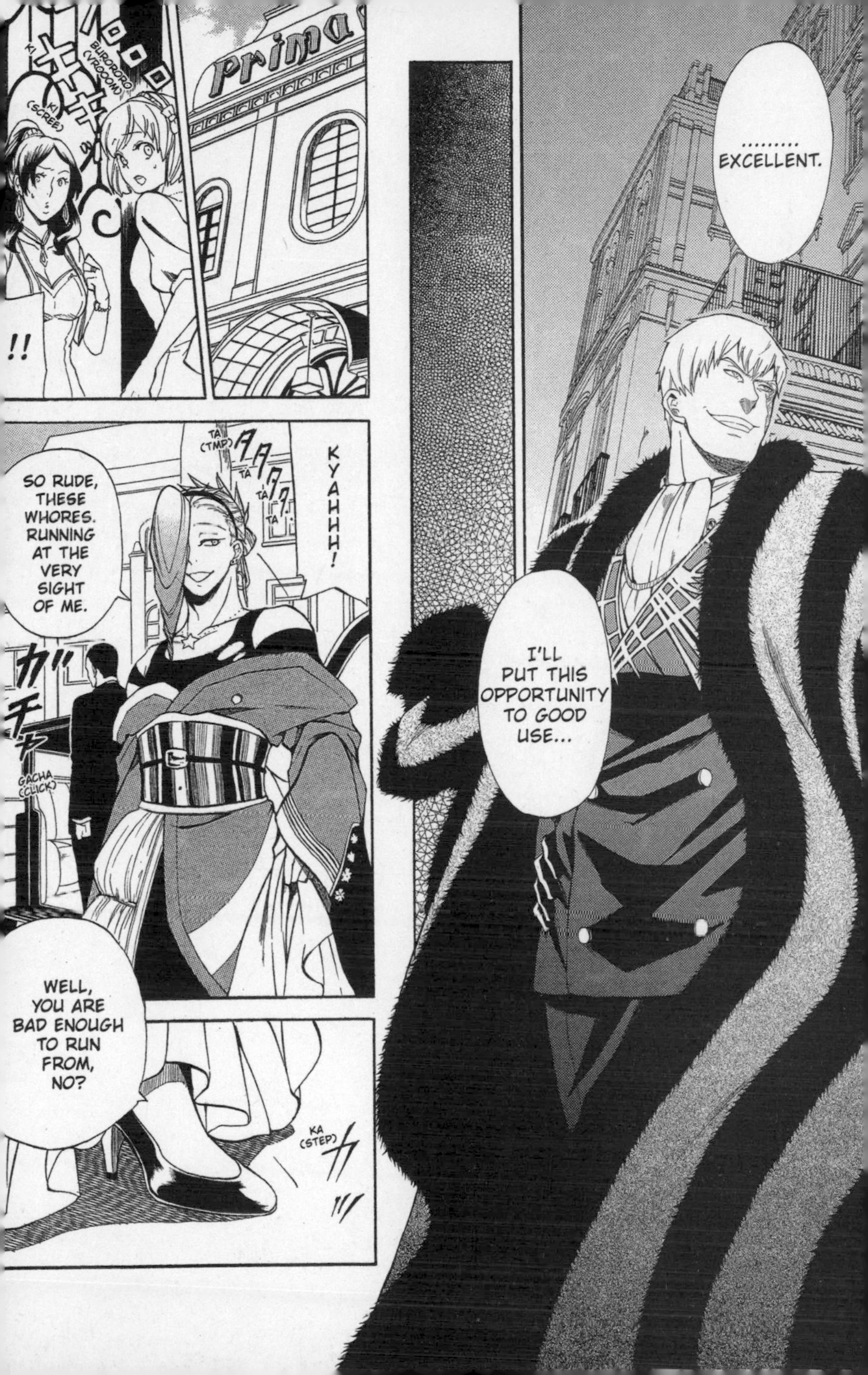

....
EXCELLENT.
I'LL PUT THIS OPPORTUNITY TO GOOD USE...
Prima
BURORORO (VROOOM)
KI
KI (SCREE)
!!
KYAHHH!
TA (TMP) TA TA TA
SO RUDE, THESE WHORES. RUNNING AT THE VERY SIGHT OF ME.
GACHA (CLICK)
WELL, YOU ARE BAD ENOUGH TO RUN FROM, NO?
KA (STEP)

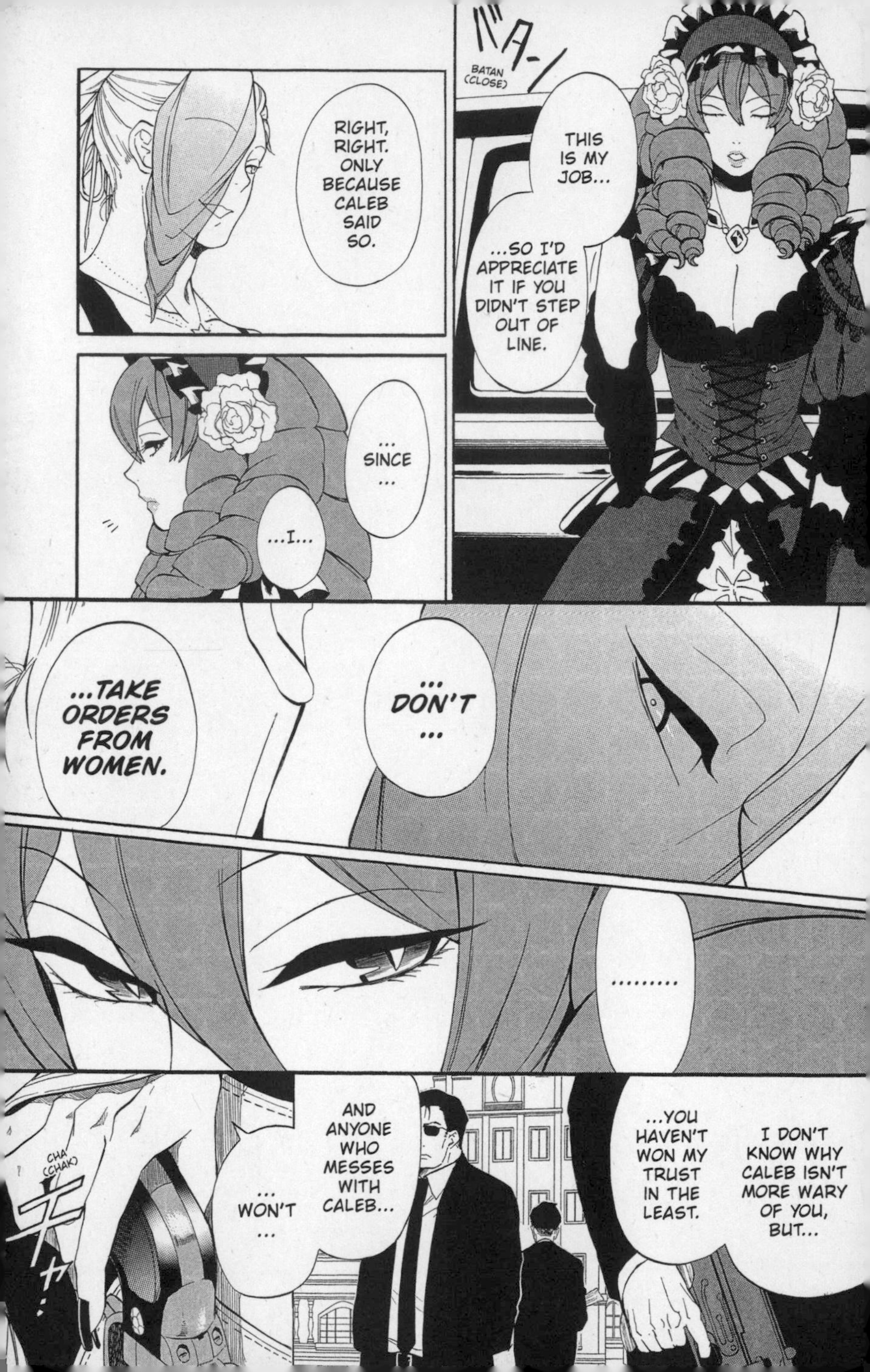
BATAN (CLOSE)
THIS IS MY JOB...
...SO I'D APPRECIATE IT IF YOU DIDN'T STEP OUT OF LINE.
RIGHT, RIGHT. ONLY BECAUSE CALEB SAID SO.
... SINCE ...
...I...
... DON'T ...
...TAKE ORDERS FROM WOMEN.
....
I DON'T KNOW WHY CALEB ISN'T MORE WARY OF YOU, BUT...
...YOU HAVEN'T WON MY TRUST IN THE LEAST.
AND ANYONE WHO MESSES WITH CALEB...
... WON'T ...
CHA (CHAK)

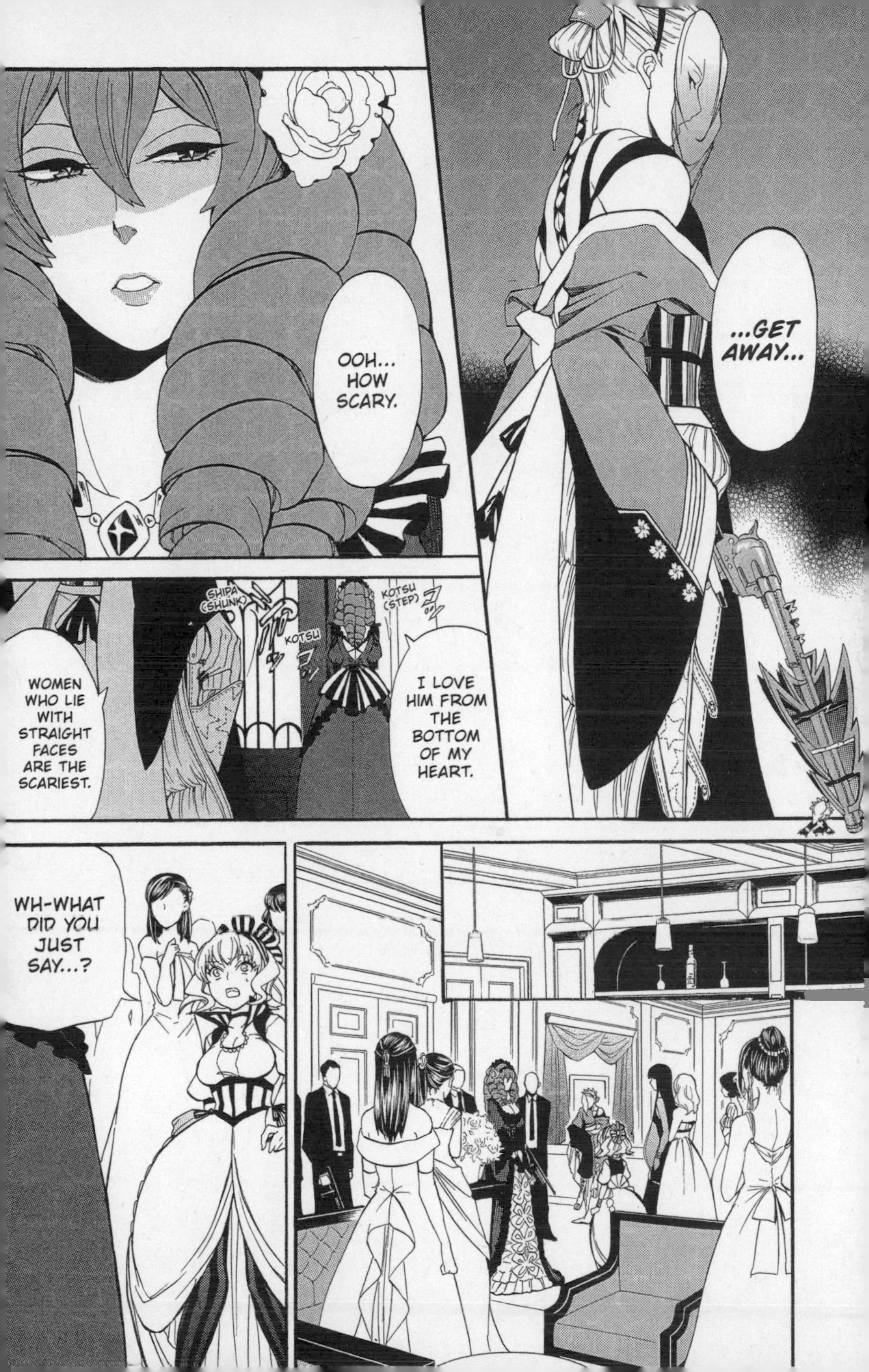
...GET AWAY...
OOH... HOW SCARY.
I LOVE HIM FROM THE BOTTOM OF MY HEART.
KOTSU (STEP)
KOTSU
SHIPA (SHUNK)
WOMEN WHO LIE WITH STRAIGHT FACES ARE THE SCARIEST.
WH-WHAT DID YOU JUST SAY...?

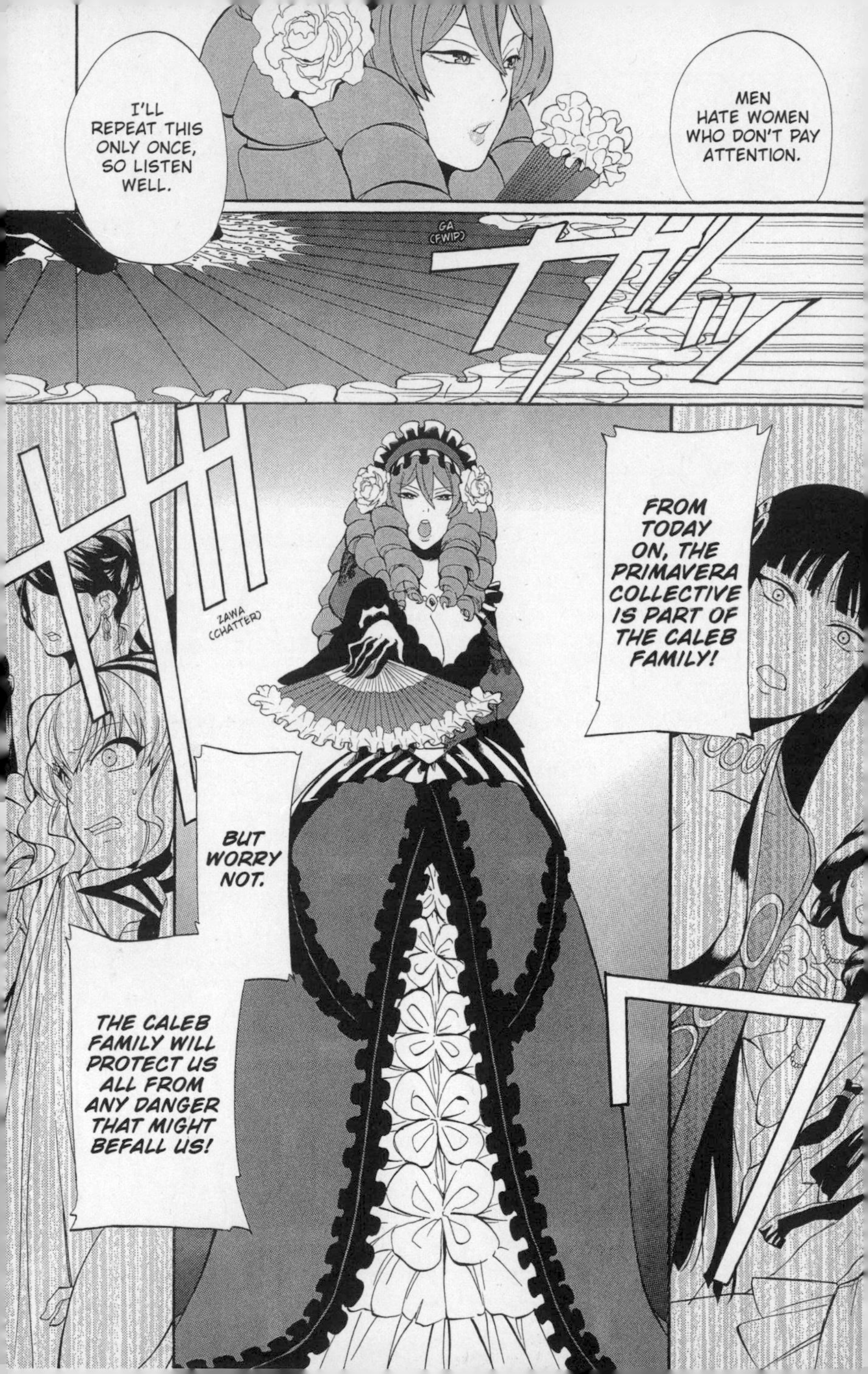
MEN HATE WOMEN WHO DON'T PAY ATTENTION.
I'LL REPEAT THIS ONLY ONCE, SO LISTEN WELL.
GA (FWIP)
FROM TODAY ON, THE PRIMAVERA COLLECTIVE IS PART OF THE CALEB FAMILY!
ZAWA (CHATTER)
BUT WORRY NOT.
THE CALEB FAMILY WILL PROTECT US ALL FROM ANY DANGER THAT MIGHT BEFALL US!

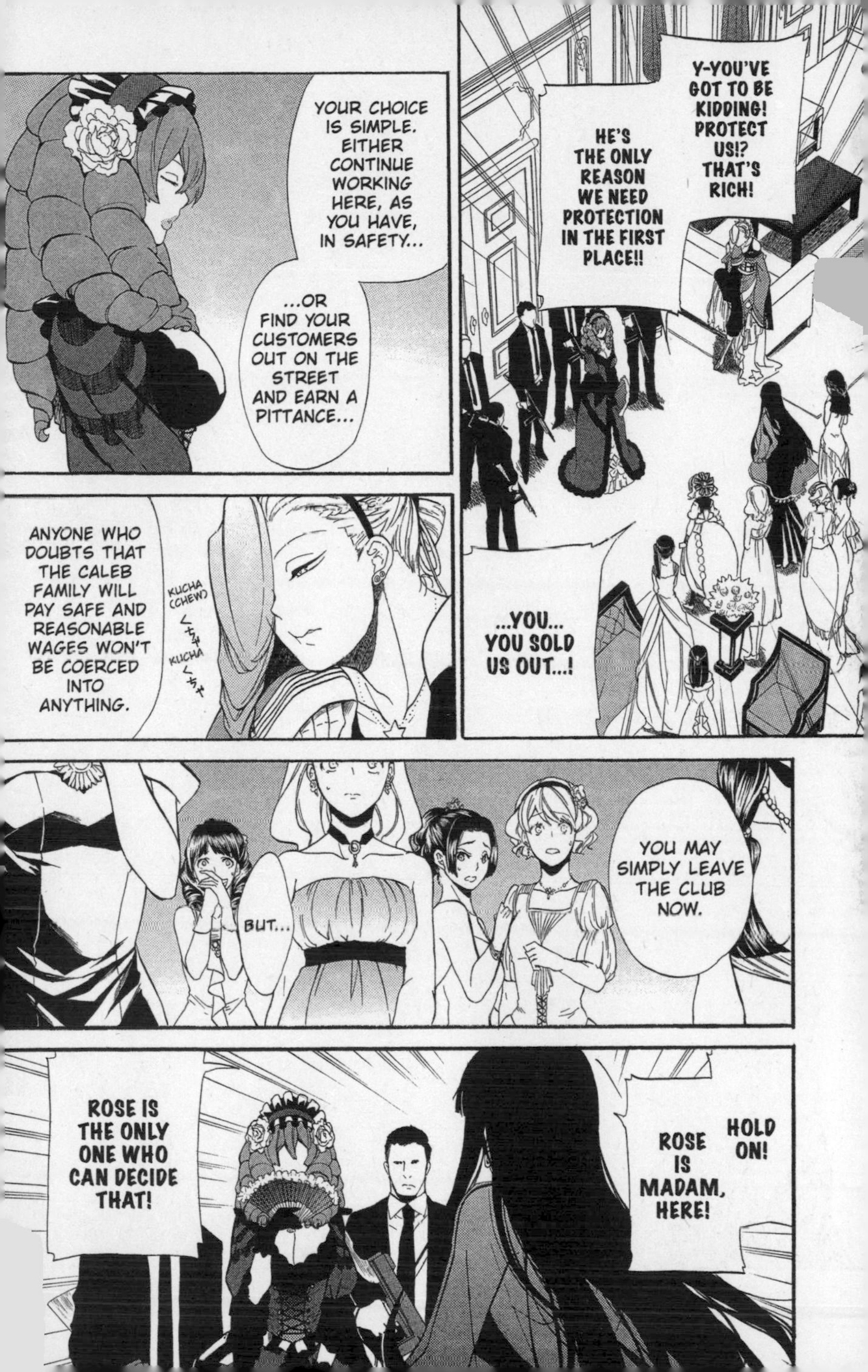
Y-YOU'VE GOT TO BE KIDDING! PROTECT US!? THAT'S RICH!
HE'S THE ONLY REASON WE NEED PROTECTION IN THE FIRST PLACE!!
...YOU... YOU SOLD US OUT...!
YOUR CHOICE IS SIMPLE. EITHER CONTINUE WORKING HERE, AS YOU HAVE, IN SAFETY...
...OR FIND YOUR CUSTOMERS OUT ON THE STREET AND EARN A PITTANCE...
ANYONE WHO DOUBTS THAT THE CALEB FAMILY WILL PAY SAFE AND REASONABLE WAGES WON'T BE COERCED INTO ANYTHING.
KUCHA (CHEW)
くちゃ
KUCHA
くちゃ
YOU MAY SIMPLY LEAVE THE CLUB NOW.
BUT...
HOLD ON!
ROSE IS MADAM, HERE!
ROSE IS THE ONLY ONE WHO CAN DECIDE THAT!

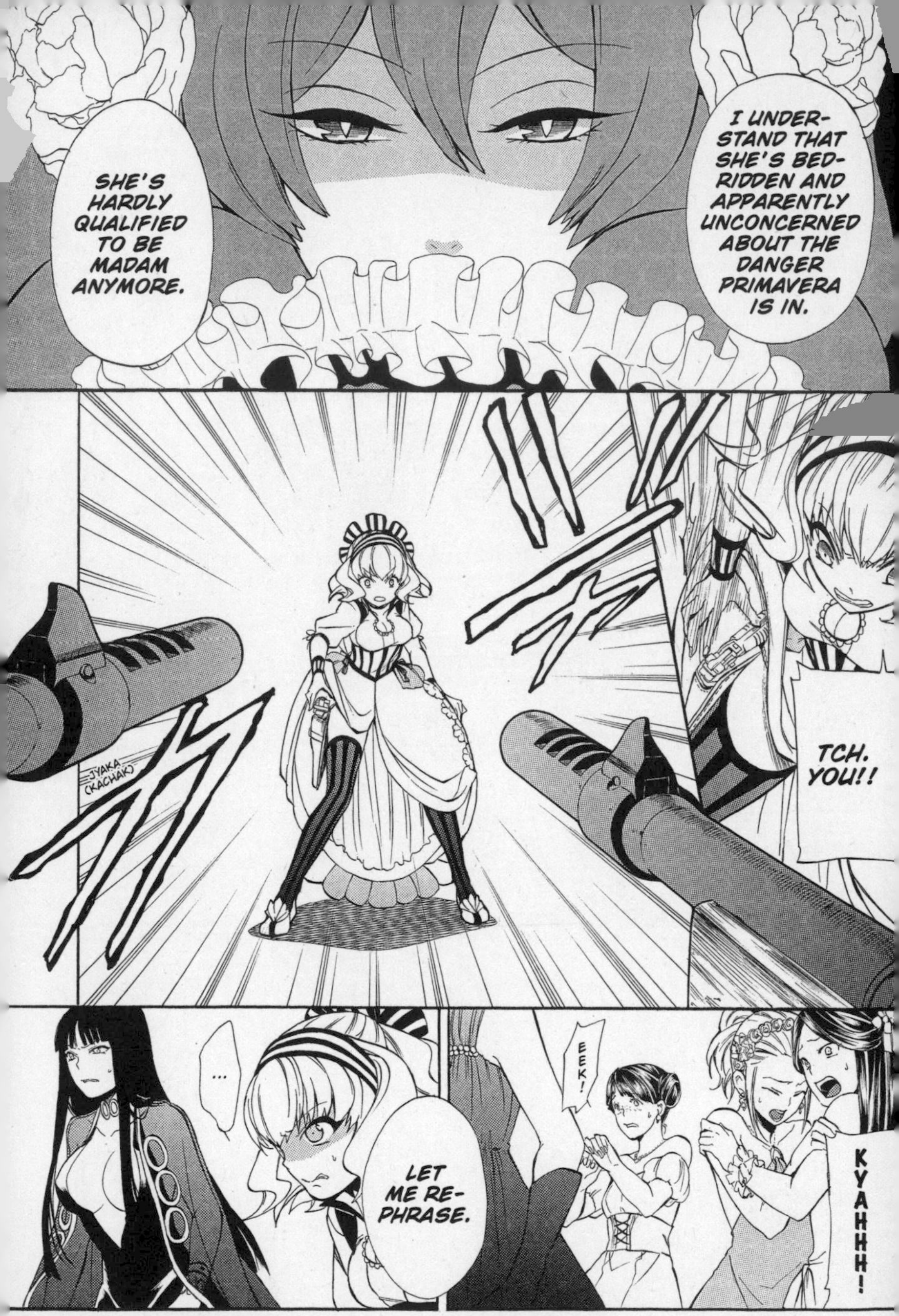
I UNDER-STAND THAT SHE'S BED-RIDDEN AND APPARENTLY UNCONCERNED ABOUT THE DANGER PRIMAVERA IS IN.
SHE'S HARDLY QUALIFIED TO BE MADAM ANYMORE.
TCH. YOU!!
JYAKA (KACHAK)
EEK!
KYAHHH!
...
LET ME RE-PHRASE.

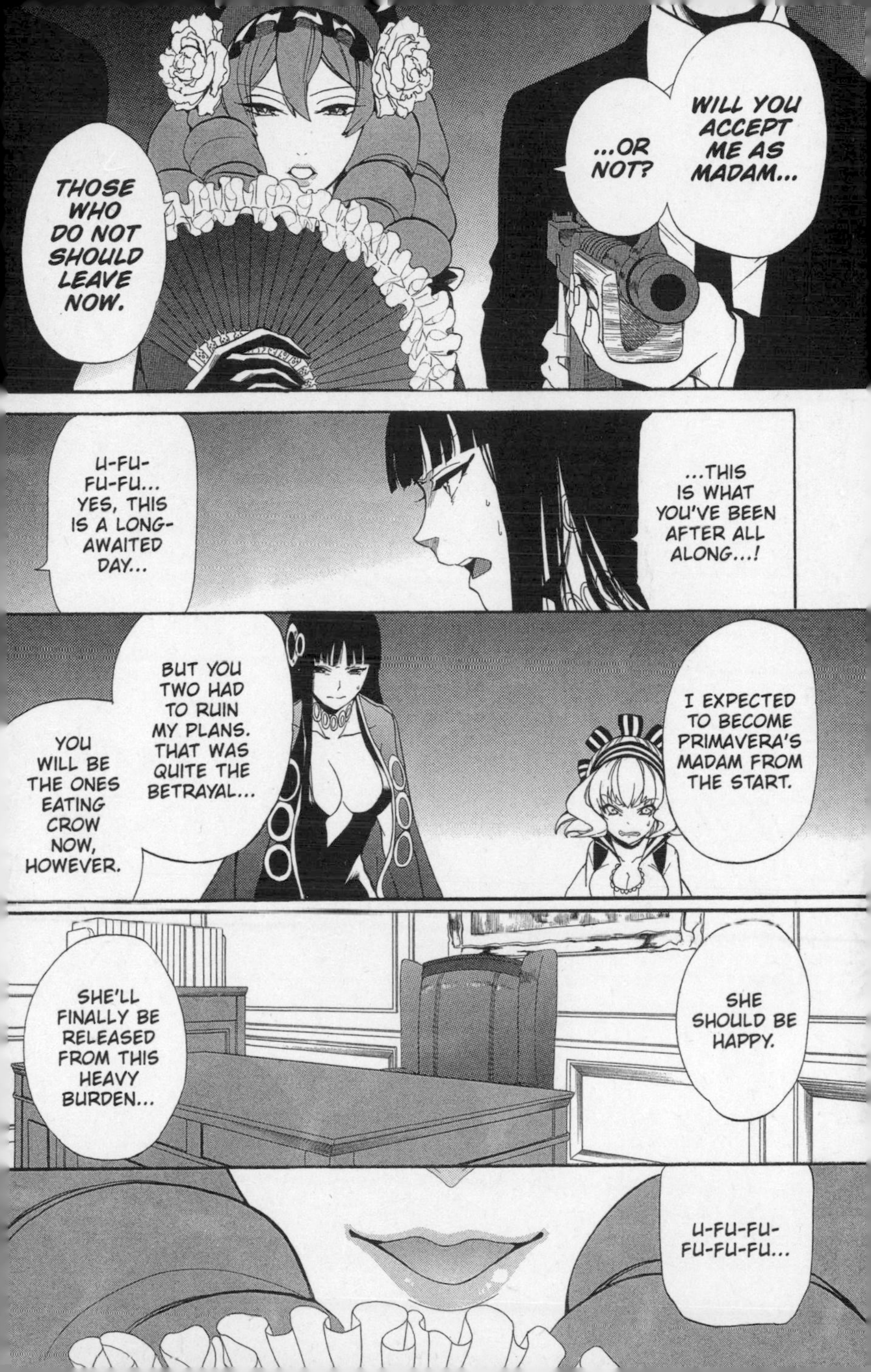
WILL YOU ACCEPT ME AS MADAM...
...OR NOT?
THOSE WHO DO NOT SHOULD LEAVE NOW.
...THIS IS WHAT YOU'VE BEEN AFTER ALL ALONG...!
U-FU-FU-FU... YES, THIS IS A LONG-AWAITED DAY...
I EXPECTED TO BECOME PRIMAVERA'S MADAM FROM THE START.
BUT YOU TWO HAD TO RUIN MY PLANS. THAT WAS QUITE THE BETRAYAL...
YOU WILL BE THE ONES EATING CROW NOW, HOWEVER.
SHE SHOULD BE HAPPY.
SHE'LL FINALLY BE RELEASED FROM THIS HEAVY BURDEN...
U-FU-FU-FU-FU-FU-FU...

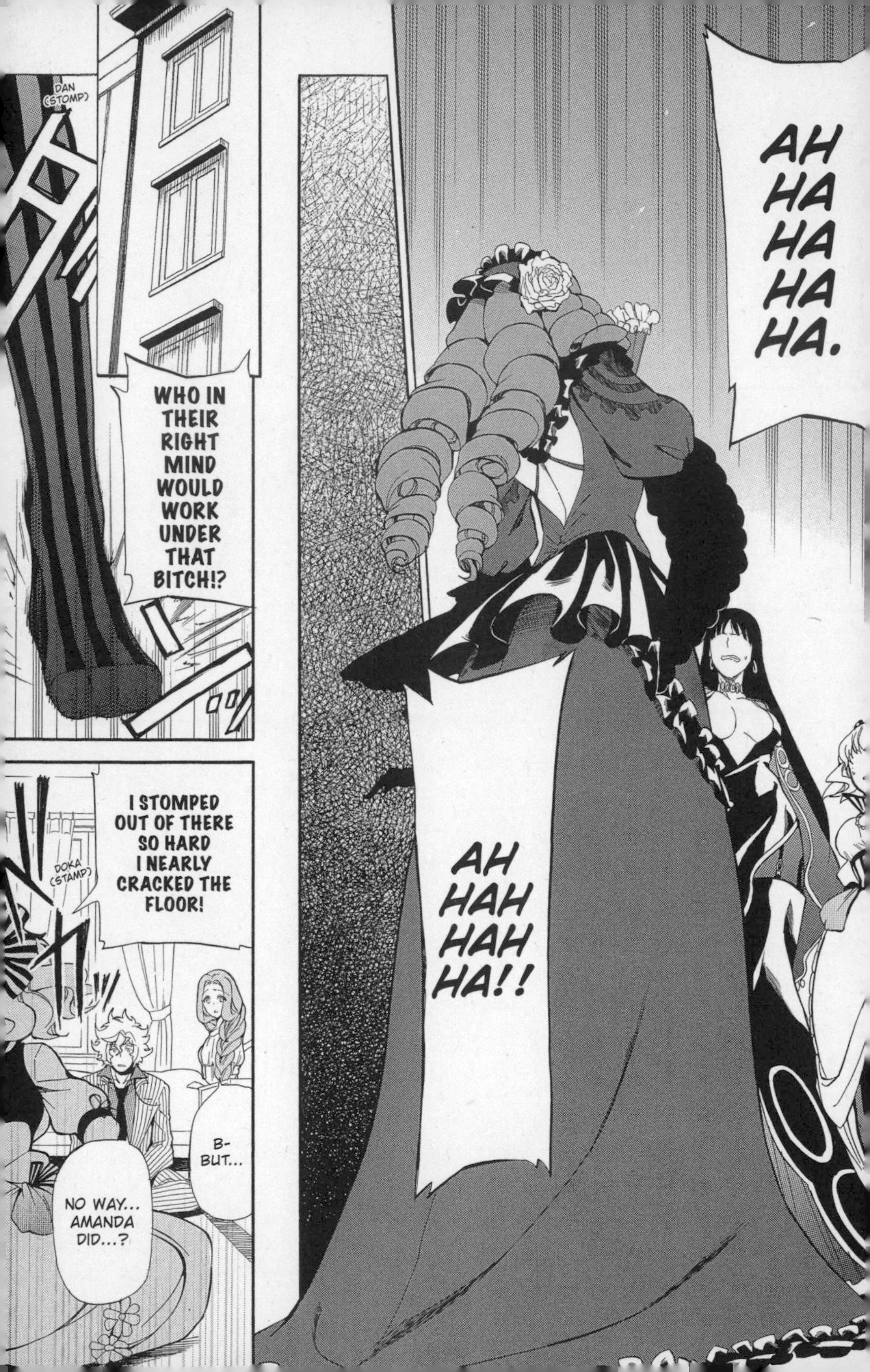
AH HA HA HA HA.
AH HAH HAH HA!!
WHO IN THEIR RIGHT MIND WOULD WORK UNDER THAT BITCH!?
DAN (STOMP)
I STOMPED OUT OF THERE SO HARD I NEARLY CRACKED THE FLOOR!
DOKA (STAMP)
B- BUT...
NO WAY... AMANDA DID...?

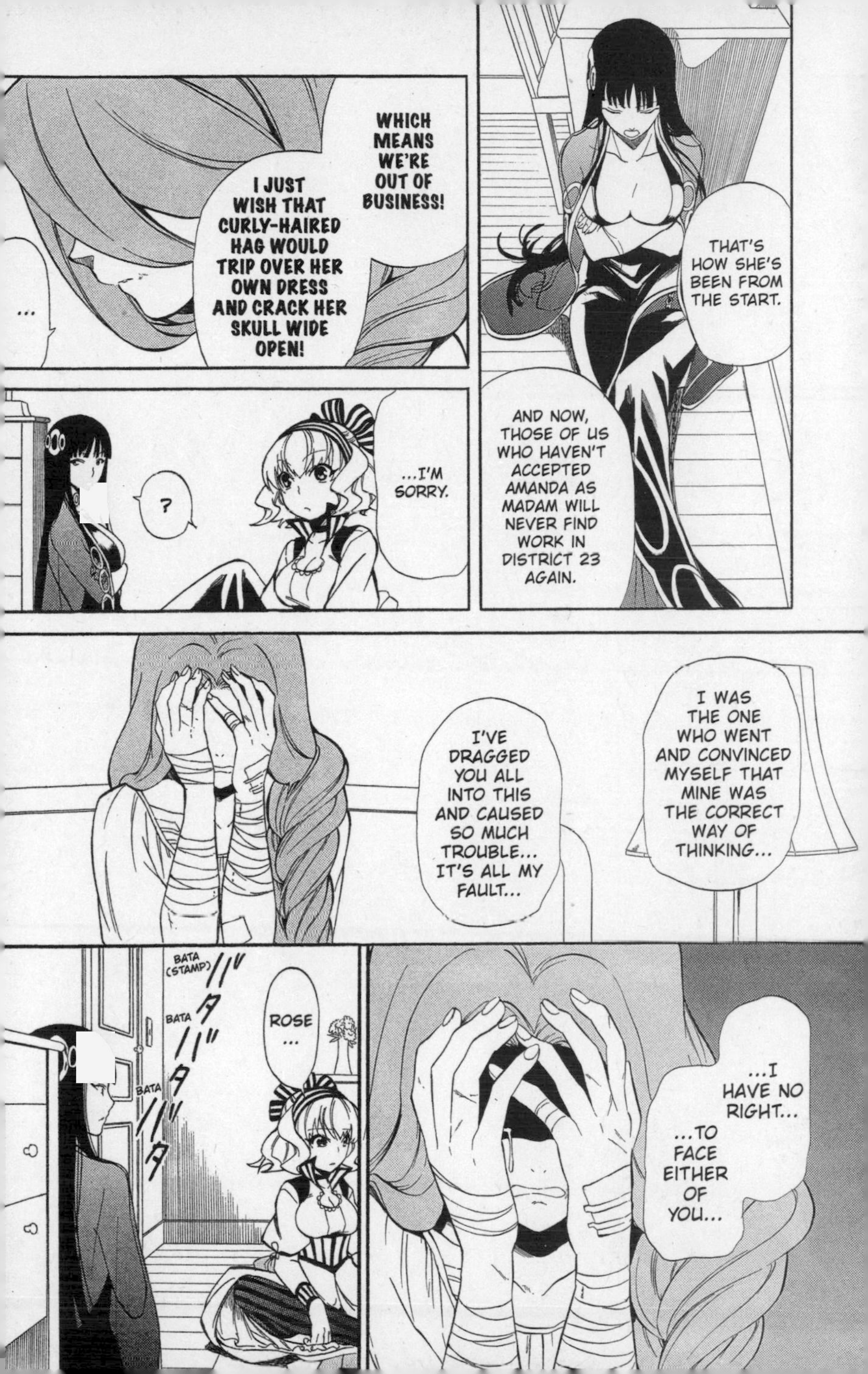
THAT'S HOW SHE'S BEEN FROM THE START.
AND NOW, THOSE OF US WHO HAVEN'T ACCEPTED AMANDA AS MADAM WILL NEVER FIND WORK IN DISTRICT 23 AGAIN.
WHICH MEANS WE'RE OUT OF BUSINESS!
I JUST WISH THAT CURLY-HAIRED HAG WOULD TRIP OVER HER OWN DRESS AND CRACK HER SKULL WIDE OPEN!
...
...I'M SORRY.
?
I WAS THE ONE WHO WENT AND CONVINCED MYSELF THAT MINE WAS THE CORRECT WAY OF THINKING...
I'VE DRAGGED YOU ALL INTO THIS AND CAUSED SO MUCH TROUBLE... IT'S ALL MY FAULT...
...I HAVE NO RIGHT...
...TO FACE EITHER OF YOU...
ROSE...
BATA (STAMP)
BATA
BATA

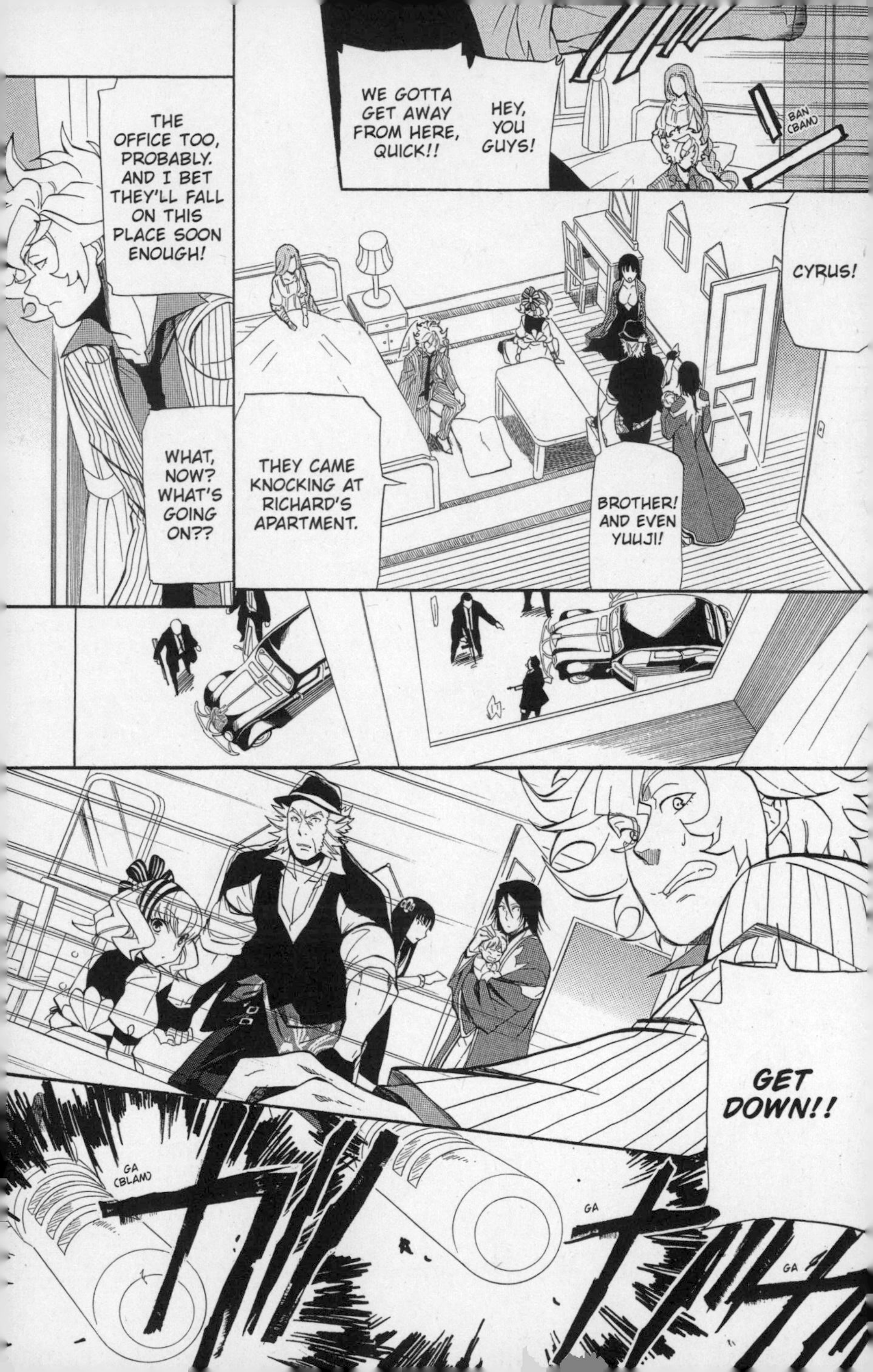
BAN (BAM)
HEY, YOU GUYS!
WE GOTTA GET AWAY FROM HERE, QUICK!!
CYRUS!
BROTHER! AND EVEN YUUJI!
THEY CAME KNOCKING AT RICHARD'S APARTMENT.
WHAT, NOW? WHAT'S GOING ON??
THE OFFICE TOO, PROBABLY. AND I BET THEY'LL FALL ON THIS PLACE SOON ENOUGH!
GET DOWN!!
GA
GA
GA (BLAM)

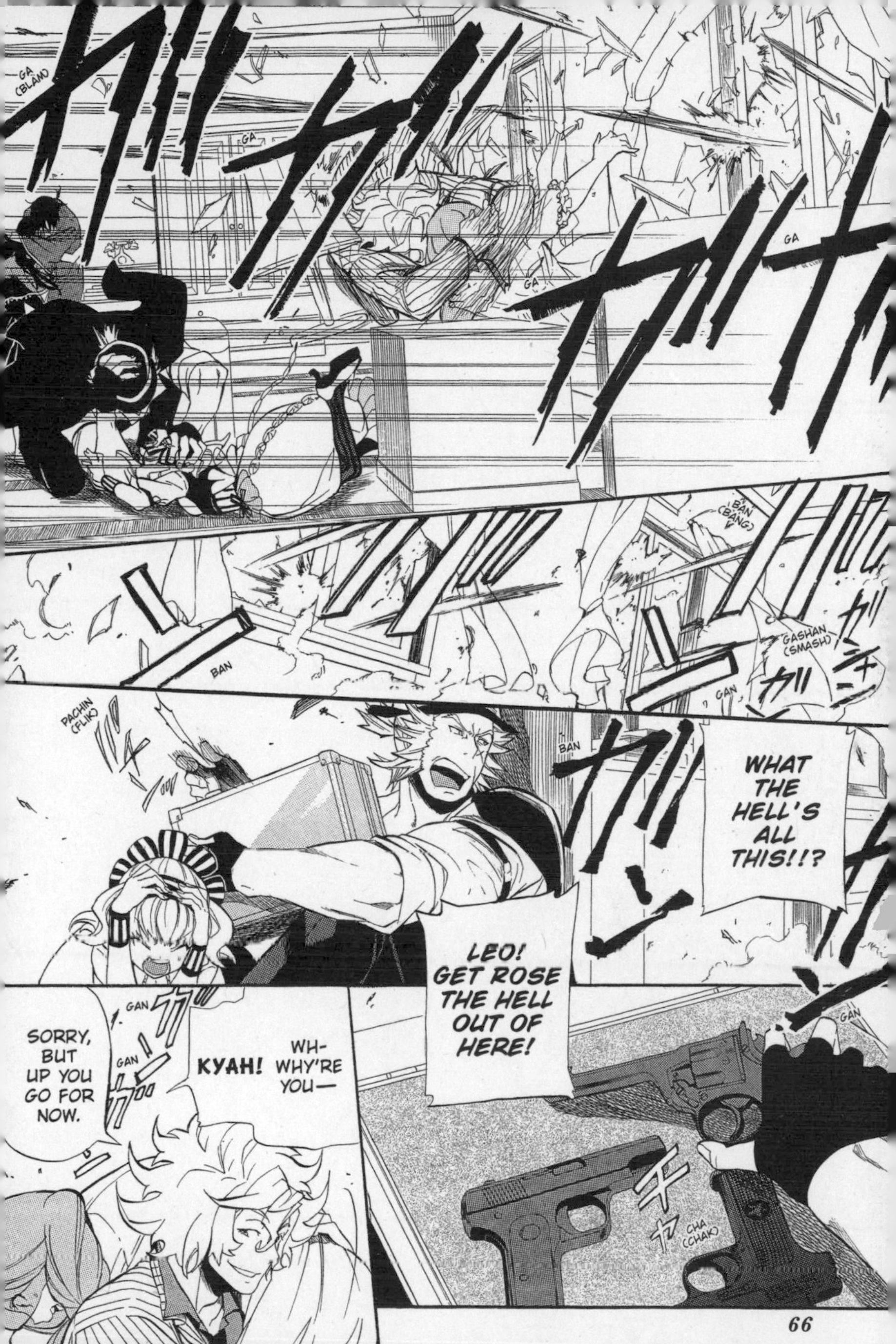
GA
GA
GA
GA (BLAM)
BAN (BANG)
GASHAN (SMASH)
BAN
WHAT THE HELL'S ALL THIS!!?
GAN
BAN
PACHIN (FLIK)
LEO! GET ROSE THE HELL OUT OF HERE!
GAN
CHA (CHAK)
WH- WHY'RE YOU—
KYAH!
GAN
GAN
SORRY, BUT UP YOU GO FOR NOW.

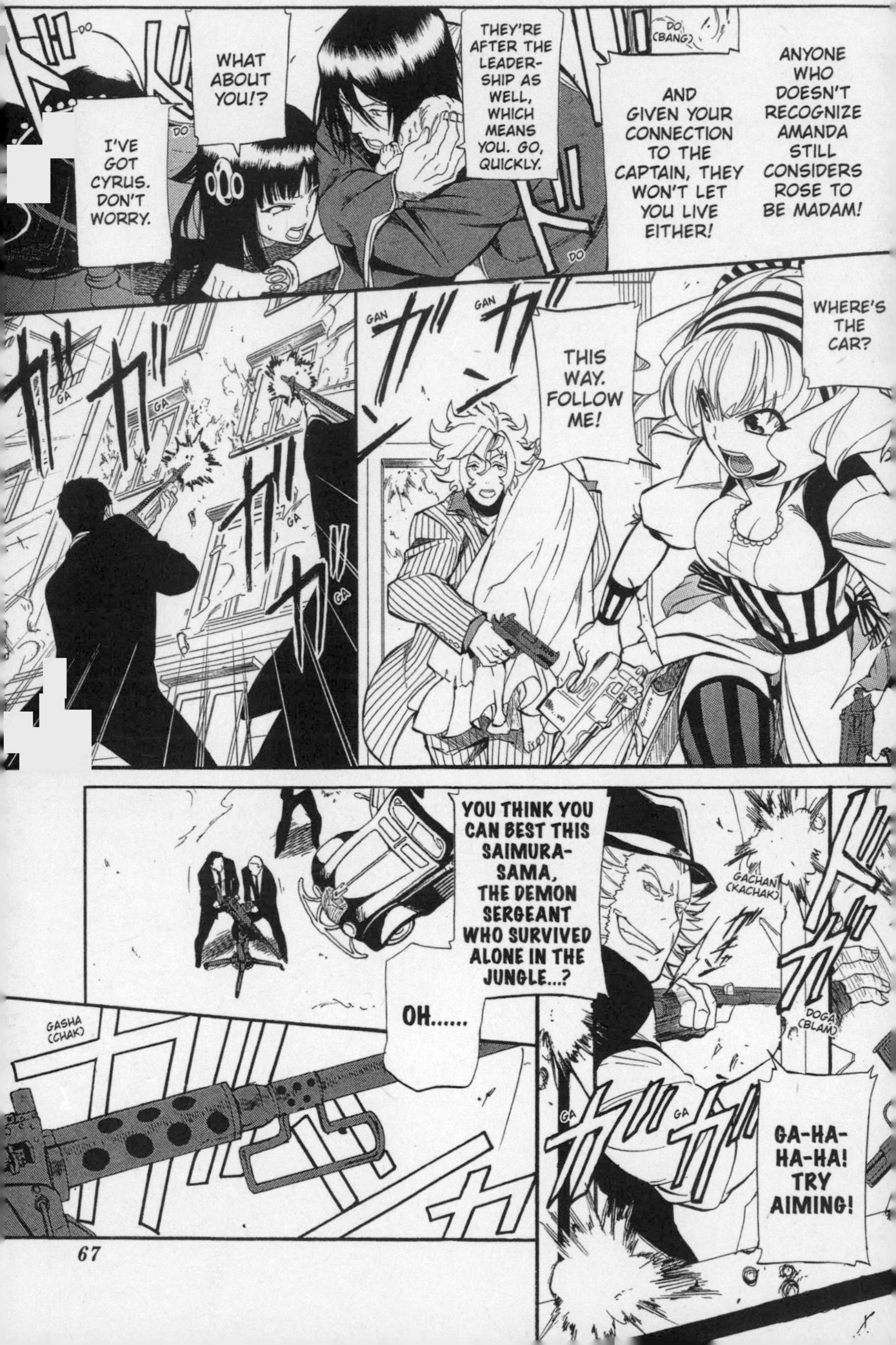
DO (BANG)
ANYONE WHO DOESN'T RECOGNIZE AMANDA STILL CONSIDERS ROSE TO BE MADAM!
AND GIVEN YOUR CONNECTION TO THE CAPTAIN, THEY WON'T LET YOU LIVE EITHER!
DO
THEY'RE AFTER THE LEADERSHIP AS WELL, WHICH MEANS YOU. GO, QUICKLY.
DO
WHAT ABOUT YOU!?
DO
I'VE GOT CYRUS. DON'T WORRY.
WHERE'S THE CAR?
GAN
GAN
THIS WAY. FOLLOW ME!
GA
GA
GA
GA
GACHAN (KACHAK)
YOU THINK YOU CAN BEST THIS SAIMURA-SAMA, THE DEMON SERGEANT WHO SURVIVED ALONE IN THE JUNGLE...?
DOGA (BLAM)
GA
GA
GA-HA-HA-HA! TRY AIMING!
OH......
GASHA (CHAK)

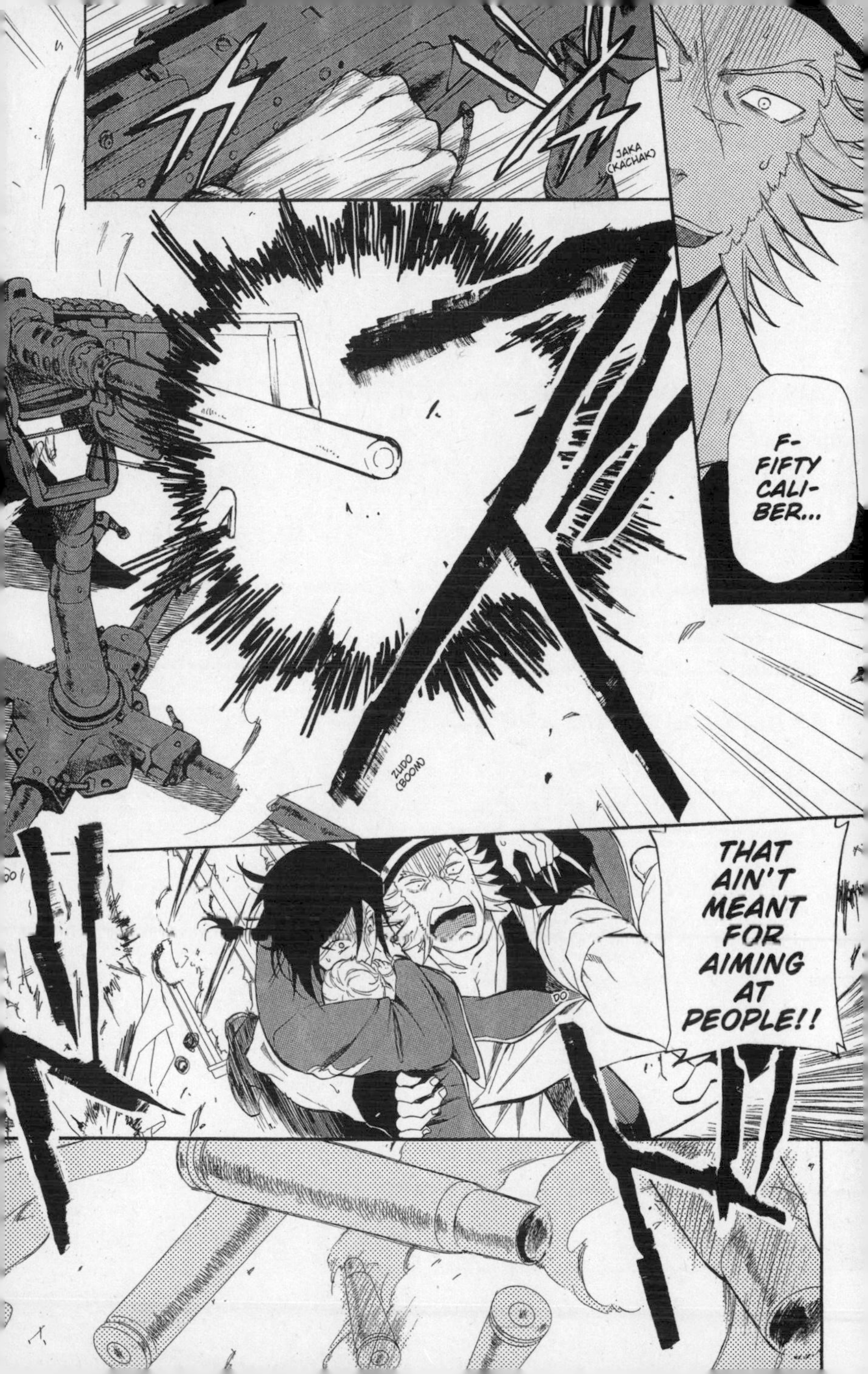
F- FIFTY CALIBER...
JAKA (KACHAK)
ZUDO (BOOM)
THAT AIN'T MEANT FOR AIMING AT PEOPLE!!
DO

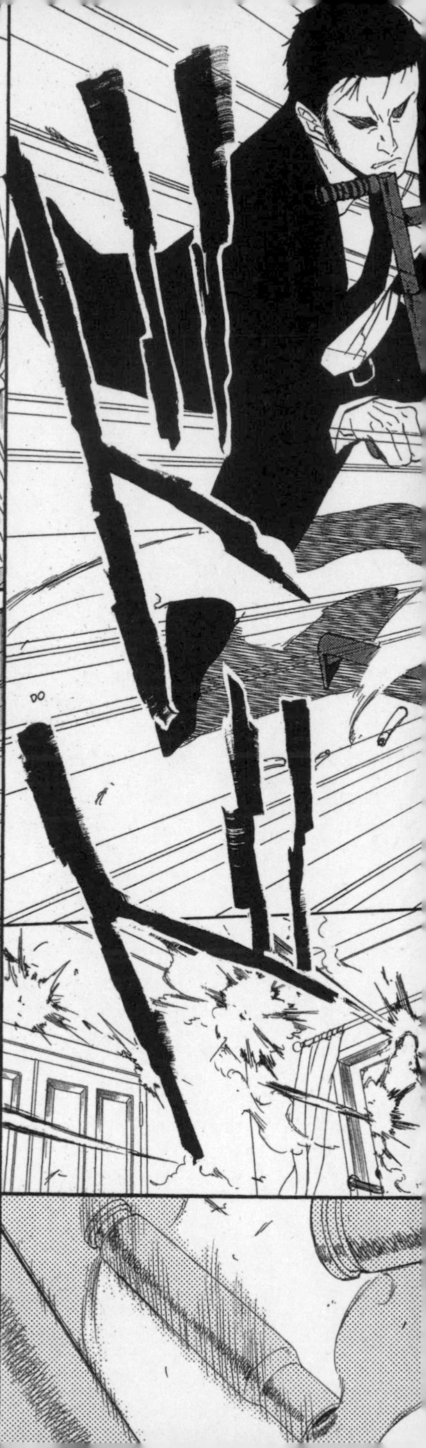
DO

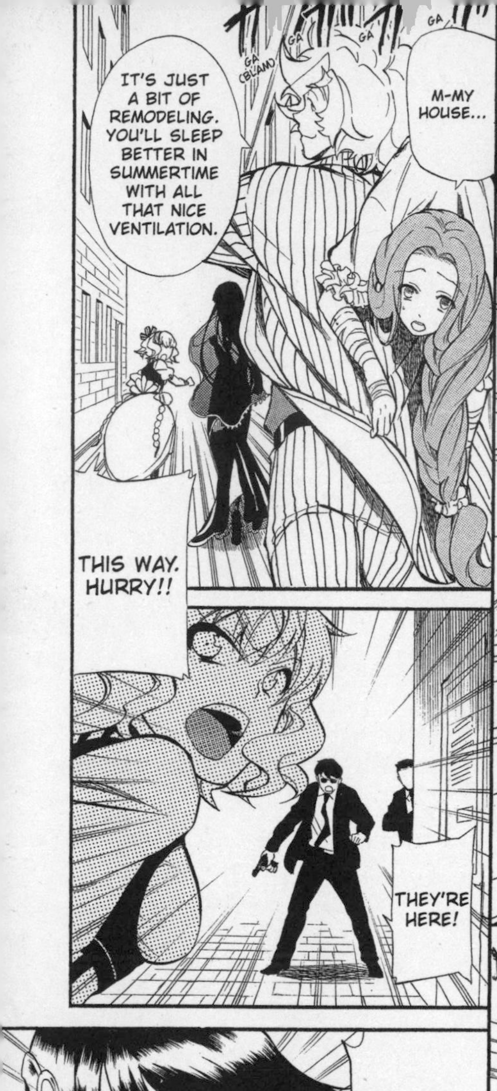
GA GA GA GA
(BLAM)
M-MY HOUSE...
IT'S JUST A BIT OF REMODELING. YOU'LL SLEEP BETTER IN SUMMERTIME WITH ALL THAT NICE VENTILATION.
THIS WAY. HURRY!!
THEY'RE HERE!
MERYL, LOOK OUT!!

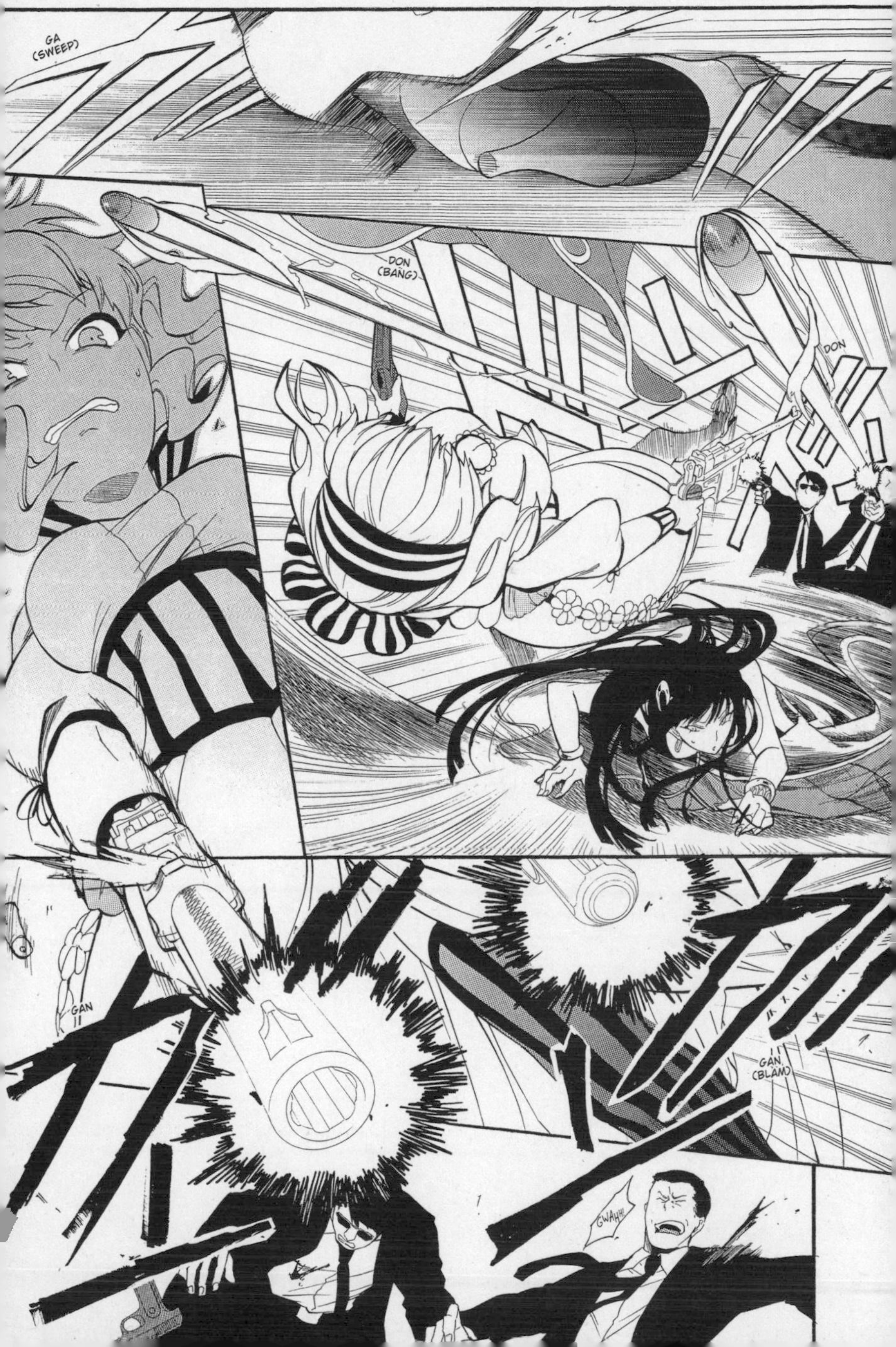
GA (SWEEP)
DON
DON (BANG)
GAN (BLAM)
GAN
GWAH!!

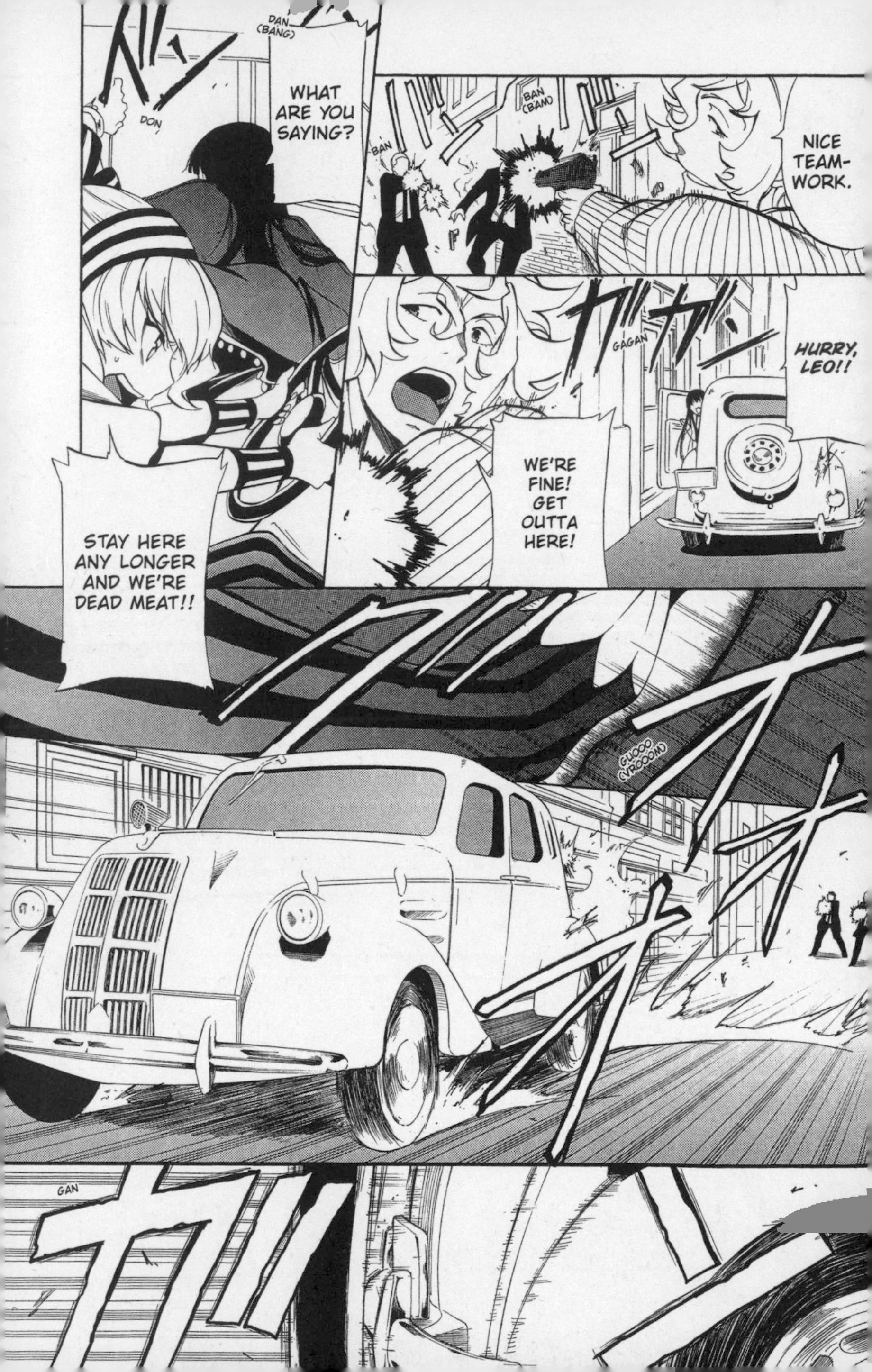
NICE TEAM-WORK.
BAN (BAM)
BAN
HURRY, LEO!!
GAGAN
WE'RE FINE! GET OUTTA HERE!
DAN (BANG)
WHAT ARE YOU SAYING?
DON
STAY HERE ANY LONGER AND WE'RE DEAD MEAT!!
GUOOO (VROOOM)
GAN

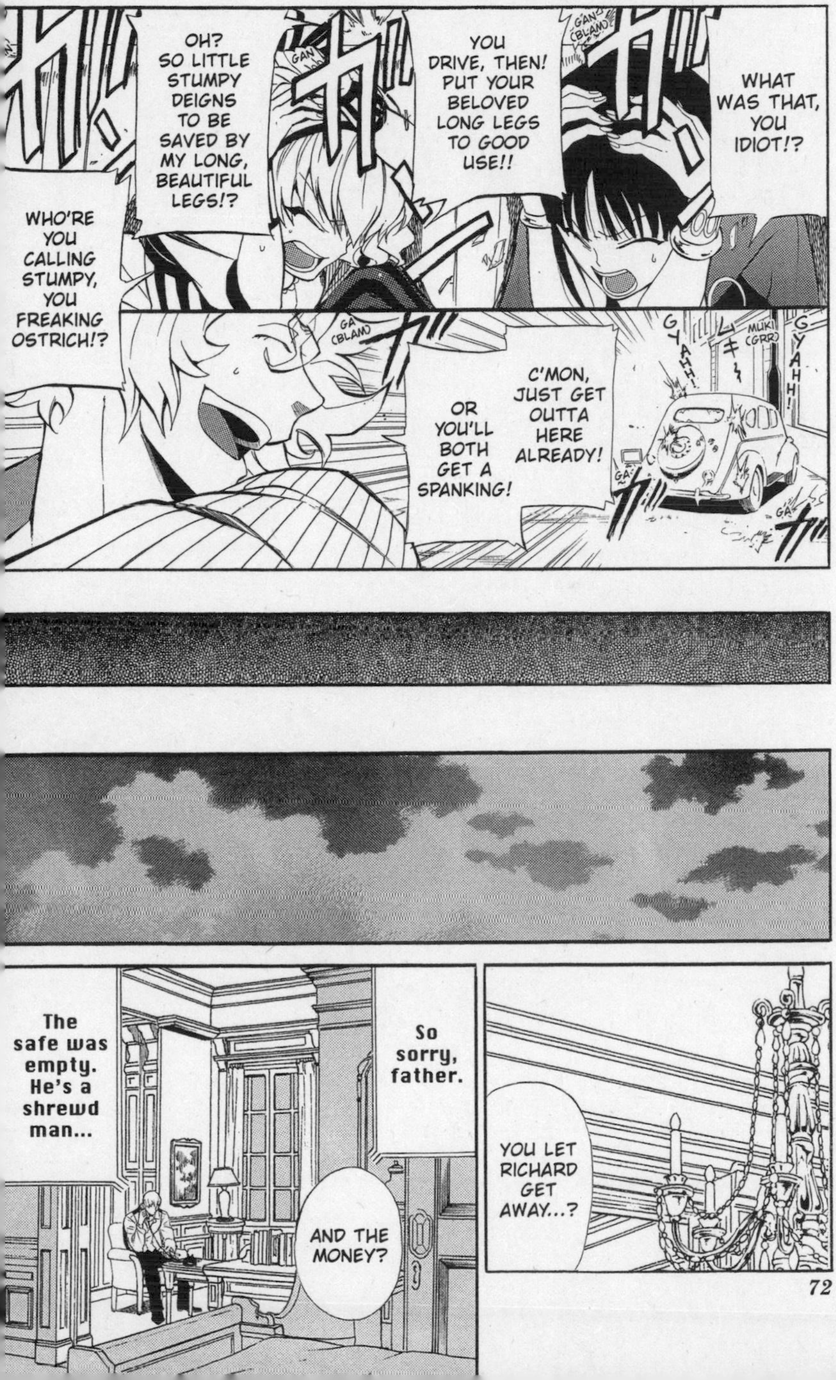
WHAT WAS THAT, YOU IDIOT!?
GAN (BLAM)
YOU DRIVE, THEN! PUT YOUR BELOVED LONG LEGS TO GOOD USE!!
GAN
OH? SO LITTLE STUMPY DEIGNS TO BE SAVED BY MY LONG, BEAUTIFUL LEGS!?
WHO'RE YOU CALLING STUMPY, YOU FREAKING OSTRICH!?
GYAHH!
MUKI (GRR)
GYAHH!
GA
GA
C'MON, JUST GET OUTTA HERE ALREADY!
OR YOU'LL BOTH GET A SPANKING!
GA (BLAM)
YOU LET RICHARD GET AWAY...?
So sorry, father.
AND THE MONEY?
The safe was empty. He's a shrewd man...

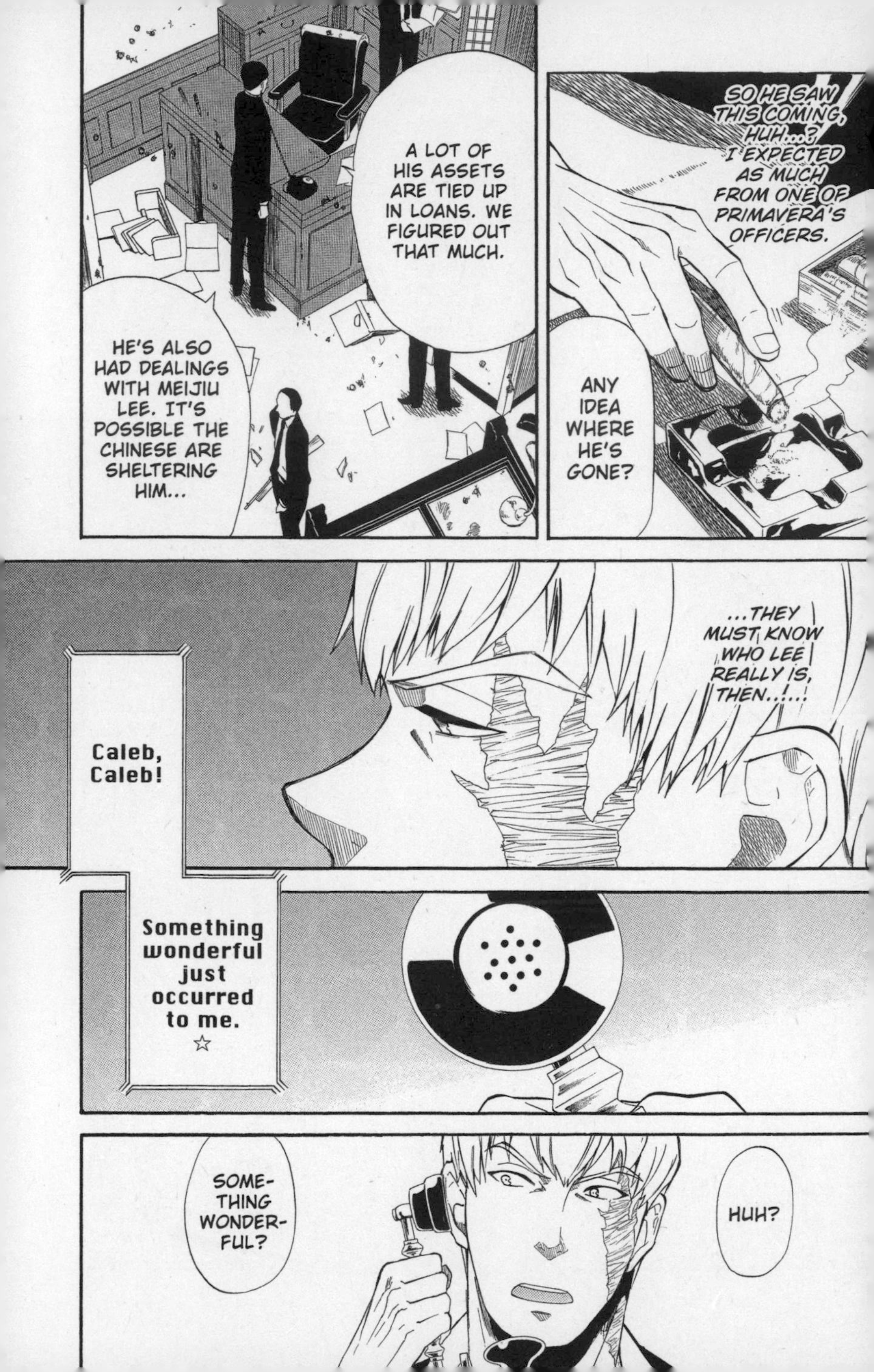
SO HE SAW THIS COMING, HUH...? I EXPECTED AS MUCH FROM ONE OF PRIMAVERA'S OFFICERS.
ANY IDEA WHERE HE'S GONE?
A LOT OF HIS ASSETS ARE TIED UP IN LOANS. WE FIGURED OUT THAT MUCH.
HE'S ALSO HAD DEALINGS WITH MEIJIU LEE. IT'S POSSIBLE THE CHINESE ARE SHELTERING HIM...
...THEY MUST KNOW WHO LEE REALLY IS, THEN.....
Caleb, Caleb!
Something wonderful just occurred to me. ☆
HUH?
SOME-THING WONDER-FUL?

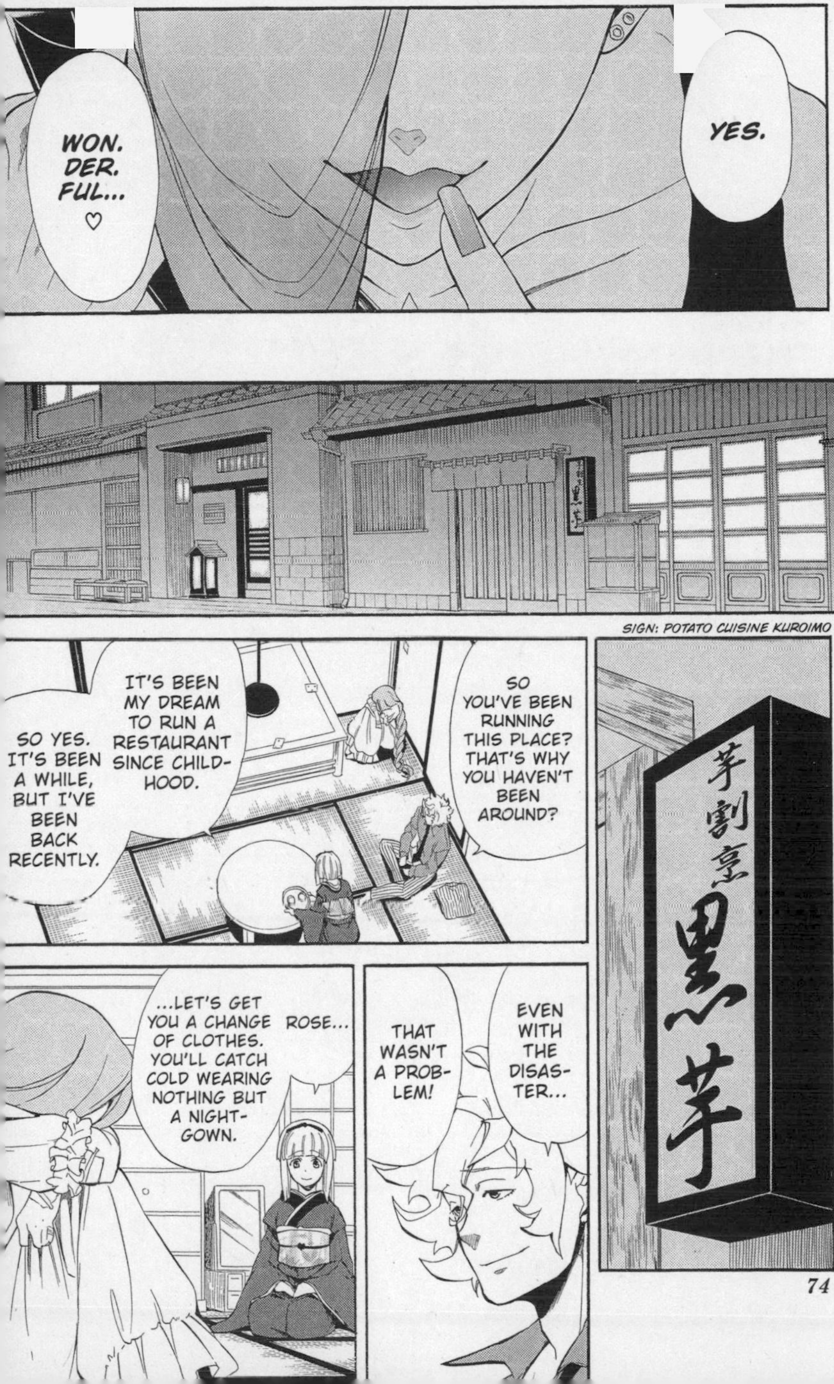
YES.
WON. DER. FUL... ♡
SIGN: POTATO CUISINE KUROIMO
芋割烹 黒芋
SO YOU'VE BEEN RUNNING THIS PLACE? THAT'S WHY YOU HAVEN'T BEEN AROUND?
IT'S BEEN MY DREAM TO RUN A RESTAURANT SINCE CHILDHOOD.
SO YES. IT'S BEEN A WHILE, BUT I'VE BEEN BACK RECENTLY.
EVEN WITH THE DISASTER...
THAT WASN'T A PROBLEM!
ROSE...
...LET'S GET YOU A CHANGE OF CLOTHES. YOU'LL CATCH COLD WEARING NOTHING BUT A NIGHTGOWN.

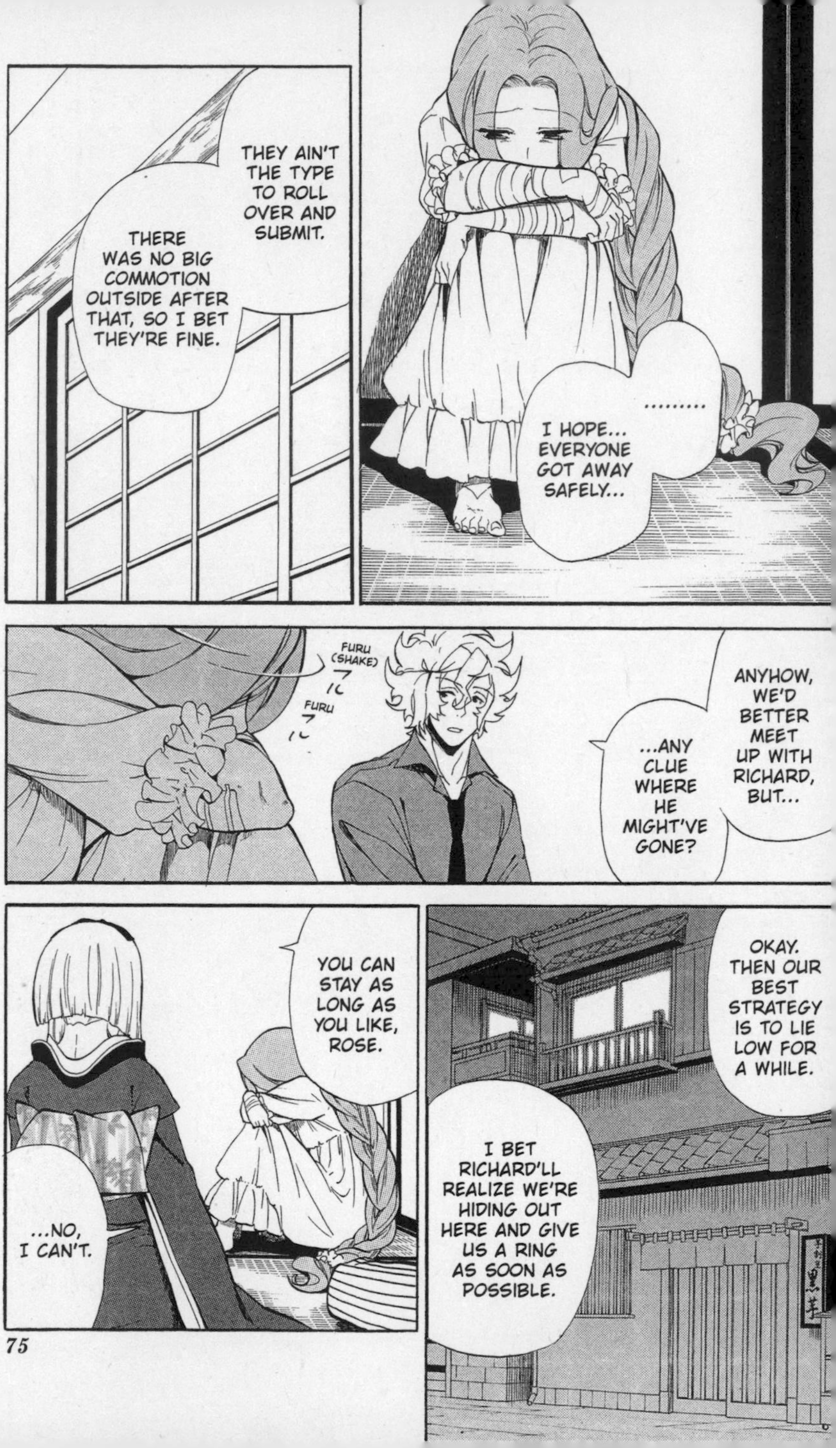
....
I HOPE... EVERYONE GOT AWAY SAFELY...
THEY AIN'T THE TYPE TO ROLL OVER AND SUBMIT.
THERE WAS NO BIG COMMOTION OUTSIDE AFTER THAT, SO I BET THEY'RE FINE.
ANYHOW, WE'D BETTER MEET UP WITH RICHARD, BUT...
...ANY CLUE WHERE HE MIGHT'VE GONE?
FURU (SHAKE)
FURU
OKAY. THEN OUR BEST STRATEGY IS TO LIE LOW FOR A WHILE.
I BET RICHARD'LL REALIZE WE'RE HIDING OUT HERE AND GIVE US A RING AS SOON AS POSSIBLE.
YOU CAN STAY AS LONG AS YOU LIKE, ROSE.
...NO, I CAN'T.

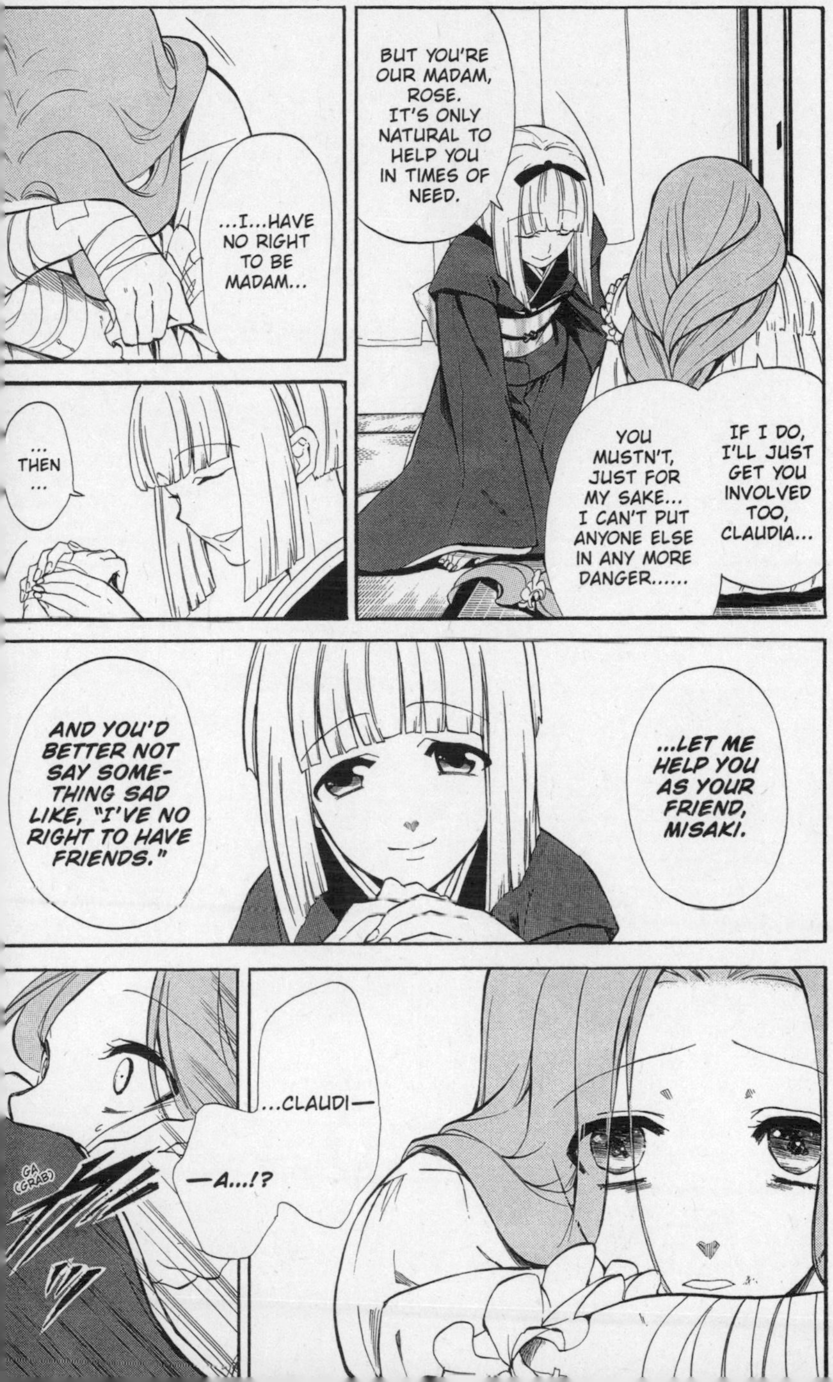
BUT YOU'RE OUR MADAM, ROSE. IT'S ONLY NATURAL TO HELP YOU IN TIMES OF NEED.
YOU MUSTN'T, JUST FOR MY SAKE... I CAN'T PUT ANYONE ELSE IN ANY MORE DANGER......
IF I DO, I'LL JUST GET YOU INVOLVED TOO, CLAUDIA...
...I...HAVE NO RIGHT TO BE MADAM...
...THEN...
...LET ME HELP YOU AS YOUR FRIEND, MISAKI.
AND YOU'D BETTER NOT SAY SOME-THING SAD LIKE, "I'VE NO RIGHT TO HAVE FRIENDS."
...CLAUDI—
—A...!?
GA (GRAB)

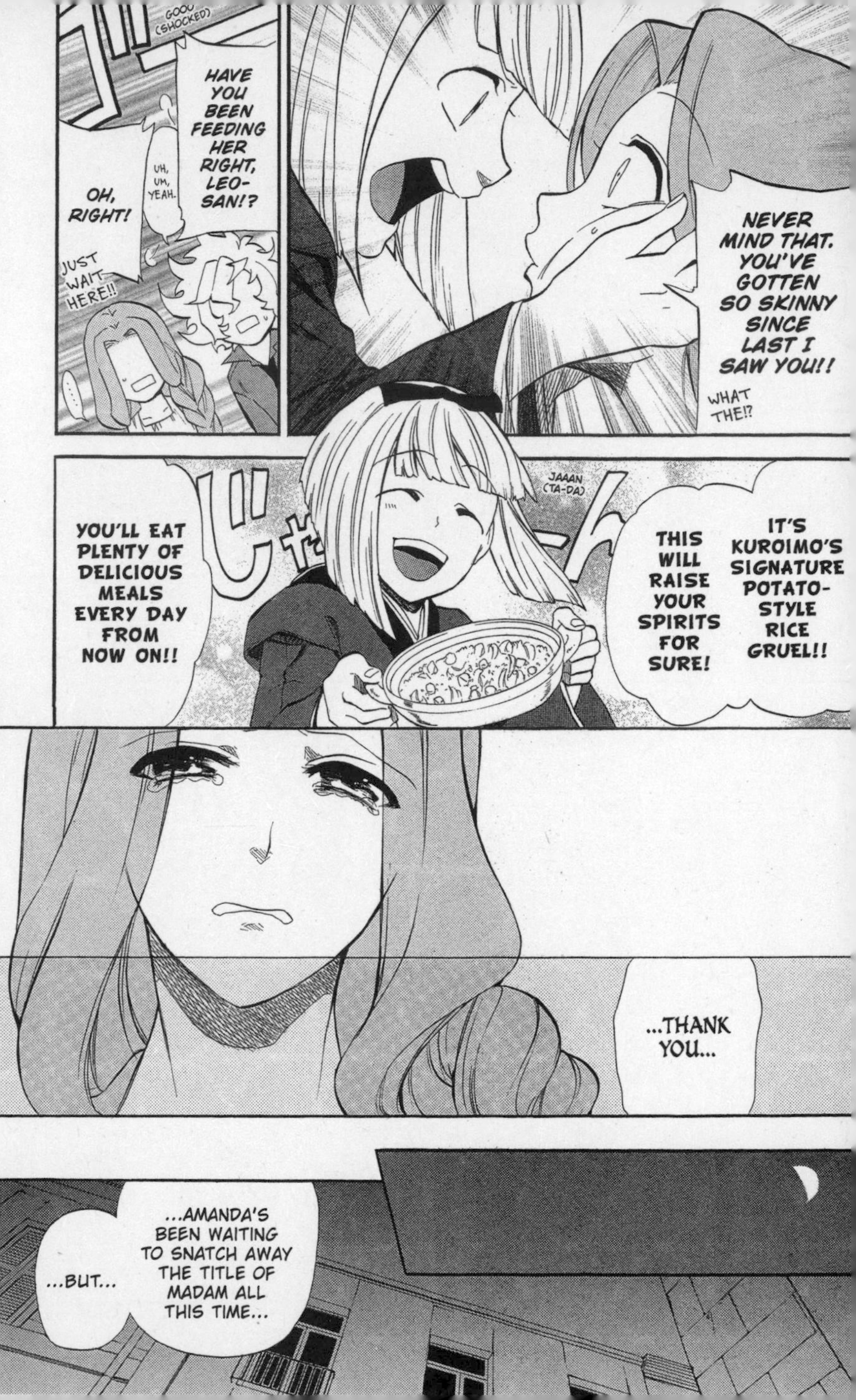
NEVER MIND THAT. YOU'VE GOTTEN SO SKINNY SINCE LAST I SAW YOU!!
WHAT THE!?
GOOU (SHOCKED)
HAVE YOU BEEN FEEDING HER RIGHT, LEO-SAN!?
UH, UM, YEAH.
OH, RIGHT!
JUST WAIT HERE!!
...
JAAAN (TA-DA)
IT'S KUROIMO'S SIGNATURE POTATO-STYLE RICE GRUEL!!
THIS WILL RAISE YOUR SPIRITS FOR SURE!
YOU'LL EAT PLENTY OF DELICIOUS MEALS EVERY DAY FROM NOW ON!!
...THANK YOU...
...AMANDA'S BEEN WAITING TO SNATCH AWAY THE TITLE OF MADAM ALL THIS TIME...
...BUT...

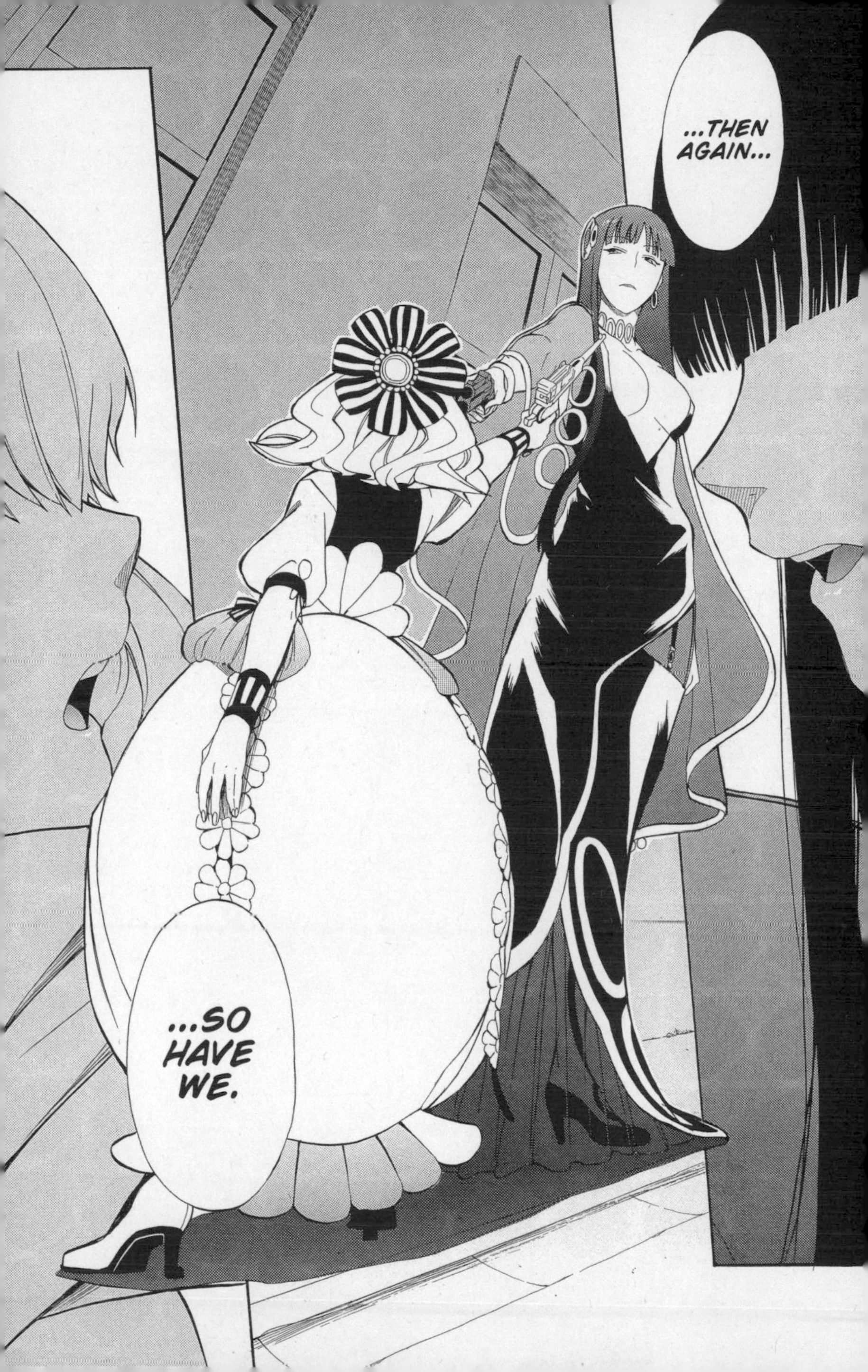
...THEN AGAIN...
...SO HAVE WE.

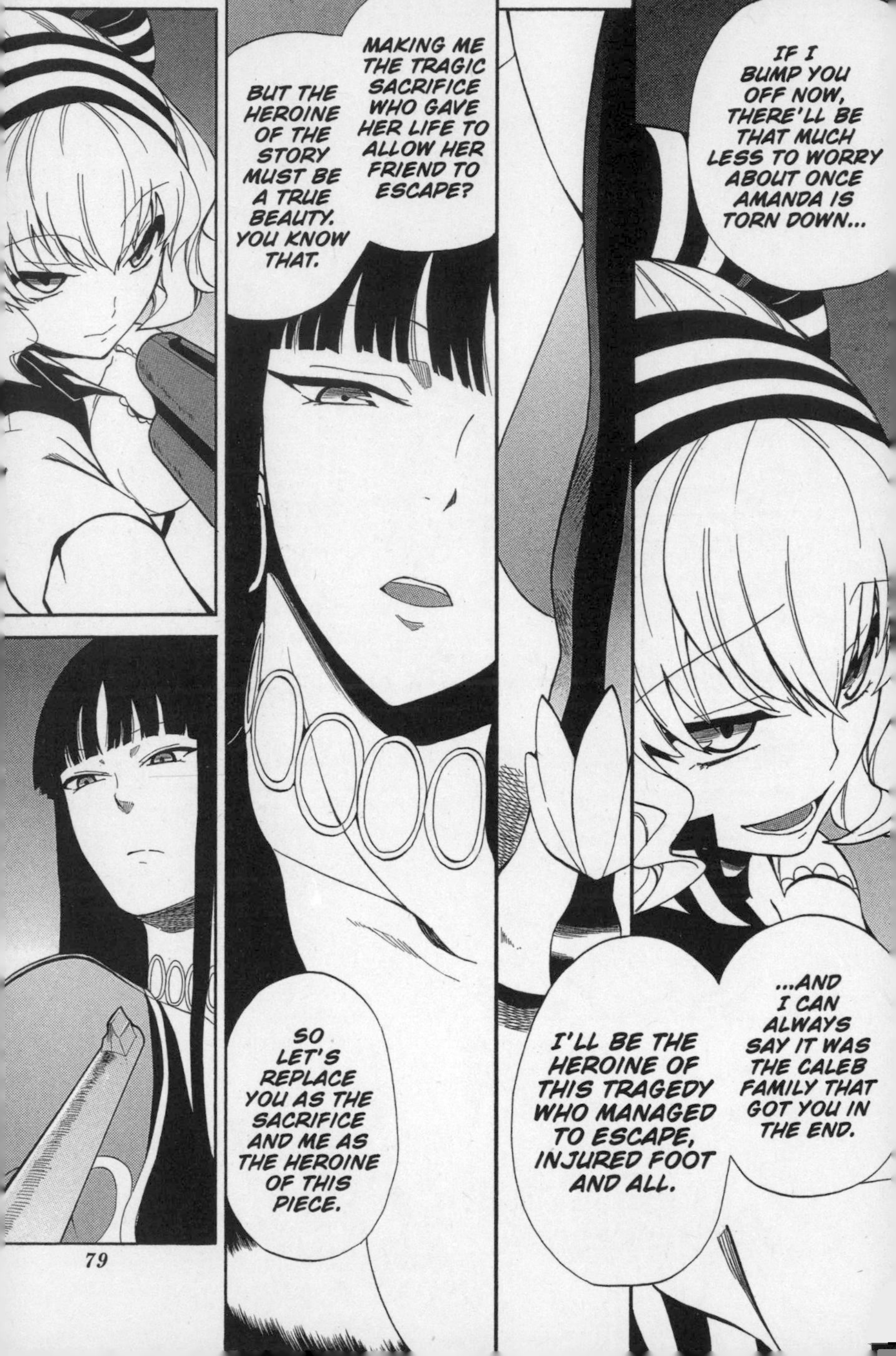
IF I BUMP YOU OFF NOW, THERE'LL BE THAT MUCH LESS TO WORRY ABOUT ONCE AMANDA IS TORN DOWN...
...AND I CAN ALWAYS SAY IT WAS THE CALEB FAMILY THAT GOT YOU IN THE END.
I'LL BE THE HEROINE OF THIS TRAGEDY WHO MANAGED TO ESCAPE, INJURED FOOT AND ALL.
MAKING ME THE TRAGIC SACRIFICE WHO GAVE HER LIFE TO ALLOW HER FRIEND TO ESCAPE?
BUT THE HEROINE OF THE STORY MUST BE A TRUE BEAUTY. YOU KNOW THAT.
SO LET'S REPLACE YOU AS THE SACRIFICE AND ME AS THE HEROINE OF THIS PIECE.

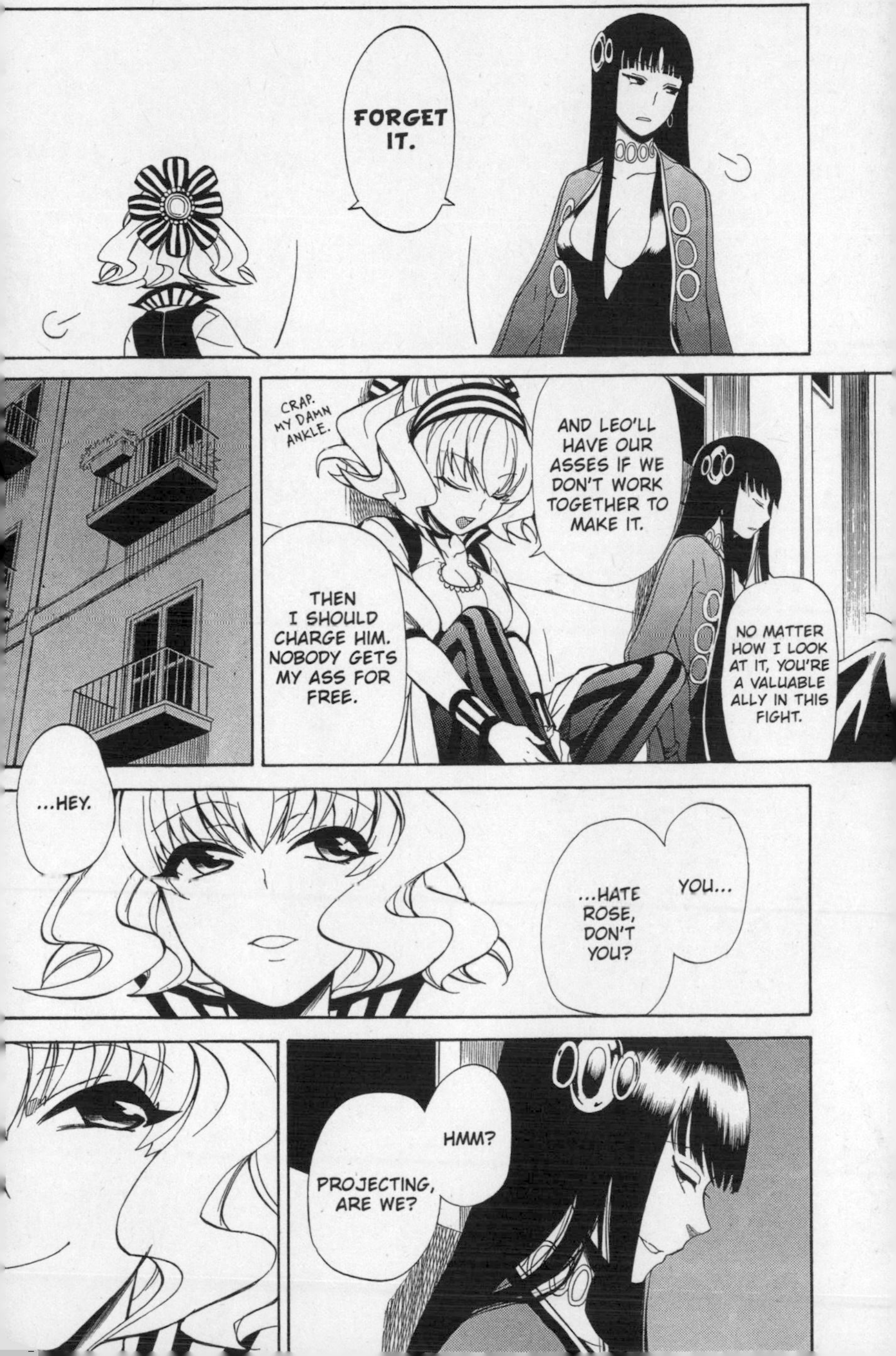
FORGET IT.
NO MATTER HOW I LOOK AT IT, YOU'RE A VALUABLE ALLY IN THIS FIGHT.
AND LEO'LL HAVE OUR ASSES IF WE DON'T WORK TOGETHER TO MAKE IT.
CRAP. MY DAMN ANKLE.
THEN I SHOULD CHARGE HIM. NOBODY GETS MY ASS FOR FREE.
YOU...
...HATE ROSE, DON'T YOU?
...HEY.
HMM?
PROJECTING, ARE WE?

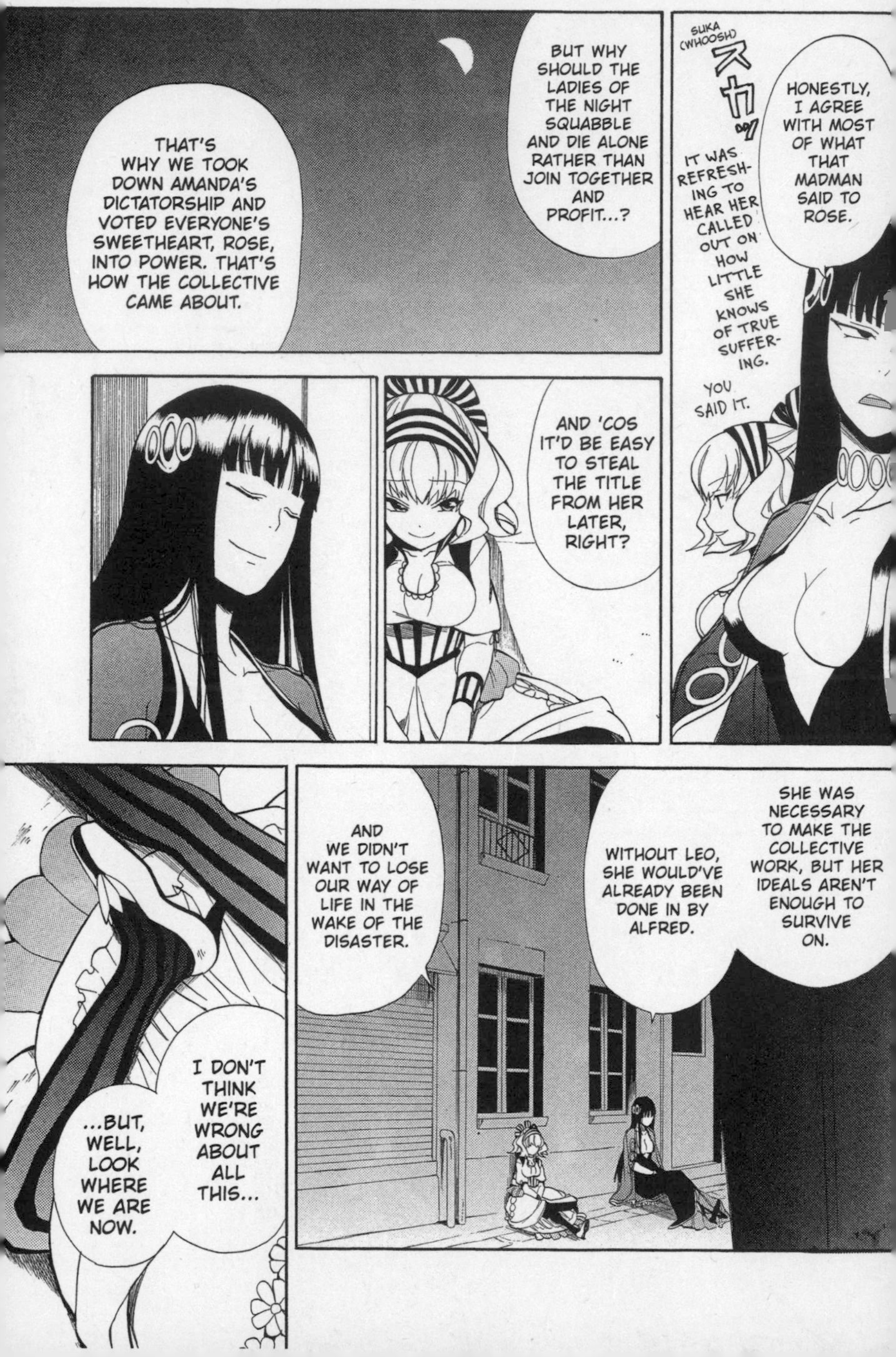
SUKA (WHOOSH)
スカ
HONESTLY, I AGREE WITH MOST OF WHAT THAT MADMAN SAID TO ROSE.
IT WAS REFRESHING TO HEAR HER CALLED OUT ON HOW LITTLE SHE KNOWS OF TRUE SUFFERING.
YOU SAID IT.
BUT WHY SHOULD THE LADIES OF THE NIGHT SQUABBLE AND DIE ALONE RATHER THAN JOIN TOGETHER AND PROFIT...?
THAT'S WHY WE TOOK DOWN AMANDA'S DICTATORSHIP AND VOTED EVERYONE'S SWEETHEART, ROSE, INTO POWER. THAT'S HOW THE COLLECTIVE CAME ABOUT.
AND 'COS IT'D BE EASY TO STEAL THE TITLE FROM HER LATER, RIGHT?
...
SHE WAS NECESSARY TO MAKE THE COLLECTIVE WORK, BUT HER IDEALS AREN'T ENOUGH TO SURVIVE ON.
WITHOUT LEO, SHE WOULD'VE ALREADY BEEN DONE IN BY ALFRED.
AND WE DIDN'T WANT TO LOSE OUR WAY OF LIFE IN THE WAKE OF THE DISASTER.
I DON'T THINK WE'RE WRONG ABOUT ALL THIS...
...BUT, WELL, LOOK WHERE WE ARE NOW.

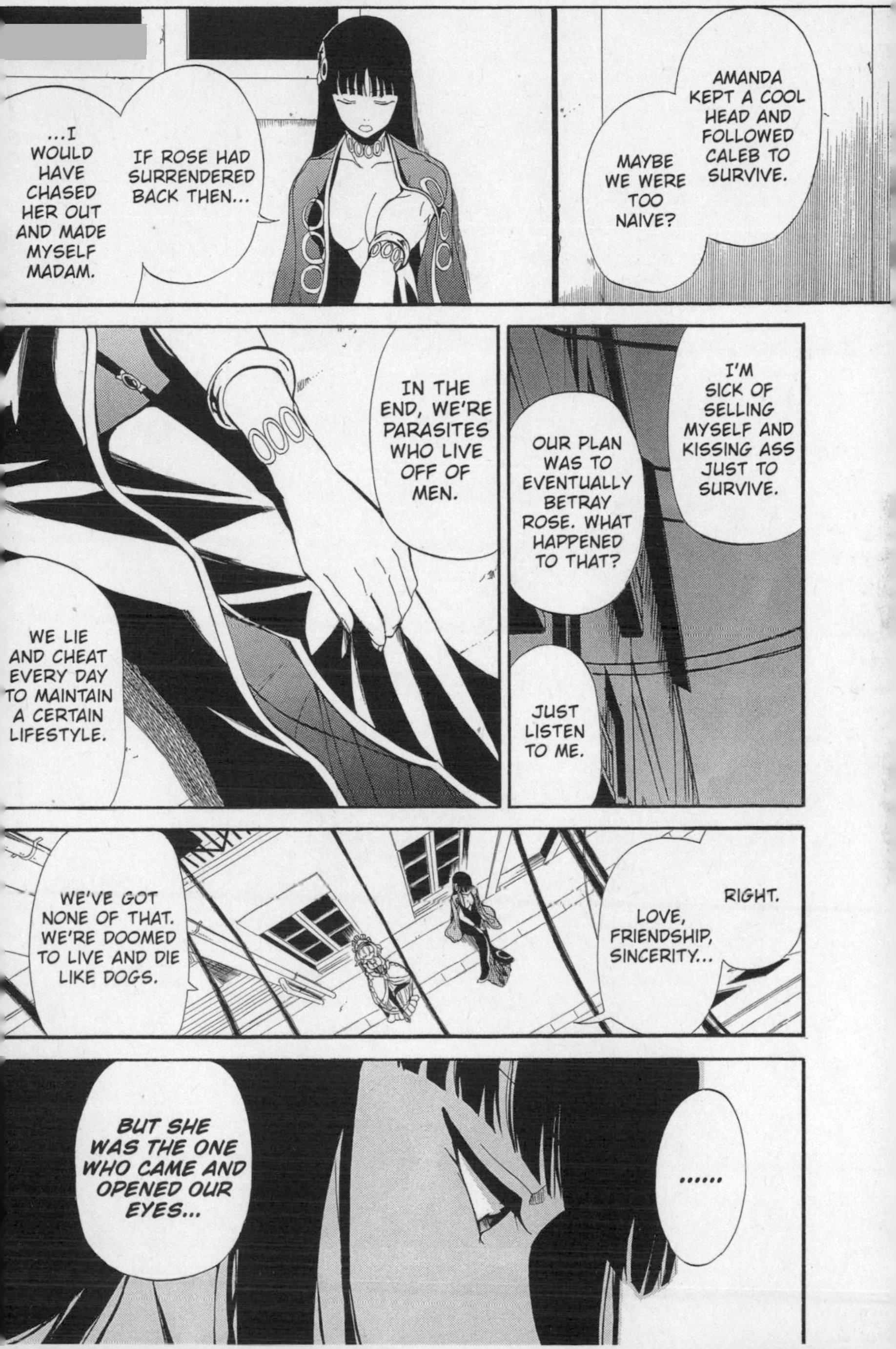
AMANDA KEPT A COOL HEAD AND FOLLOWED CALEB TO SURVIVE.
MAYBE WE WERE TOO NAIVE?
IF ROSE HAD SURRENDERED BACK THEN...
...I WOULD HAVE CHASED HER OUT AND MADE MYSELF MADAM.
I'M SICK OF SELLING MYSELF AND KISSING ASS JUST TO SURVIVE.
OUR PLAN WAS TO EVENTUALLY BETRAY ROSE. WHAT HAPPENED TO THAT?
JUST LISTEN TO ME.
IN THE END, WE'RE PARASITES WHO LIVE OFF OF MEN.
WE LIE AND CHEAT EVERY DAY TO MAINTAIN A CERTAIN LIFESTYLE.
RIGHT.
LOVE, FRIENDSHIP, SINCERITY...
WE'VE GOT NONE OF THAT. WE'RE DOOMED TO LIVE AND DIE LIKE DOGS.
......
BUT SHE WAS THE ONE WHO CAME AND OPENED OUR EYES...

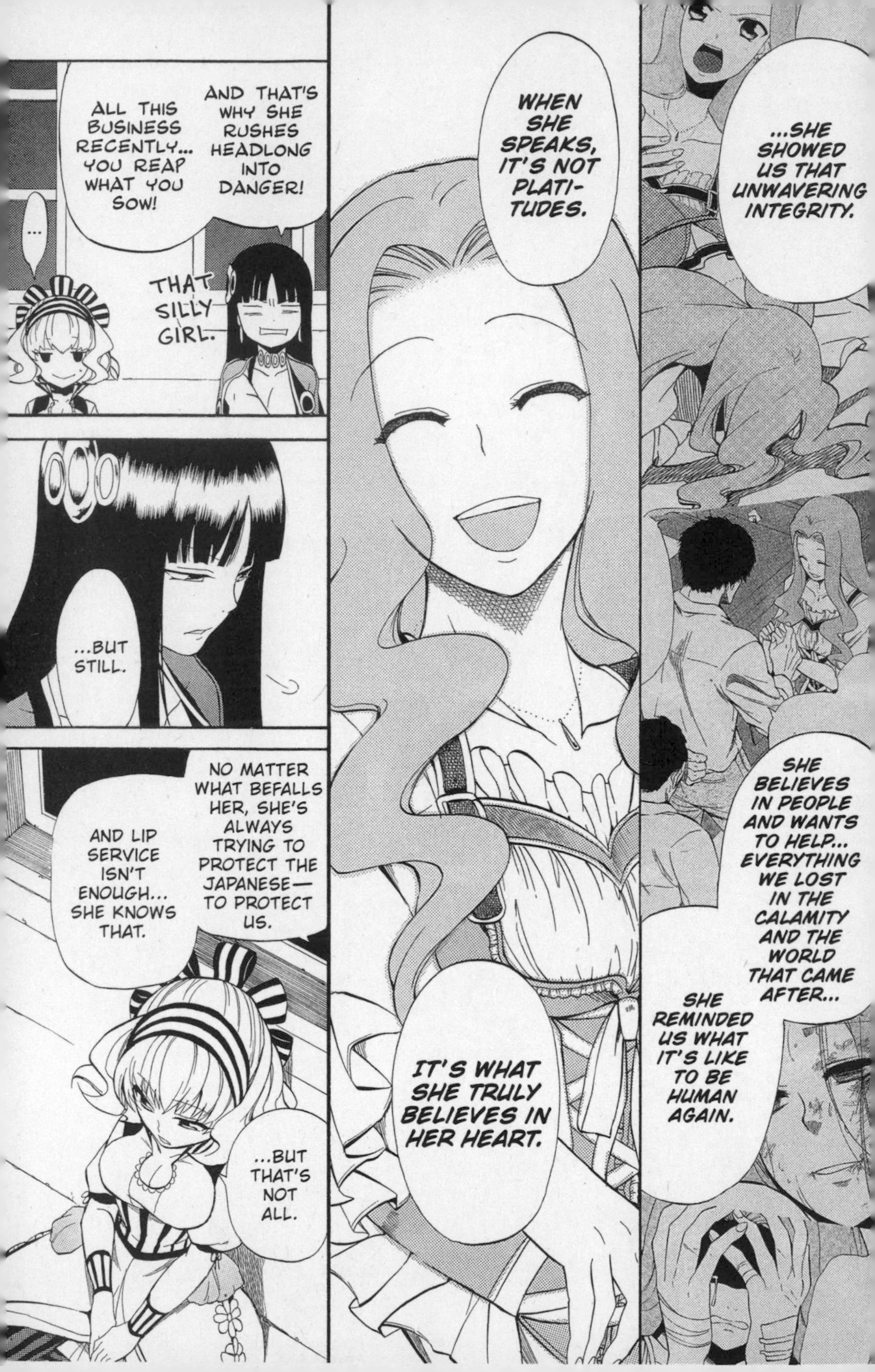
ALL THIS BUSINESS RECENTLY... YOU REAP WHAT YOU SOW!
AND THAT'S WHY SHE RUSHES HEADLONG INTO DANGER!
...
THAT SILLY GIRL.
...BUT STILL.
NO MATTER WHAT BEFALLS HER, SHE'S ALWAYS TRYING TO PROTECT THE JAPANESE— TO PROTECT US.
AND LIP SERVICE ISN'T ENOUGH... SHE KNOWS THAT.
...BUT THAT'S NOT ALL.
WHEN SHE SPEAKS, IT'S NOT PLATITUDES.
IT'S WHAT SHE TRULY BELIEVES IN HER HEART.
...SHE SHOWED US THAT UNWAVERING INTEGRITY.
SHE BELIEVES IN PEOPLE AND WANTS TO HELP... EVERYTHING WE LOST IN THE CALAMITY AND THE WORLD THAT CAME AFTER...
SHE REMINDED US WHAT IT'S LIKE TO BE HUMAN AGAIN.

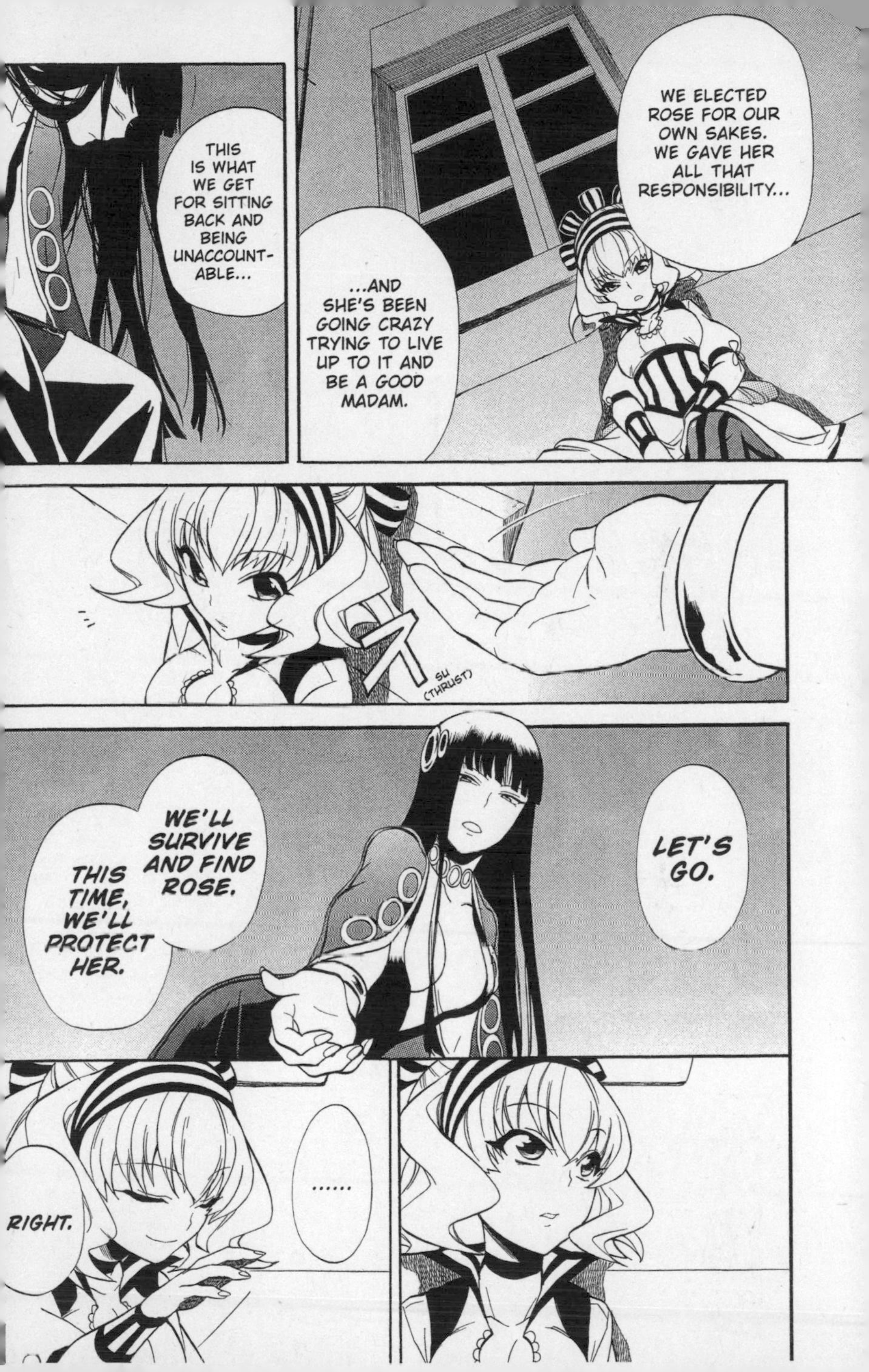
WE ELECTED ROSE FOR OUR OWN SAKES. WE GAVE HER ALL THAT RESPONSIBILITY...
...AND SHE'S BEEN GOING CRAZY TRYING TO LIVE UP TO IT AND BE A GOOD MADAM.
THIS IS WHAT WE GET FOR SITTING BACK AND BEING UNACCOUNT-ABLE...
SU (THRUST)
LET'S GO.
WE'LL SURVIVE AND FIND ROSE.
THIS TIME, WE'LL PROTECT HER.
......
RIGHT.

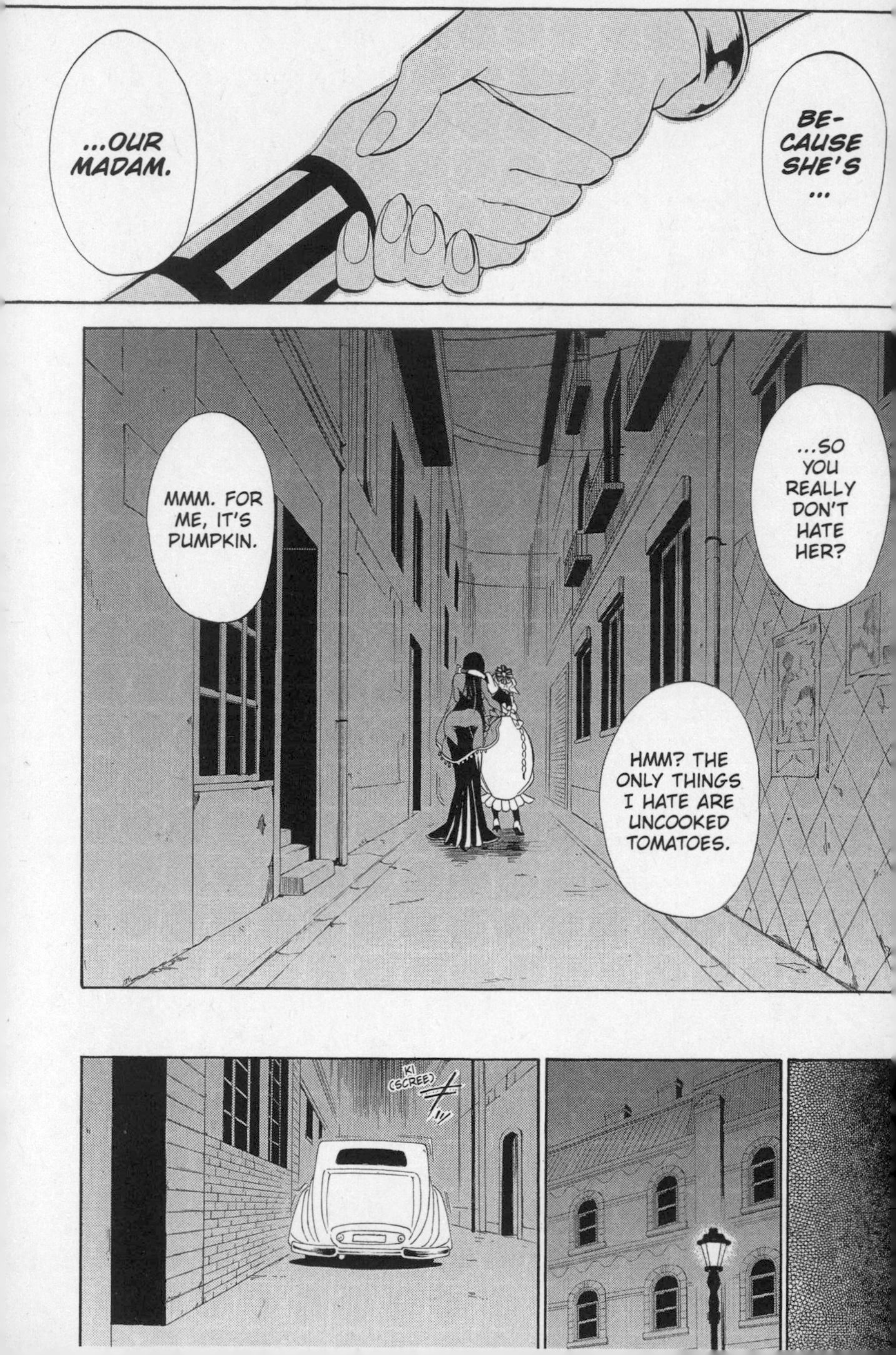
BE-CAUSE SHE'S ...
...OUR MADAM.
...SO YOU REALLY DON'T HATE HER?
HMM? THE ONLY THINGS I HATE ARE UNCOOKED TOMATOES.
MMM. FOR ME, IT'S PUMPKIN.
KI (SCREE)

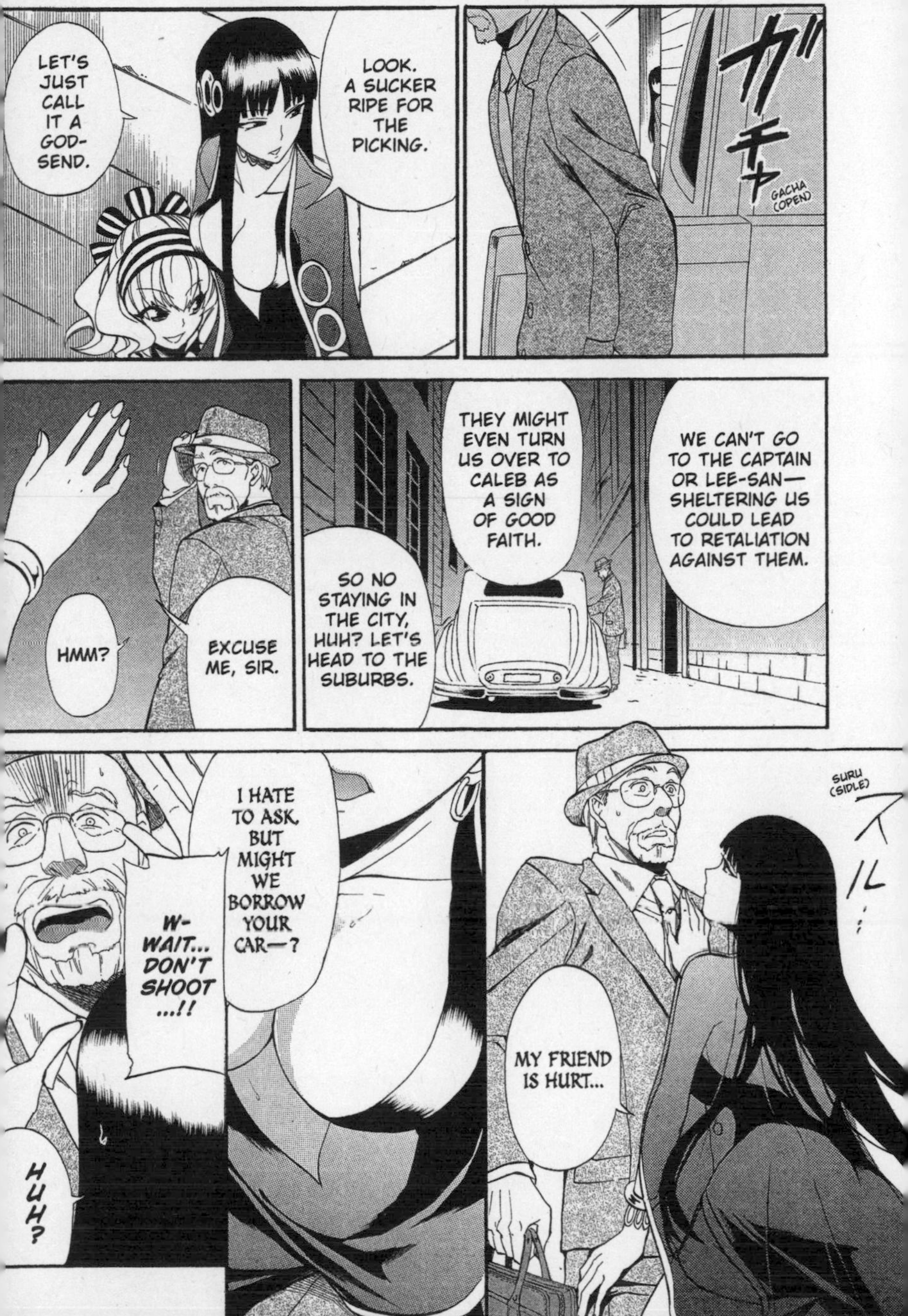
ガチャ
GACHA (OPEN)
LOOK. A SUCKER RIPE FOR THE PICKING.
LET'S JUST CALL IT A GOD-SEND.
WE CAN'T GO TO THE CAPTAIN OR LEE-SAN— SHELTERING US COULD LEAD TO RETALIATION AGAINST THEM.
THEY MIGHT EVEN TURN US OVER TO CALEB AS A SIGN OF GOOD FAITH.
SO NO STAYING IN THE CITY, HUH? LET'S HEAD TO THE SUBURBS.
EXCUSE ME, SIR.
HMM?
スル
SURU (SIDLE)
MY FRIEND IS HURT...
I HATE TO ASK, BUT MIGHT WE BORROW YOUR CAR—?
W-WAIT... DON'T SHOOT ...!!
HUH?

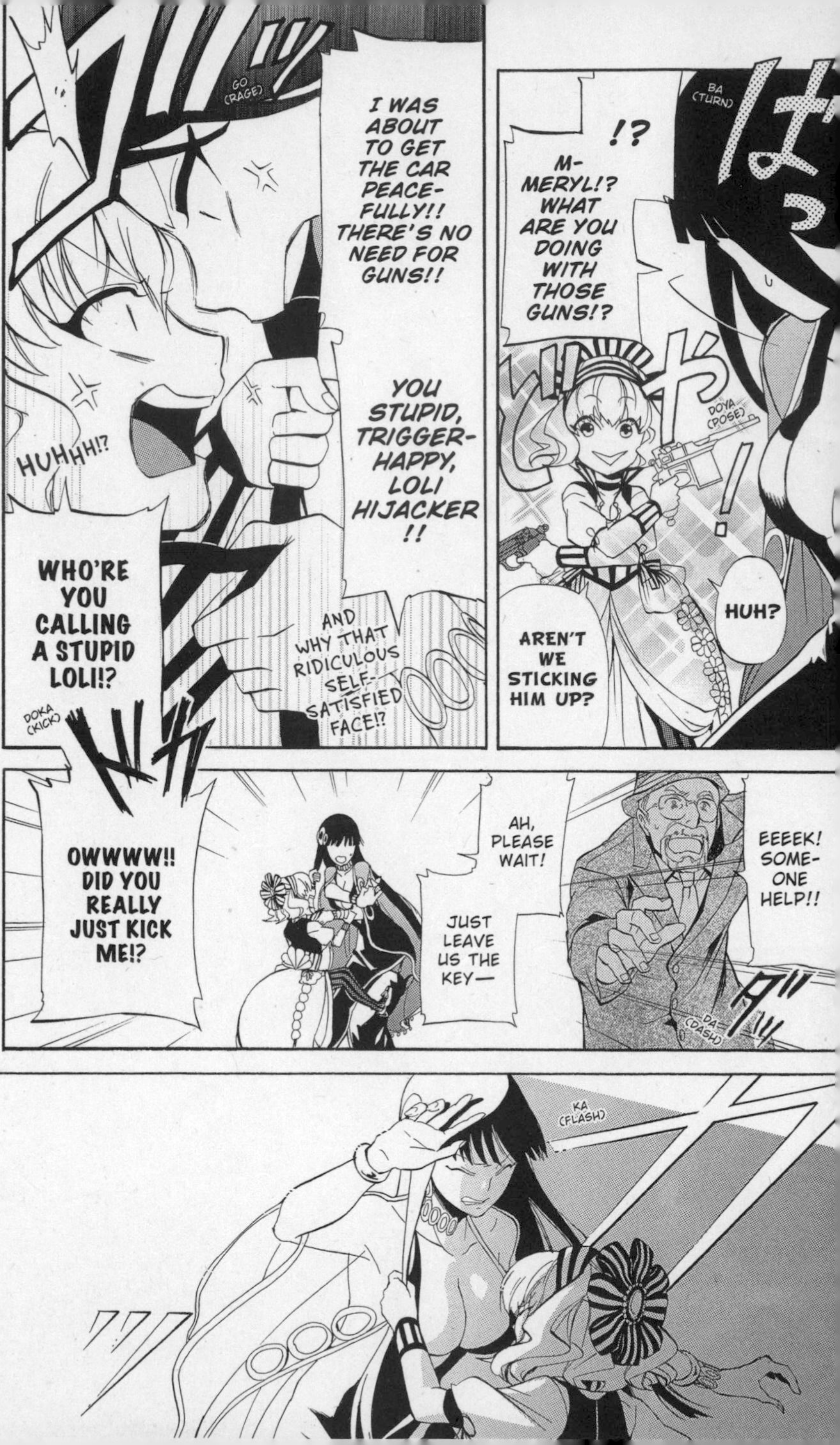
BA (TURN)
!?
M-MERYL!? WHAT ARE YOU DOING WITH THOSE GUNS!?
DOYA (POSE)
HUH?
AREN'T WE STICKING HIM UP?
GO (RAGE)
I WAS ABOUT TO GET THE CAR PEACE-FULLY!! THERE'S NO NEED FOR GUNS!!
YOU STUPID, TRIGGER-HAPPY, LOLI HIJACKER!!
AND WHY THAT RIDICULOUS SELF-SATISFIED FACE!?
HUHHH!?
WHO'RE YOU CALLING A STUPID LOLI!?
DOKA (KICK)
EEEEK! SOME-ONE HELP!!
DA (DASH)
AH, PLEASE WAIT!
JUST LEAVE US THE KEY—
OWWWW!! DID YOU REALLY JUST KICK ME!?
KA (FLASH)

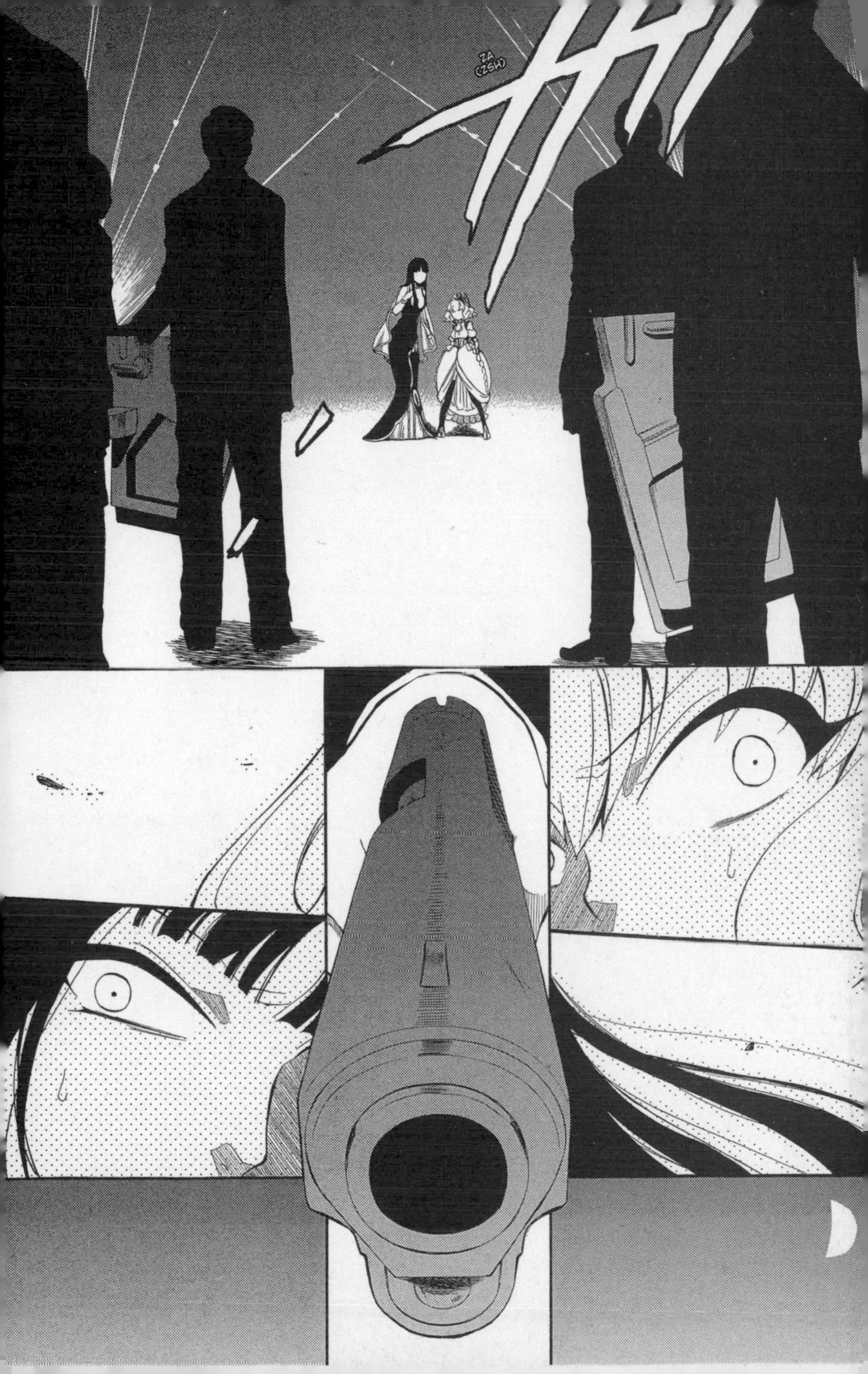
ZA
(ZSH)

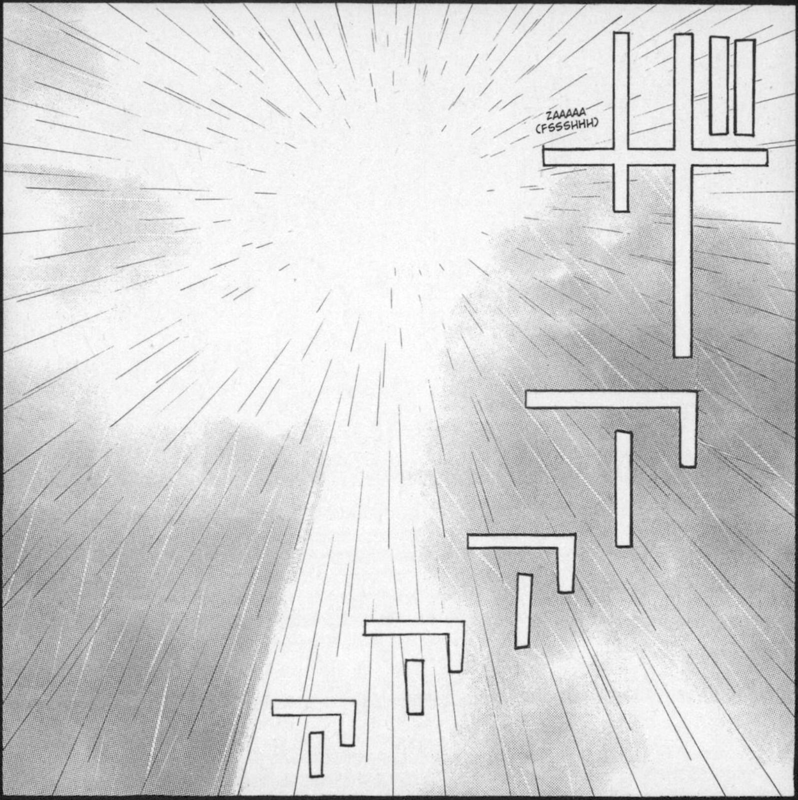
ZAAAAA
(FSSSHHH)

Scene: 12

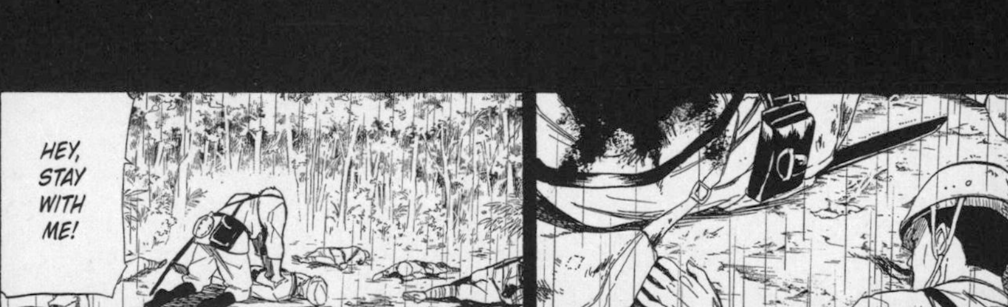
HEY, STAY WITH ME!

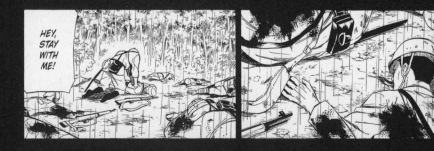

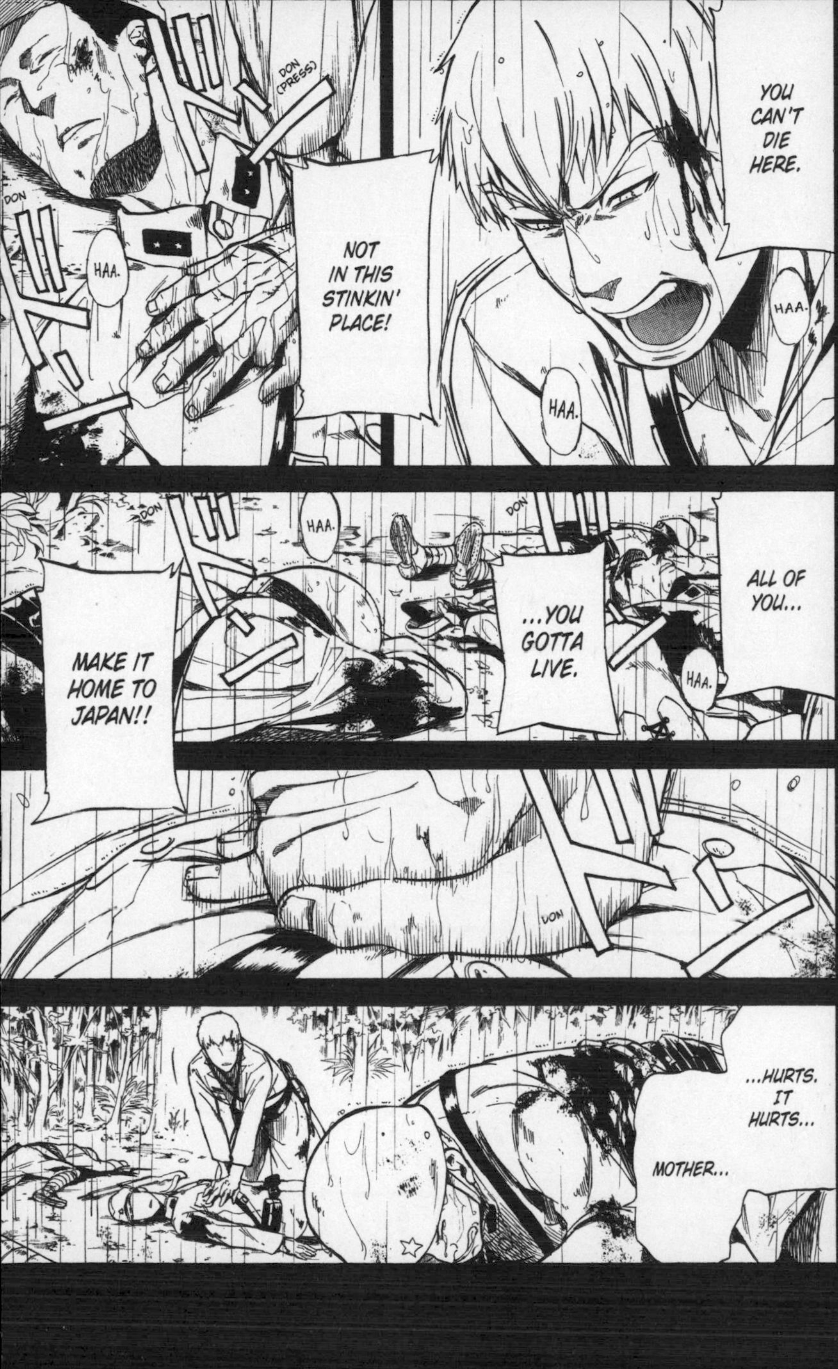
YOU CAN'T DIE HERE.
HAA.
HAA.
NOT IN THIS STINKIN' PLACE!
DON (PRESS)
DON
HAA.
ALL OF YOU...
HAA.
...YOU GOTTA LIVE.
DON
HAA.
DON
MAKE IT HOME TO JAPAN!!
DON
...HURTS. IT HURTS...
MOTHER...

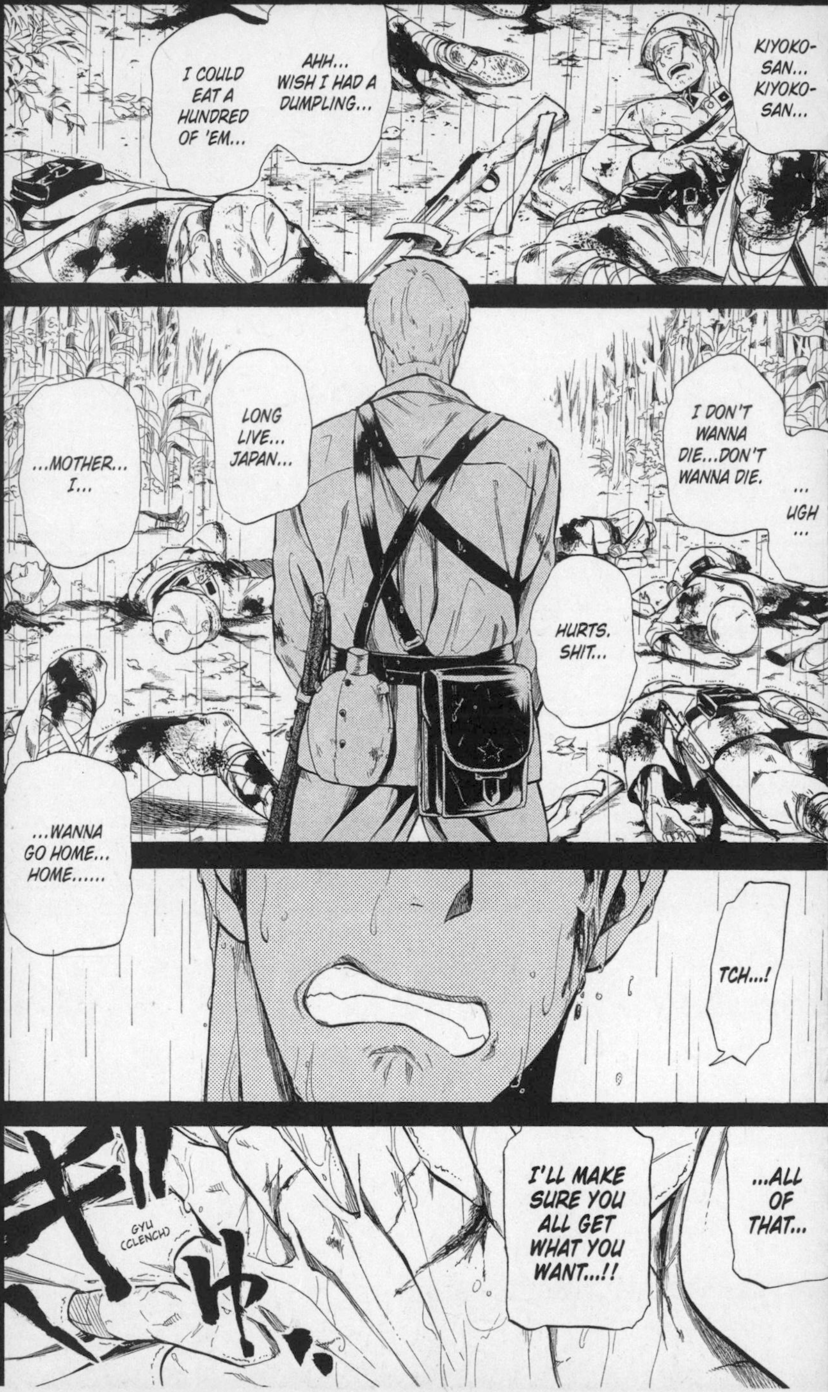
KIYOKO-SAN... KIYOKO-SAN...
AHH... WISH I HAD A DUMPLING...
I COULD EAT A HUNDRED OF 'EM...
I DON'T WANNA DIE...DON'T WANNA DIE.
...UGH...
LONG LIVE... JAPAN...
...MOTHER... I...
HURTS. SHIT...
...WANNA GO HOME... HOME......
TCH...!
...ALL OF THAT...
I'LL MAKE SURE YOU ALL GET WHAT YOU WANT...!!
GYU (CLENCH)
ギュッ

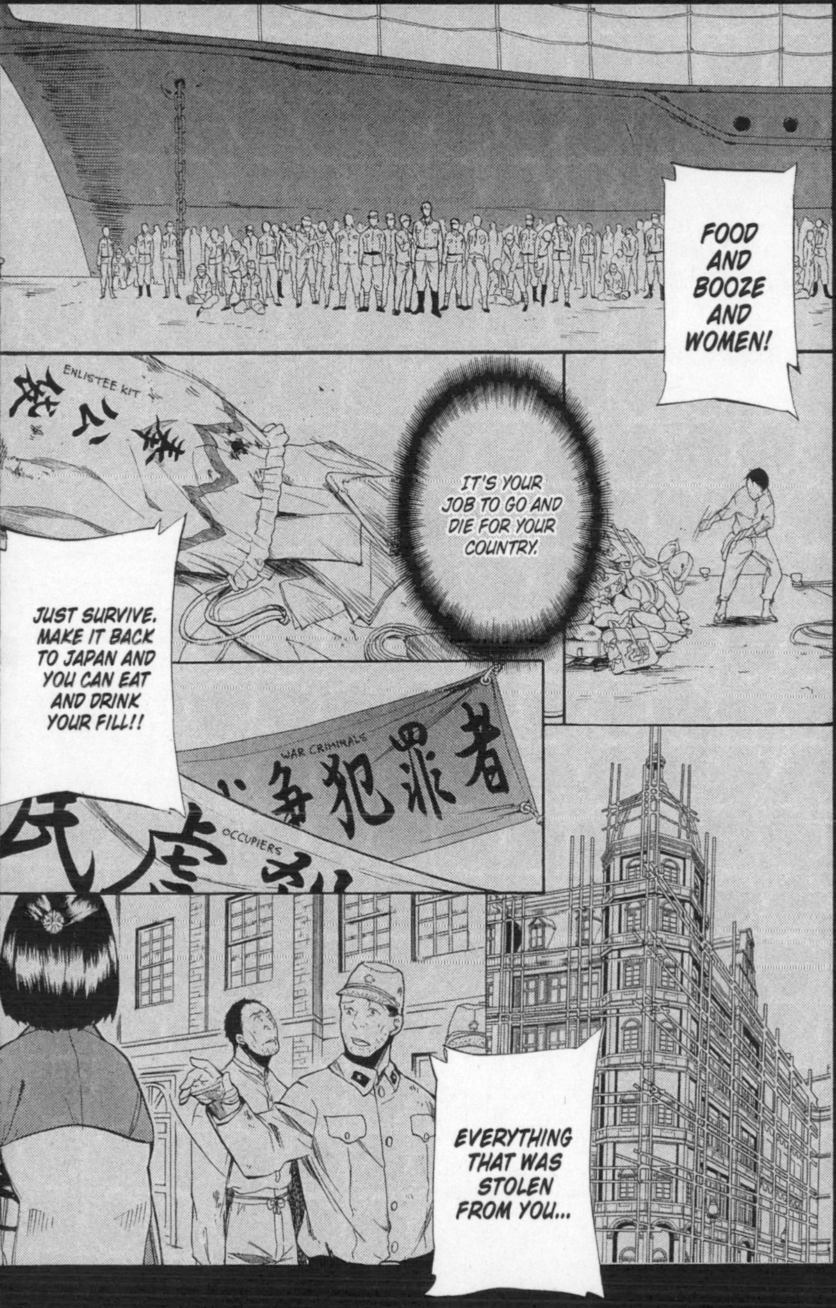
FOOD AND BOOZE AND WOMEN!
ENLISTEE KIT
IT'S YOUR JOB TO GO AND DIE FOR YOUR COUNTRY.
JUST SURVIVE. MAKE IT BACK TO JAPAN AND YOU CAN EAT AND DRINK YOUR FILL!!
WAR CRIMINALS
OCCUPIERS
EVERYTHING THAT WAS STOLEN FROM YOU...

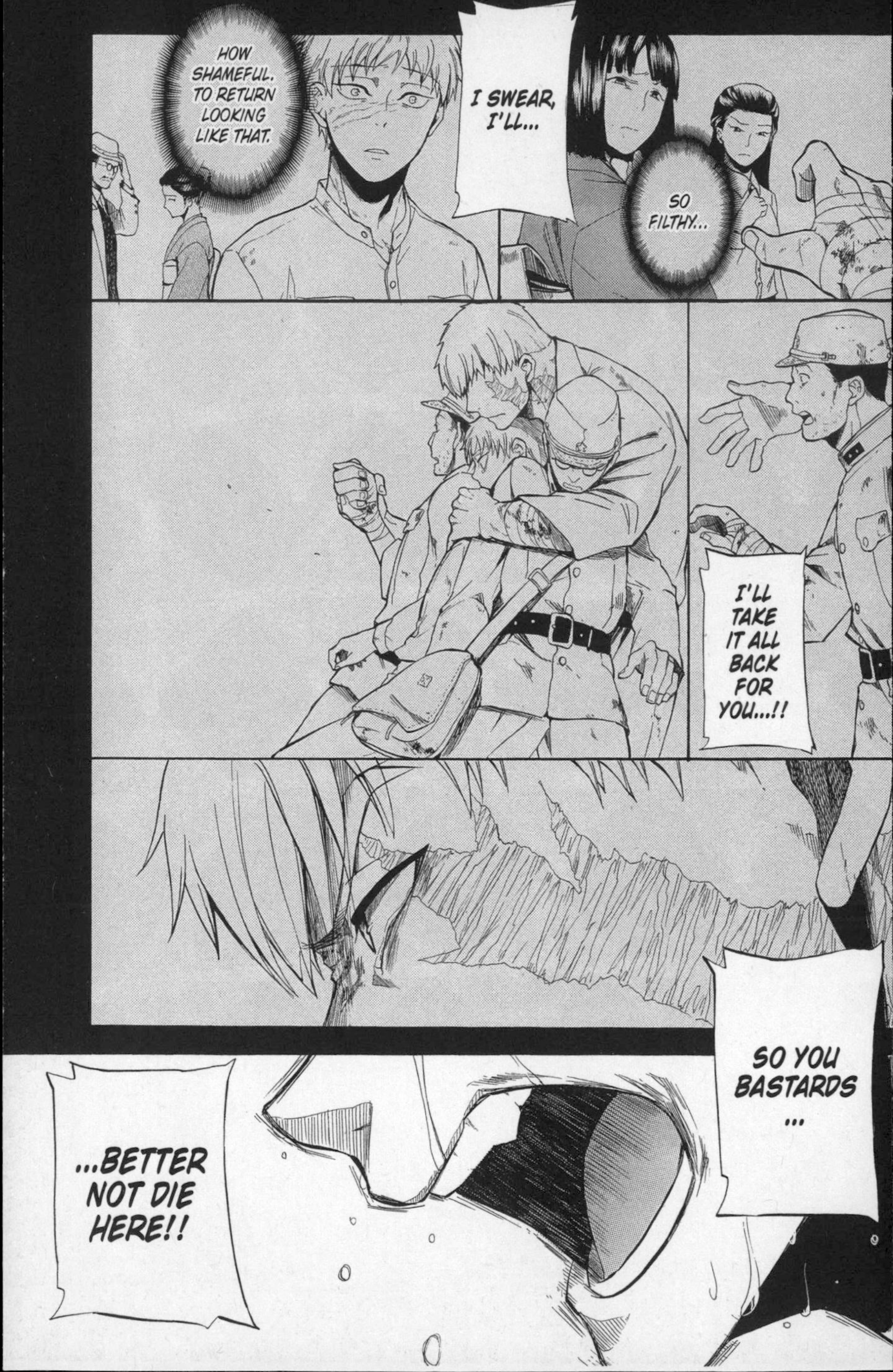
SO FILTHY...
I SWEAR, I'LL...
HOW SHAMEFUL. TO RETURN LOOKING LIKE THAT.
I'LL TAKE IT ALL BACK FOR YOU...!!
SO YOU BASTARDS ...
...BETTER NOT DIE HERE!!

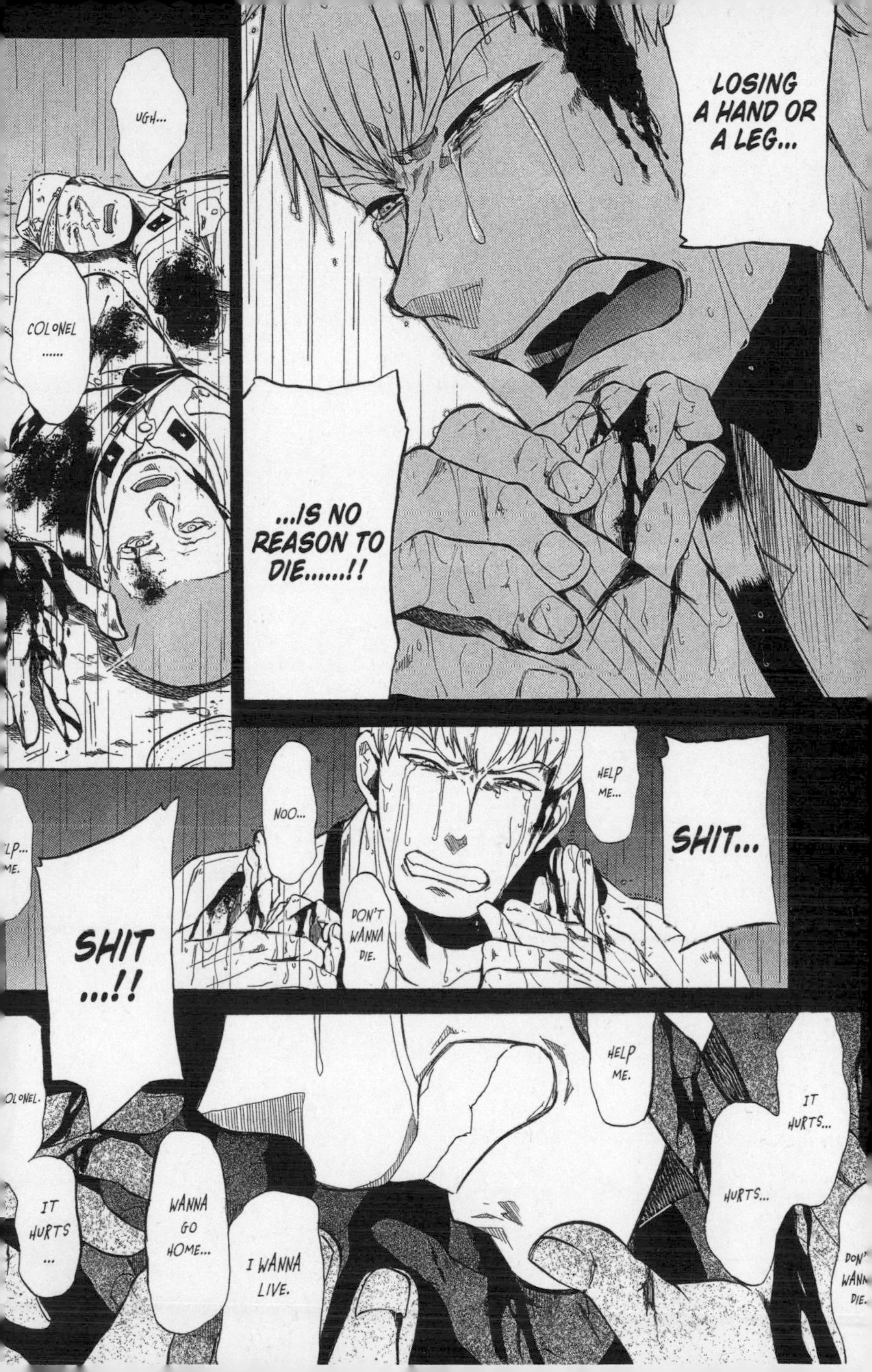
LOSING A HAND OR A LEG...
...IS NO REASON TO DIE......!!
UGH...
COLONEL ......
SHIT...
HELP ME...
NOO...
DON'T WANNA DIE.
SHIT ...!!
IT HURTS...
HURTS...
HELP ME.
I WANNA LIVE.
WANNA GO HOME...
IT HURTS ...

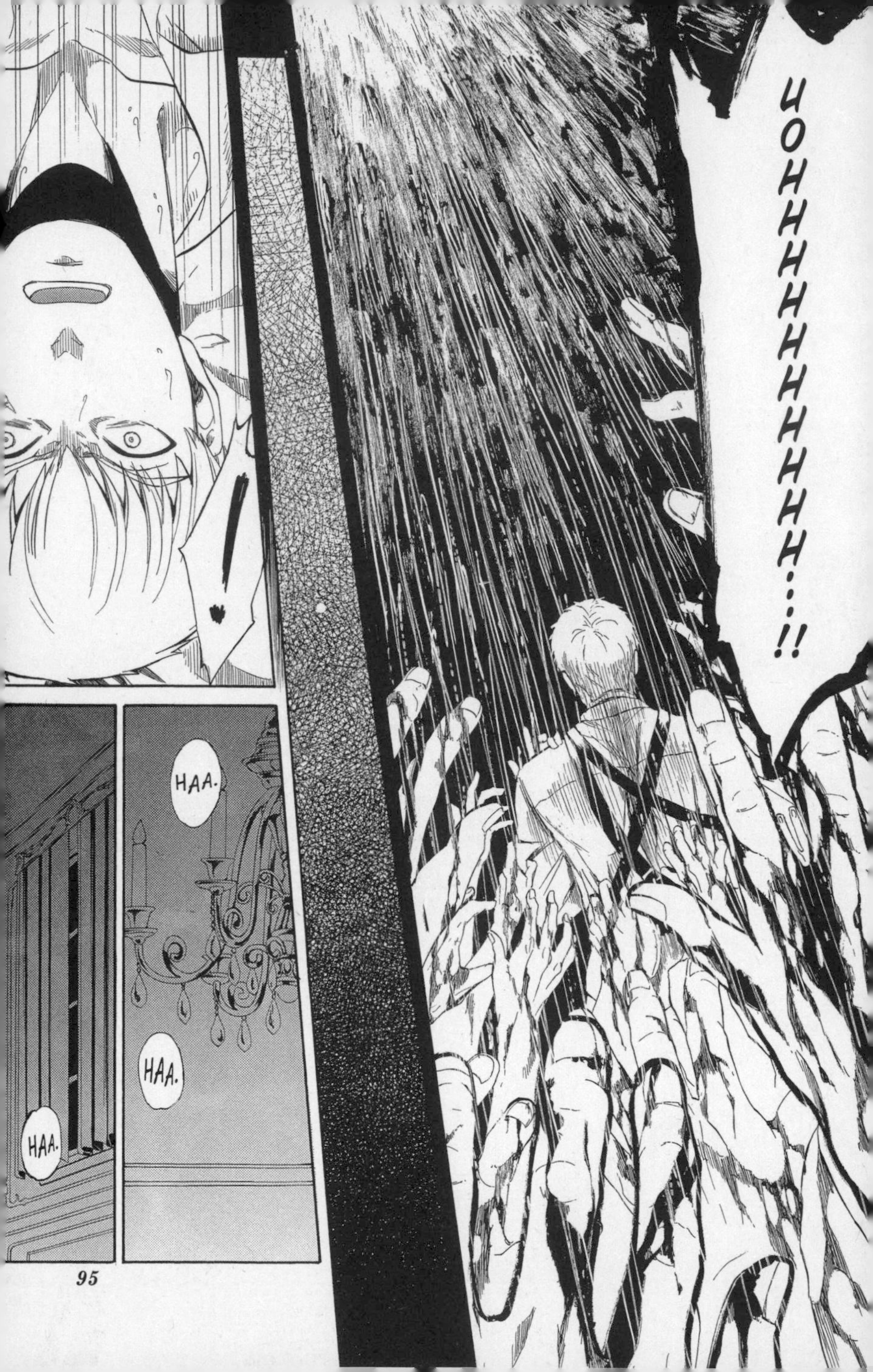

UOHHHHHHHHH...!!
HAA.
HAA.
HAA.

...I KNOW...
JUST HANG
ON A BIT
LONGER...

I'LL
SAVE
YOU
ALL...

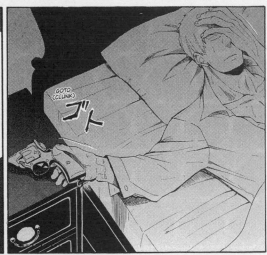

GOTO
(CLUNK)
ゴト

DOTA
(TMP)

BAN
(BAM)

COLONEL!
COLONEL!!

HEY.
I'VE
GOT MY
EYES,
RIGHT!?

GA
(GRAB)

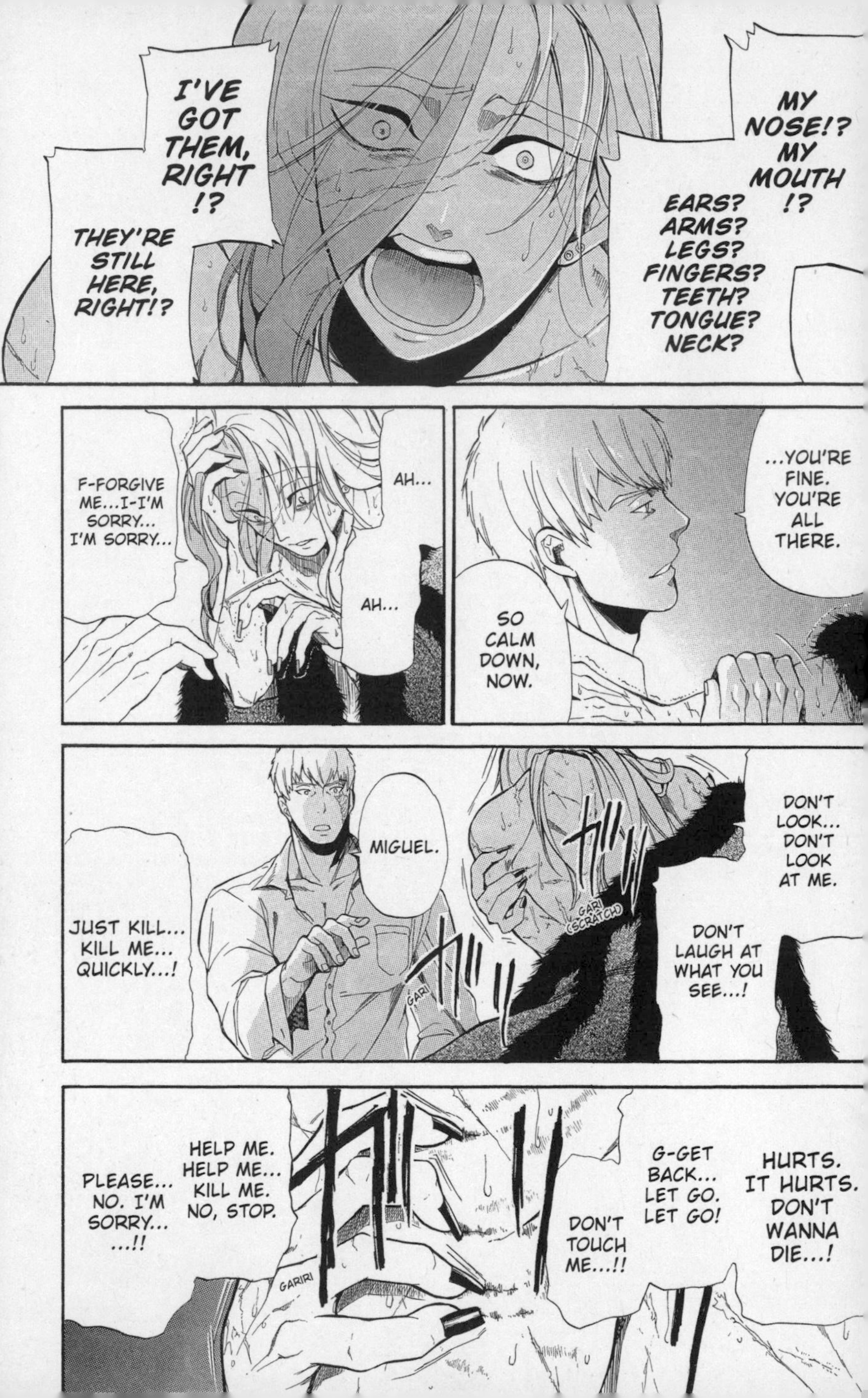
MY NOSE!? MY MOUTH !?
EARS? ARMS? LEGS? FINGERS? TEETH? TONGUE? NECK?
I'VE GOT THEM, RIGHT !?
THEY'RE STILL HERE, RIGHT!?
...YOU'RE FINE. YOU'RE ALL THERE.
SO CALM DOWN, NOW.
AH...
AH...
F-FORGIVE ME...I-I'M SORRY... I'M SORRY...
DON'T LOOK... DON'T LOOK AT ME.
DON'T LAUGH AT WHAT YOU SEE...!
GARI (SCRATCH)
MIGUEL.
GARI
JUST KILL... KILL ME... QUICKLY...!
HURTS. IT HURTS. DON'T WANNA DIE...!
G-GET BACK... LET GO. LET GO!
DON'T TOUCH ME...!!
HELP ME. HELP ME... KILL ME. NO, STOP.
PLEASE... NO. I'M SORRY... ...!!
GARIRI

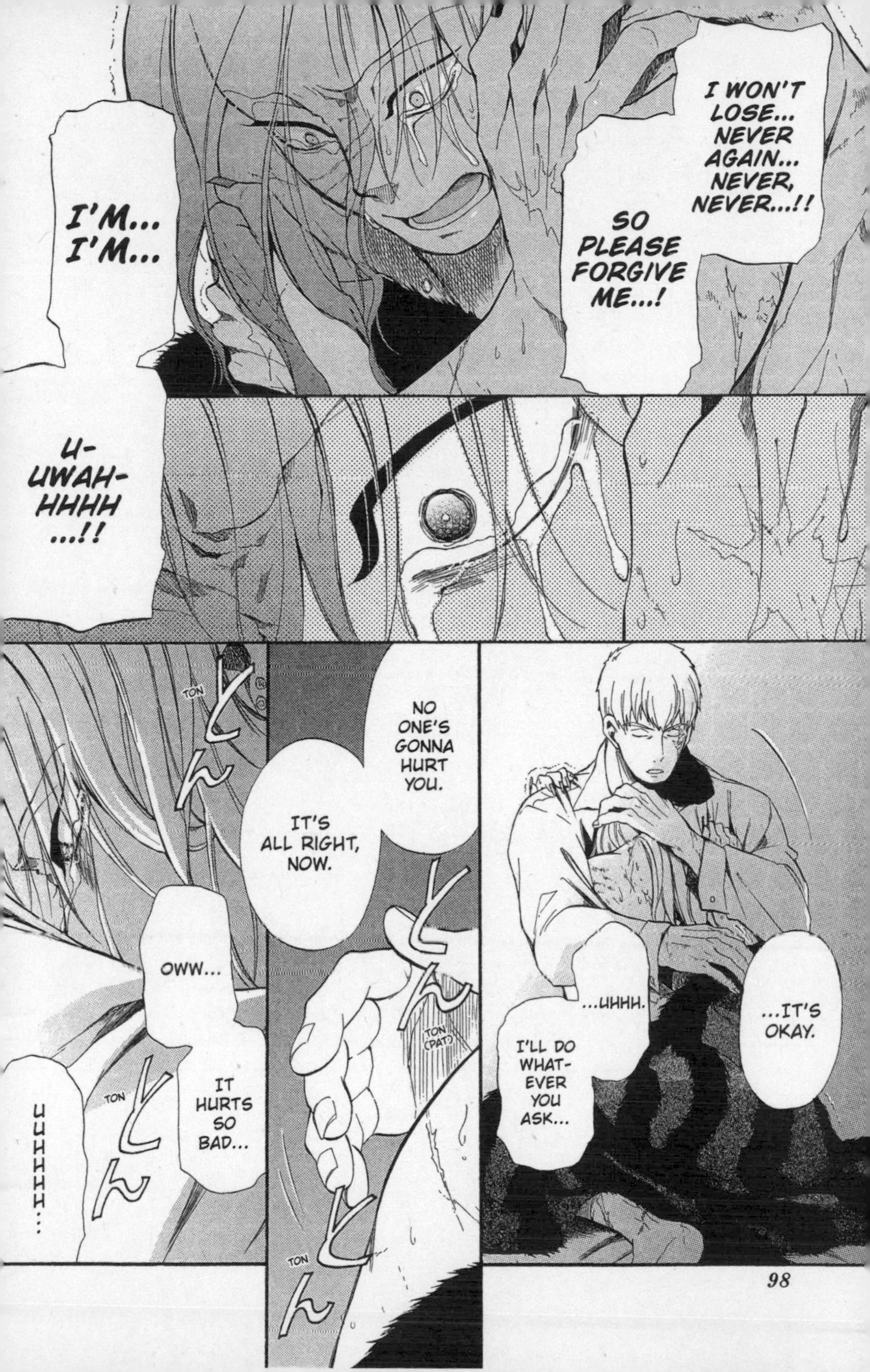
I WON'T LOSE... NEVER AGAIN... NEVER, NEVER...!!
SO PLEASE FORGIVE ME...!
I'M... I'M...
U-UWAH-HHHH...!!
...IT'S OKAY.
...UHHH.
I'LL DO WHATEVER YOU ASK...
NO ONE'S GONNA HURT YOU.
IT'S ALL RIGHT, NOW.
TON (PAT)
TON
TON
OWW...
IT HURTS SO BAD...
TON
UHHHHH...

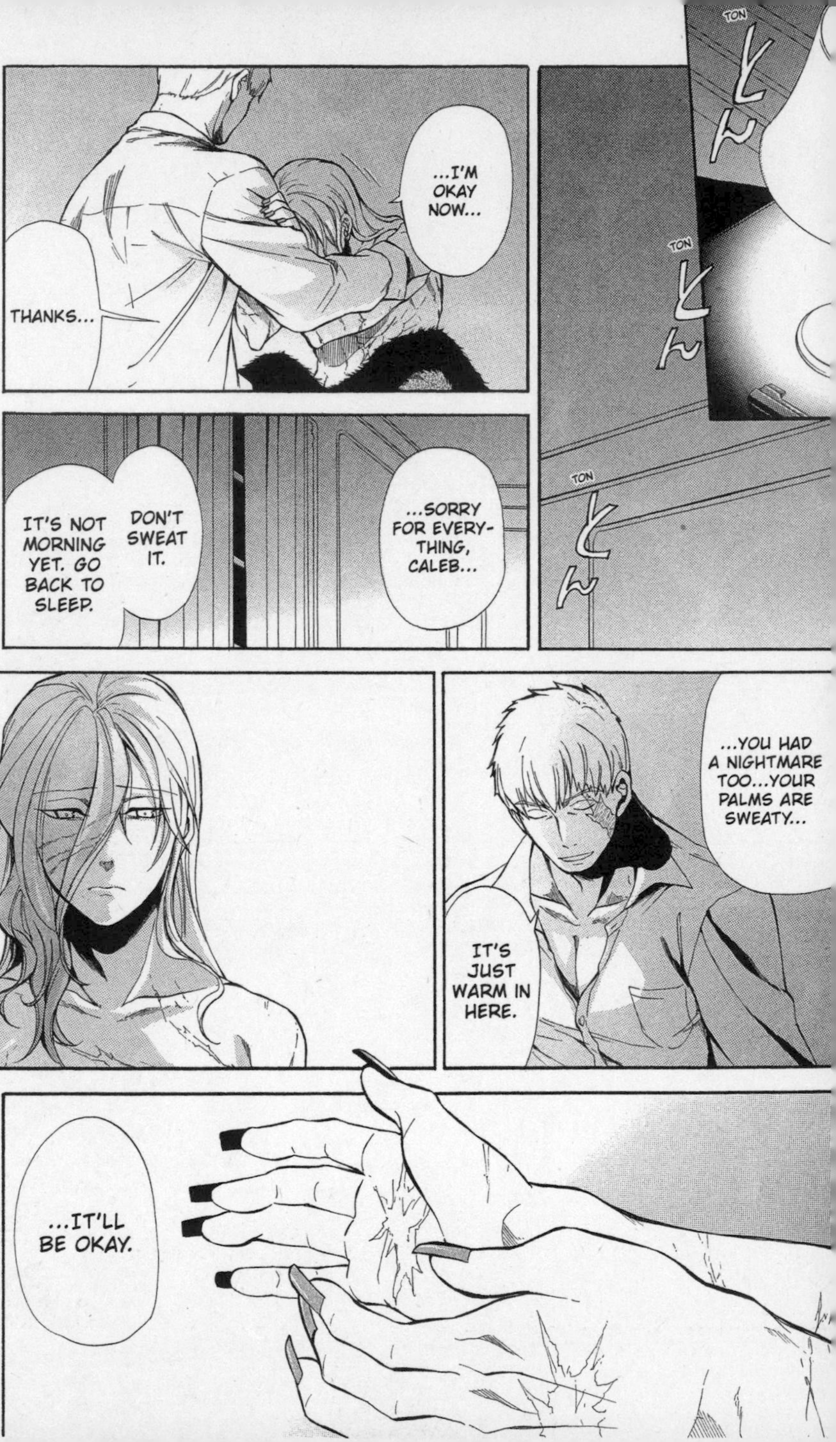
TON
とん
TON
とん
TON
とん
...I'M OKAY NOW...
THANKS...
...SORRY FOR EVERY-THING, CALEB...
DON'T SWEAT IT.
IT'S NOT MORNING YET. GO BACK TO SLEEP.
...YOU HAD A NIGHTMARE TOO...YOUR PALMS ARE SWEATY...
IT'S JUST WARM IN HERE.
...IT'LL BE OKAY.

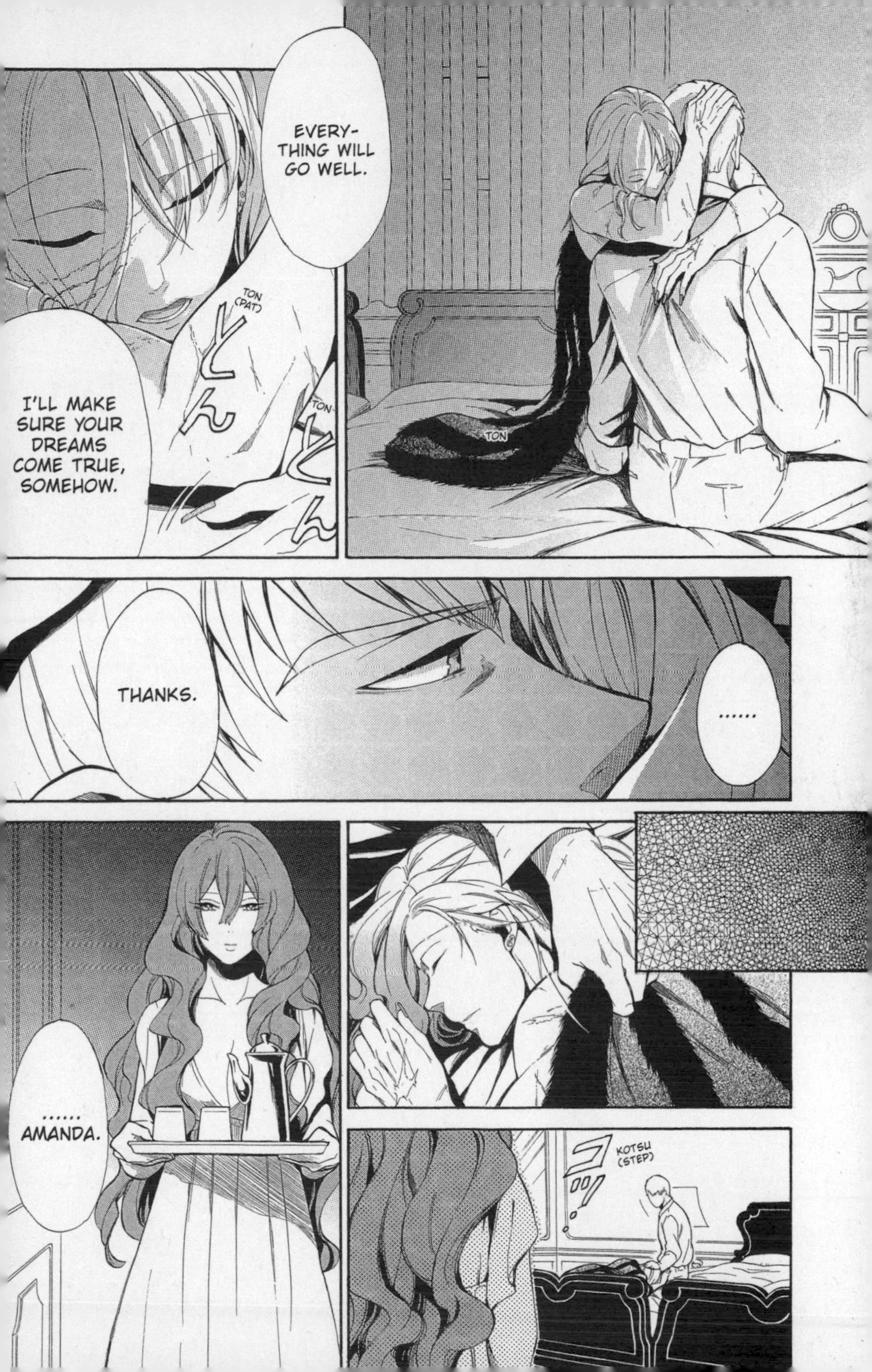
TON
EVERY-THING WILL GO WELL.
TON (PAT)
TON
I'LL MAKE SURE YOUR DREAMS COME TRUE, SOMEHOW.
......
THANKS.
KOTSU (STEP)
...... AMANDA.

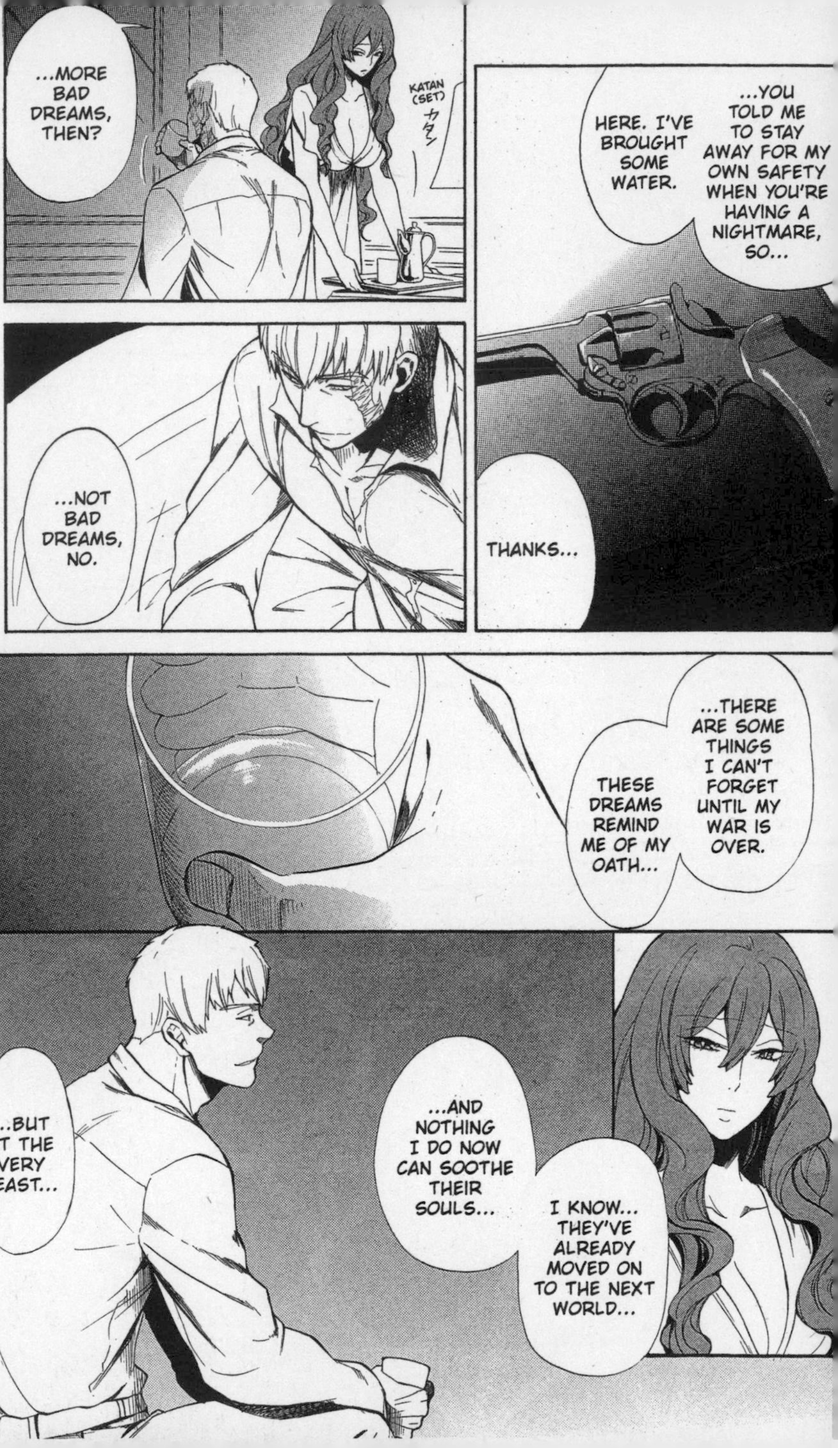
...YOU TOLD ME TO STAY AWAY FOR MY OWN SAFETY WHEN YOU'RE HAVING A NIGHTMARE, SO...
HERE. I'VE BROUGHT SOME WATER.
THANKS...
...MORE BAD DREAMS, THEN?
KATAN (SET)
カタン
...NOT BAD DREAMS, NO.
...THERE ARE SOME THINGS I CAN'T FORGET UNTIL MY WAR IS OVER.
THESE DREAMS REMIND ME OF MY OATH...
I KNOW... THEY'VE ALREADY MOVED ON TO THE NEXT WORLD...
...AND NOTHING I DO NOW CAN SOOTHE THEIR SOULS...
...BUT AT THE VERY LEAST...

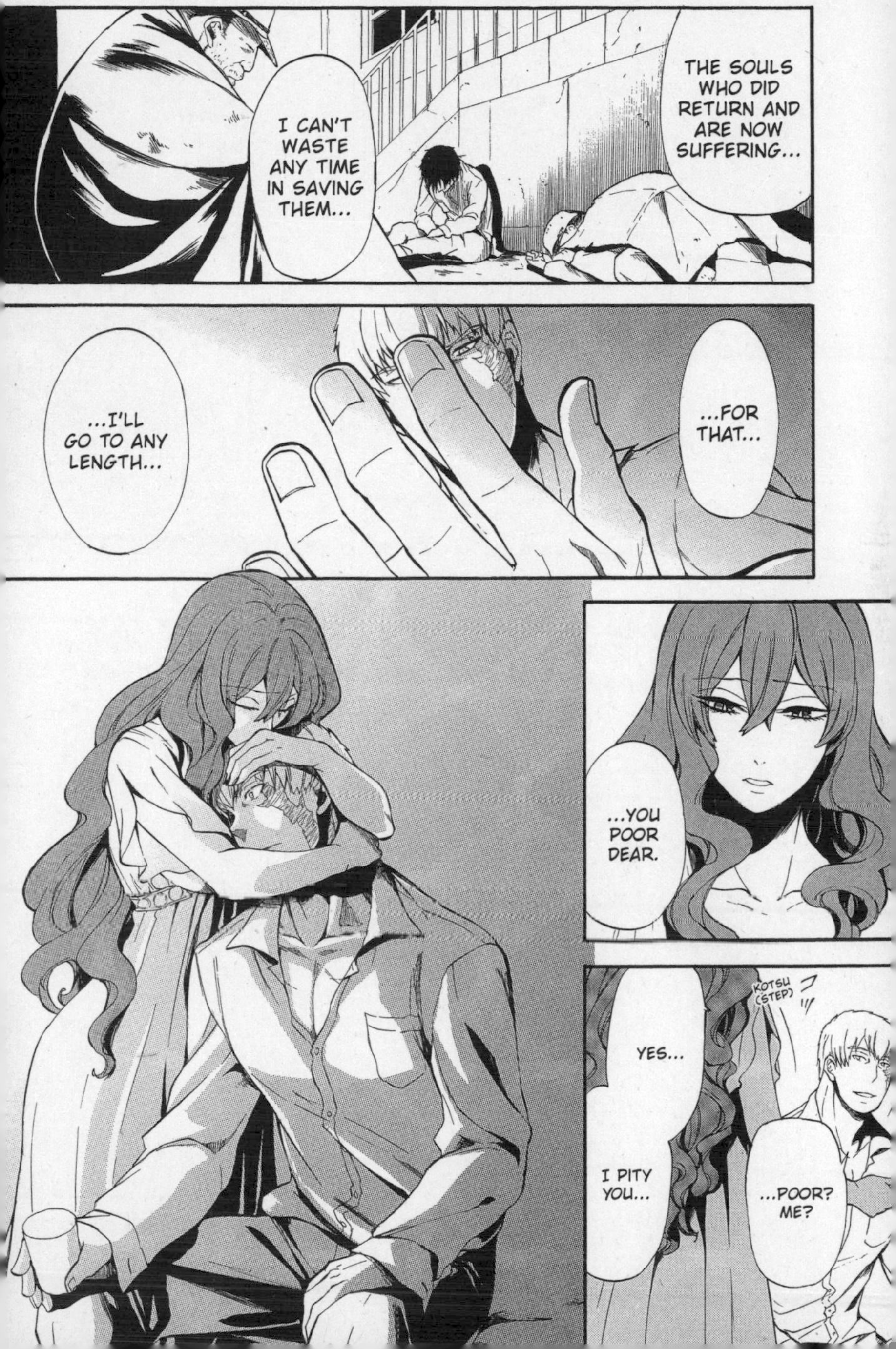
THE SOULS WHO DID RETURN AND ARE NOW SUFFERING...
I CAN'T WASTE ANY TIME IN SAVING THEM...
...FOR THAT...
...I'LL GO TO ANY LENGTH...
...YOU POOR DEAR.
KOTSU (STEP)
...POOR? ME?
YES...
I PITY YOU...

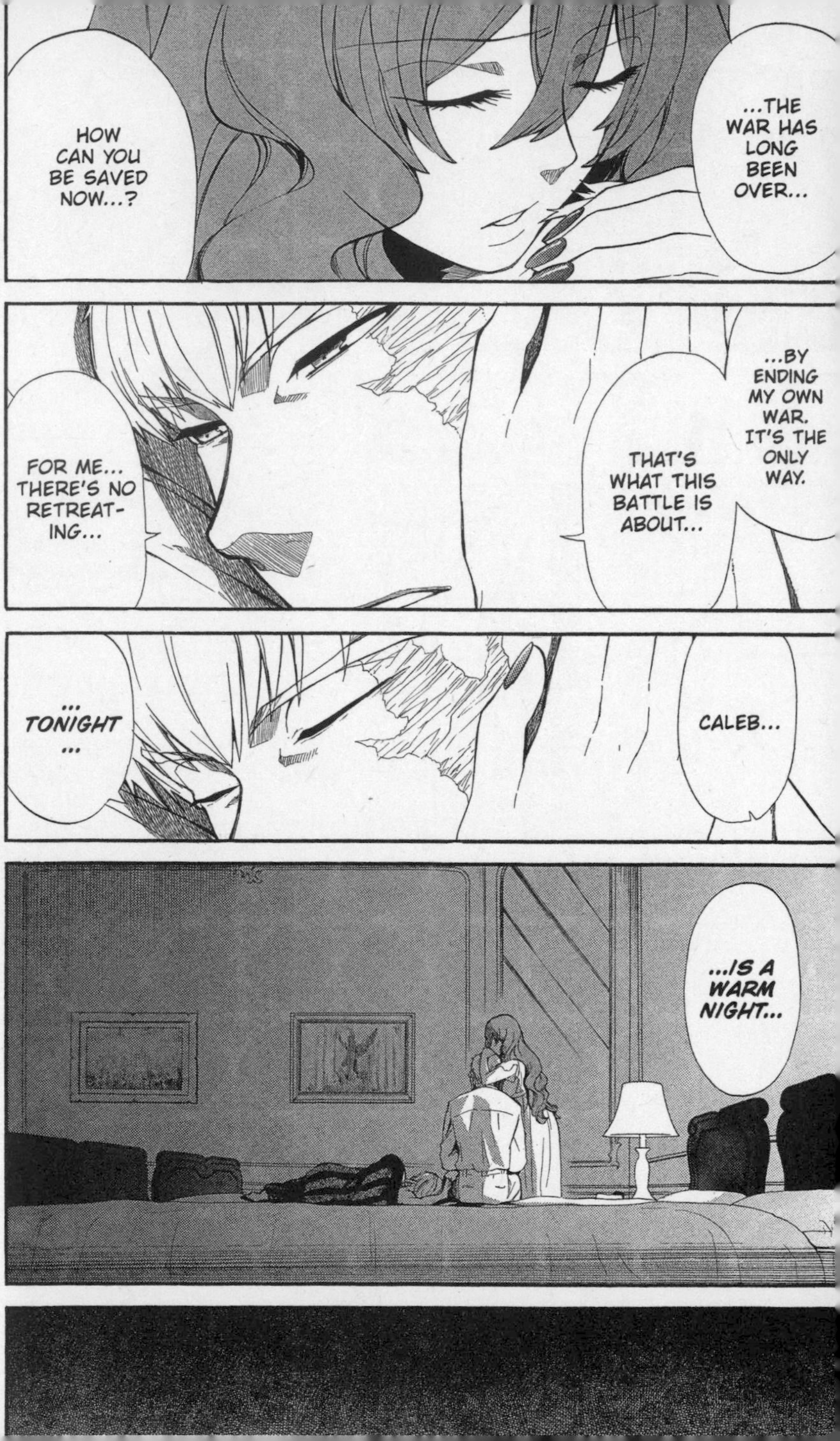
...THE WAR HAS LONG BEEN OVER...
HOW CAN YOU BE SAVED NOW...?
...BY ENDING MY OWN WAR. IT'S THE ONLY WAY.
THAT'S WHAT THIS BATTLE IS ABOUT...
FOR ME... THERE'S NO RETREAT-ING...
CALEB...
...TONIGHT...
...IS A WARM NIGHT...

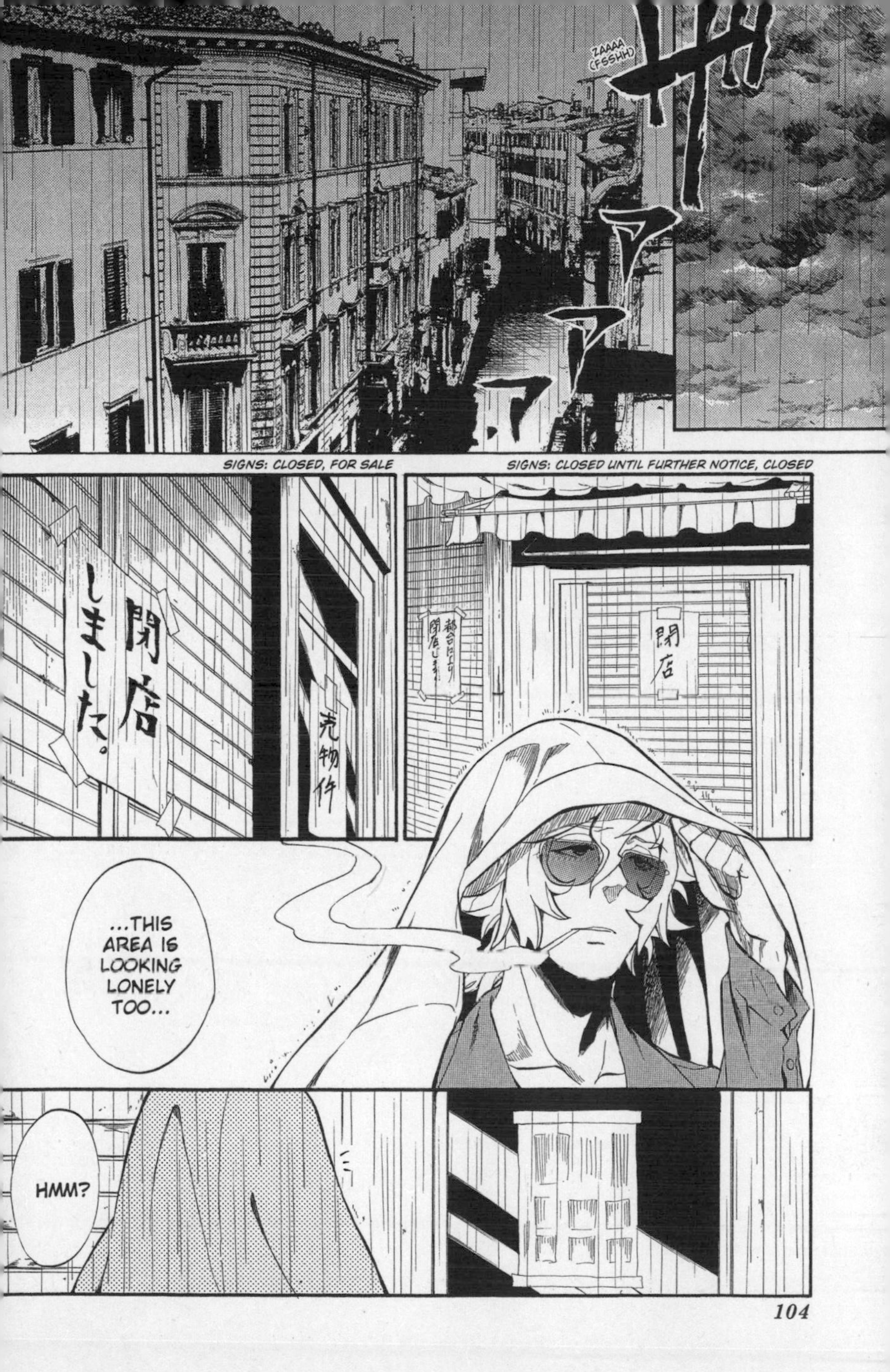
ZAAAA (FSSHH)
SIGNS: CLOSED UNTIL FURTHER NOTICE, CLOSED
都合により閉店します
閉店
SIGNS: CLOSED, FOR SALE
閉店しました。
売物件
...THIS AREA IS LOOKING LONELY TOO...
HMM?

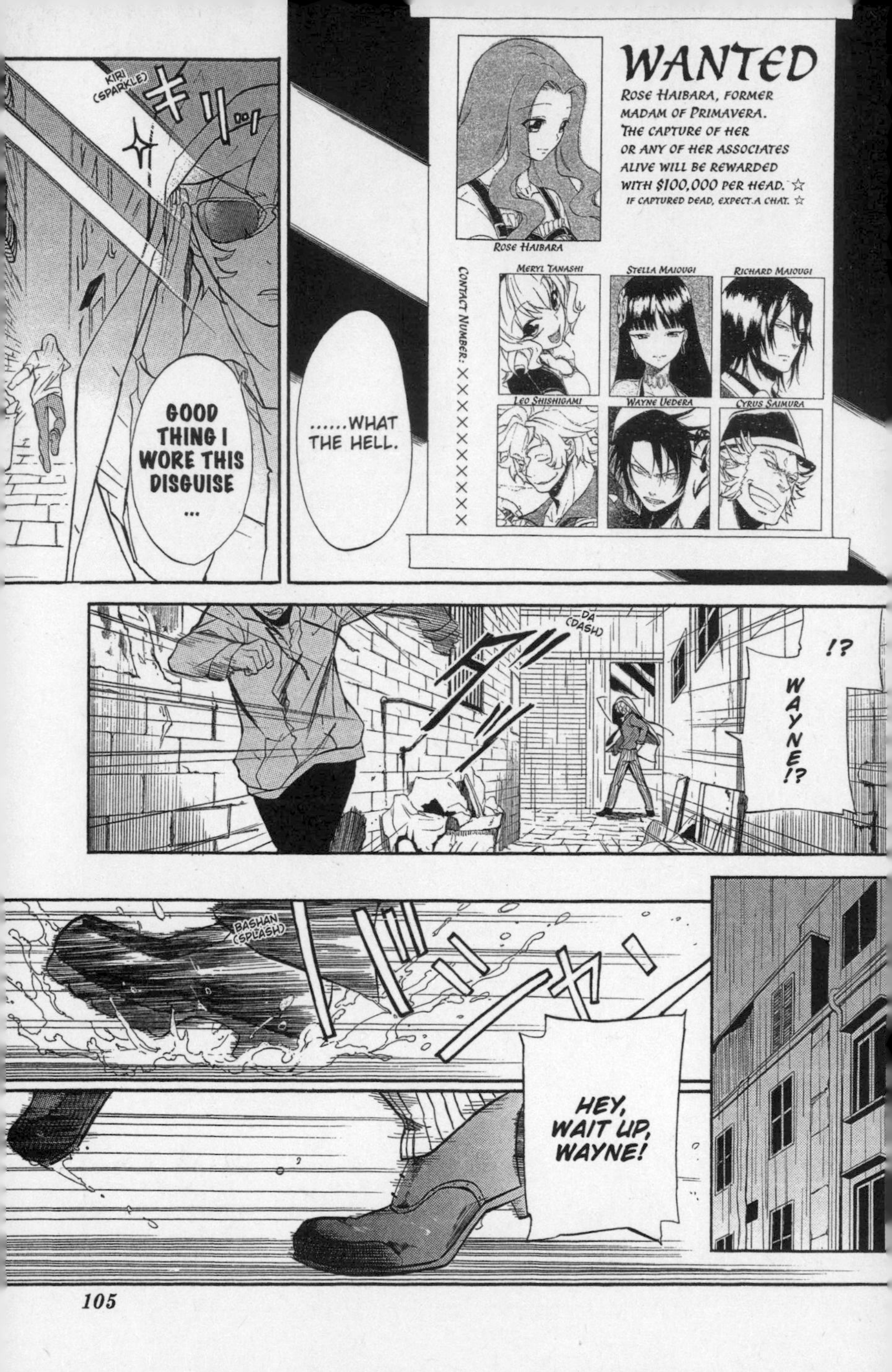
WANTED
ROSE HAIBARA, FORMER MADAM OF PRIMAVERA. THE CAPTURE OF HER OR ANY OF HER ASSOCIATES ALIVE WILL BE REWARDED WITH $100,000 PER HEAD. ☆
IF CAPTURED DEAD, EXPECT A CHAT. ☆
ROSE HAIBARA
CONTACT NUMBER: ××××××××××××
MERYL TANASHI
STELLA MAIOUGI
RICHARD MAIOUGI
LEO SHISHIGAMI
WAYNE UEDERA
CYRUS SAIMURA
......WHAT THE HELL.
KIRI (SPARKLE)
GOOD THING I WORE THIS DISGUISE ...
!? WAYNE!?
DA (DASH)
HEY, WAIT UP, WAYNE!
BASHAN (SPLASH)

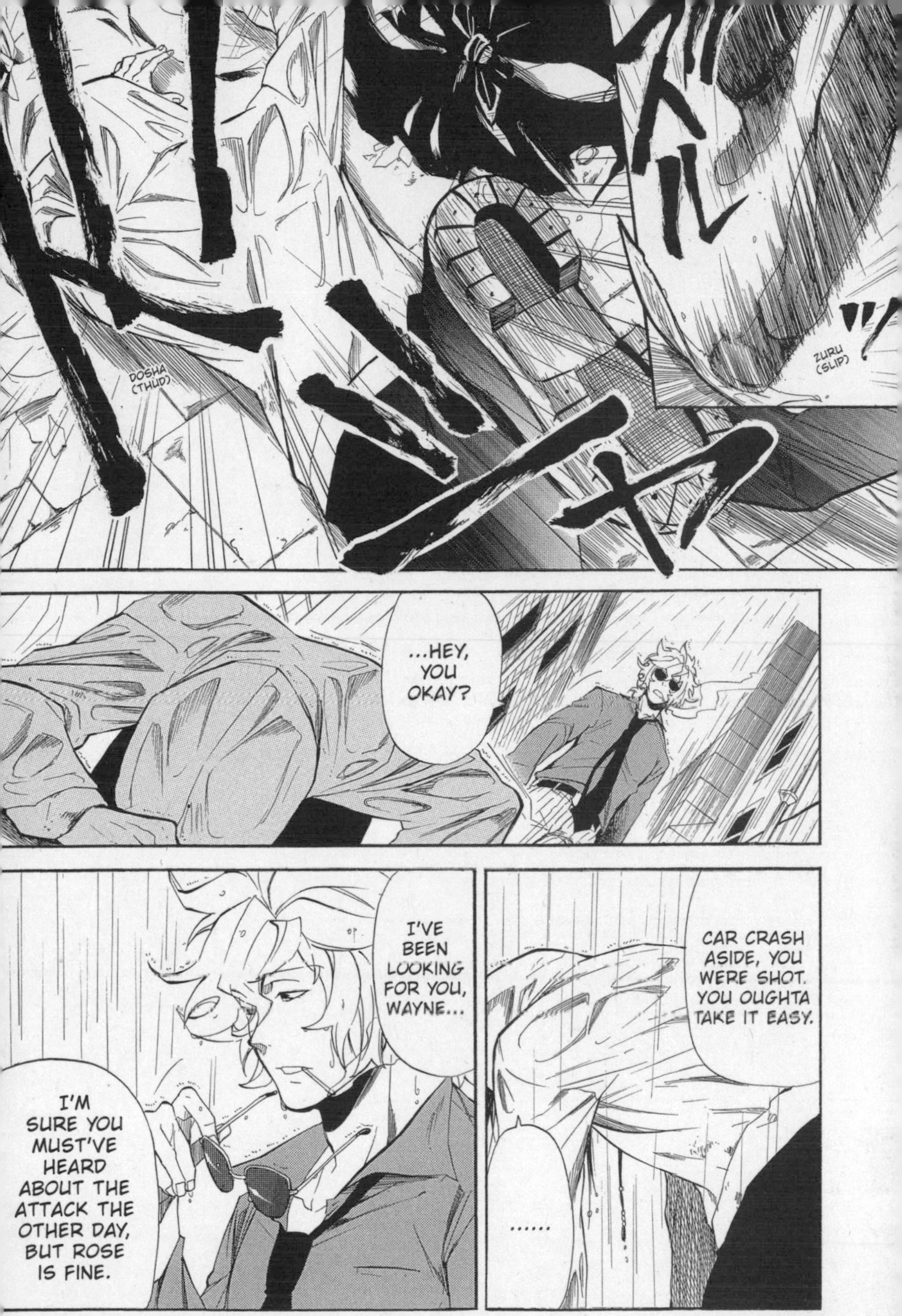
ZURU (SLIP)
DOSHA (THUD)
...HEY, YOU OKAY?
CAR CRASH ASIDE, YOU WERE SHOT. YOU OUGHTA TAKE IT EASY.
......
I'VE BEEN LOOKING FOR YOU, WAYNE...
I'M SURE YOU MUST'VE HEARD ABOUT THE ATTACK THE OTHER DAY, BUT ROSE IS FINE.

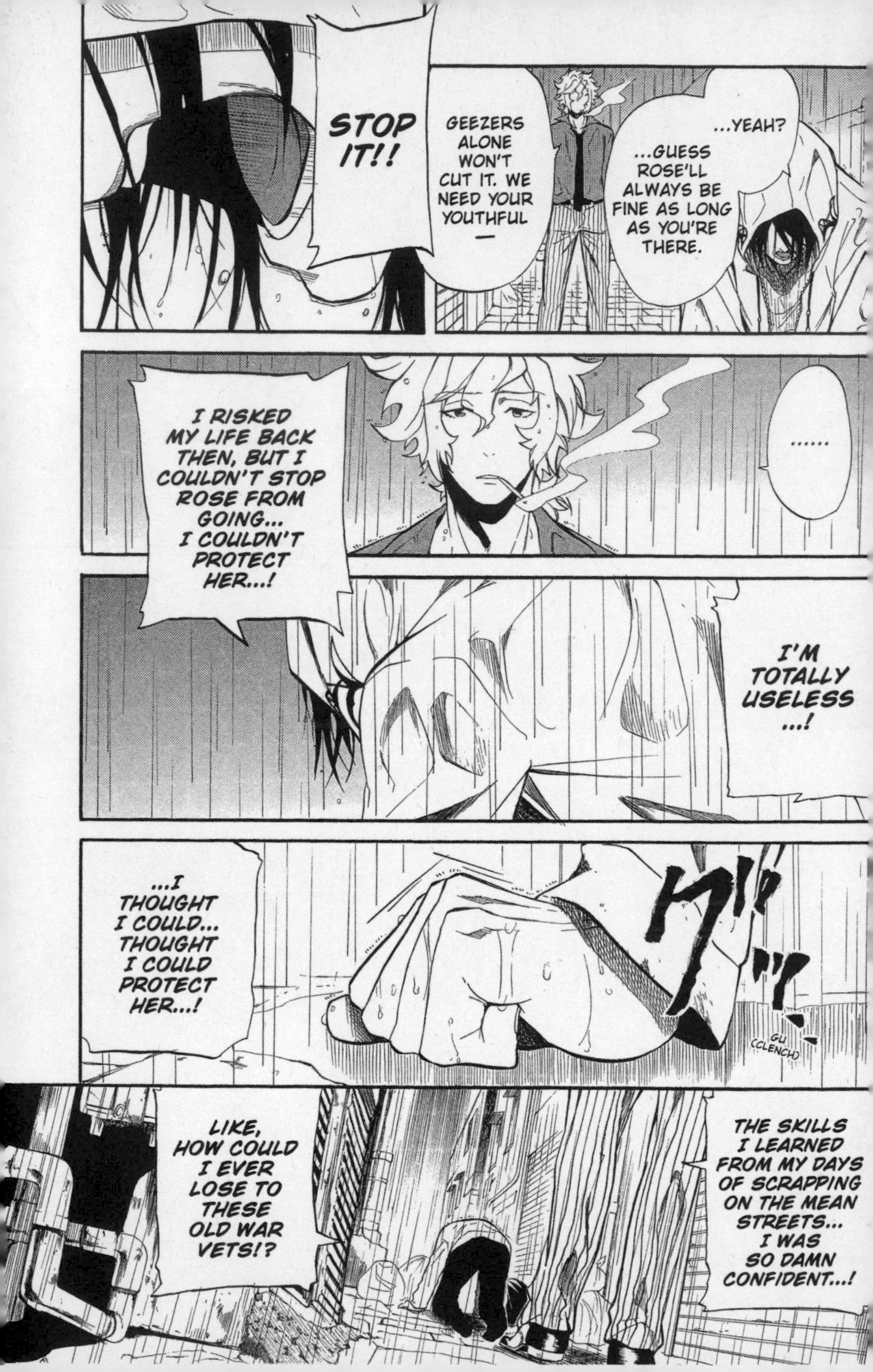
...YEAH?
...GUESS ROSE'LL ALWAYS BE FINE AS LONG AS YOU'RE THERE.
GEEZERS ALONE WON'T CUT IT. WE NEED YOUR YOUTHFUL —
STOP IT!!
......
I RISKED MY LIFE BACK THEN, BUT I COULDN'T STOP ROSE FROM GOING... I COULDN'T PROTECT HER...!
I'M TOTALLY USELESS ...!
GU (CLENCH)
...I THOUGHT I COULD... THOUGHT I COULD PROTECT HER...!
THE SKILLS I LEARNED FROM MY DAYS OF SCRAPPING ON THE MEAN STREETS... I WAS SO DAMN CONFIDENT...!
LIKE, HOW COULD I EVER LOSE TO THESE OLD WAR VETS!?

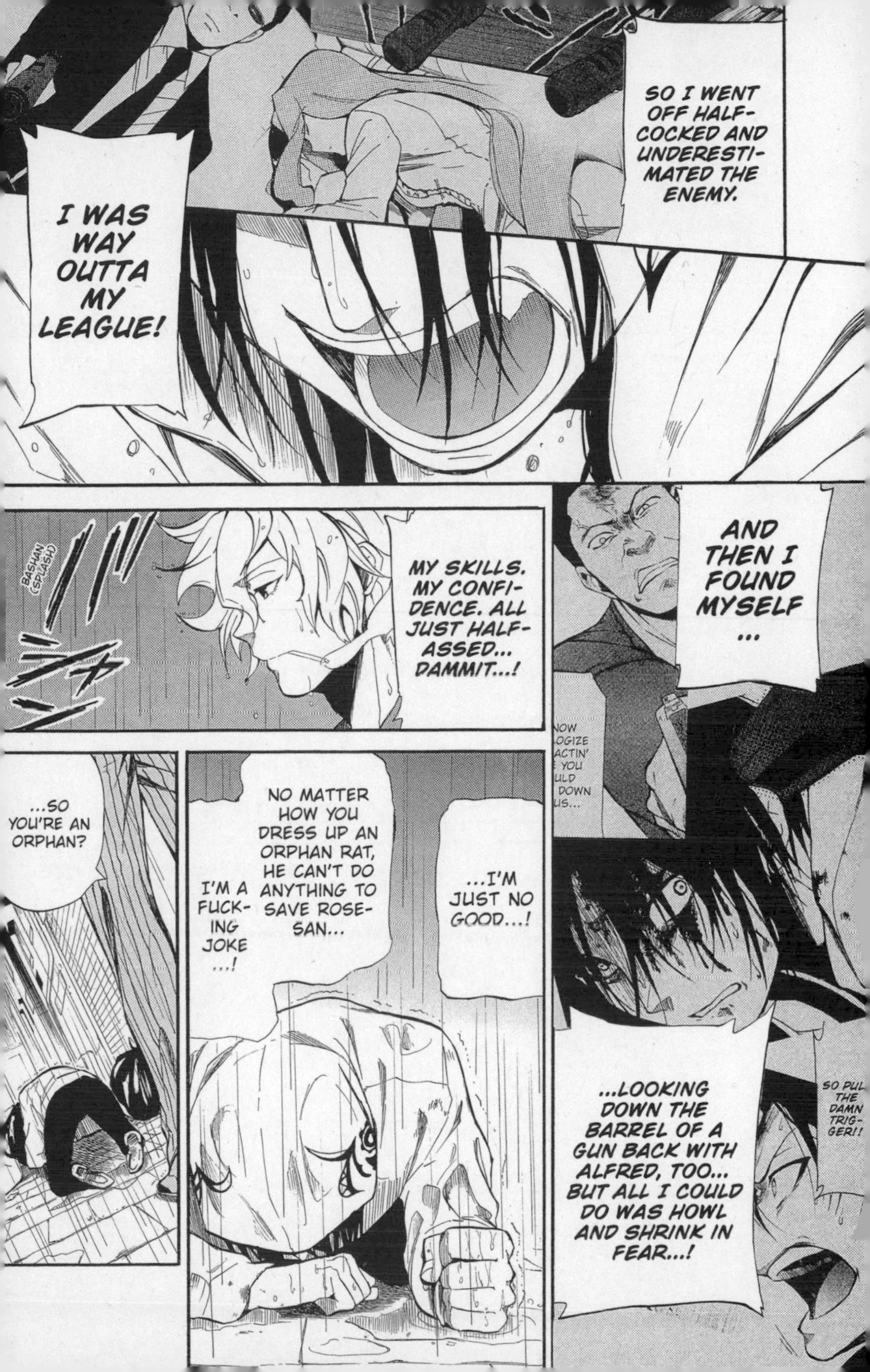
SO I WENT OFF HALF-COCKED AND UNDERESTIMATED THE ENEMY.
I WAS WAY OUTTA MY LEAGUE!
AND THEN I FOUND MYSELF ...
...LOOKING DOWN THE BARREL OF A GUN BACK WITH ALFRED, TOO... BUT ALL I COULD DO WAS HOWL AND SHRINK IN FEAR...!
SO PULL THE DAMN TRIGGER!!
MY SKILLS. MY CONFIDENCE. ALL JUST HALF-ASSED... DAMMIT...!
BASHAN (SPLASH)
...I'M JUST NO GOOD...!
NO MATTER HOW YOU DRESS UP AN ORPHAN RAT, HE CAN'T DO ANYTHING TO SAVE ROSE-SAN...
I'M A FUCKING JOKE ...!
...SO YOU'RE AN ORPHAN?

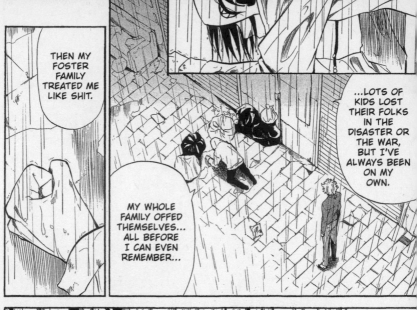

...LOTS OF KIDS LOST THEIR FOLKS IN THE DISASTER OR THE WAR, BUT I'VE ALWAYS BEEN ON MY OWN.
MY WHOLE FAMILY OFFED THEMSELVES... ALL BEFORE I CAN EVEN REMEMBER...
THEN MY FOSTER FAMILY TREATED ME LIKE SHIT.
THEY KEPT ME IN THE SHED AND TOSSED ME LEFTOVERS WHILE EATING MEAT THEM-SELVES.
WASN'T RARE FOR ME NOT TO EAT AT ALL.
AND IF ANYTHING WENT MISSING OR GOT BROKEN, THEY'D BLAME ME AND BEAT ME HALFWAY TO HELL...
...SO YOU RAN AWAY, THEN...?
YEAH...

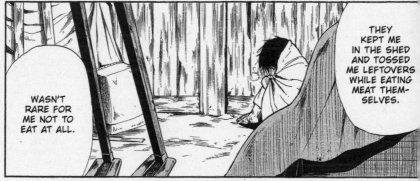

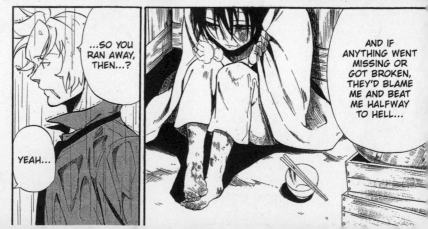

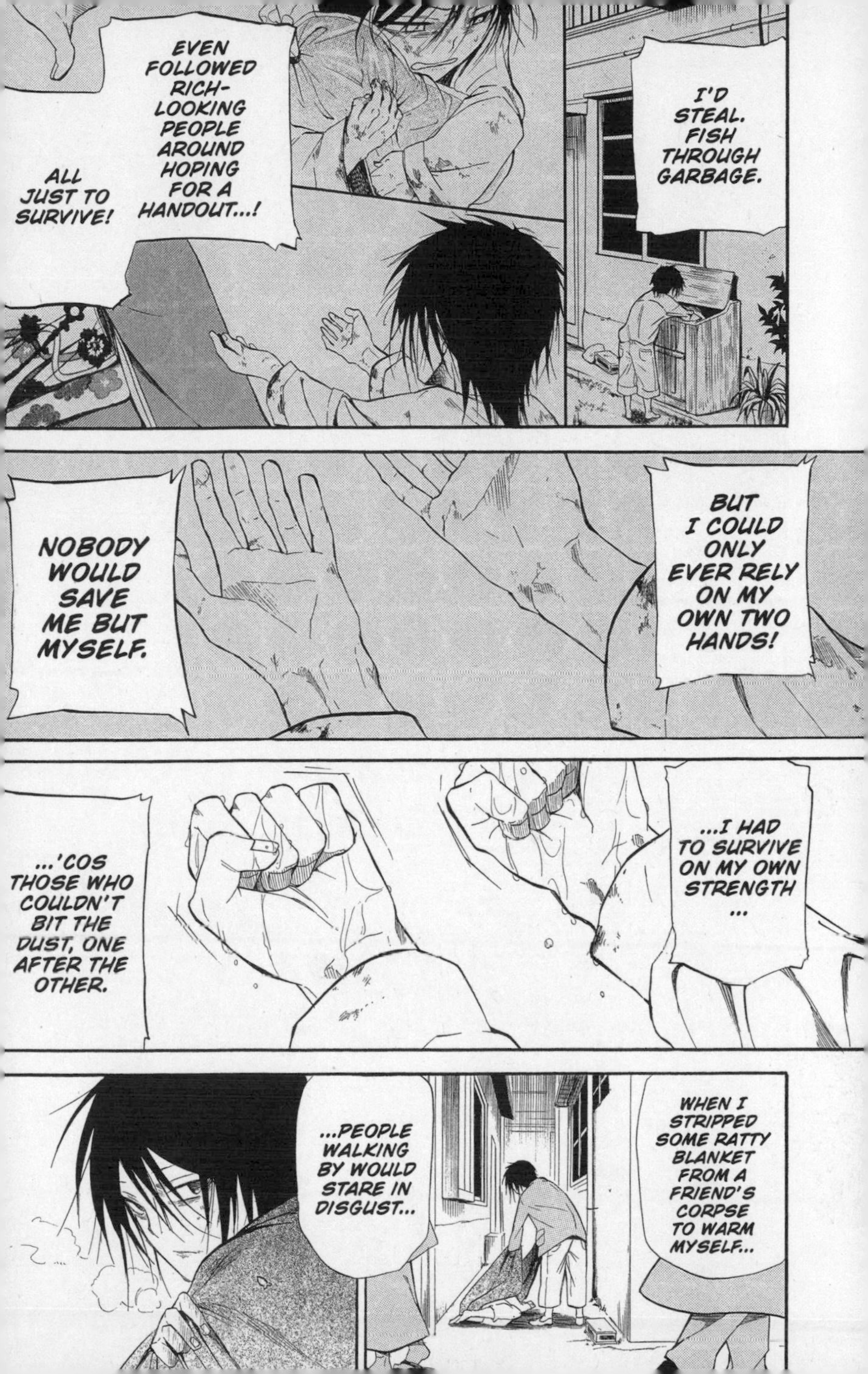
I'D STEAL. FISH THROUGH GARBAGE.
EVEN FOLLOWED RICH-LOOKING PEOPLE AROUND HOPING FOR A HANDOUT...!
ALL JUST TO SURVIVE!
BUT I COULD ONLY EVER RELY ON MY OWN TWO HANDS!
NOBODY WOULD SAVE ME BUT MYSELF.
...I HAD TO SURVIVE ON MY OWN STRENGTH...
...'COS THOSE WHO COULDN'T BIT THE DUST, ONE AFTER THE OTHER.
WHEN I STRIPPED SOME RATTY BLANKET FROM A FRIEND'S CORPSE TO WARM MYSELF...
...PEOPLE WALKING BY WOULD STARE IN DISGUST...

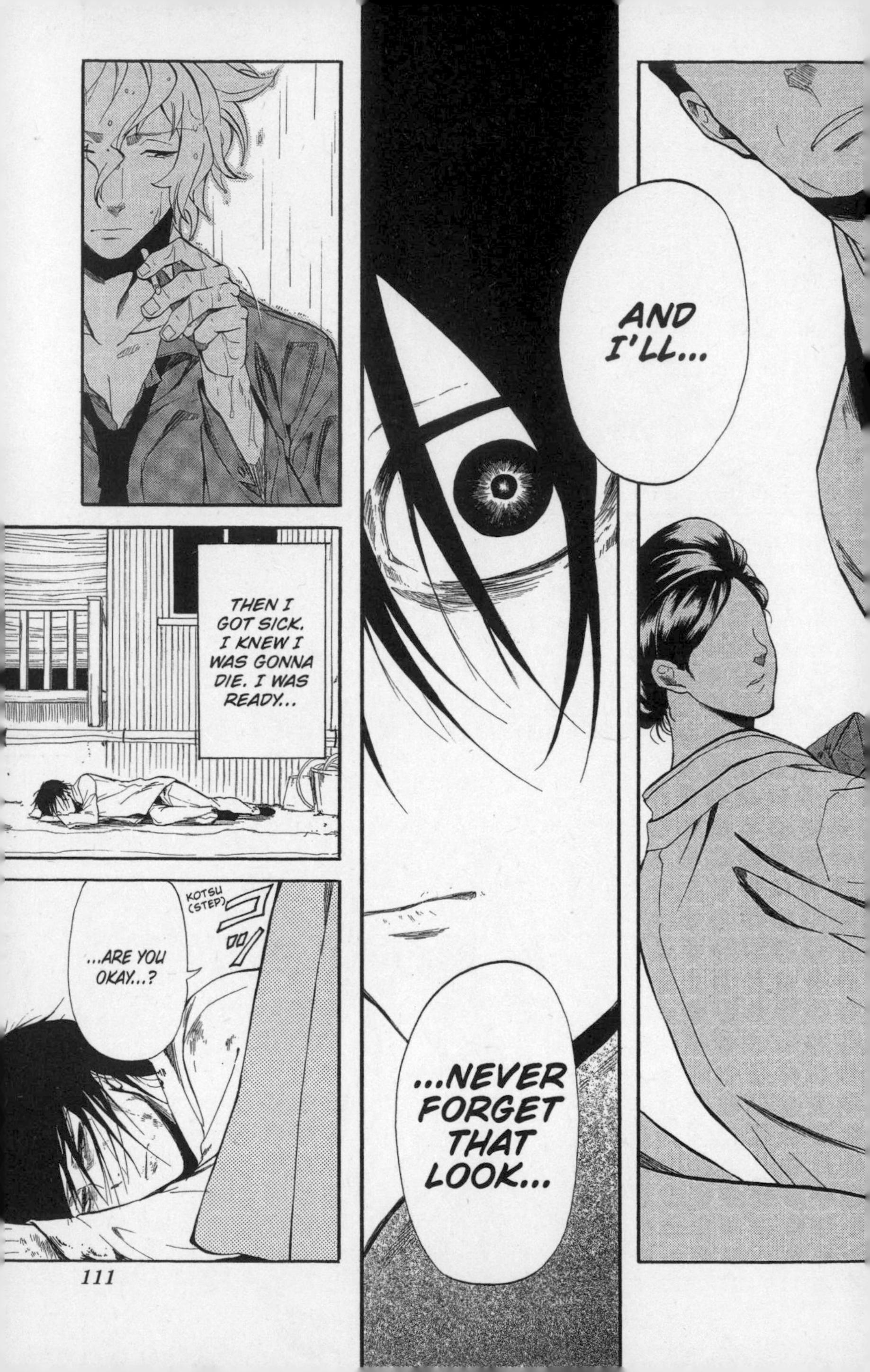
AND I'LL...
...NEVER FORGET THAT LOOK...
THEN I GOT SICK. I KNEW I WAS GONNA DIE. I WAS READY...
KOTSU (STEP)
...ARE YOU OKAY...?

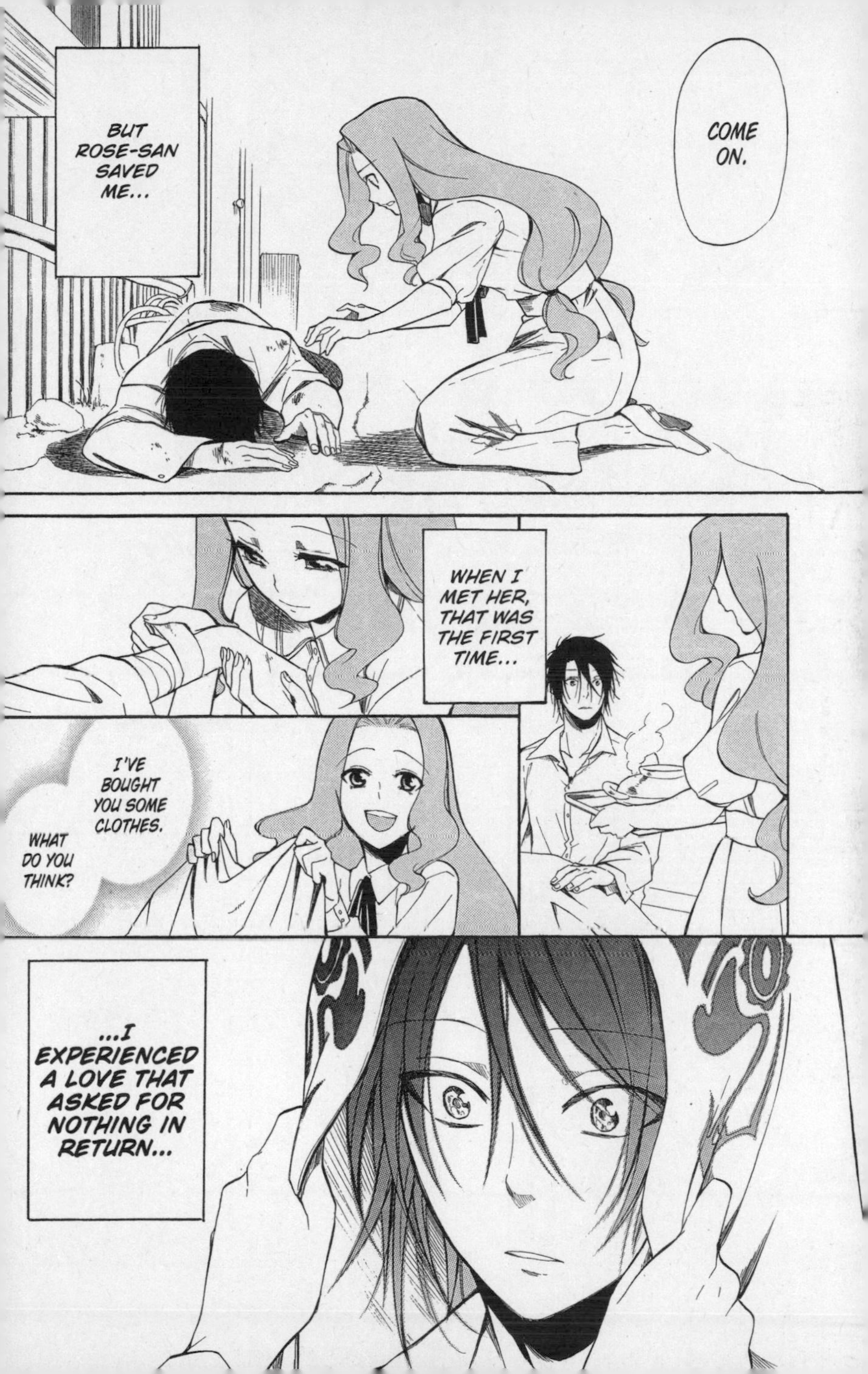
COME ON.
BUT ROSE-SAN SAVED ME...
WHEN I MET HER, THAT WAS THE FIRST TIME...
I'VE BOUGHT YOU SOME CLOTHES.
WHAT DO YOU THINK?
...I EXPERIENCED A LOVE THAT ASKED FOR NOTHING IN RETURN...

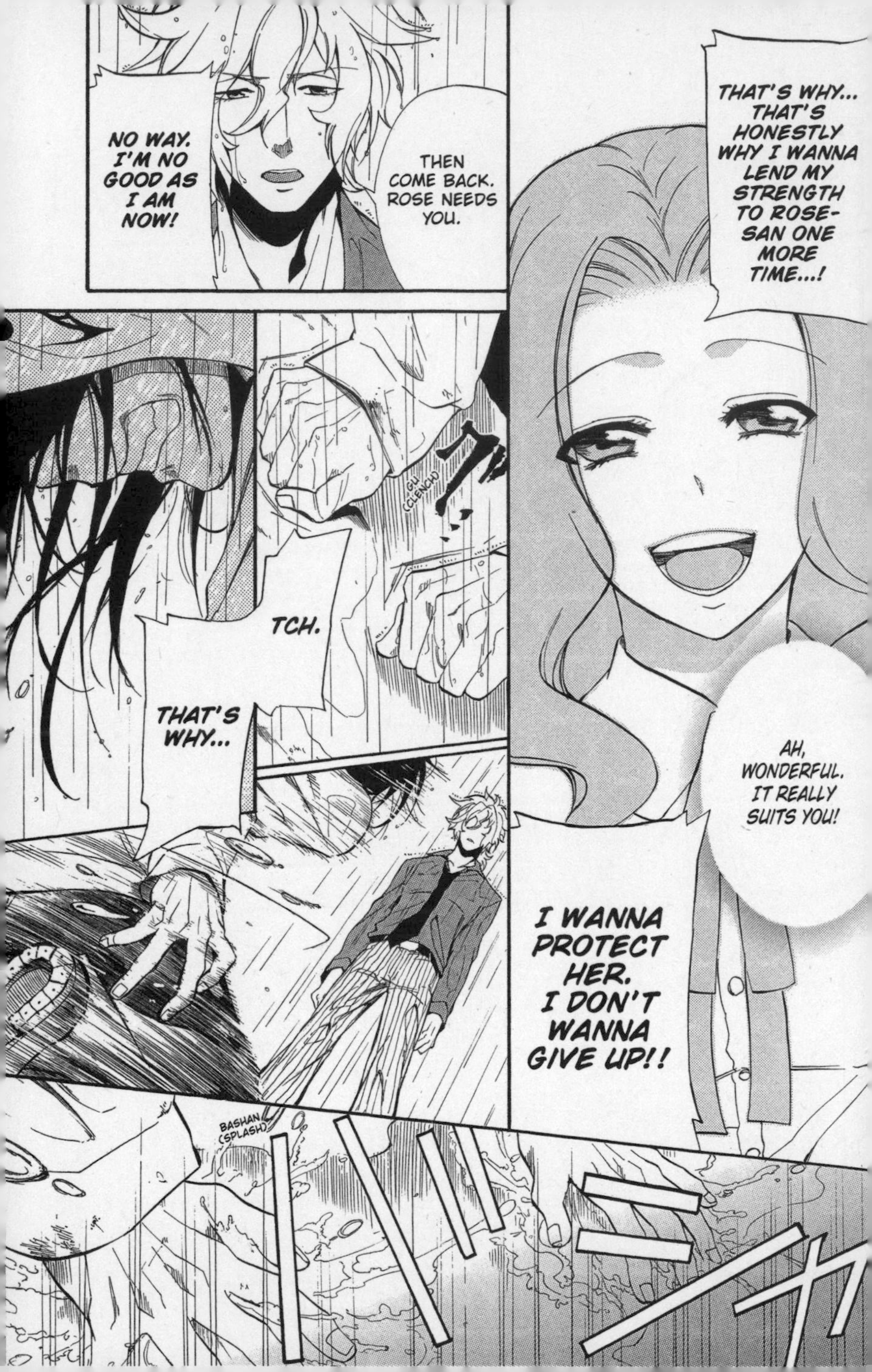
THAT'S WHY... THAT'S HONESTLY WHY I WANNA LEND MY STRENGTH TO ROSE-SAN ONE MORE TIME...!
AH, WONDERFUL. IT REALLY SUITS YOU!
I WANNA PROTECT HER. I DON'T WANNA GIVE UP!!
THEN COME BACK. ROSE NEEDS YOU.
NO WAY. I'M NO GOOD AS I AM NOW!
GU (CLENCH)
TCH.
THAT'S WHY...
BASHAN (SPLASH)

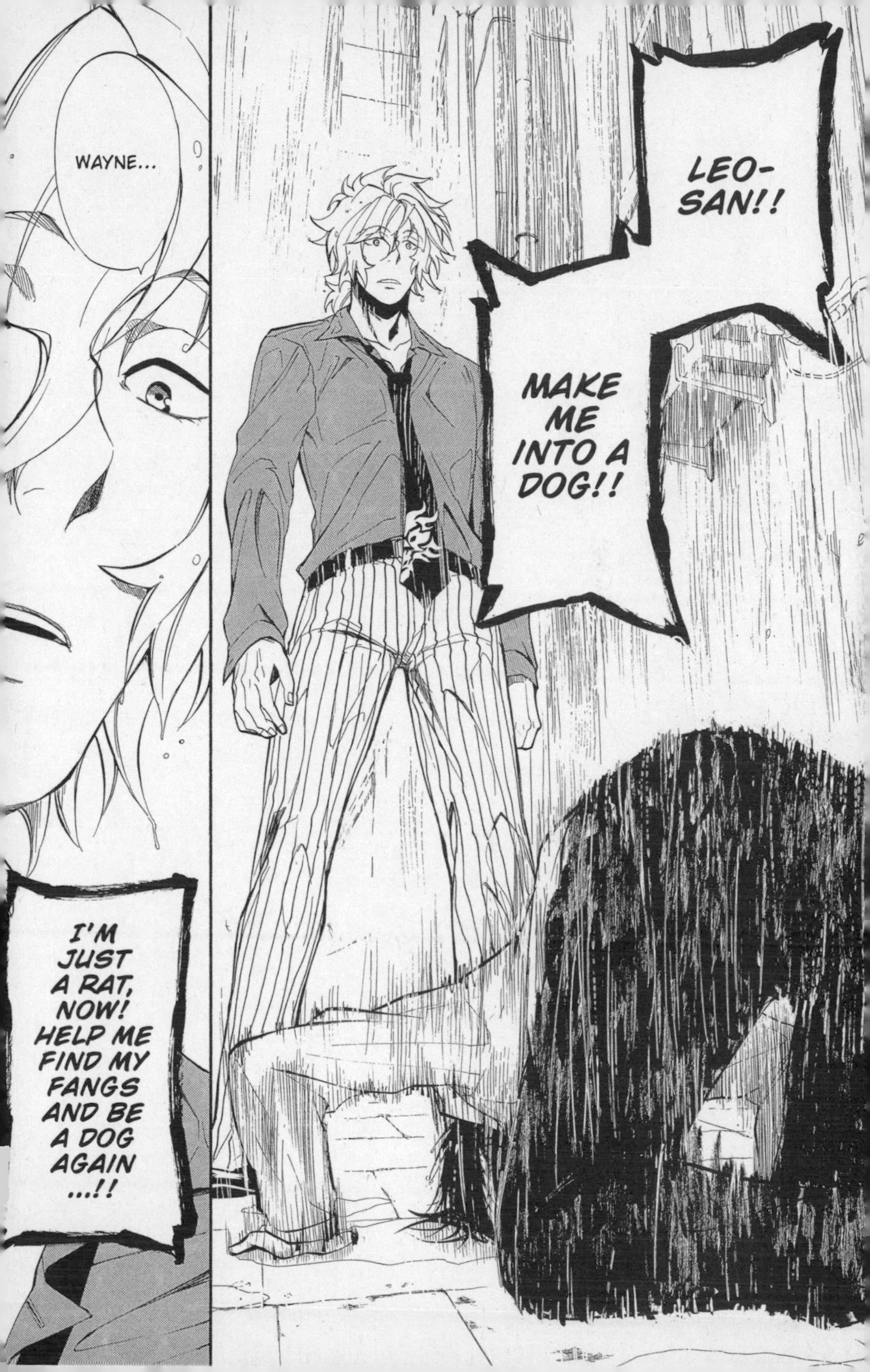
LEO-SAN!!
MAKE ME INTO A DOG!!
WAYNE...
I'M JUST A RAT, NOW! HELP ME FIND MY FANGS AND BE A DOG AGAIN ...!!

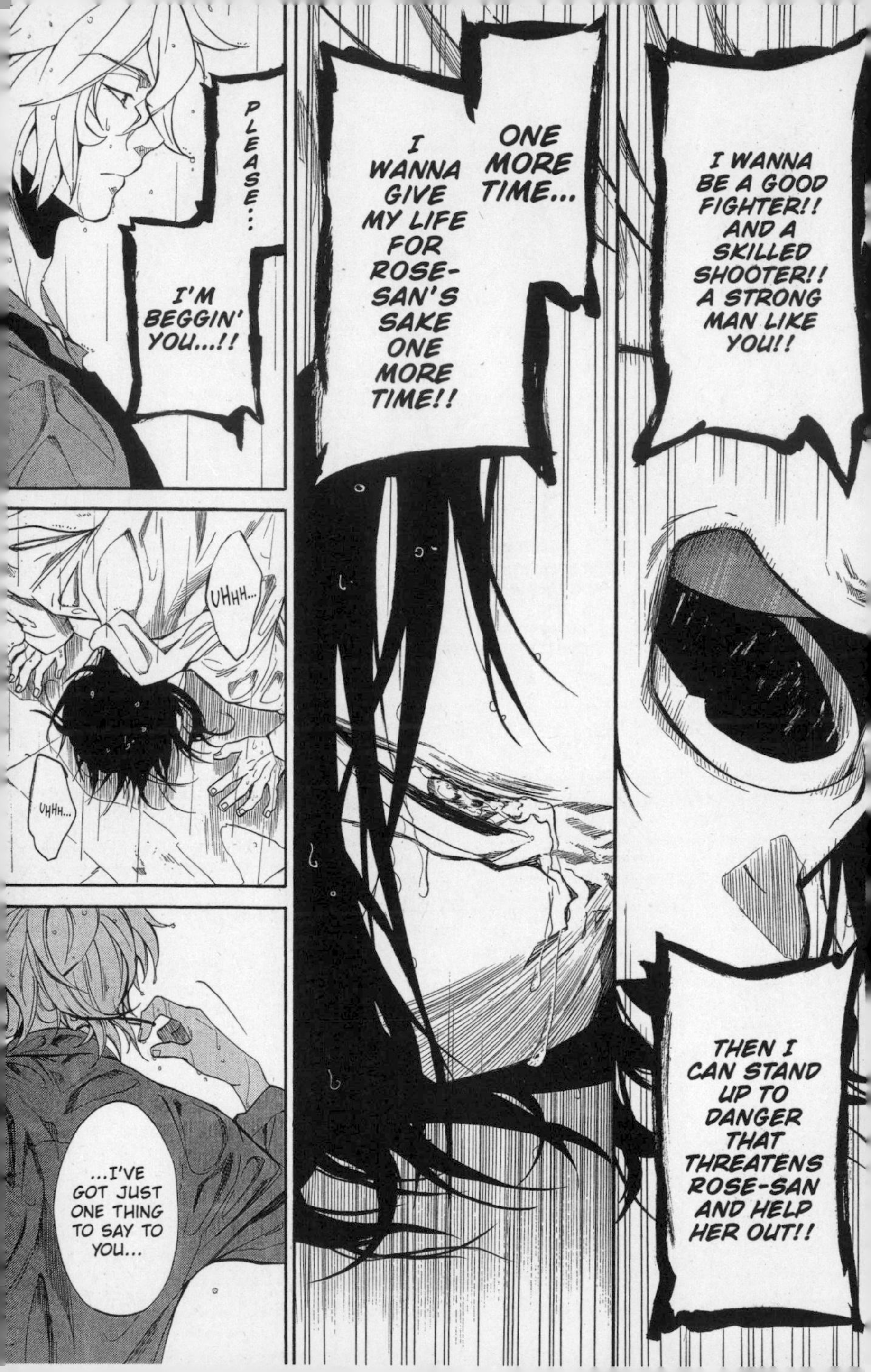
I WANNA BE A GOOD FIGHTER!! AND A SKILLED SHOOTER!! A STRONG MAN LIKE YOU!!
THEN I CAN STAND UP TO DANGER THAT THREATENS ROSE-SAN AND HELP HER OUT!!
ONE MORE TIME...
I WANNA GIVE MY LIFE FOR ROSE-SAN'S SAKE ONE MORE TIME!!
PLEASE...
I'M BEGGIN' YOU...!!
UHHH...
UHHH...
...I'VE GOT JUST ONE THING TO SAY TO YOU...

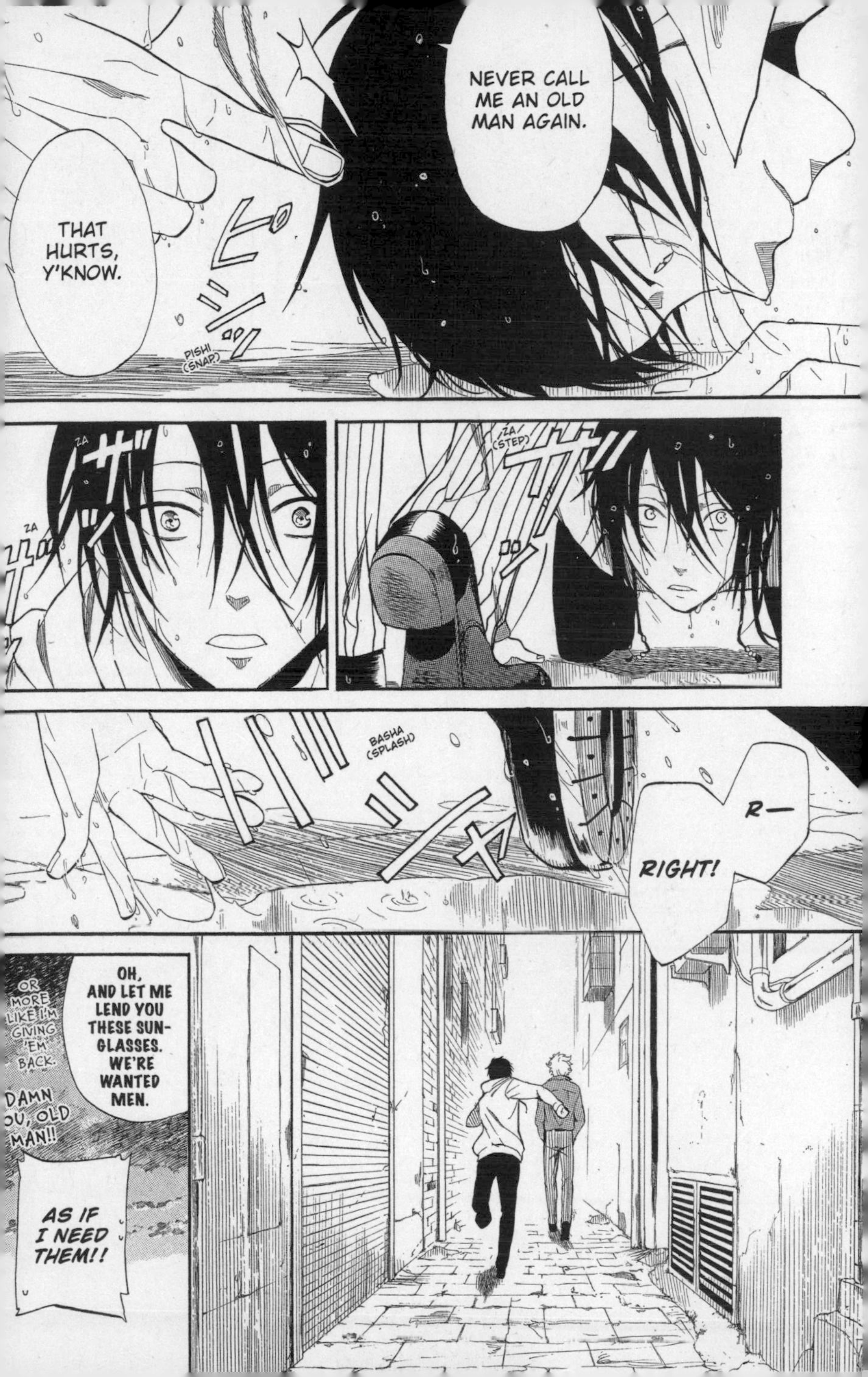
NEVER CALL ME AN OLD MAN AGAIN.
PISHI (SNAP)
THAT HURTS, Y'KNOW.
ZA (STEP)
ZA
ZA
R— RIGHT!
BASHA (SPLASH)
OH, AND LET ME LEND YOU THESE SUN-GLASSES. WE'RE WANTED MEN.
OR MORE LIKE I'M GIVING 'EM BACK.
DAMN OU, OLD MAN!!
AS IF I NEED THEM!!

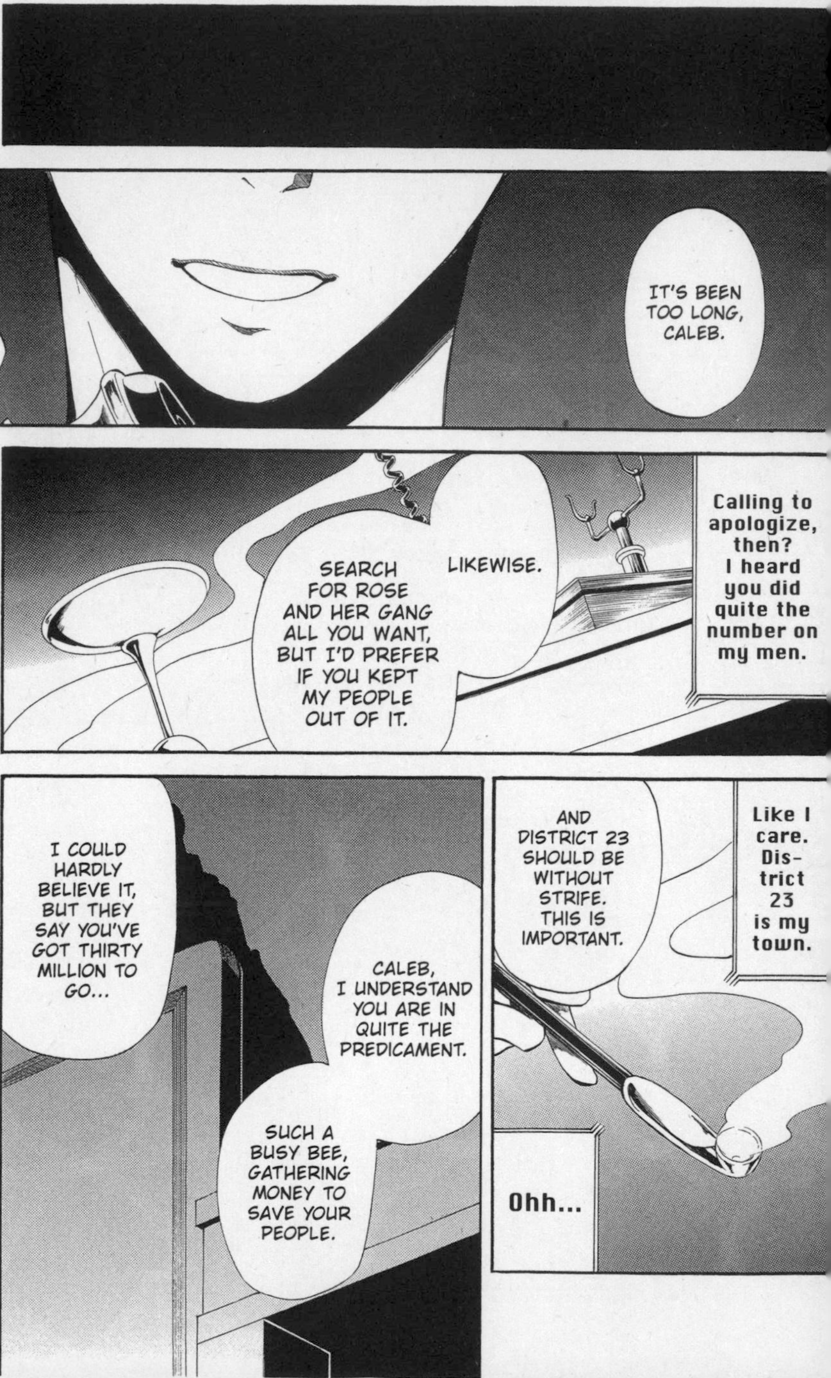
IT'S BEEN TOO LONG, CALEB.
Calling to apologize, then? I heard you did quite the number on my men.
LIKEWISE.
SEARCH FOR ROSE AND HER GANG ALL YOU WANT, BUT I'D PREFER IF YOU KEPT MY PEOPLE OUT OF IT.
AND DISTRICT 23 SHOULD BE WITHOUT STRIFE. THIS IS IMPORTANT.
Like I care. Dis-trict 23 is my town.
Ohh...
CALEB, I UNDERSTAND YOU ARE IN QUITE THE PREDICAMENT.
I COULD HARDLY BELIEVE IT, BUT THEY SAY YOU'VE GOT THIRTY MILLION TO GO...
SUCH A BUSY BEE, GATHERING MONEY TO SAVE YOUR PEOPLE.

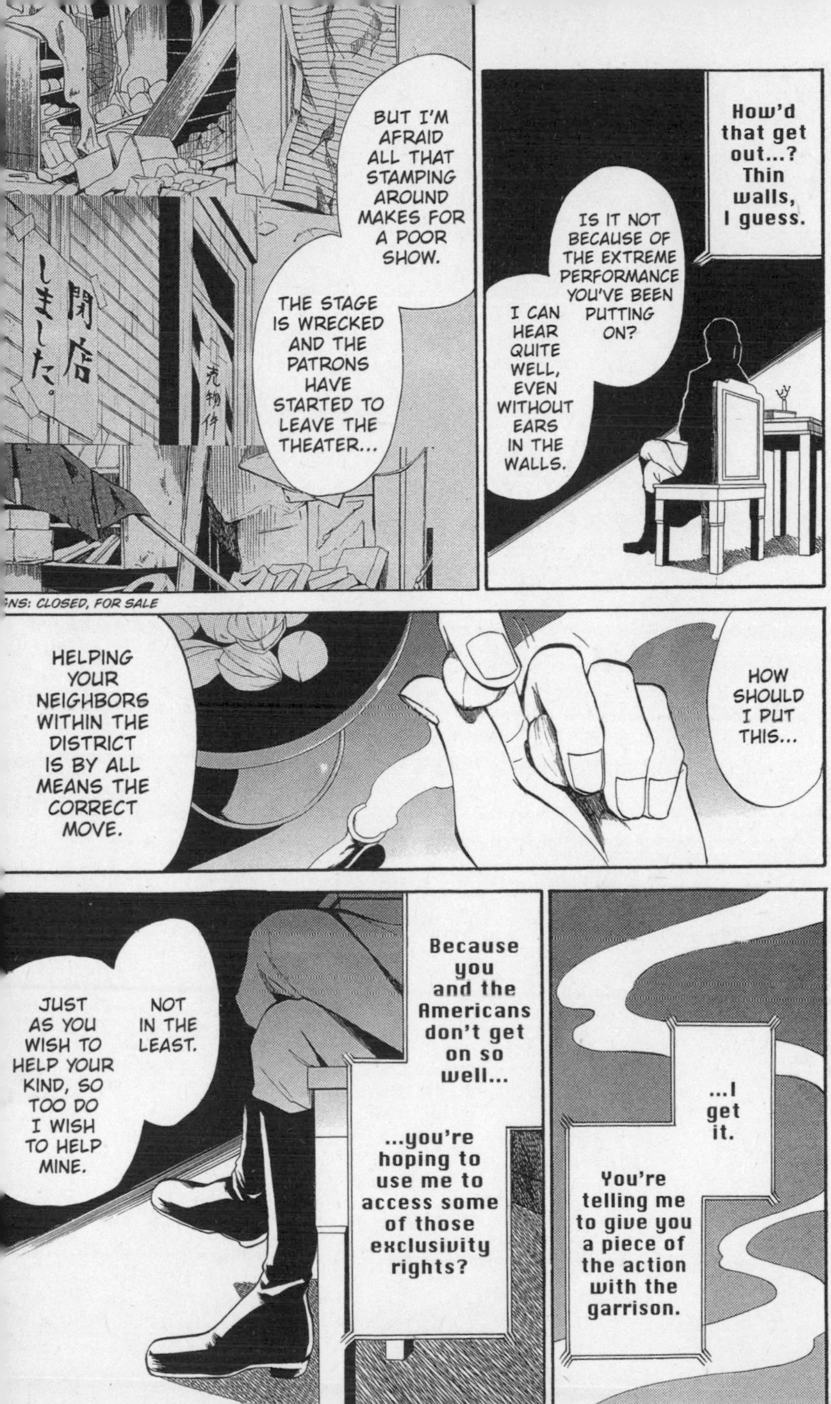
How'd that get out...? Thin walls, I guess.
IS IT NOT BECAUSE OF THE EXTREME PERFORMANCE YOU'VE BEEN PUTTING ON?
I CAN HEAR QUITE WELL, EVEN WITHOUT EARS IN THE WALLS.
BUT I'M AFRAID ALL THAT STAMPING AROUND MAKES FOR A POOR SHOW.
THE STAGE IS WRECKED AND THE PATRONS HAVE STARTED TO LEAVE THE THEATER...
閉店しました。
売物件
GNS: CLOSED, FOR SALE
HOW SHOULD I PUT THIS...
HELPING YOUR NEIGHBORS WITHIN THE DISTRICT IS BY ALL MEANS THE CORRECT MOVE.
...I get it.
You're telling me to give you a piece of the action with the garrison.
Because you and the Americans don't get on so well...
...you're hoping to use me to access some of those exclusivity rights?
NOT IN THE LEAST.
JUST AS YOU WISH TO HELP YOUR KIND, SO TOO DO I WISH TO HELP MINE.

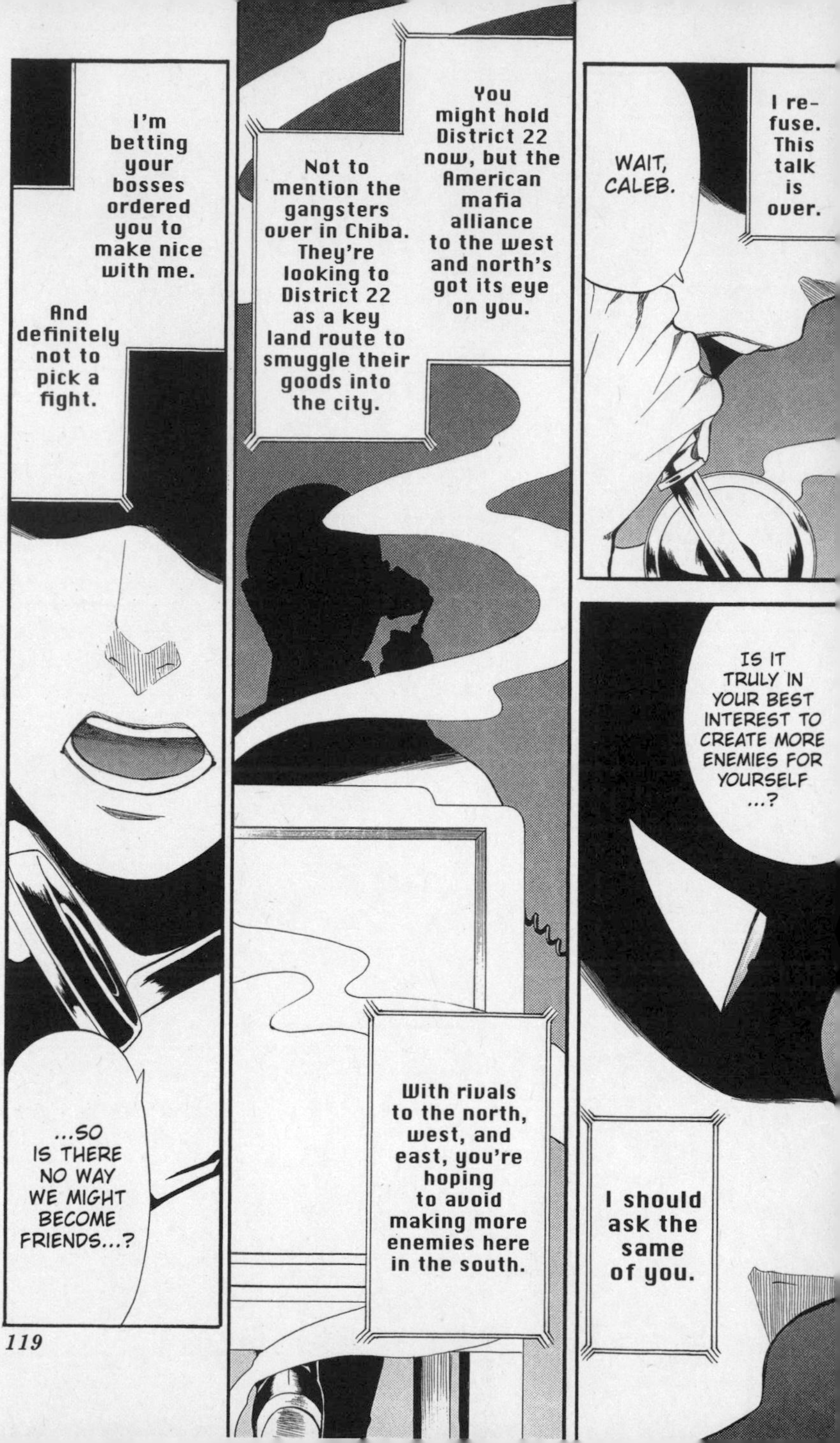
I re-fuse. This talk is over.
WAIT, CALEB.
IS IT TRULY IN YOUR BEST INTEREST TO CREATE MORE ENEMIES FOR YOURSELF ...?
I should ask the same of you.
You might hold District 22 now, but the American mafia alliance to the west and north's got its eye on you.
Not to mention the gangsters over in Chiba. They're looking to District 22 as a key land route to smuggle their goods into the city.
With rivals to the north, west, and east, you're hoping to avoid making more enemies here in the south.
I'm betting your bosses ordered you to make nice with me.
And definitely not to pick a fight.
...SO IS THERE NO WAY WE MIGHT BECOME FRIENDS...?

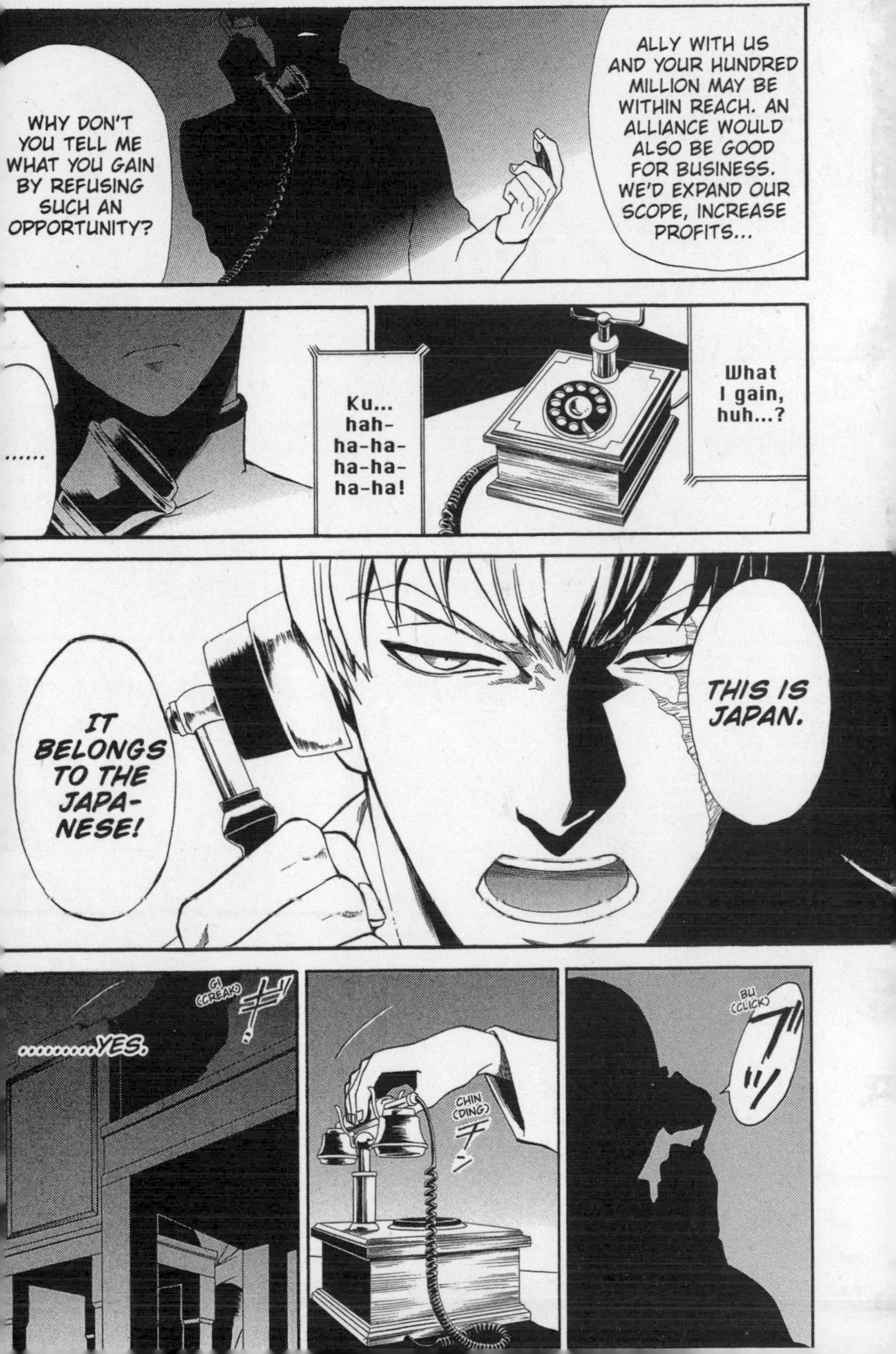
ALLY WITH US AND YOUR HUNDRED MILLION MAY BE WITHIN REACH. AN ALLIANCE WOULD ALSO BE GOOD FOR BUSINESS. WE'D EXPAND OUR SCOPE, INCREASE PROFITS...
WHY DON'T YOU TELL ME WHAT YOU GAIN BY REFUSING SUCH AN OPPORTUNITY?
What I gain, huh...?
Ku... hah-ha-ha-ha-ha-ha-ha!
......
THIS IS JAPAN.
IT BELONGS TO THE JAPANESE!
BU (CLICK)
CHIN (DING)
GI (CREAK)
..........YES.

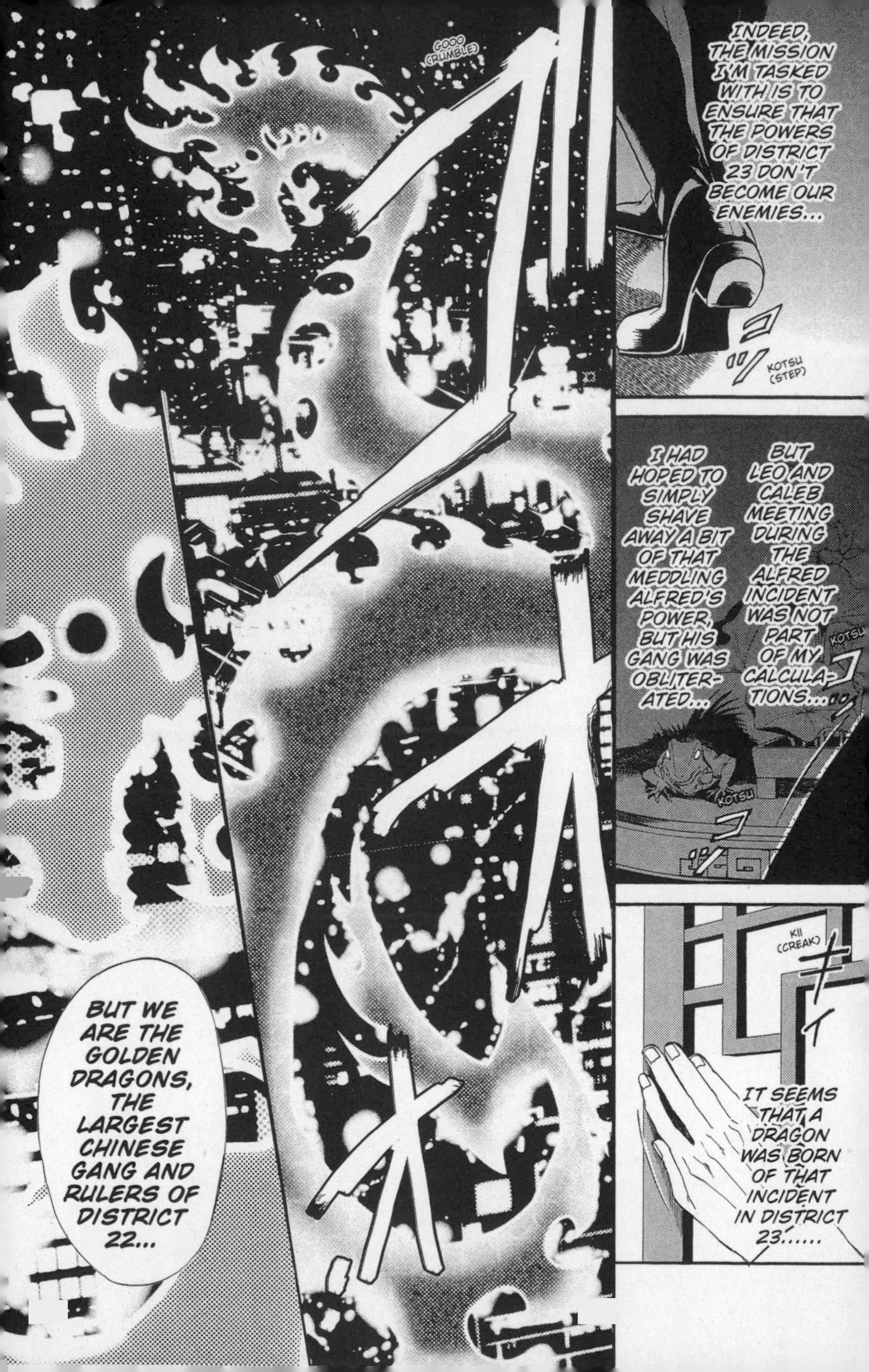
INDEED, THE MISSION I'M TASKED WITH IS TO ENSURE THAT THE POWERS OF DISTRICT 23 DON'T BECOME OUR ENEMIES...
KOTSU (STEP)
BUT LEO AND CALEB MEETING DURING THE ALFRED INCIDENT WAS NOT PART OF MY CALCULATIONS...
I HAD HOPED TO SIMPLY SHAVE AWAY A BIT OF THAT MEDDLING ALFRED'S POWER, BUT HIS GANG WAS OBLITERATED...
KOTSU
KOTSU
KII (CREAK)
IT SEEMS THAT A DRAGON WAS BORN OF THAT INCIDENT IN DISTRICT 23......
GOOO (RUMBLE)
BUT WE ARE THE GOLDEN DRAGONS, THE LARGEST CHINESE GANG AND RULERS OF DISTRICT 22...

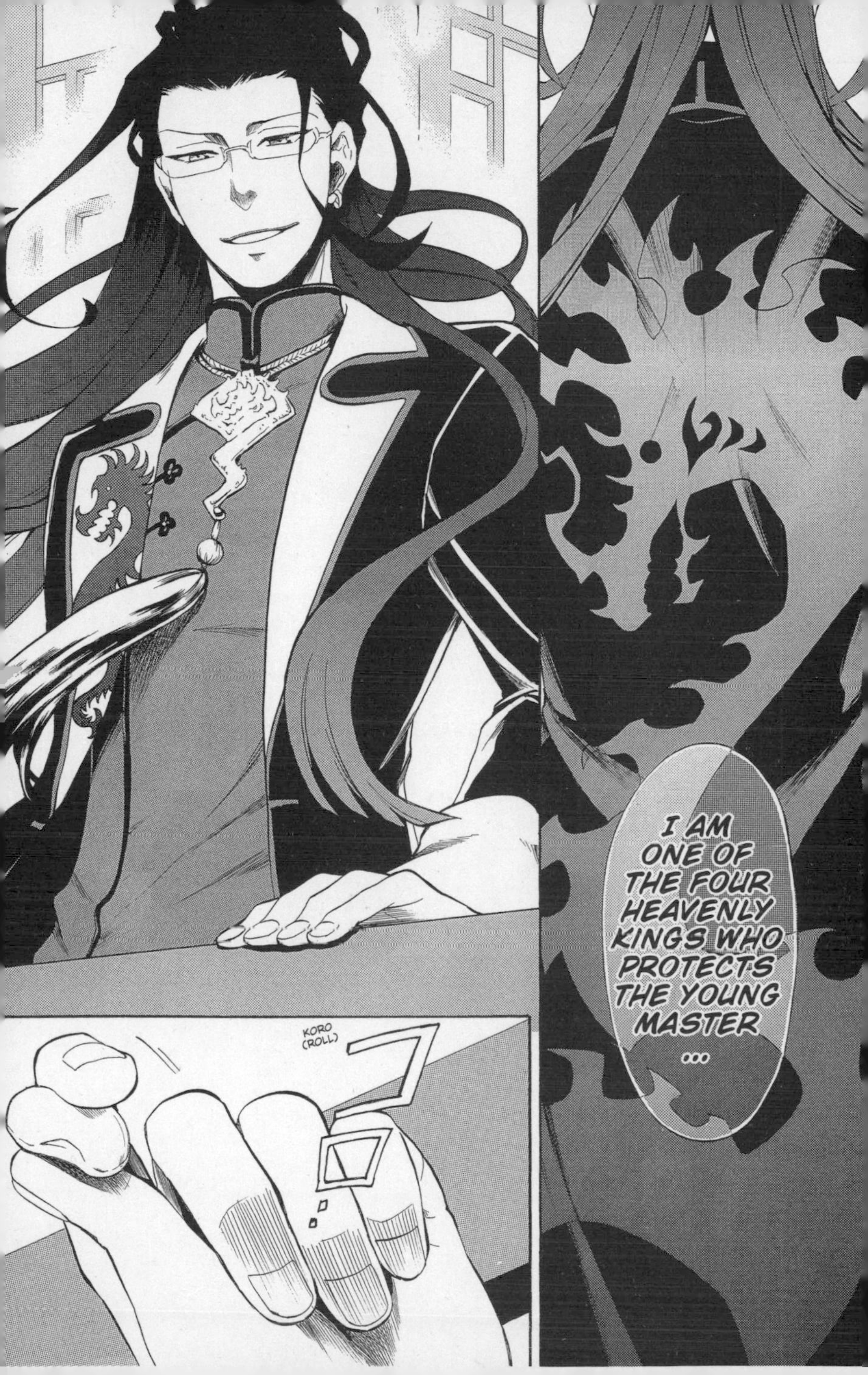
I AM ONE OF THE FOUR HEAVENLY KINGS WHO PROTECTS THE YOUNG MASTER ...
KORO (ROLL)

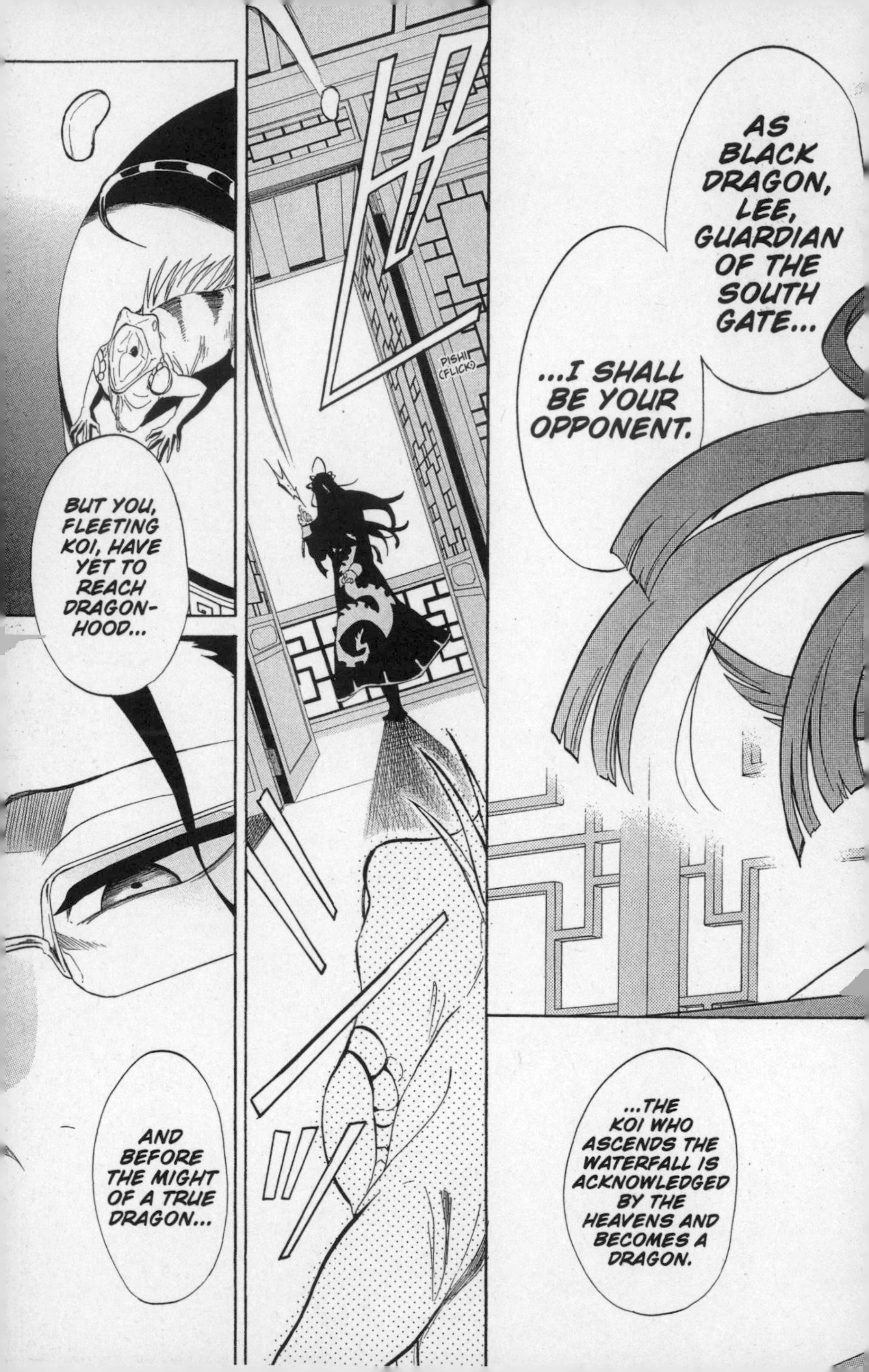
AS BLACK DRAGON, LEE, GUARDIAN OF THE SOUTH GATE...
...I SHALL BE YOUR OPPONENT.
...THE KOI WHO ASCENDS THE WATERFALL IS ACKNOWLEDGED BY THE HEAVENS AND BECOMES A DRAGON.
PISHI (FLICK)
BUT YOU, FLEETING KOI, HAVE YET TO REACH DRAGON-HOOD...
AND BEFORE THE MIGHT OF A TRUE DRAGON...

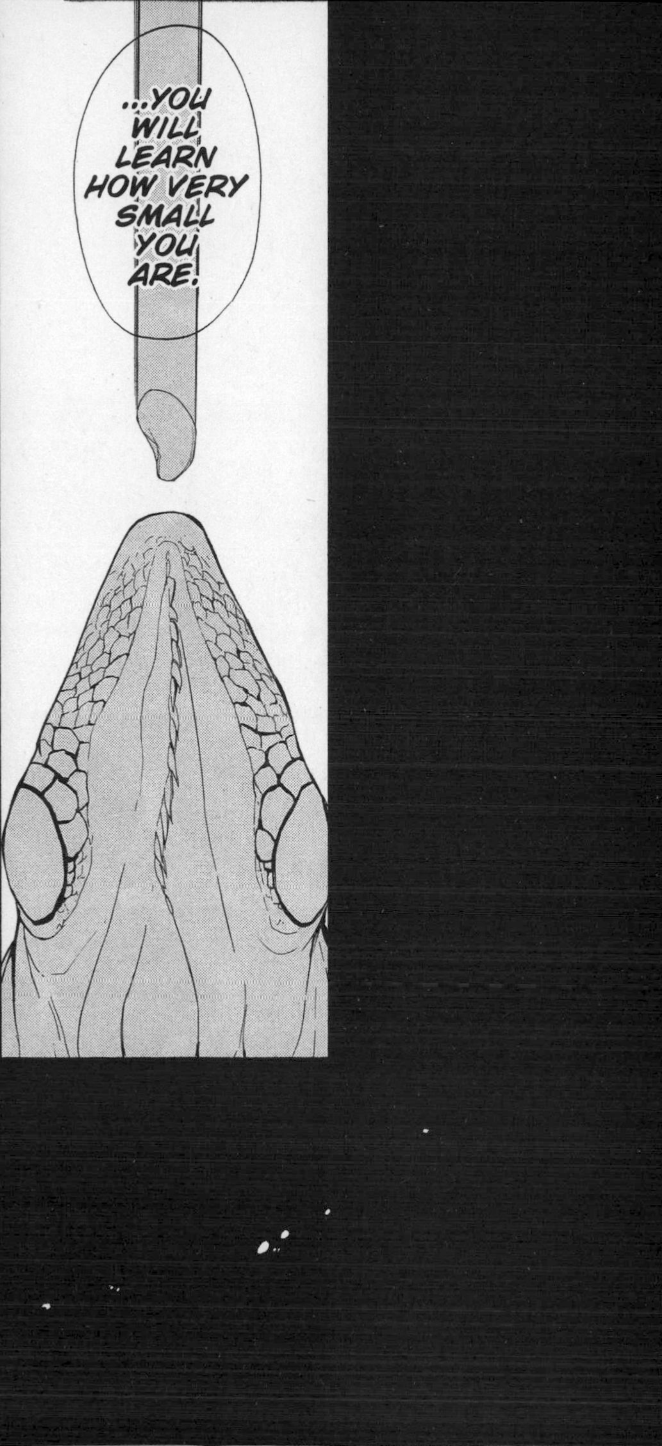
...YOU WILL LEARN HOW VERY SMALL YOU ARE.

Scene: 13

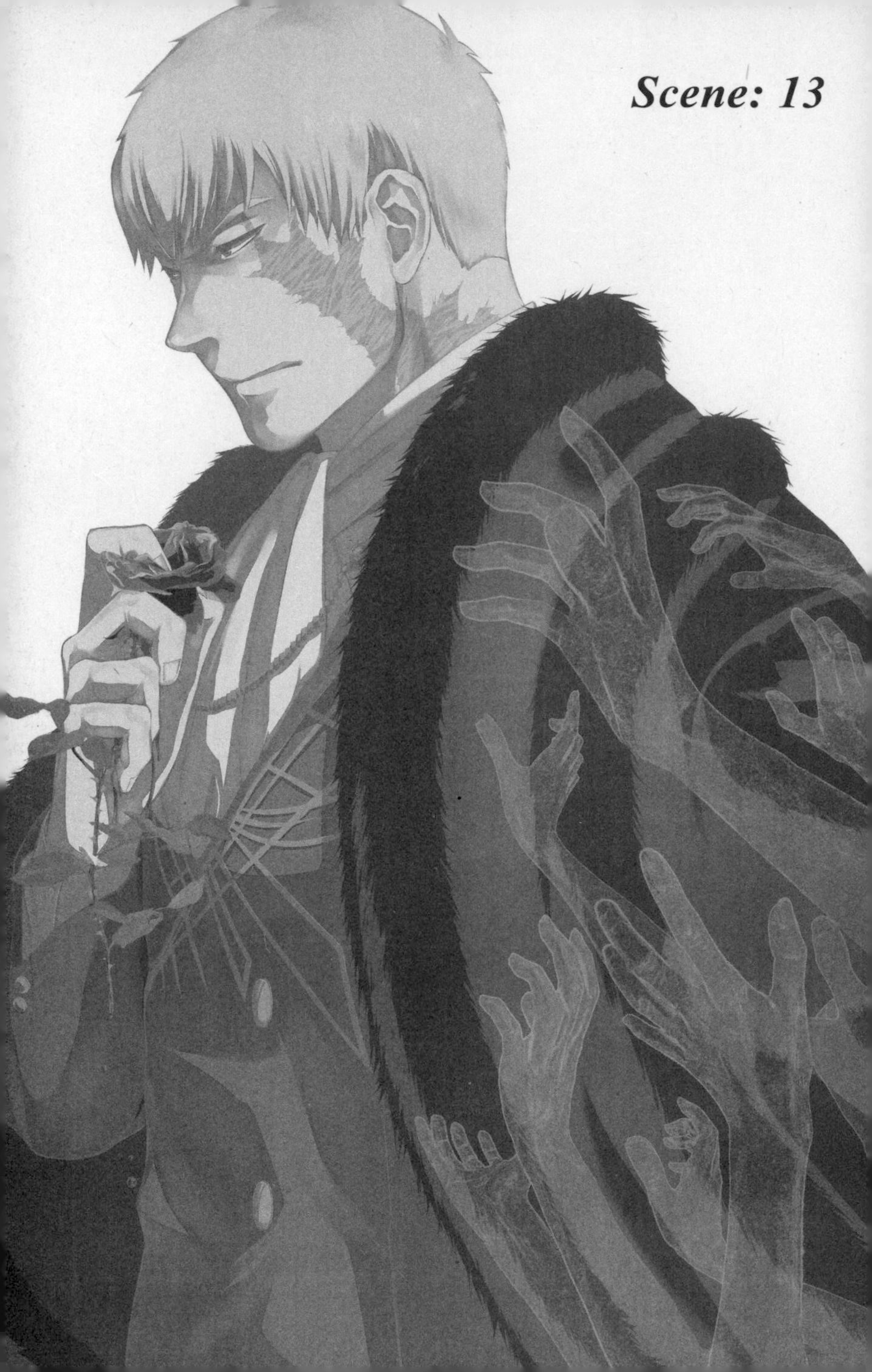

ROSE GUNS DAYS

Season 1

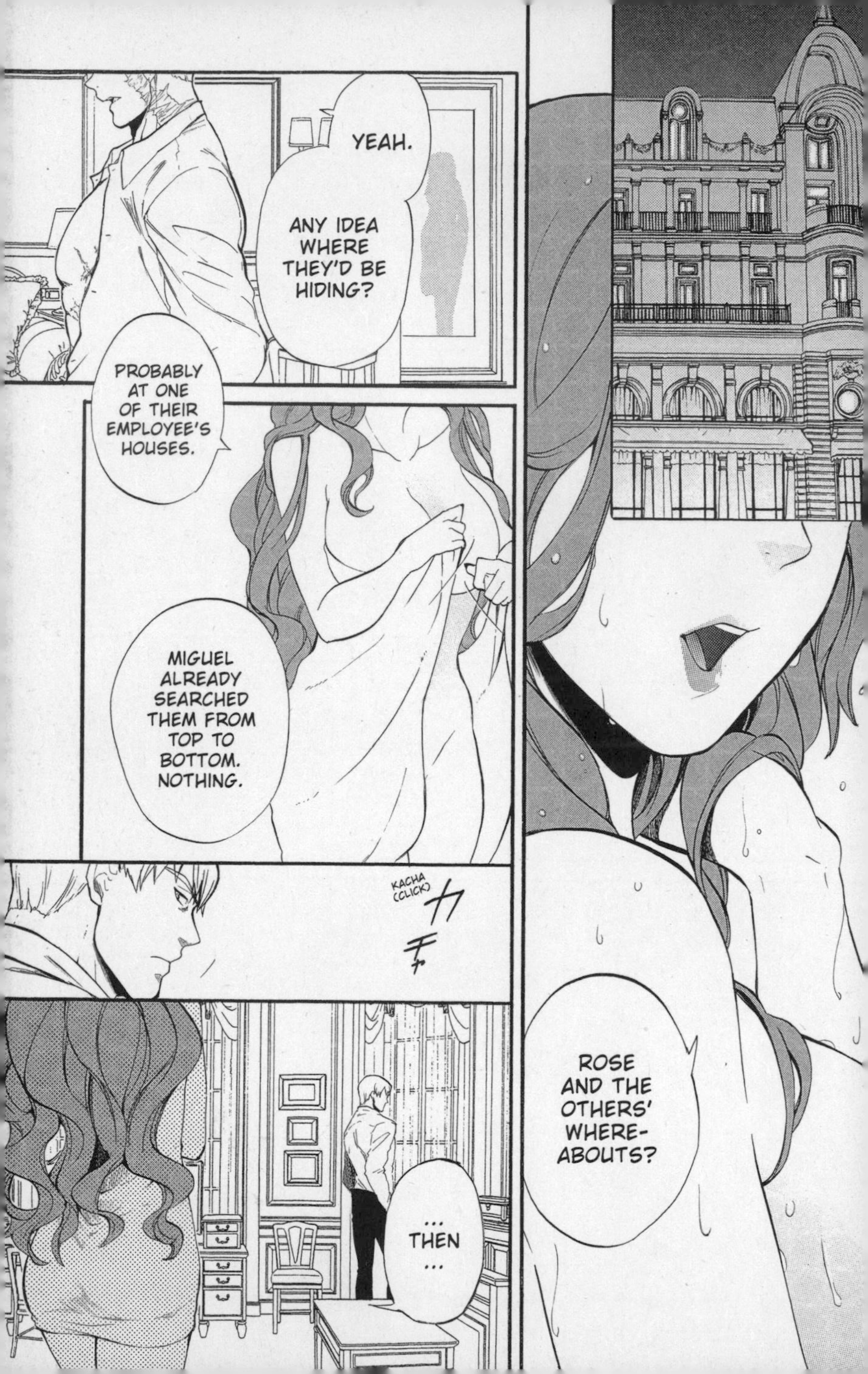
ROSE AND THE OTHERS' WHERE-ABOUTS?
YEAH.
ANY IDEA WHERE THEY'D BE HIDING?
PROBABLY AT ONE OF THEIR EMPLOYEE'S HOUSES.
MIGUEL ALREADY SEARCHED THEM FROM TOP TO BOTTOM. NOTHING.
KACHA (CLICK)
...THEN...

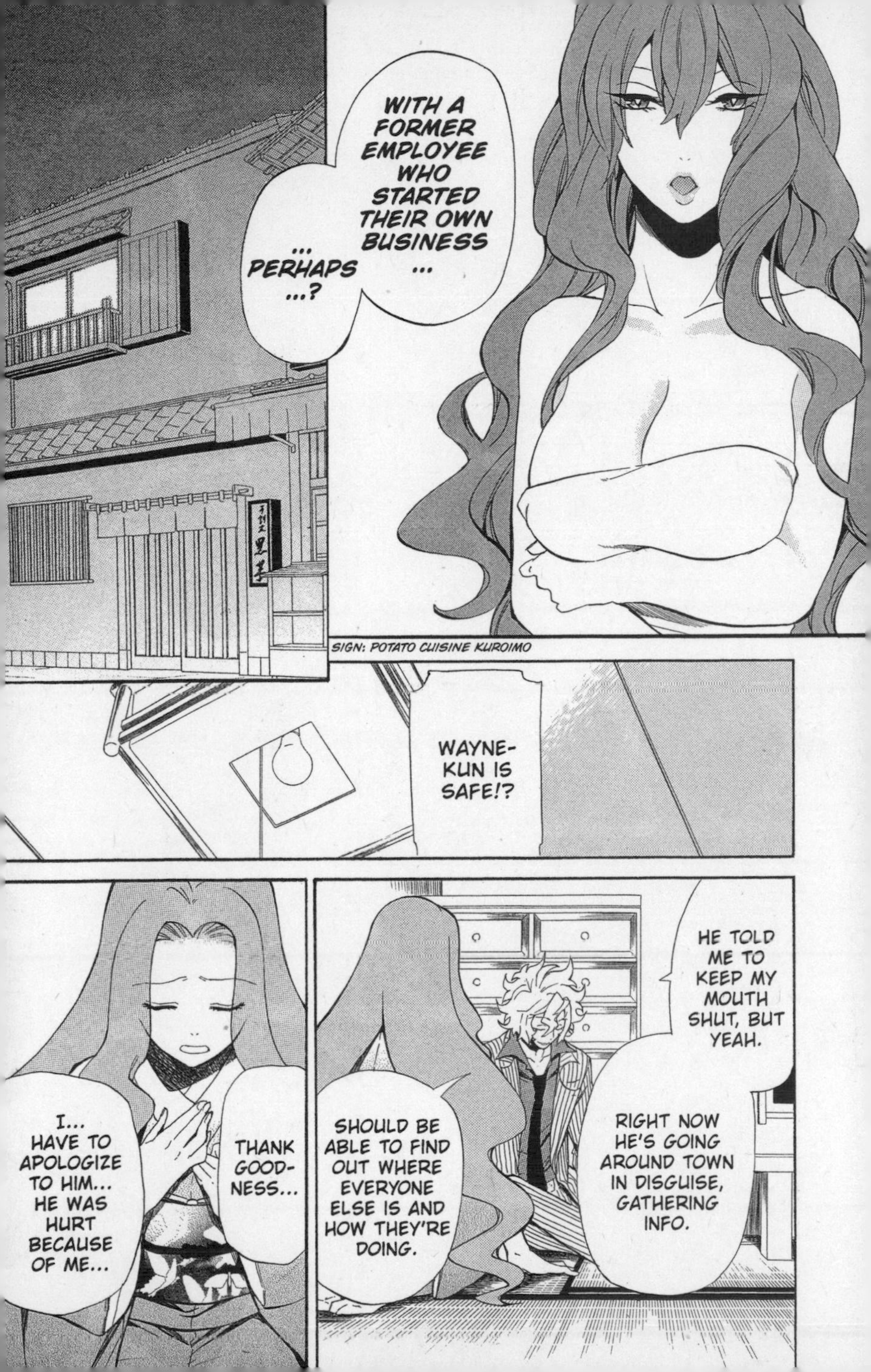
WITH A FORMER EMPLOYEE WHO STARTED THEIR OWN BUSINESS ...
... PERHAPS ...?
SIGN: POTATO CUISINE KUROIMO
WAYNE-KUN IS SAFE!?
HE TOLD ME TO KEEP MY MOUTH SHUT, BUT YEAH.
RIGHT NOW HE'S GOING AROUND TOWN IN DISGUISE, GATHERING INFO.
SHOULD BE ABLE TO FIND OUT WHERE EVERYONE ELSE IS AND HOW THEY'RE DOING.
THANK GOOD-NESS...
I... HAVE TO APOLOGIZE TO HIM... HE WAS HURT BECAUSE OF ME...

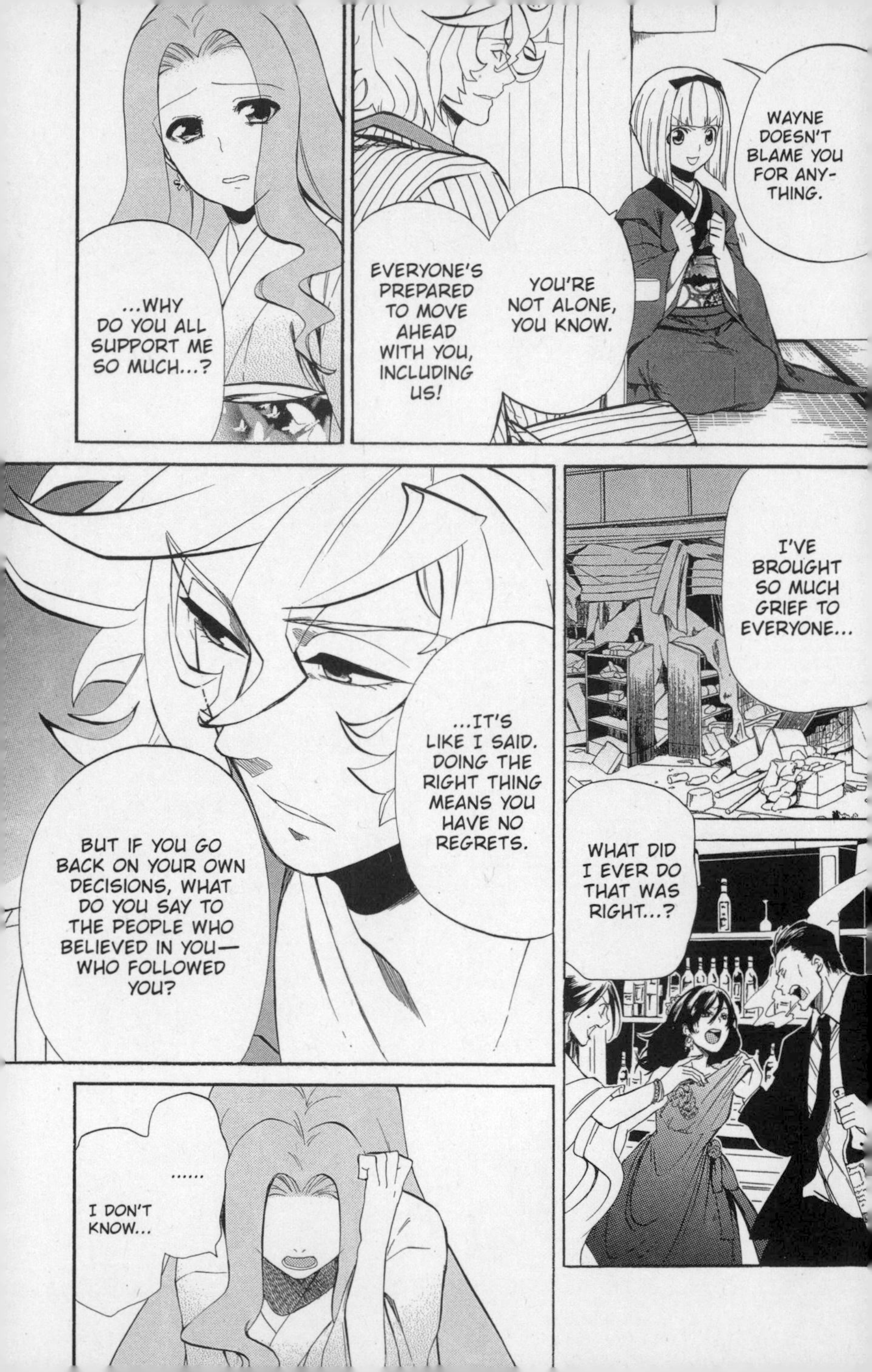
WAYNE DOESN'T BLAME YOU FOR ANY-THING.
YOU'RE NOT ALONE, YOU KNOW.
EVERYONE'S PREPARED TO MOVE AHEAD WITH YOU, INCLUDING US!
...WHY DO YOU ALL SUPPORT ME SO MUCH...?
I'VE BROUGHT SO MUCH GRIEF TO EVERYONE...
WHAT DID I EVER DO THAT WAS RIGHT...?
...IT'S LIKE I SAID. DOING THE RIGHT THING MEANS YOU HAVE NO REGRETS.
BUT IF YOU GO BACK ON YOUR OWN DECISIONS, WHAT DO YOU SAY TO THE PEOPLE WHO BELIEVED IN YOU—WHO FOLLOWED YOU?
......
I DON'T KNOW...

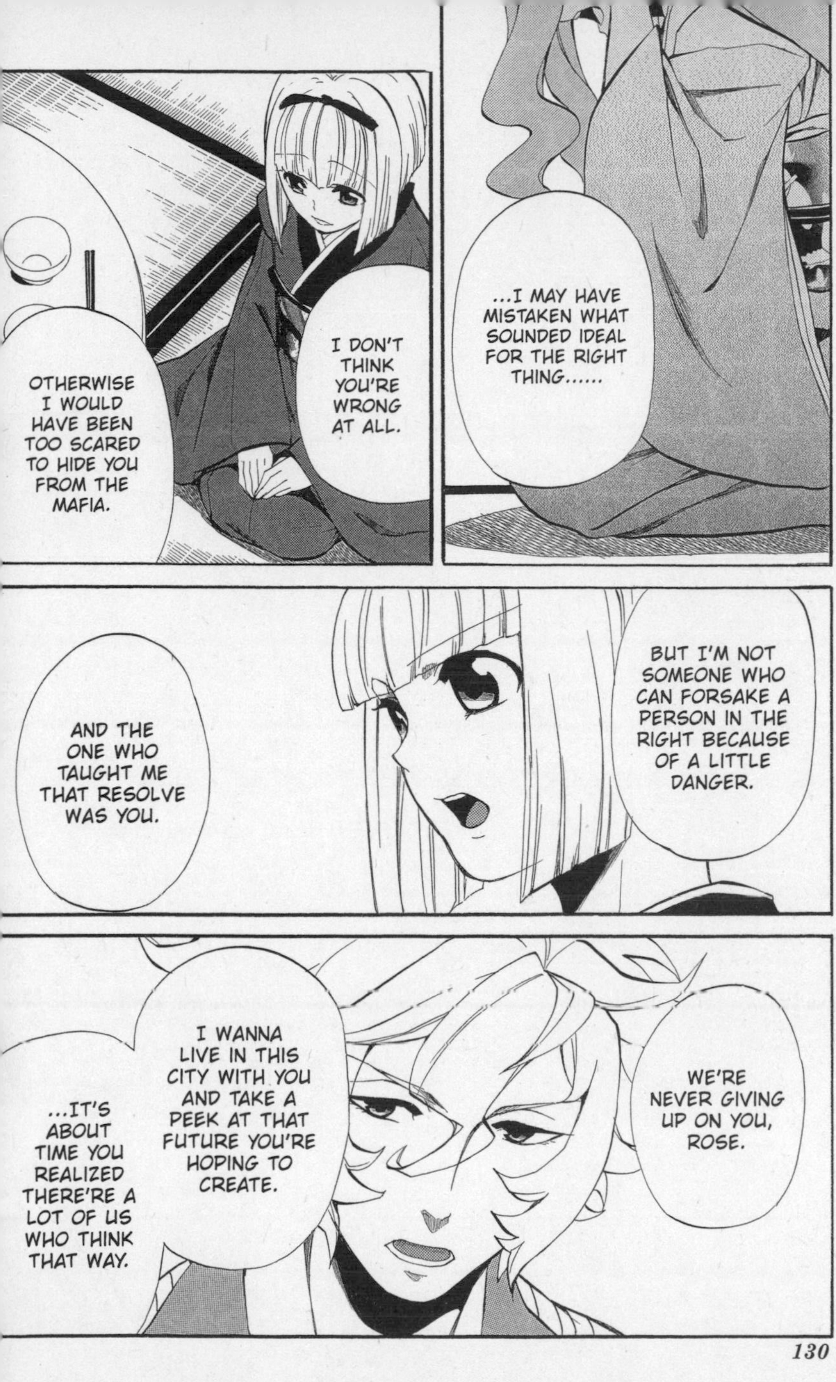
...I MAY HAVE MISTAKEN WHAT SOUNDED IDEAL FOR THE RIGHT THING......
I DON'T THINK YOU'RE WRONG AT ALL.
OTHERWISE I WOULD HAVE BEEN TOO SCARED TO HIDE YOU FROM THE MAFIA.
BUT I'M NOT SOMEONE WHO CAN FORSAKE A PERSON IN THE RIGHT BECAUSE OF A LITTLE DANGER.
AND THE ONE WHO TAUGHT ME THAT RESOLVE WAS YOU.
WE'RE NEVER GIVING UP ON YOU, ROSE.
I WANNA LIVE IN THIS CITY WITH YOU AND TAKE A PEEK AT THAT FUTURE YOU'RE HOPING TO CREATE.
...IT'S ABOUT TIME YOU REALIZED THERE'RE A LOT OF US WHO THINK THAT WAY.

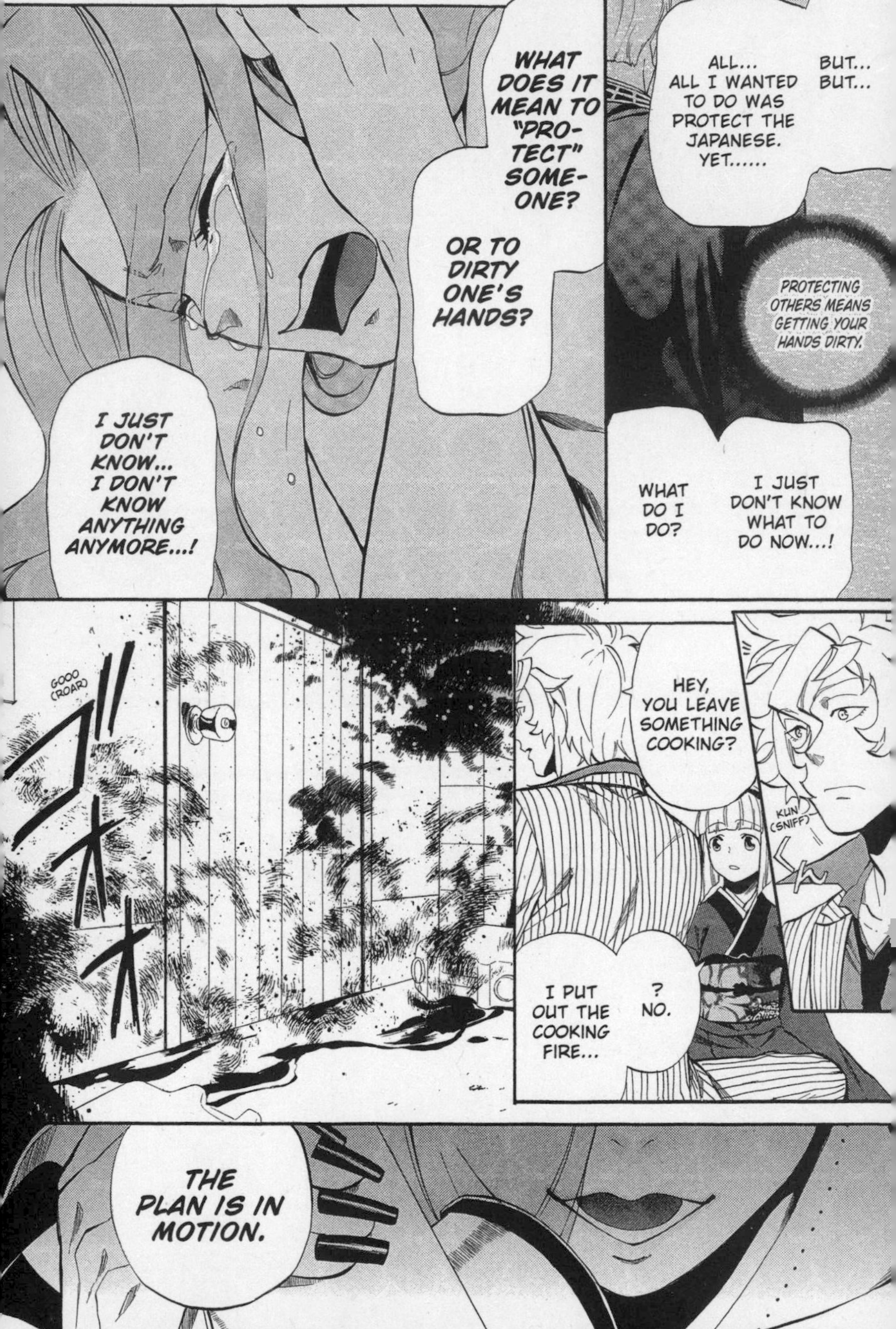
BUT... BUT...
ALL... ALL I WANTED TO DO WAS PROTECT THE JAPANESE. YET......
PROTECTING OTHERS MEANS GETTING YOUR HANDS DIRTY.
I JUST DON'T KNOW WHAT TO DO NOW...!
WHAT DO I DO?
WHAT DOES IT MEAN TO "PRO-TECT" SOME-ONE?
OR TO DIRTY ONE'S HANDS?
I JUST DON'T KNOW... I DON'T KNOW ANYTHING ANYMORE...!
KUN (SNIFF)
HEY, YOU LEAVE SOMETHING COOKING?
? NO.
I PUT OUT THE COOKING FIRE...
GOOO (ROAR)
THE PLAN IS IN MOTION.

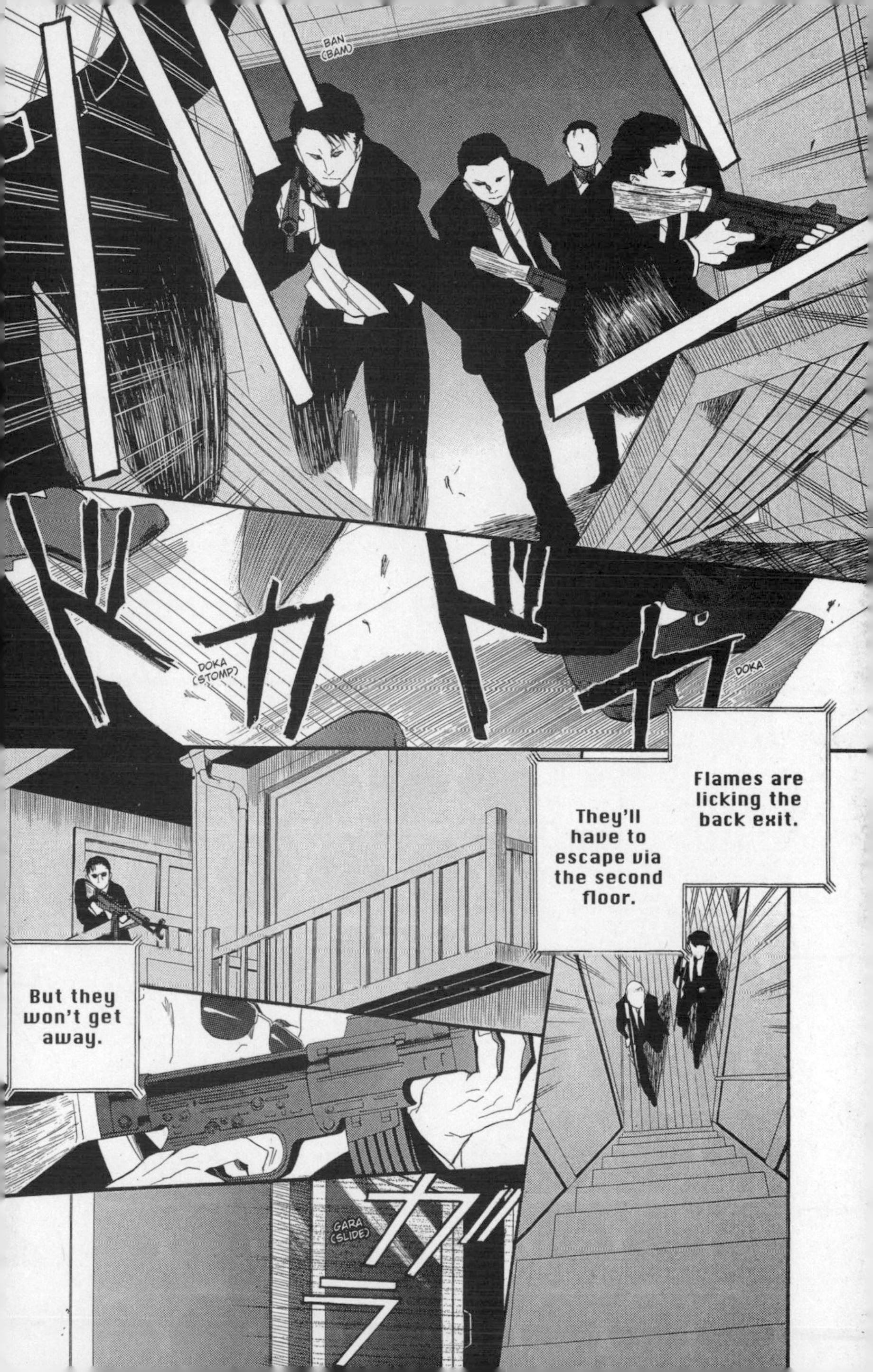
BAN (BAM)
DOKA
DOKA (STOMP)
Flames are licking the back exit.
They'll have to escape via the second floor.
But they won't get away.
GARA (SLIDE)

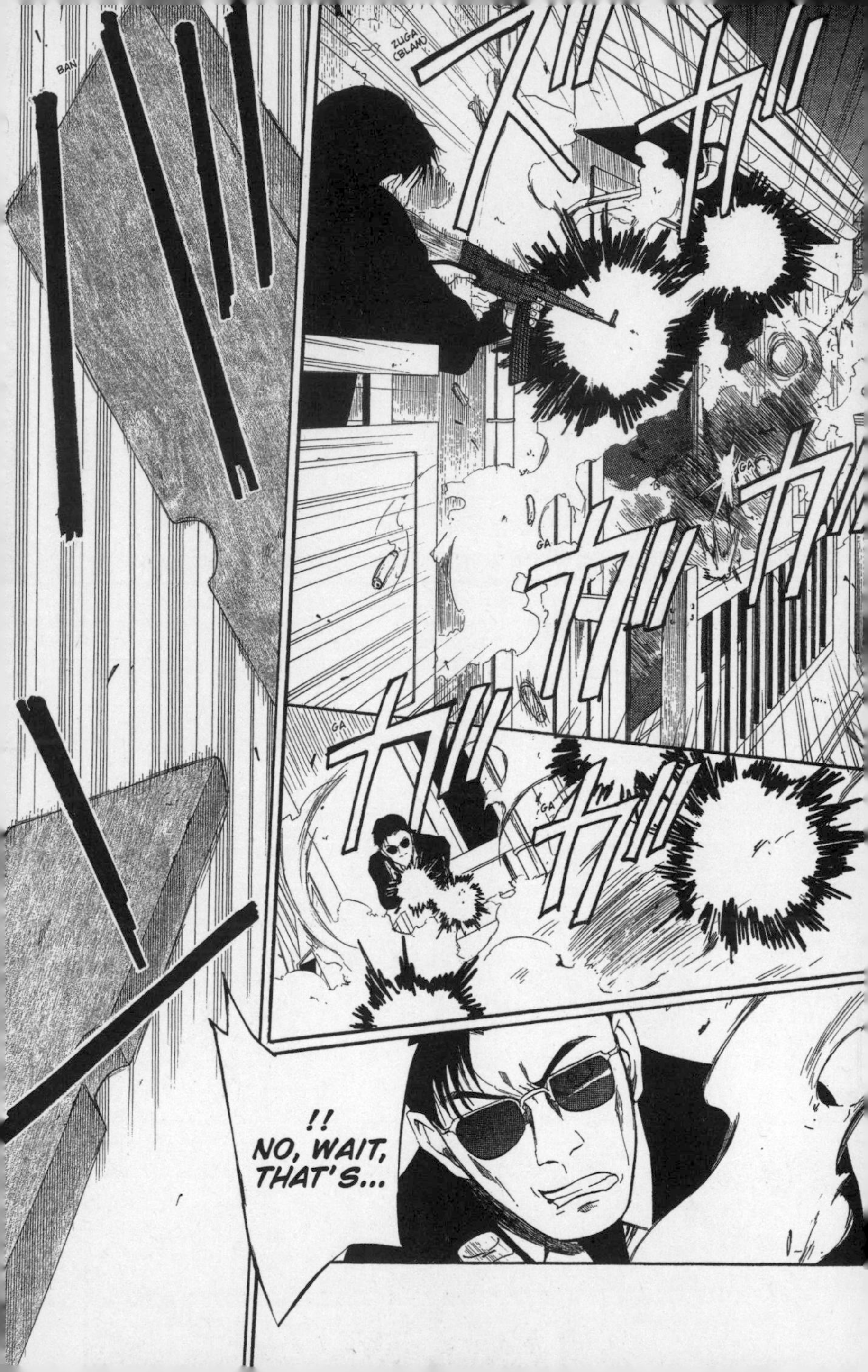
ZUGA (BLAM)
GA
GA
GA
GA
!!
NO, WAIT, THAT'S...
BAN

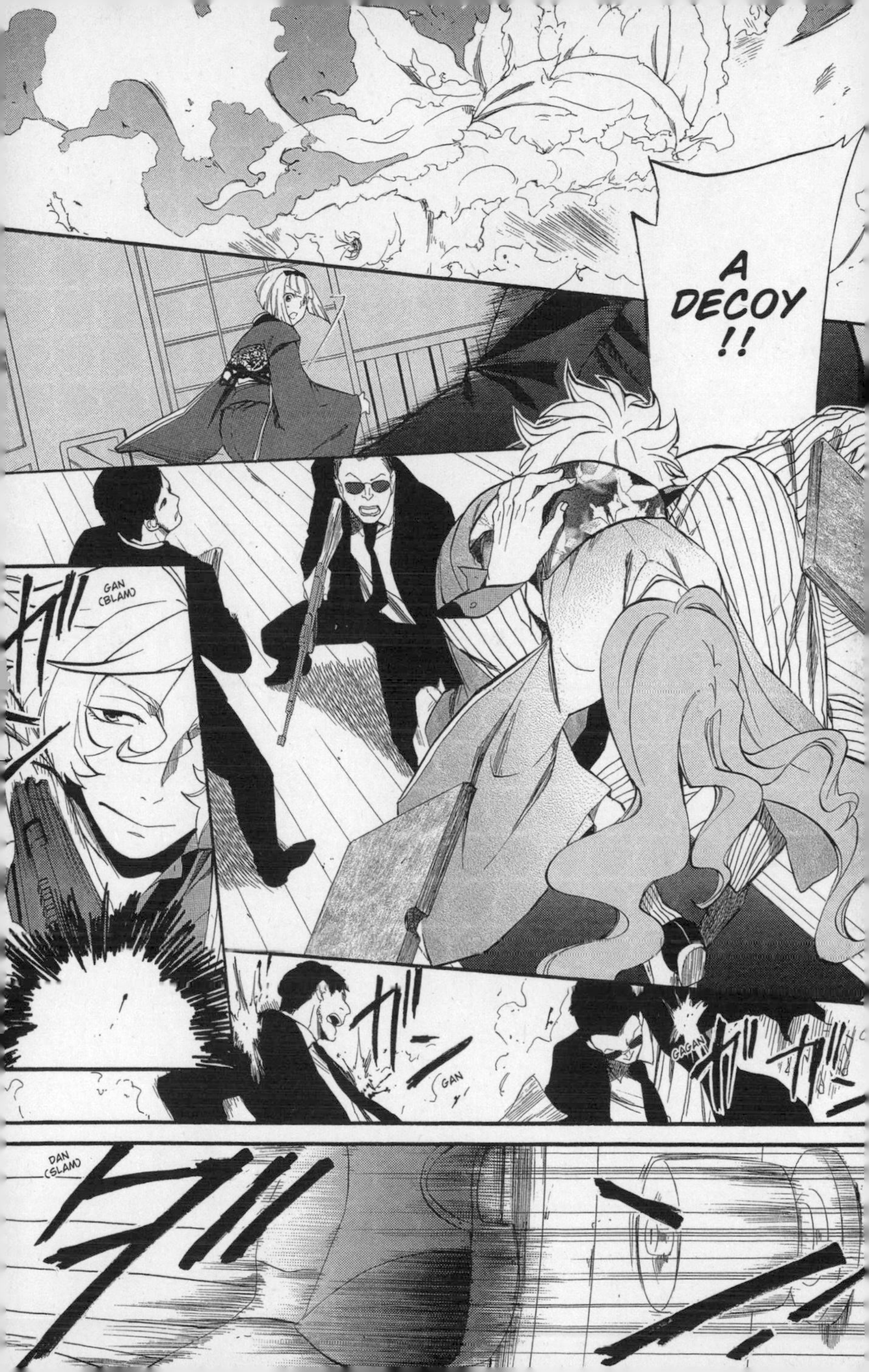
A DECOY !!
GAN (BLAM)
GAGAN
GAN
DAN (SLAM)

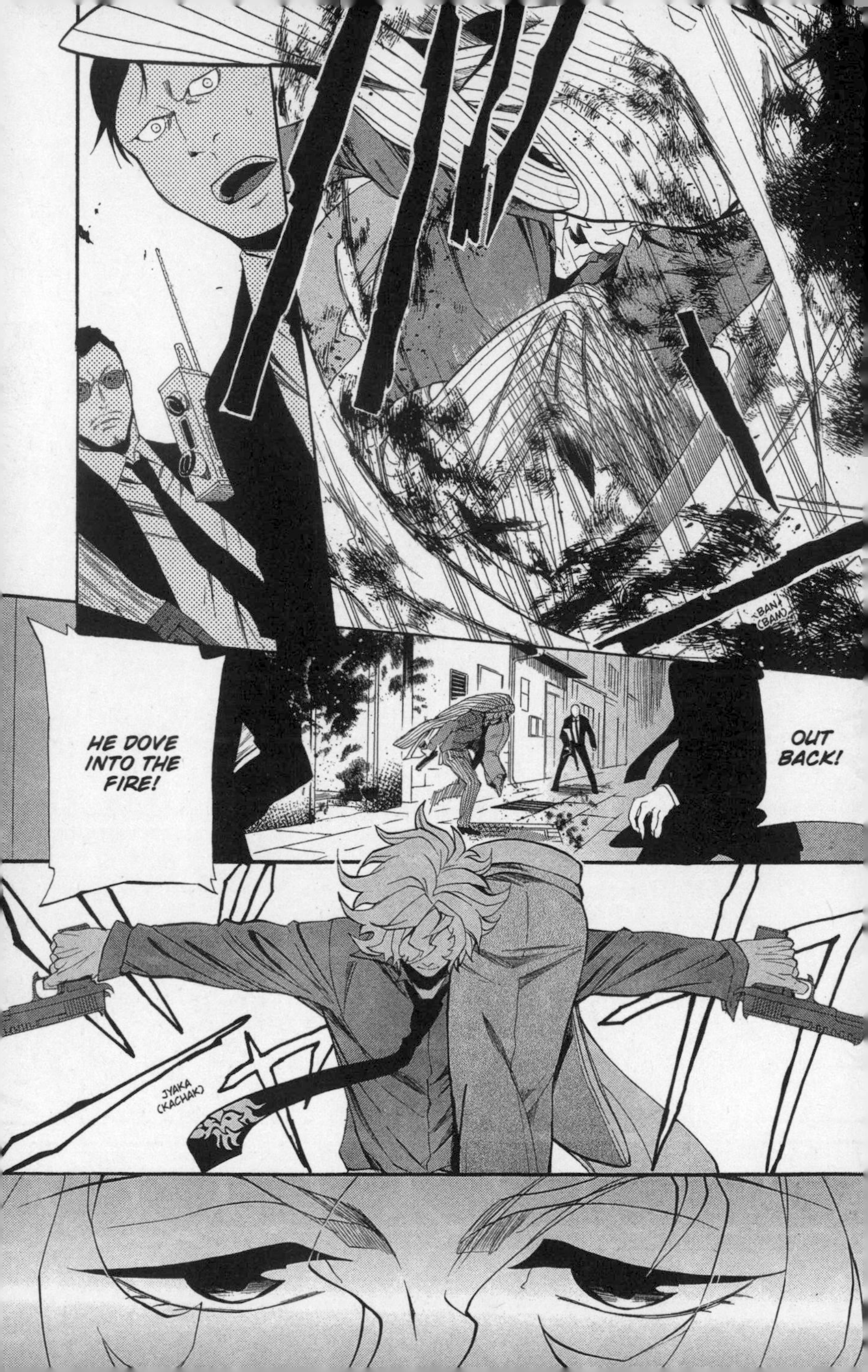
BAN (BAM)
OUT BACK!
HE DOVE INTO THE FIRE!
JYAKA (KACHAK)

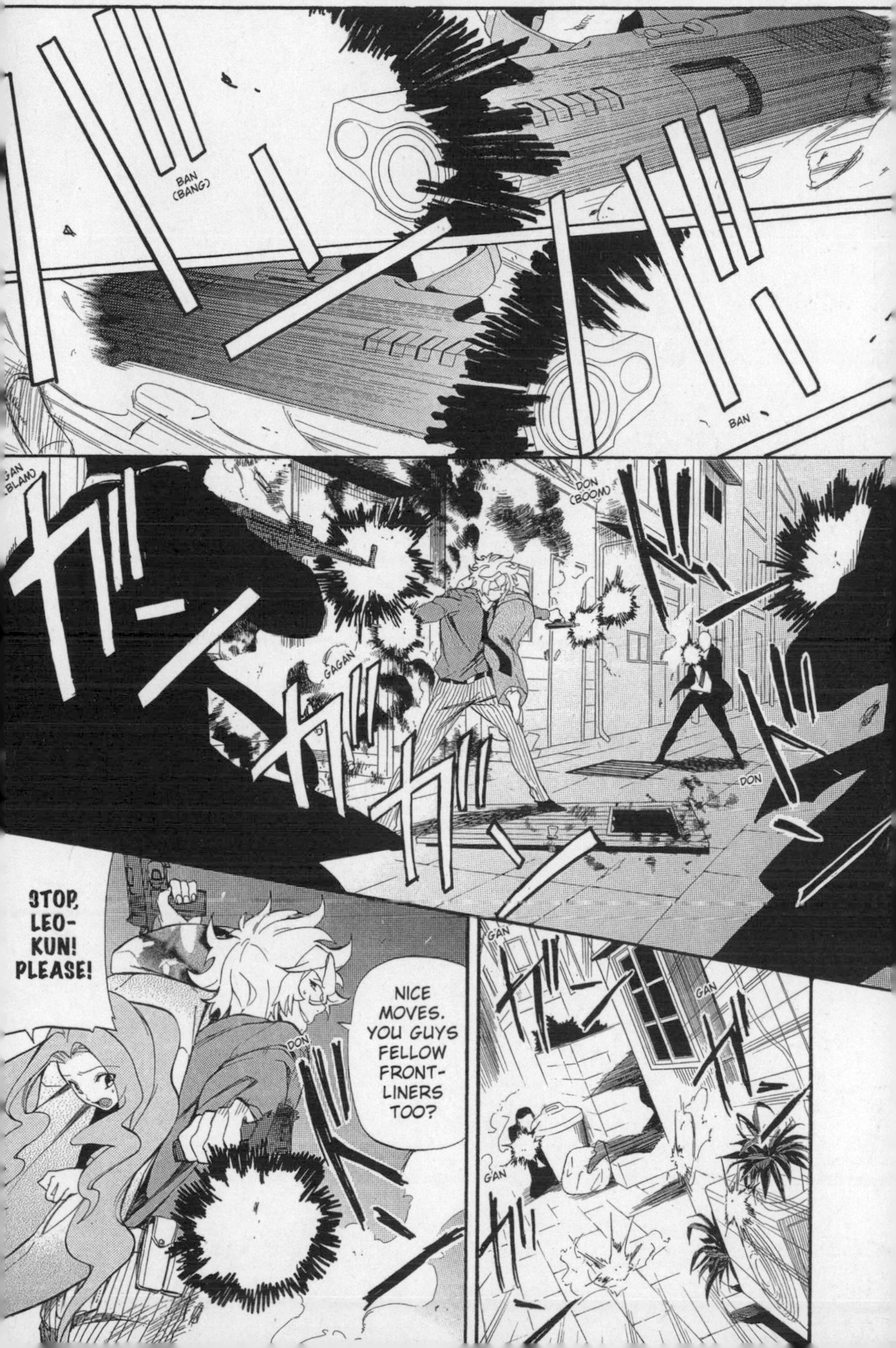
BAN (BANG)
BAN
DON (BOOM)
GAN (BLAM
GAGAN
DON
GAN
GAN
GAN
NICE MOVES. YOU GUYS FELLOW FRONT-LINERS TOO?
STOP, LEO-KUN! PLEASE!
DON

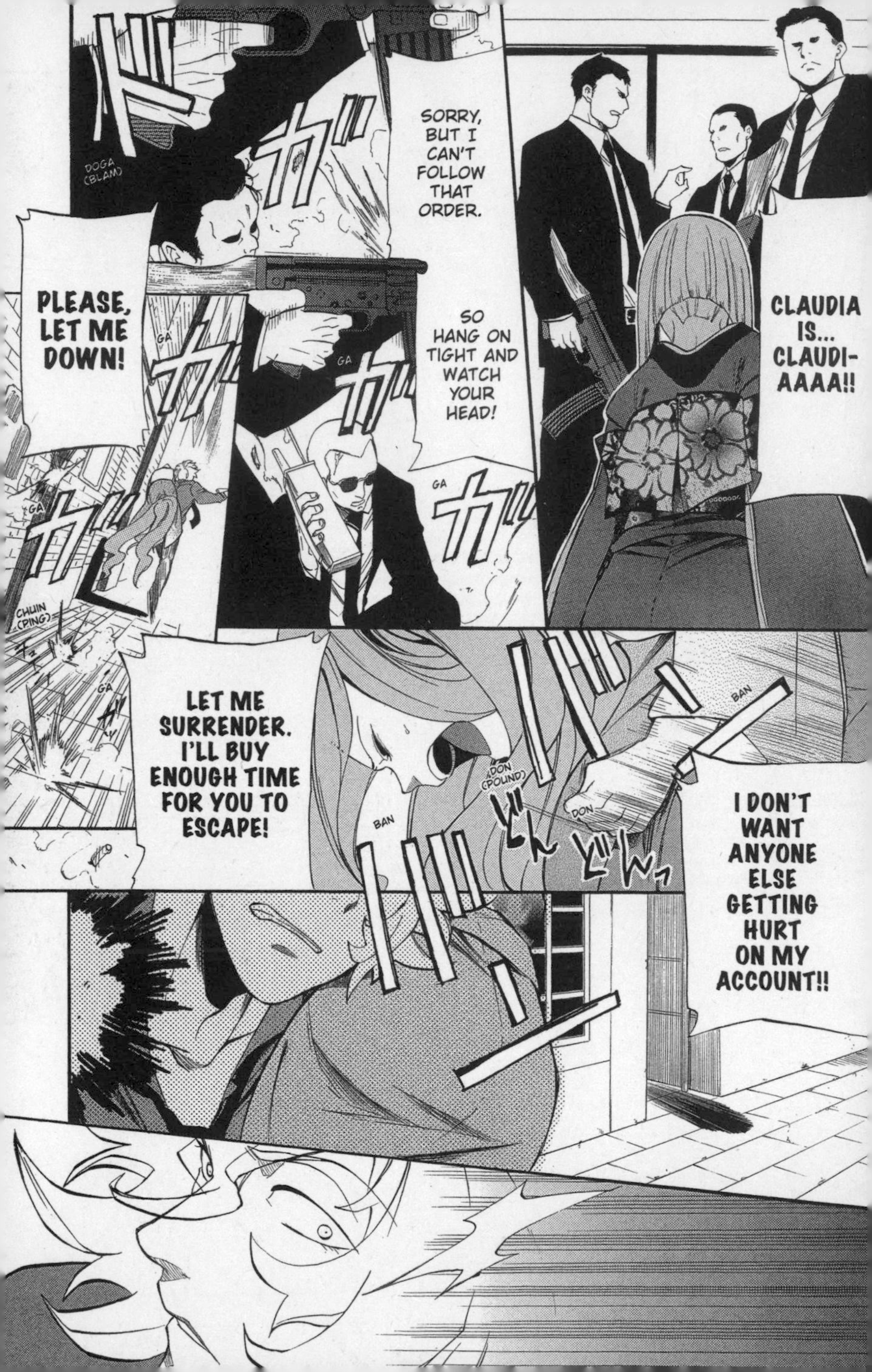
CLAUDIA IS... CLAUDI-AAAA!!
SORRY, BUT I CAN'T FOLLOW THAT ORDER.
SO HANG ON TIGHT AND WATCH YOUR HEAD!
GA
GA
DOGA (BLAM)
PLEASE, LET ME DOWN!
GA
GA
CHUIN (PING)
I DON'T WANT ANYONE ELSE GETTING HURT ON MY ACCOUNT!!
BAN
DON
DON (POUND)
BAN
LET ME SURRENDER. I'LL BUY ENOUGH TIME FOR YOU TO ESCAPE!
GA

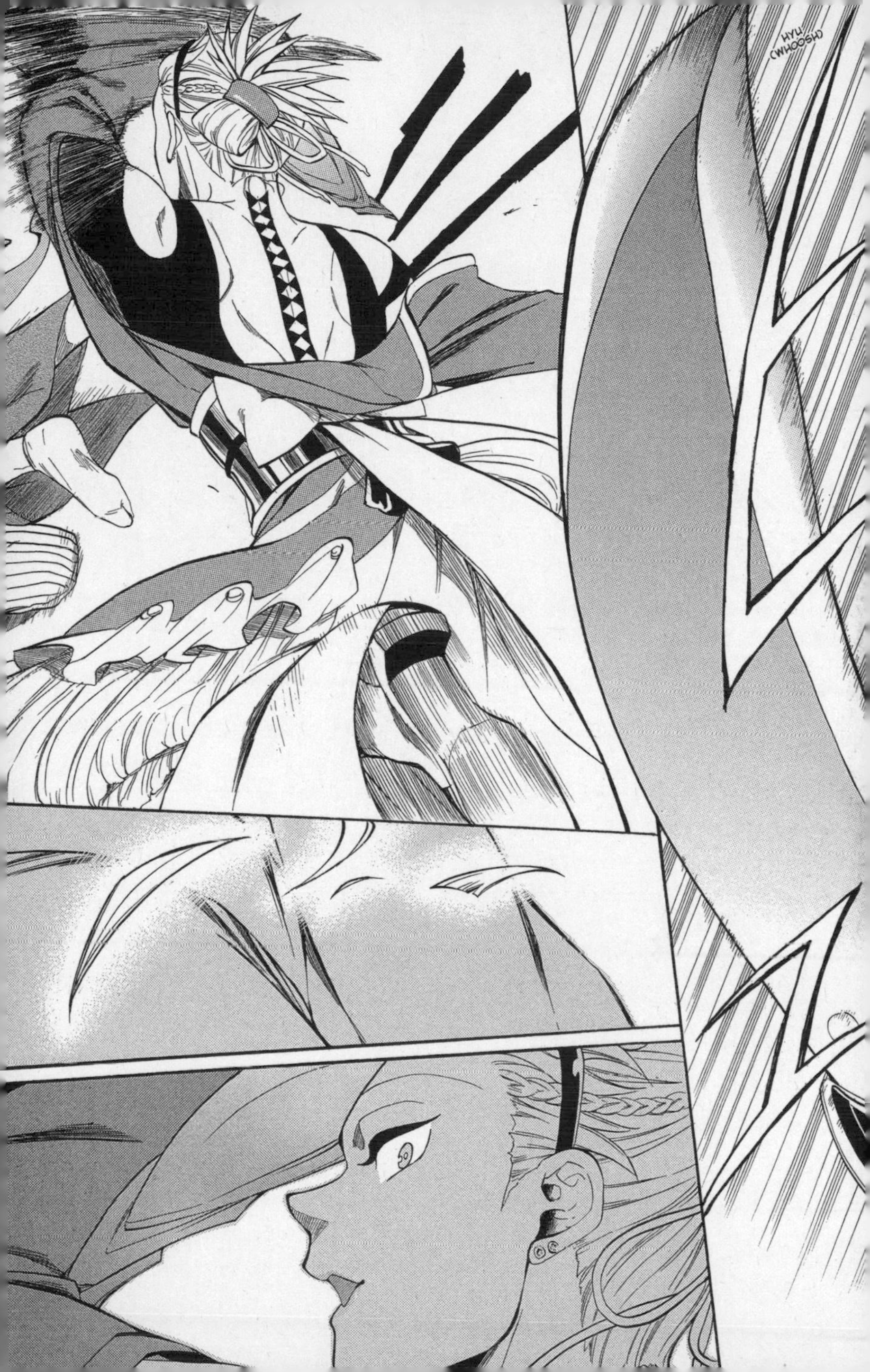
HYU (WHOOSH)

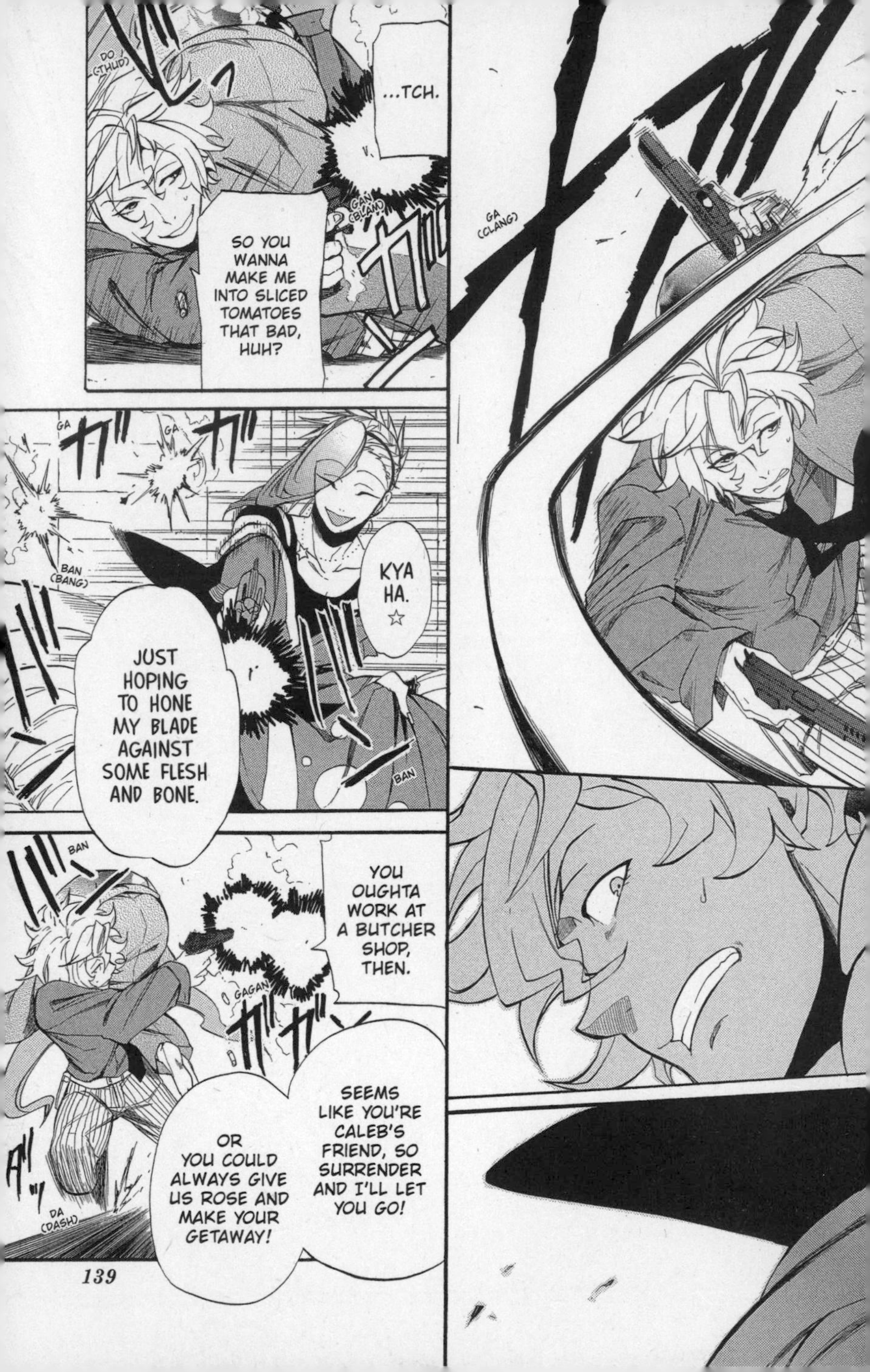

GA (CLANG)
DO (THUD)
...TCH.
GAN (BLAM)
SO YOU WANNA MAKE ME INTO SLICED TOMATOES THAT BAD, HUH?
KYA HA. ☆
GA
GA
BAN (BANG)
JUST HOPING TO HONE MY BLADE AGAINST SOME FLESH AND BONE.
BAN
YOU OUGHTA WORK AT A BUTCHER SHOP, THEN.
BAN
GAGAN
SEEMS LIKE YOU'RE CALEB'S FRIEND, SO SURRENDER AND I'LL LET YOU GO!
OR YOU COULD ALWAYS GIVE US ROSE AND MAKE YOUR GETAWAY!
DA (DASH)

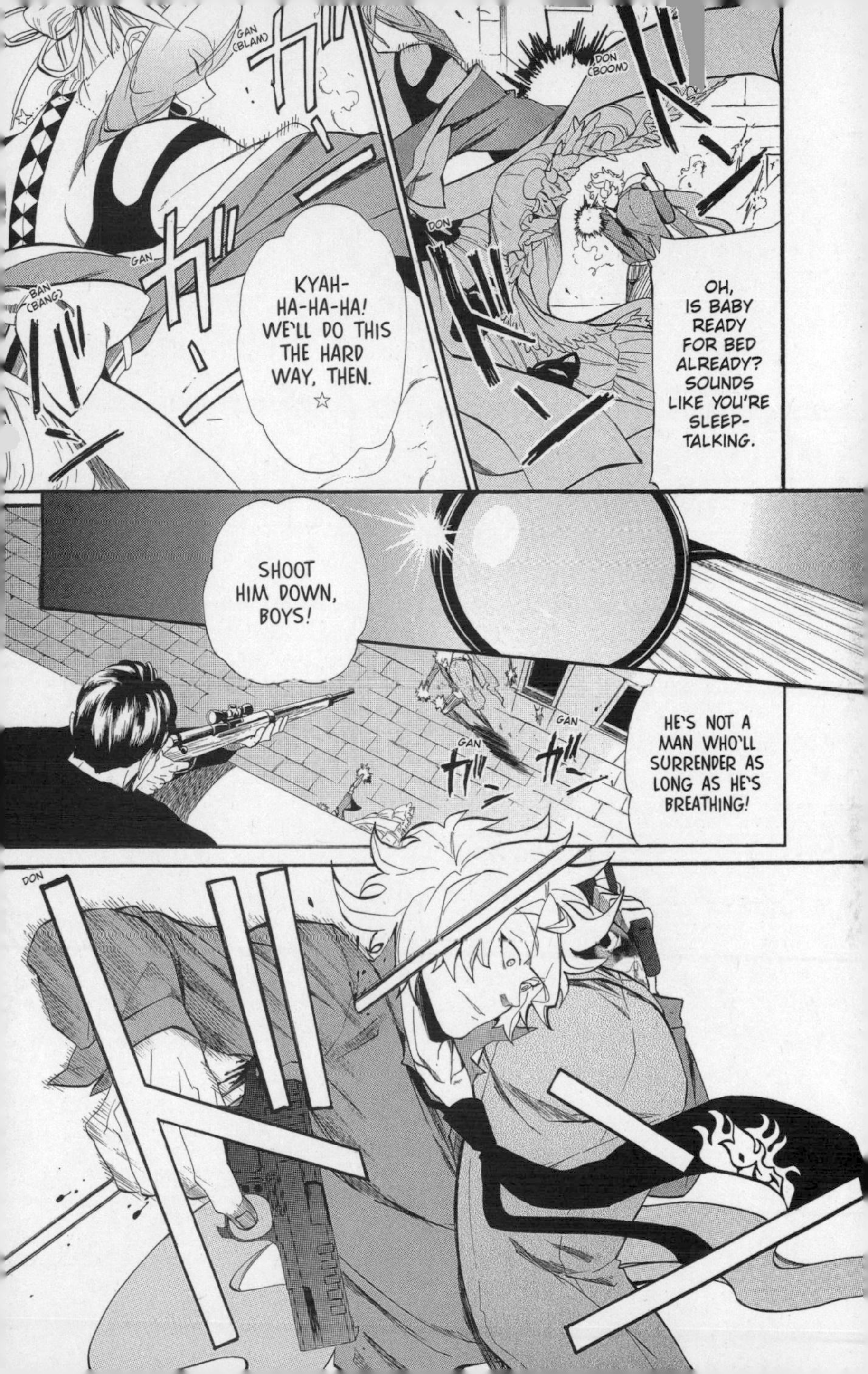
OH, IS BABY READY FOR BED ALREADY? SOUNDS LIKE YOU'RE SLEEP-TALKING.
DON (BOOM)
DON
GAN (BLAM)
KYAH-HA-HA-HA! WE'LL DO THIS THE HARD WAY, THEN. ☆
GAN
BAN (BANG)
HE'S NOT A MAN WHO'LL SURRENDER AS LONG AS HE'S BREATHING!
GAN
GAN
SHOOT HIM DOWN, BOYS!
DON

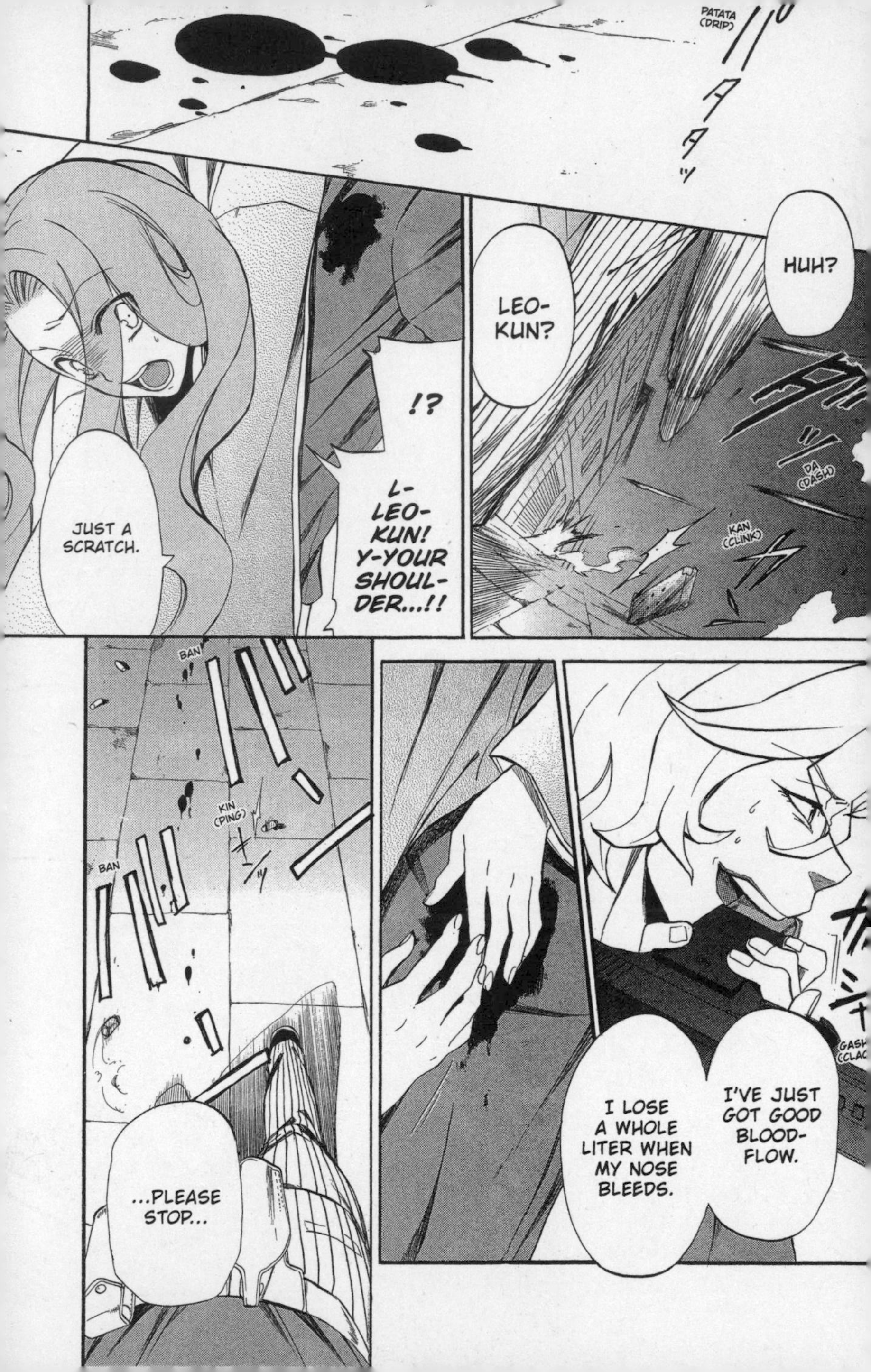
PATATA (DRIP)
HUH?
LEO-KUN?
DA (DASH)
KAN (CLINK)
!?
L-LEO-KUN! Y-YOUR SHOULDER...!!
JUST A SCRATCH.
GASH (CLAC
I'VE JUST GOT GOOD BLOOD-FLOW.
I LOSE A WHOLE LITER WHEN MY NOSE BLEEDS.
BAN
KIN (PING)
BAN
...PLEASE STOP...

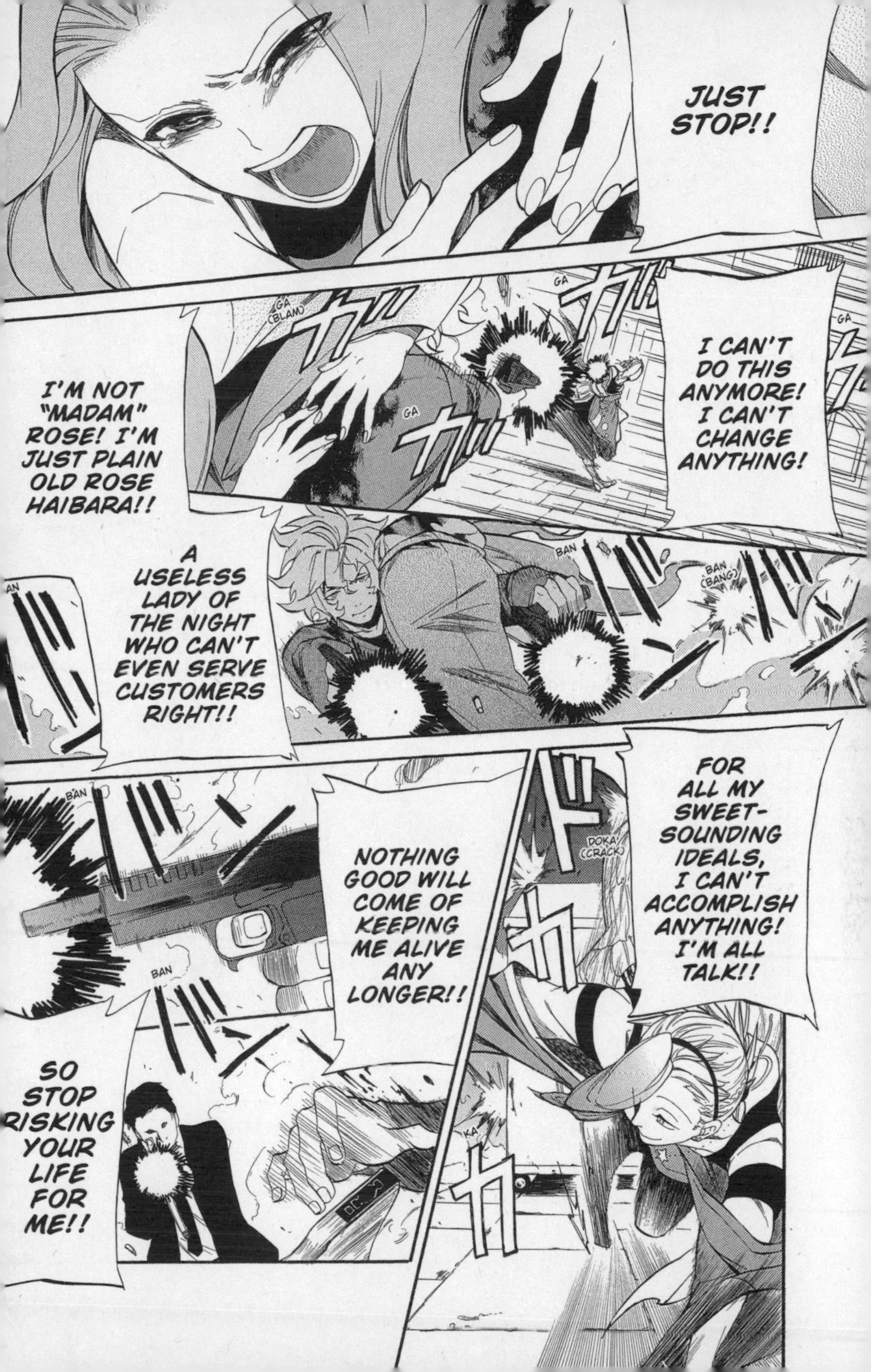
JUST STOP!!
GA
GA
GA (BLAM)
GA
I CAN'T DO THIS ANYMORE! I CAN'T CHANGE ANYTHING!
I'M NOT "MADAM" ROSE! I'M JUST PLAIN OLD ROSE HAIBARA!!
BAN
BAN (BANG)
A USELESS LADY OF THE NIGHT WHO CAN'T EVEN SERVE CUSTOMERS RIGHT!!
BAN
DOKA (CRACK)
FOR ALL MY SWEET-SOUNDING IDEALS, I CAN'T ACCOMPLISH ANYTHING! I'M ALL TALK!!
KA
BAN
NOTHING GOOD WILL COME OF KEEPING ME ALIVE ANY LONGER!!
BAN
SO STOP RISKING YOUR LIFE FOR ME!!

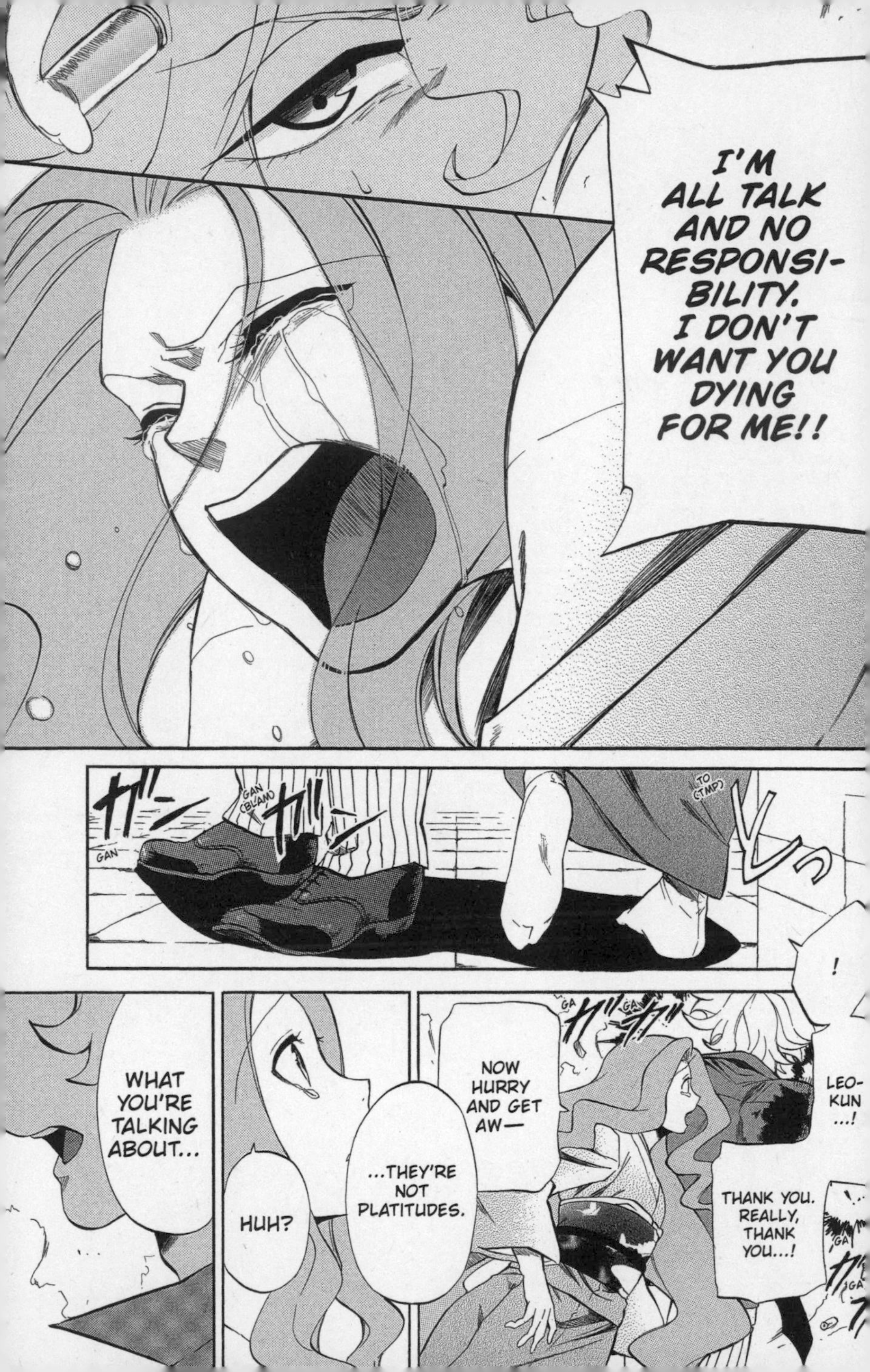

I'M ALL TALK AND NO RESPONSI-BILITY. I DON'T WANT YOU DYING FOR ME!!
TO (TMP)
GAN (BLAM)
GAN
!
GA
GA
LEO-KUN ...!
THANK YOU. REALLY, THANK YOU...!
GA
GA
NOW HURRY AND GET AW—
...THEY'RE NOT PLATITUDES.
HUH?
WHAT YOU'RE TALKING ABOUT...

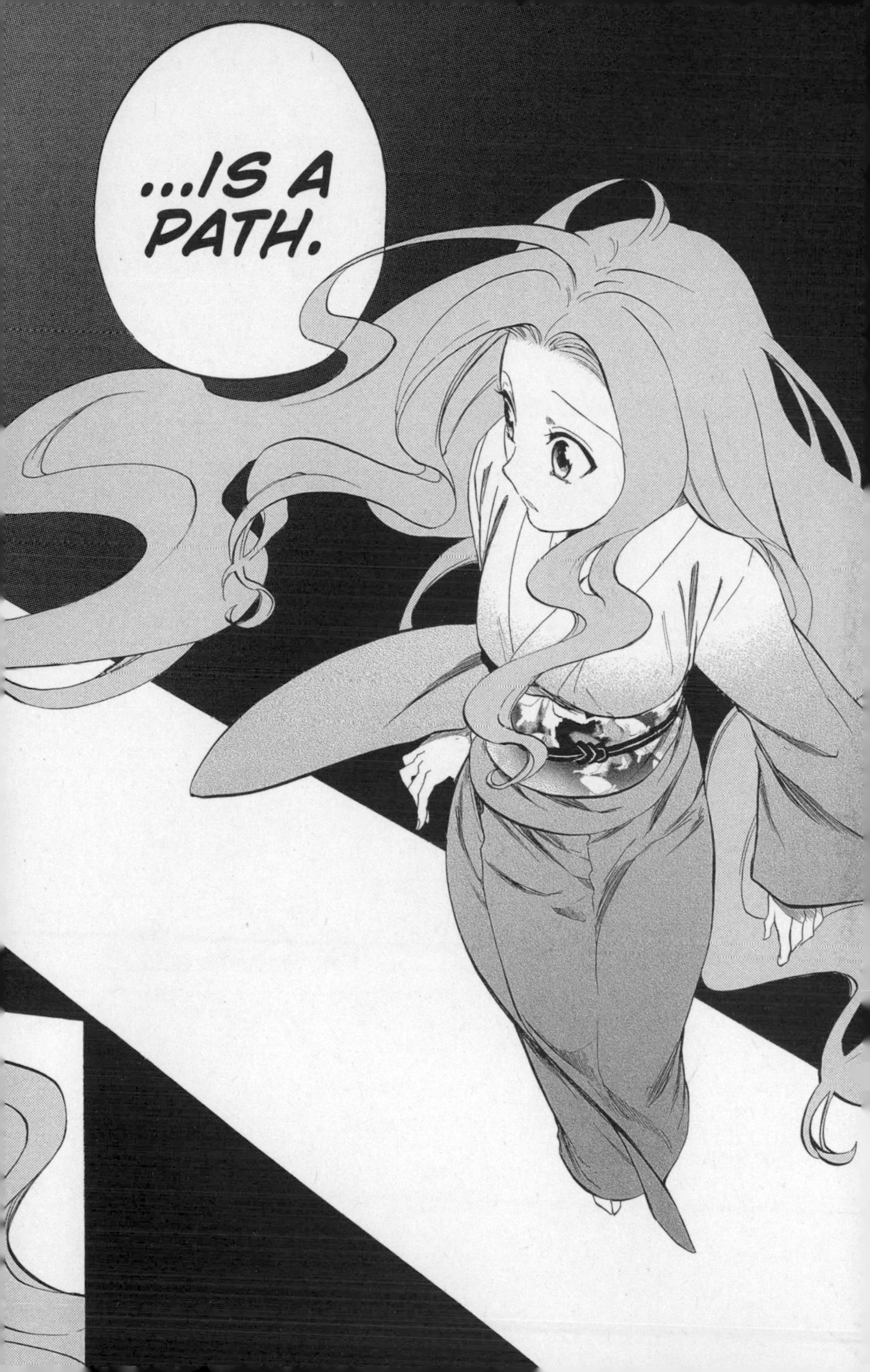
...IS A PATH.

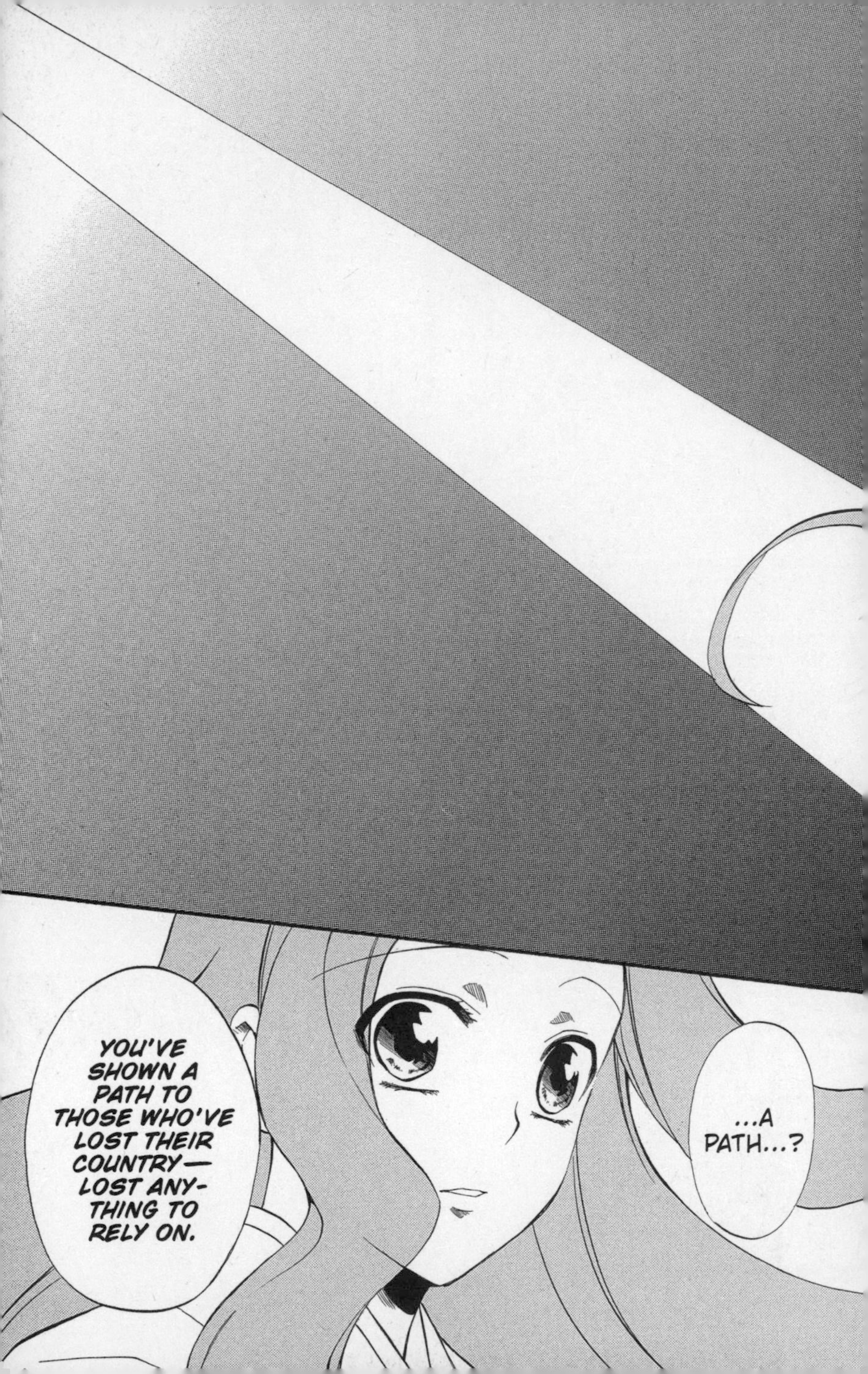
YOU'VE SHOWN A PATH TO THOSE WHO'VE LOST THEIR COUNTRY—LOST ANY-THING TO RELY ON.
...A PATH...?

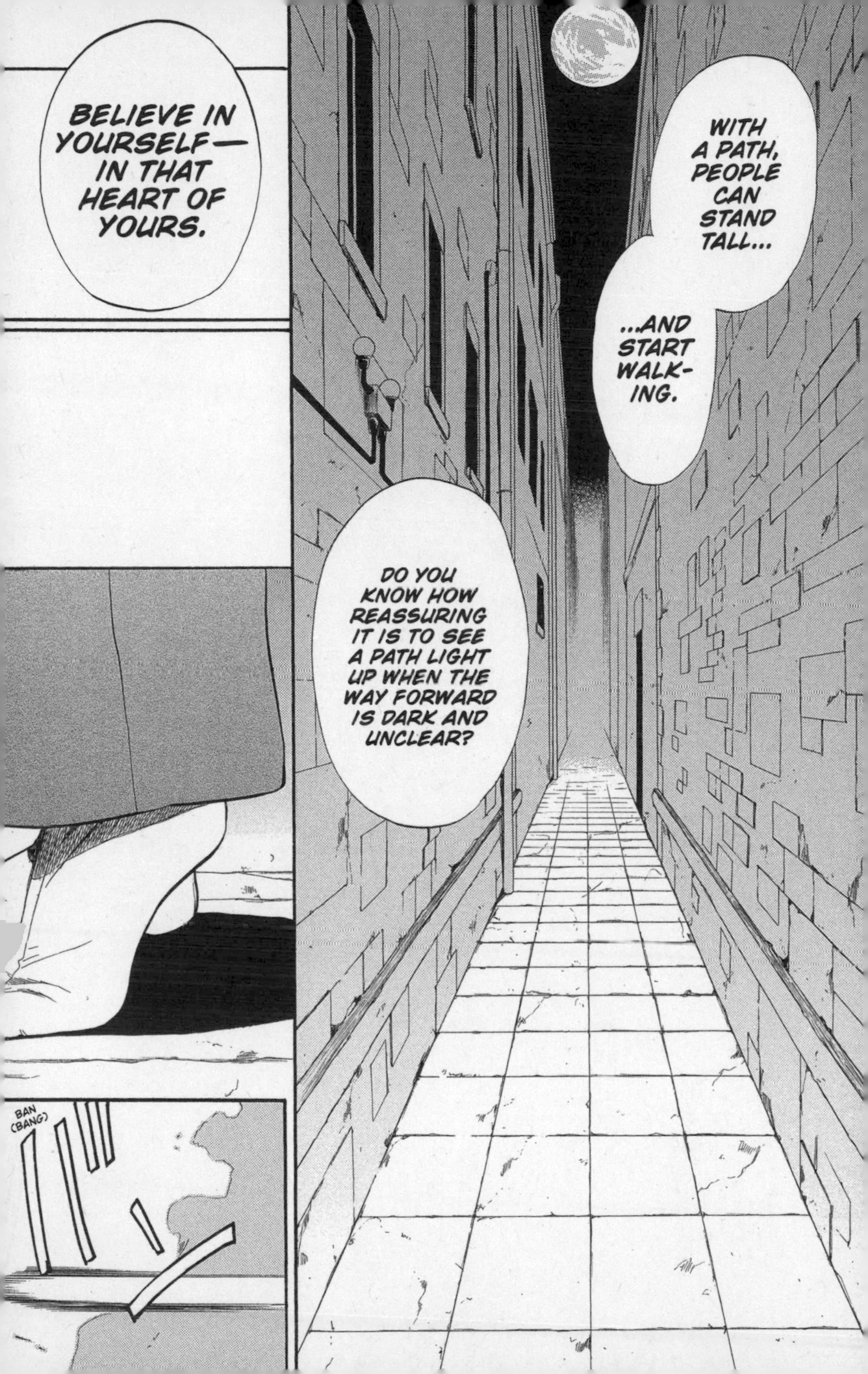
WITH A PATH, PEOPLE CAN STAND TALL...
...AND START WALK-ING.
DO YOU KNOW HOW REASSURING IT IS TO SEE A PATH LIGHT UP WHEN THE WAY FORWARD IS DARK AND UNCLEAR?
BELIEVE IN YOURSELF— IN THAT HEART OF YOURS.
BAN (BANG)

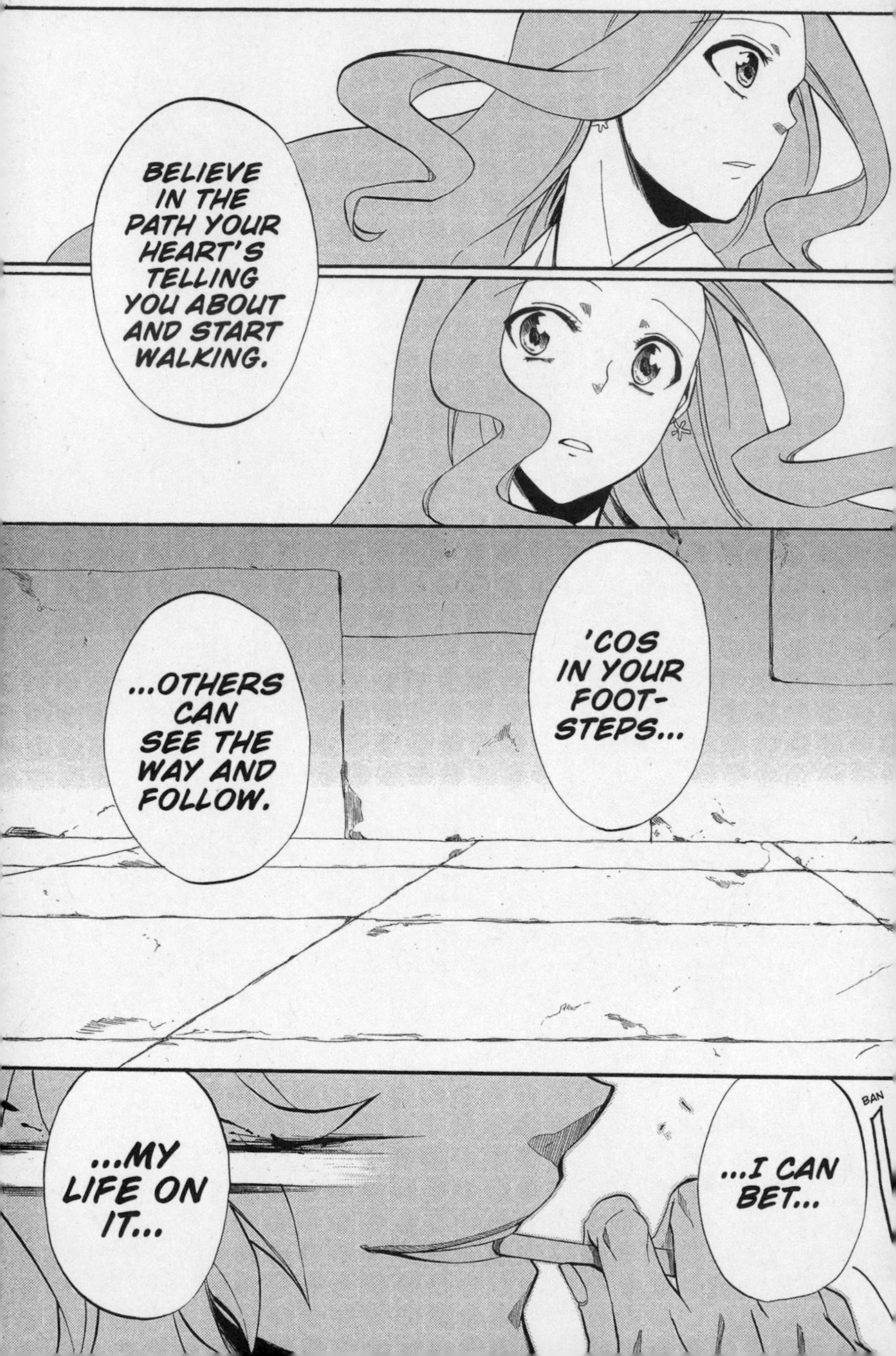
BELIEVE IN THE PATH YOUR HEART'S TELLING YOU ABOUT AND START WALKING.
'COS IN YOUR FOOT-STEPS...
...OTHERS CAN SEE THE WAY AND FOLLOW.
BAN
...I CAN BET...
...MY LIFE ON IT...

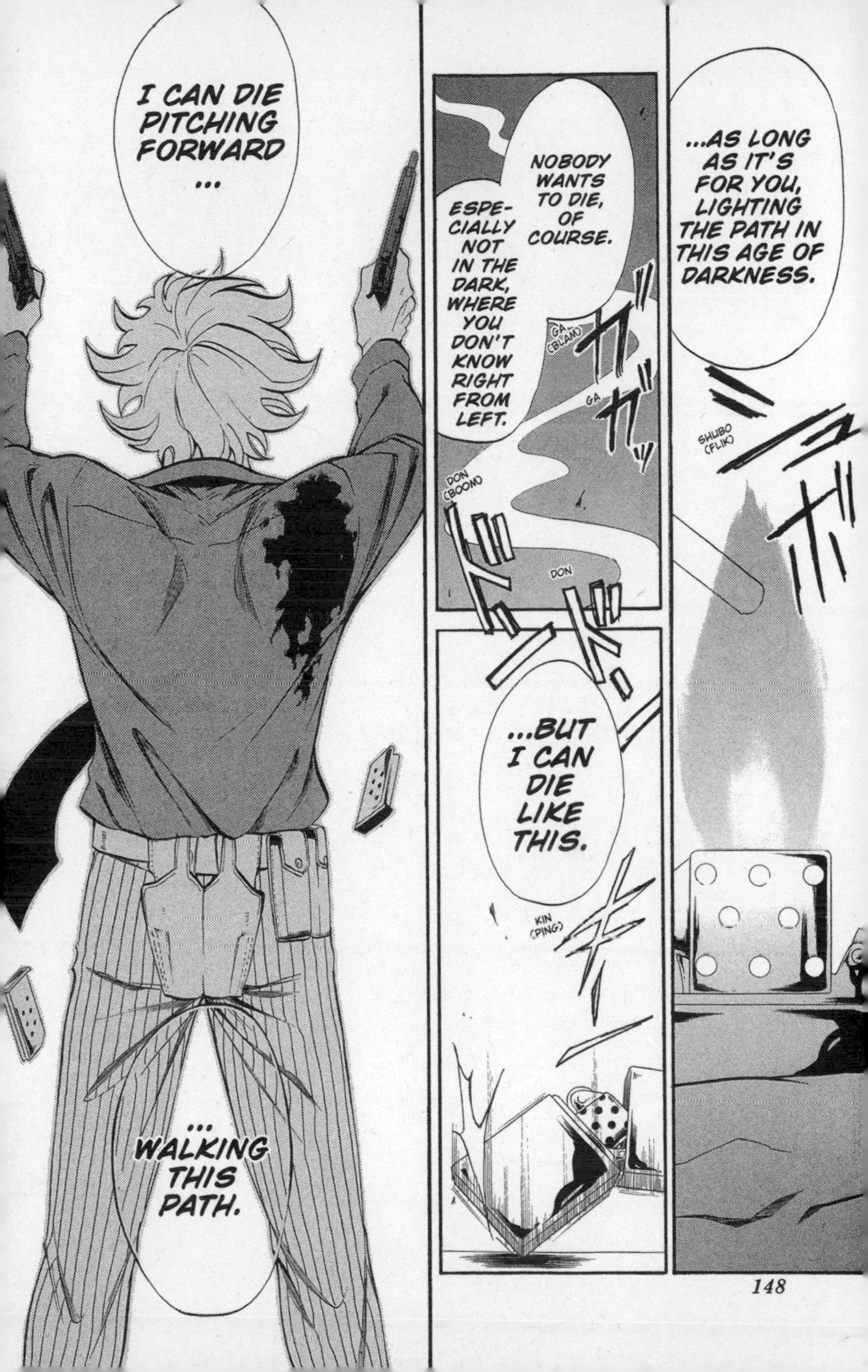

...AS LONG AS IT'S FOR YOU, LIGHTING THE PATH IN THIS AGE OF DARKNESS.
SHUBO (FLIK)
NOBODY WANTS TO DIE, OF COURSE.
ESPE-CIALLY NOT IN THE DARK, WHERE YOU DON'T KNOW RIGHT FROM LEFT.
GA (BLAM)
GA
DON (BOOM)
DON
...BUT I CAN DIE LIKE THIS.
KIN (PING)
I CAN DIE PITCHING FORWARD ...
... WALKING THIS PATH.

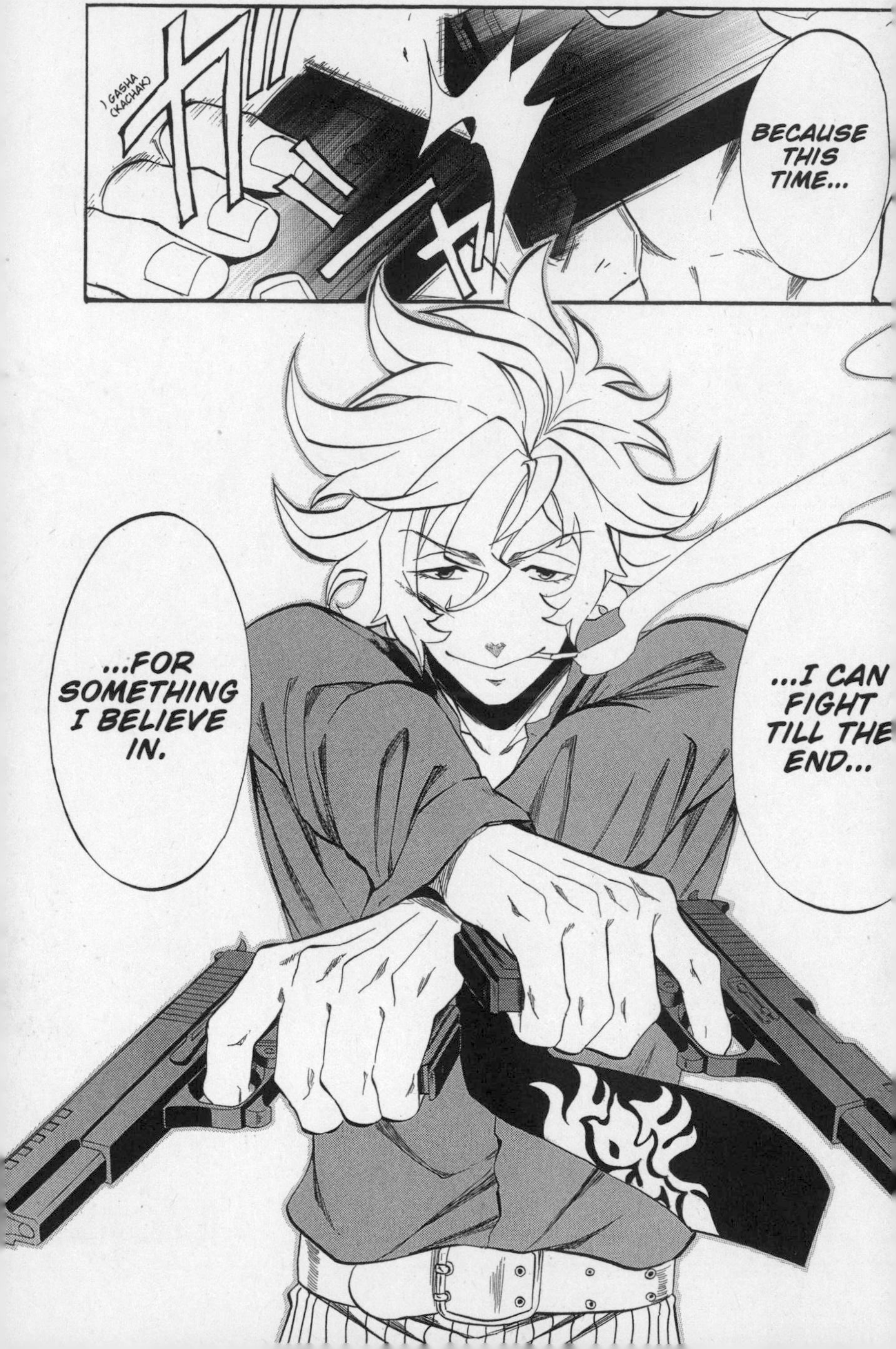
BECAUSE THIS TIME...
GASHA (KACHAK)
...I CAN FIGHT TILL THE END...
...FOR SOMETHING I BELIEVE IN.

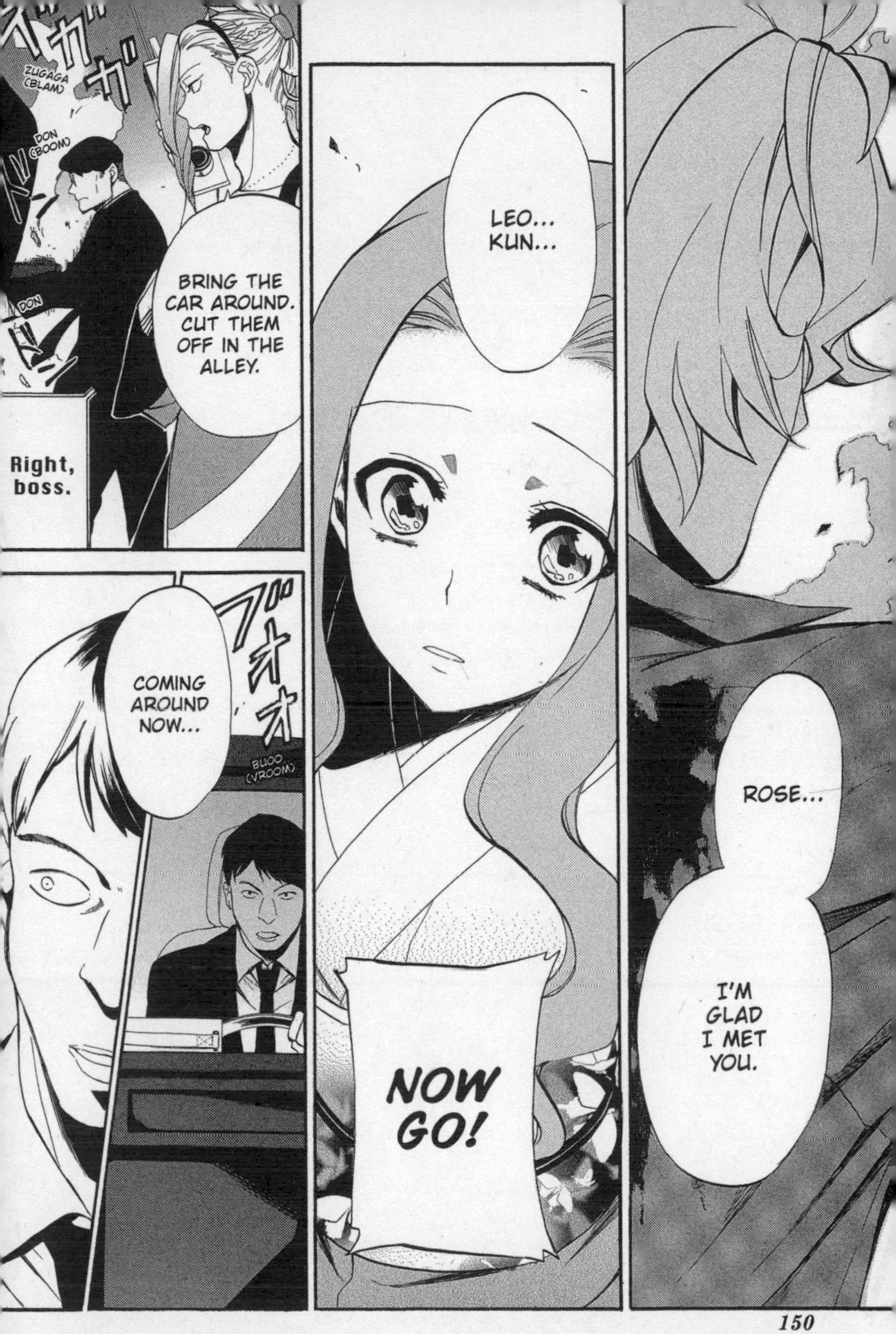
ROSE...
I'M GLAD I MET YOU.
LEO... KUN...
NOW GO!
ZUGAGA (BLAM)
DON (BOOM)
BRING THE CAR AROUND. CUT THEM OFF IN THE ALLEY.
DON
Right, boss.
COMING AROUND NOW...
BUOO (VROOM)

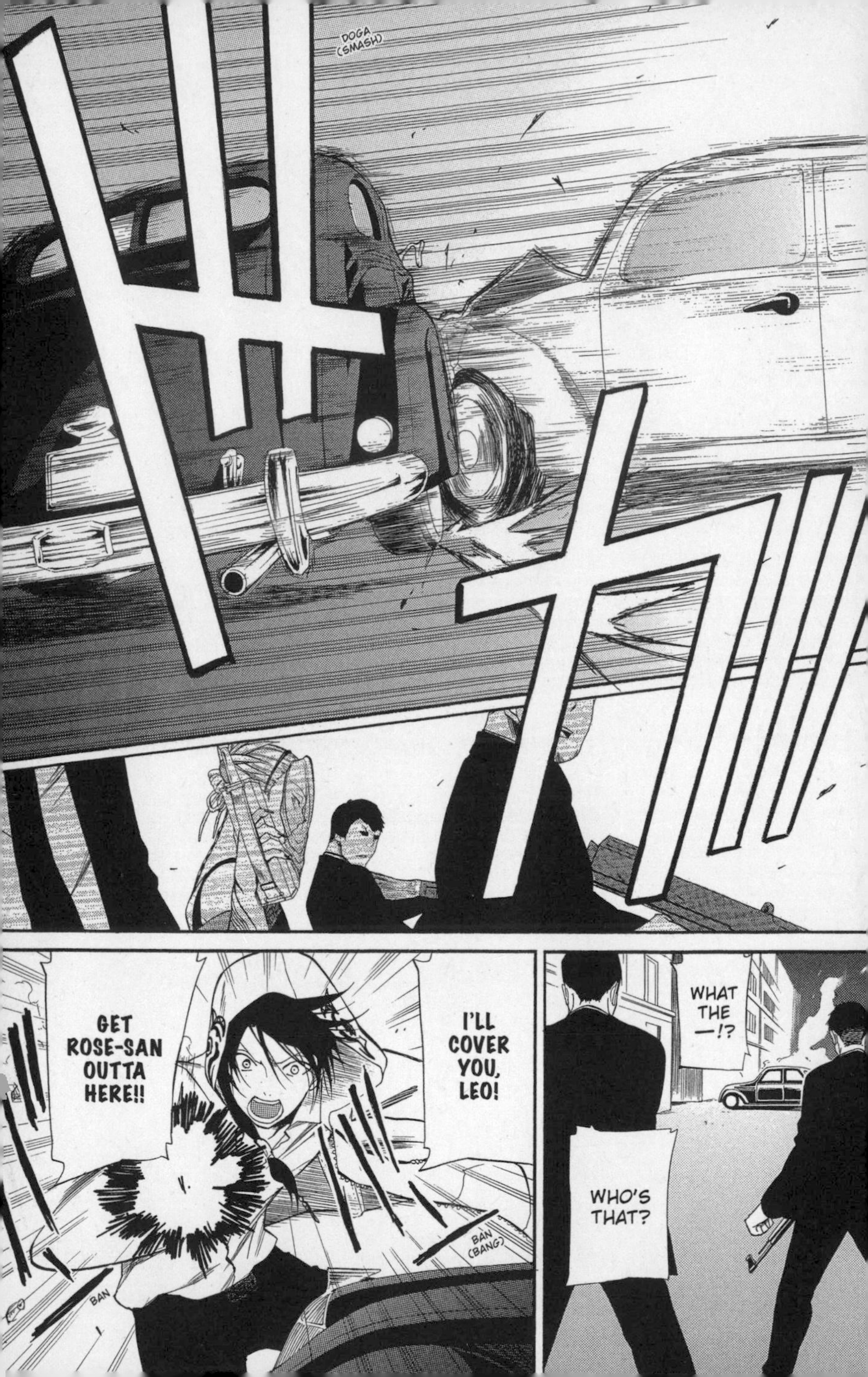
DOGA (SMASH)
WHAT THE—!?
WHO'S THAT?
I'LL COVER YOU, LEO!
GET ROSE-SAN OUTTA HERE!!
BAN (BANG)
BAN

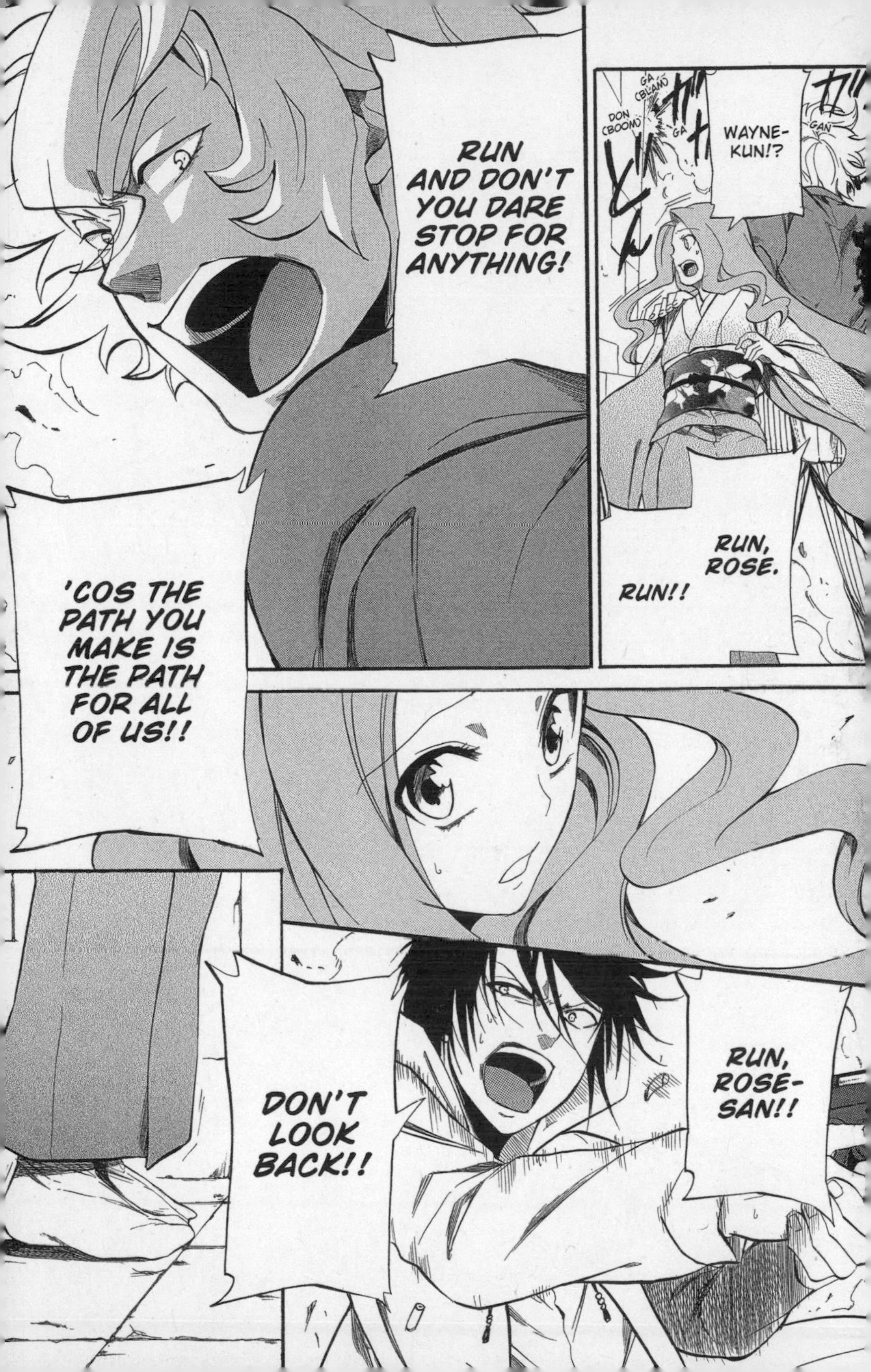

GA (BLAM)
DON (BOOM)
GA
GAN
WAYNE-KUN!?
RUN, ROSE.
RUN!!
RUN AND DON'T YOU DARE STOP FOR ANYTHING!
'COS THE PATH YOU MAKE IS THE PATH FOR ALL OF US!!
RUN, ROSE-SAN!!
DON'T LOOK BACK!!

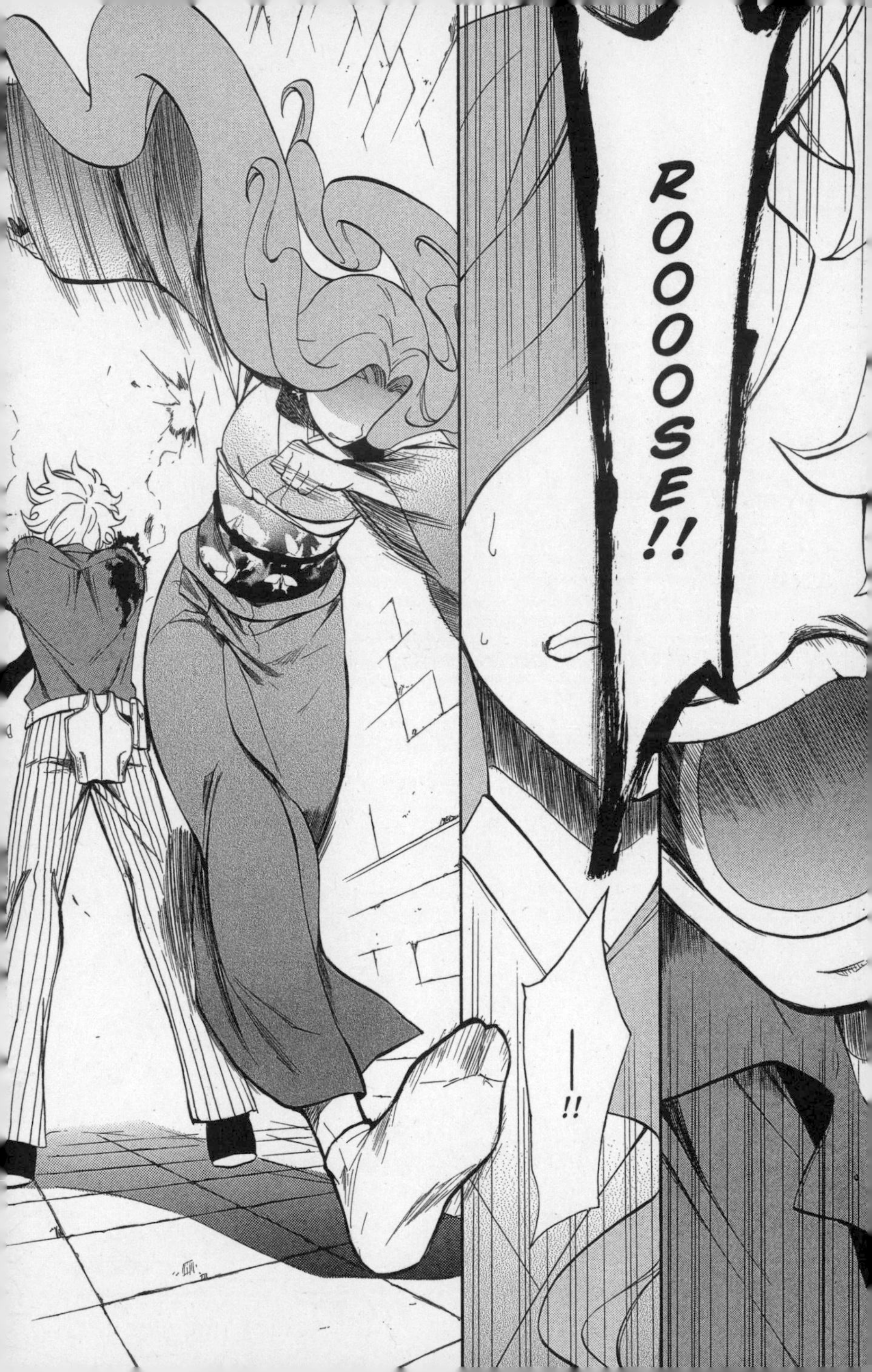
ROOOOOSE!!
—!!

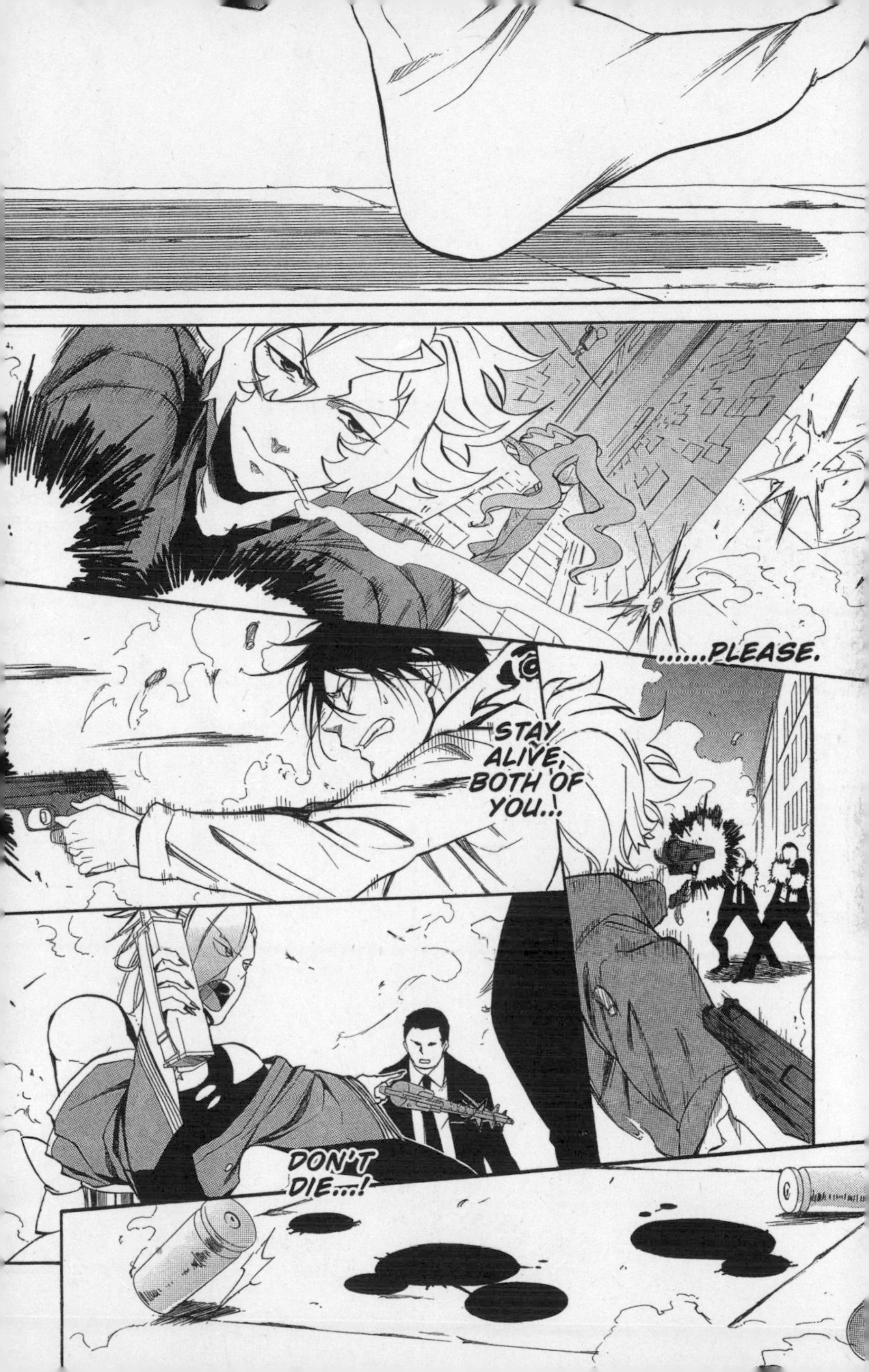
......PLEASE.
STAY ALIVE, BOTH OF YOU..!
DON'T DIE...!

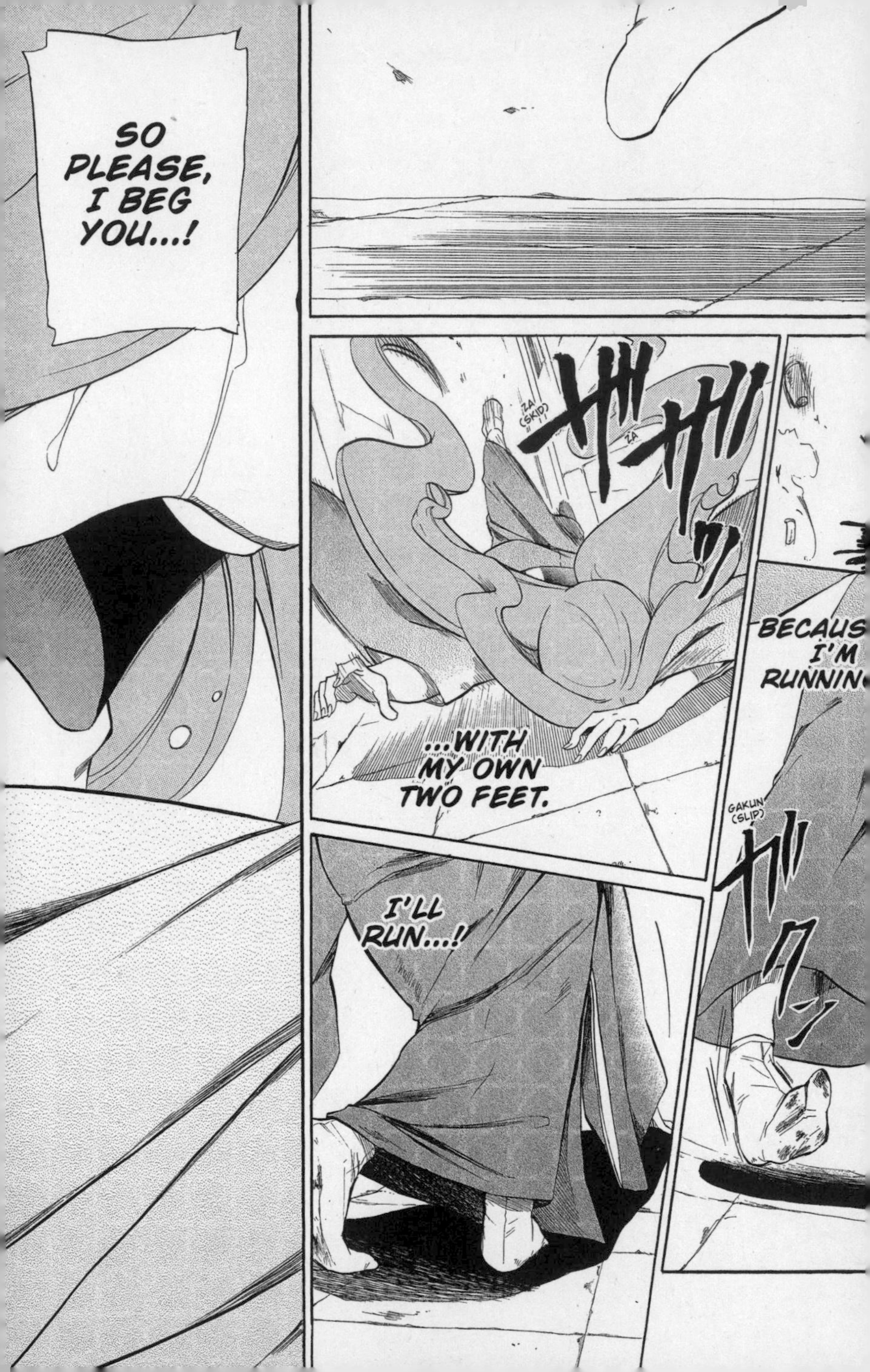
BECAUS I'M RUNNIN
ZA (SKID)
ZA
...WITH MY OWN TWO FEET.
GAKUN (SLIP)
I'LL RUN...!
SO PLEASE, I BEG YOU...!

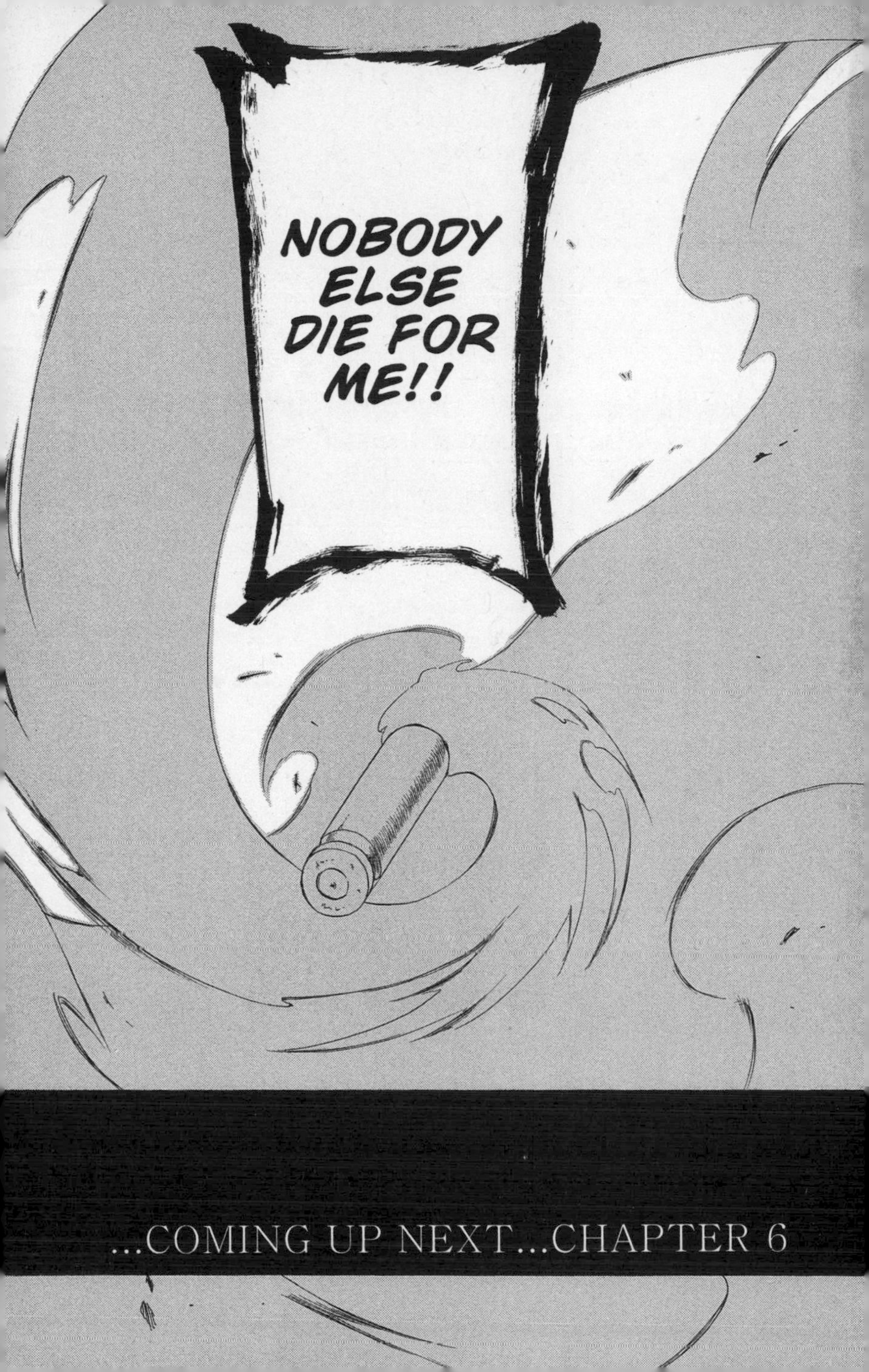
NOBODY ELSE DIE FOR ME!!
...COMING UP NEXT...CHAPTER 6

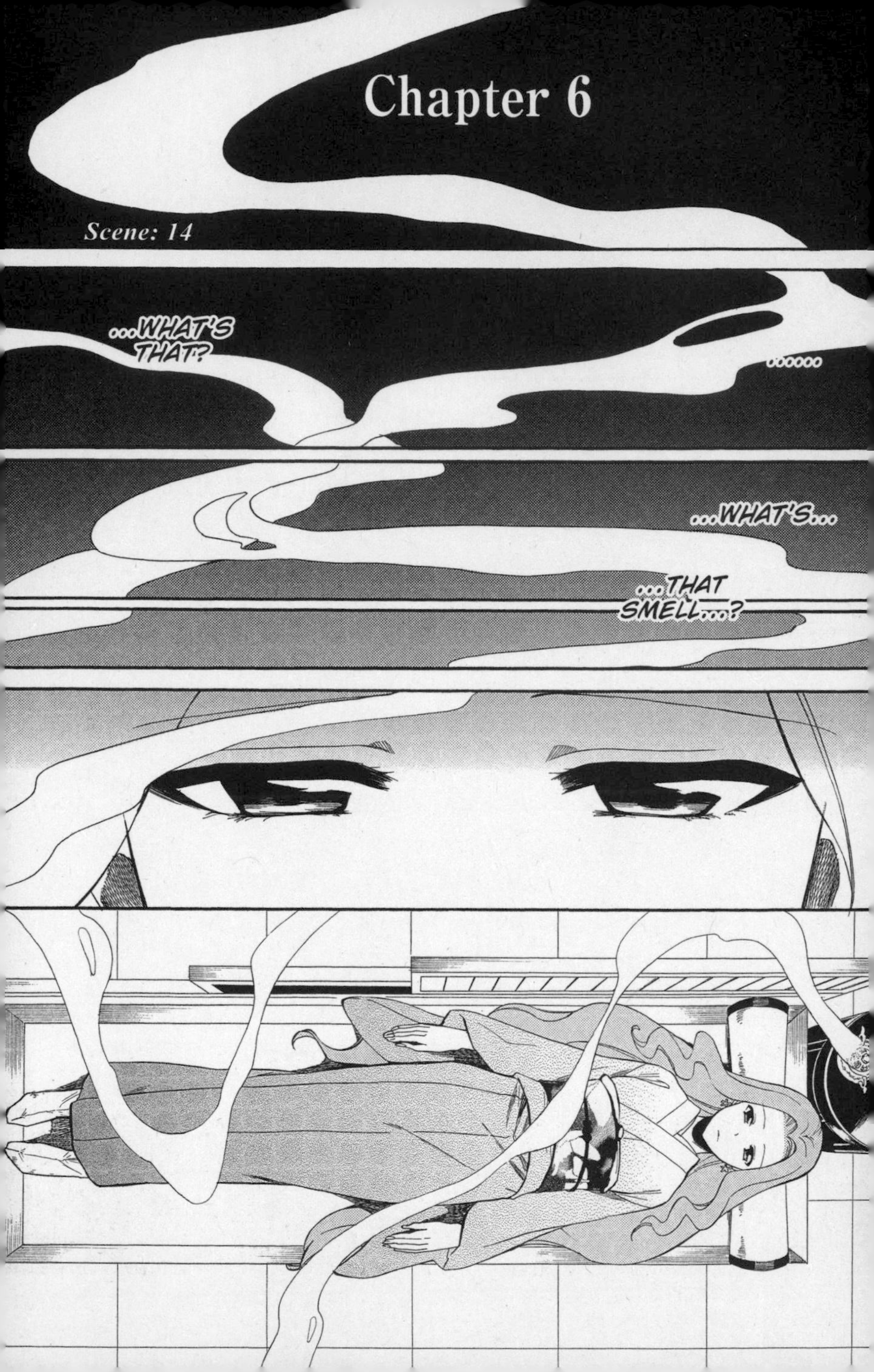
Chapter 6
Scene: 14
......
...WHAT'S THAT?
...WHAT'S...
...THAT SMELL...?

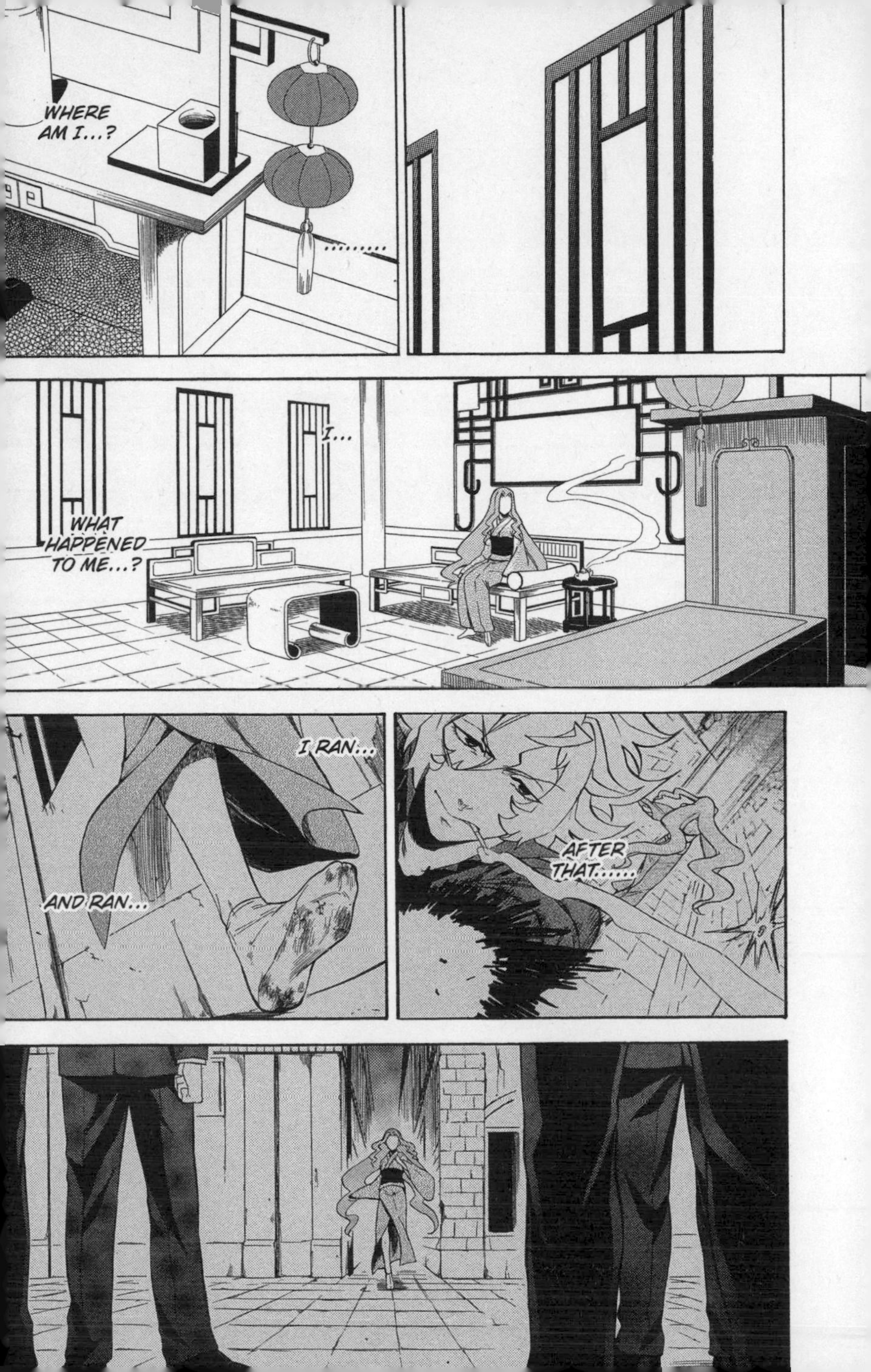
WHERE AM I...?
....
I...
WHAT HAPPENED TO ME...?
AFTER THAT......
I RAN...
AND RAN...

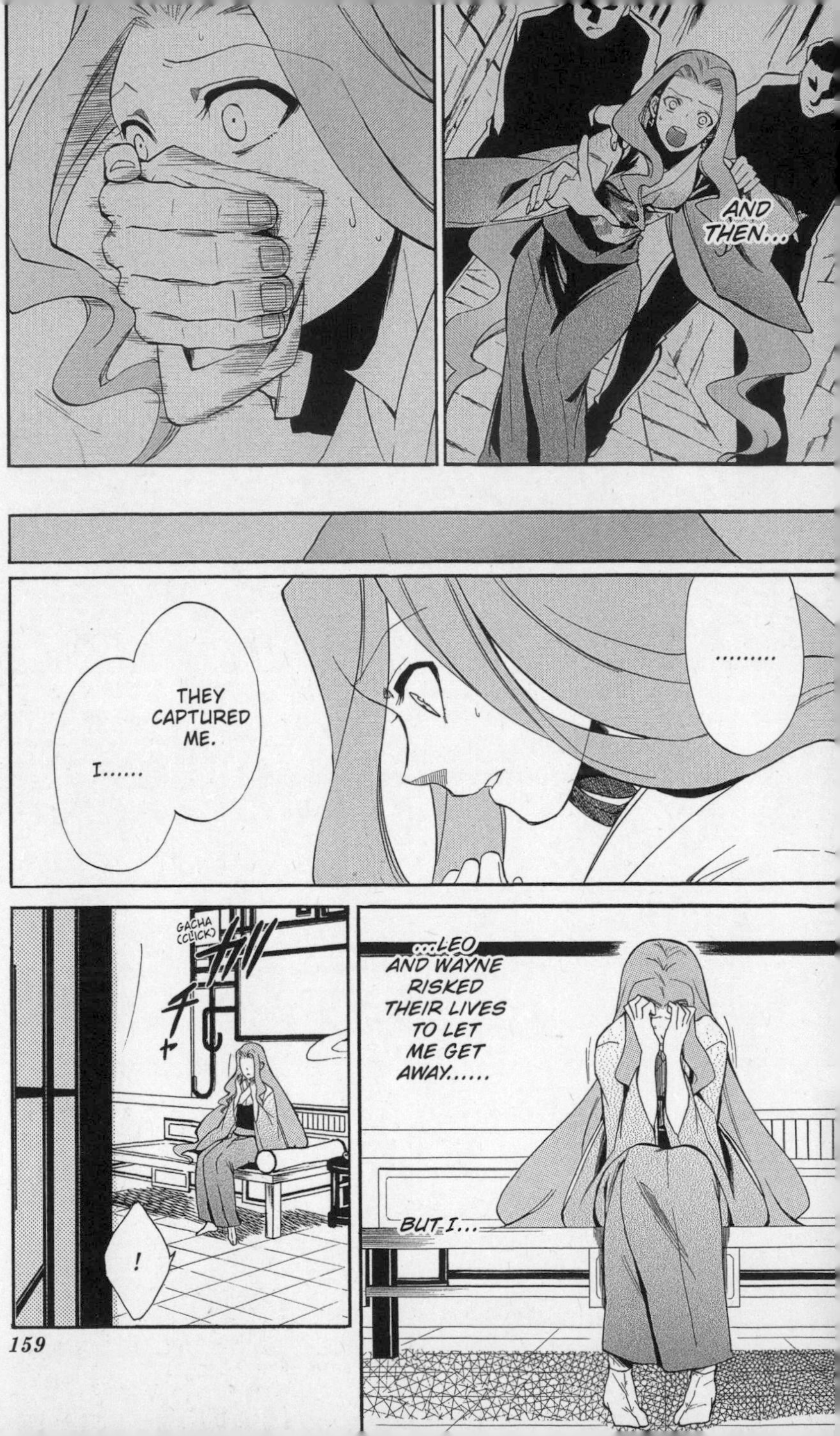
AND THEN...
....
THEY CAPTURED ME.
I......
...LEO AND WAYNE RISKED THEIR LIVES TO LET ME GET AWAY......
BUT I...
GACHA (CLICK)
!

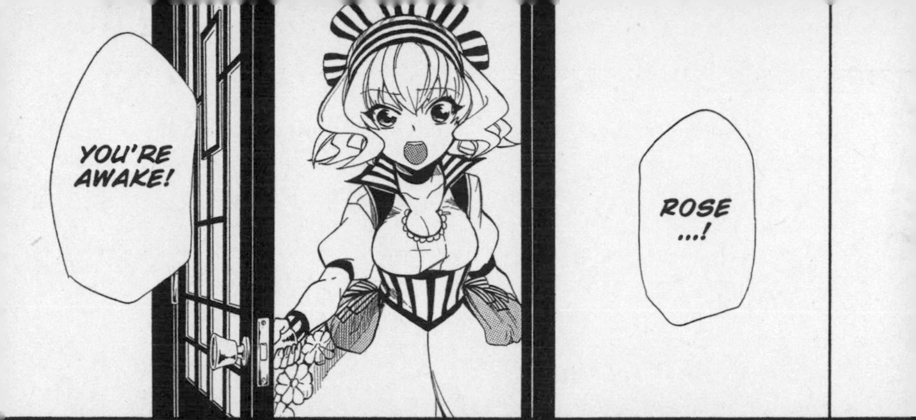
ROSE ...!
YOU'RE AWAKE!

Scene: 14

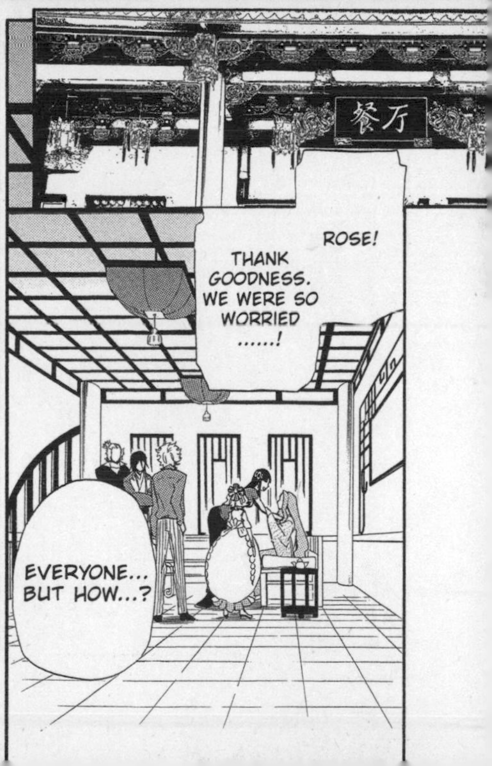
ROSE!
THANK GOODNESS. WE WERE SO WORRIED ......!
EVERYONE... BUT HOW...?

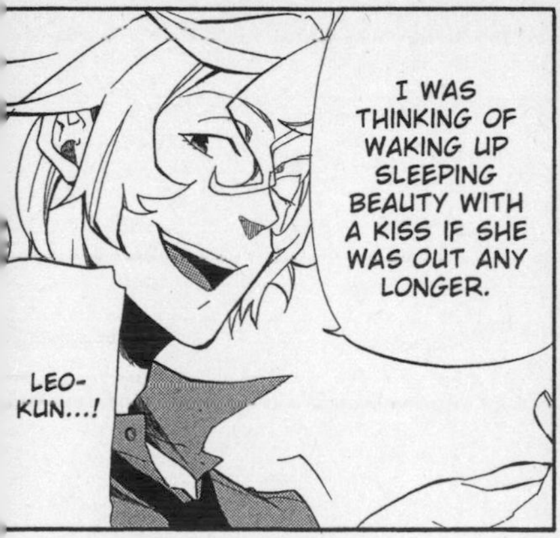
I WAS THINKING OF WAKING UP SLEEPING BEAUTY WITH A KISS IF SHE WAS OUT ANY LONGER.
LEO-KUN...!

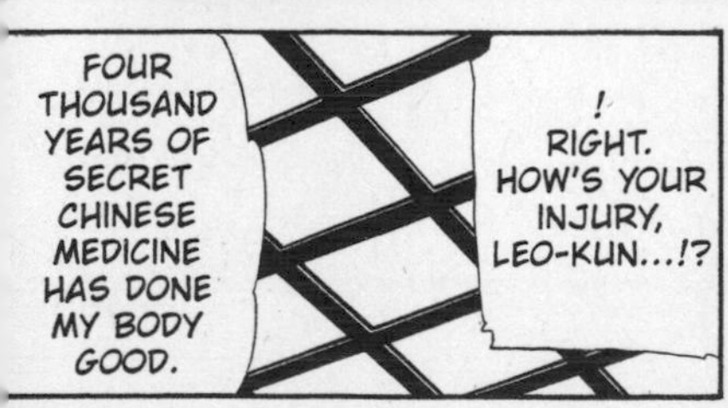
! RIGHT. HOW'S YOUR INJURY, LEO-KUN...!?
FOUR THOUSAND YEARS OF SECRET CHINESE MEDICINE HAS DONE MY BODY GOOD.

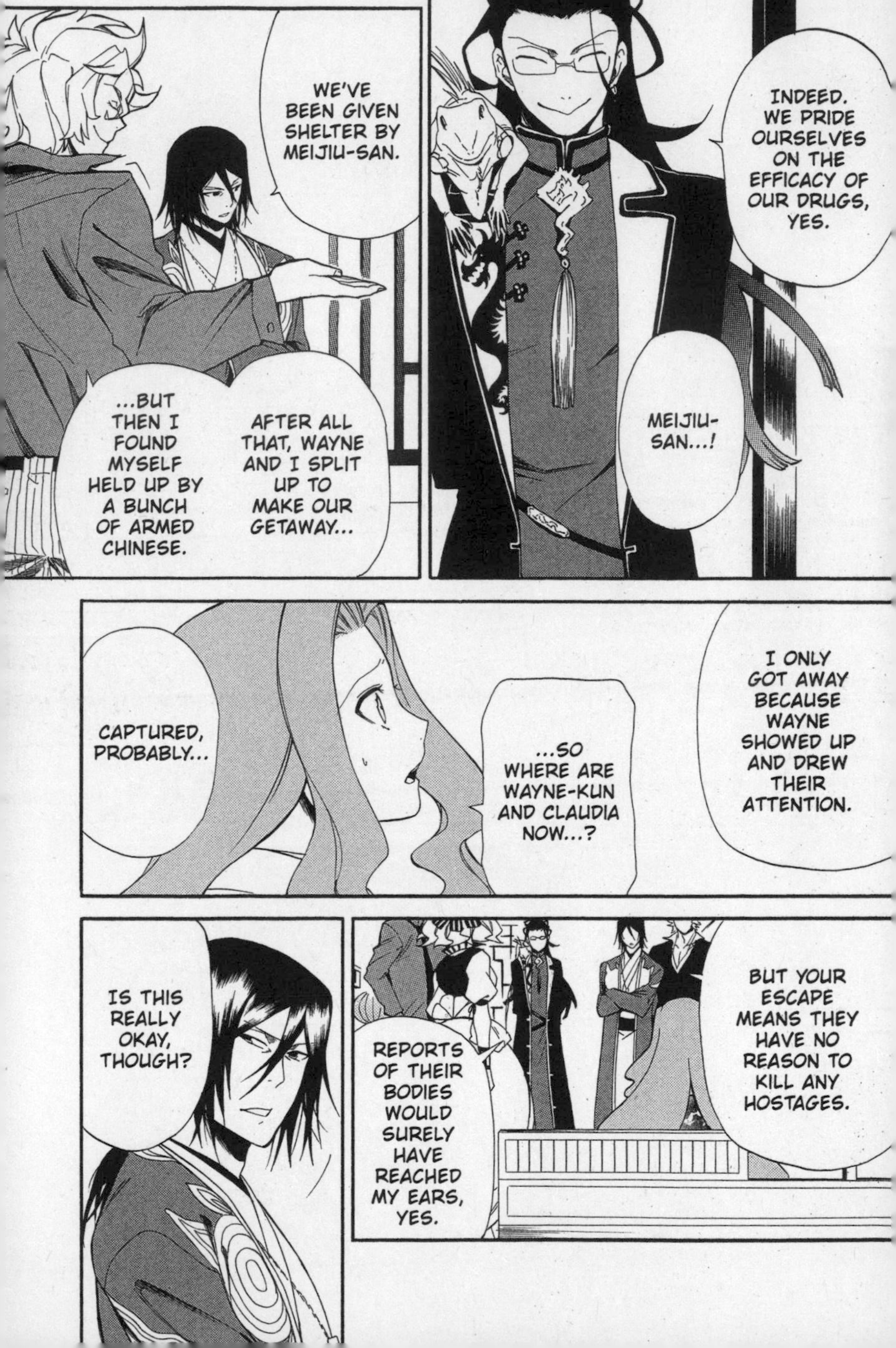
INDEED. WE PRIDE OURSELVES ON THE EFFICACY OF OUR DRUGS, YES.
MEIJIU-SAN...!
WE'VE BEEN GIVEN SHELTER BY MEIJIU-SAN.
AFTER ALL THAT, WAYNE AND I SPLIT UP TO MAKE OUR GETAWAY...
...BUT THEN I FOUND MYSELF HELD UP BY A BUNCH OF ARMED CHINESE.
I ONLY GOT AWAY BECAUSE WAYNE SHOWED UP AND DREW THEIR ATTENTION.
...SO WHERE ARE WAYNE-KUN AND CLAUDIA NOW...?
CAPTURED, PROBABLY...
BUT YOUR ESCAPE MEANS THEY HAVE NO REASON TO KILL ANY HOSTAGES.
REPORTS OF THEIR BODIES WOULD SURELY HAVE REACHED MY EARS, YES.
IS THIS REALLY OKAY, THOUGH?

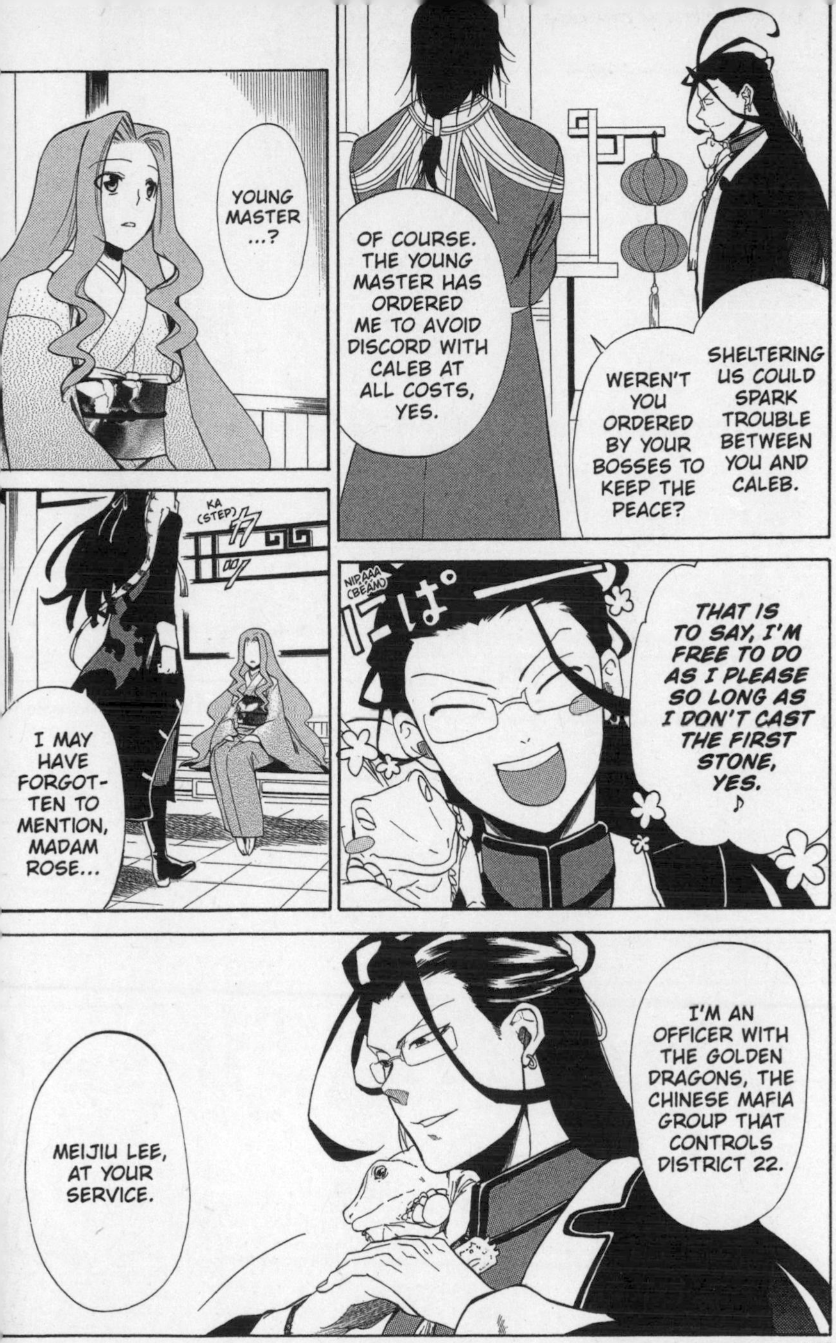
SHELTERING US COULD SPARK TROUBLE BETWEEN YOU AND CALEB.
WEREN'T YOU ORDERED BY YOUR BOSSES TO KEEP THE PEACE?
OF COURSE. THE YOUNG MASTER HAS ORDERED ME TO AVOID DISCORD WITH CALEB AT ALL COSTS, YES.
YOUNG MASTER ...?
NIPAAA (BEAM)
THAT IS TO SAY, I'M FREE TO DO AS I PLEASE SO LONG AS I DON'T CAST THE FIRST STONE, YES. ♪
KA (STEP)
I MAY HAVE FORGOT-TEN TO MENTION, MADAM ROSE...
I'M AN OFFICER WITH THE GOLDEN DRAGONS, THE CHINESE MAFIA GROUP THAT CONTROLS DISTRICT 22.
MEIJIU LEE, AT YOUR SERVICE.

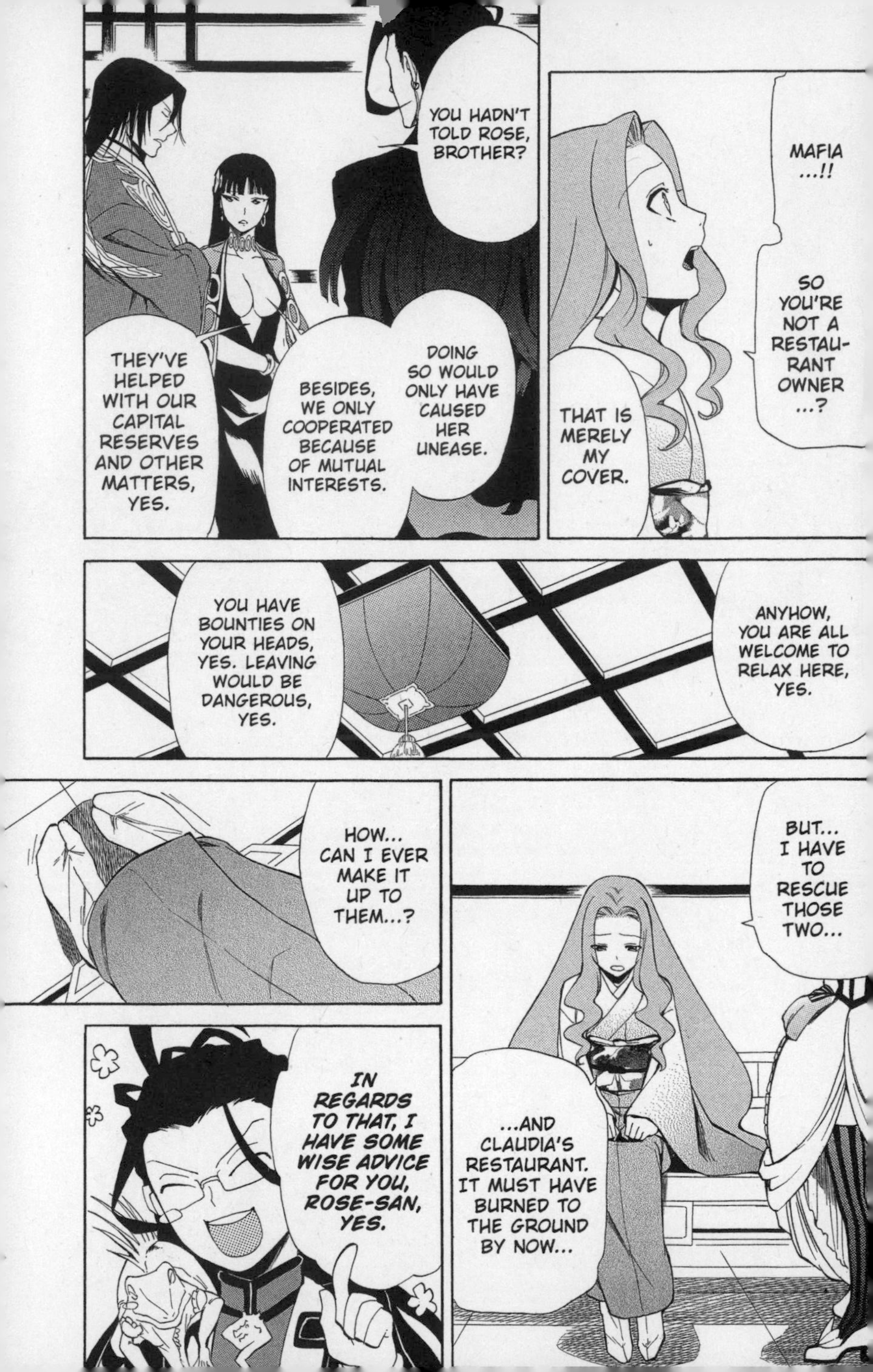
MAFIA ...!!
SO YOU'RE NOT A RESTAURANT OWNER ...?
THAT IS MERELY MY COVER.
YOU HADN'T TOLD ROSE, BROTHER?
DOING SO WOULD ONLY HAVE CAUSED HER UNEASE.
BESIDES, WE ONLY COOPERATED BECAUSE OF MUTUAL INTERESTS.
THEY'VE HELPED WITH OUR CAPITAL RESERVES AND OTHER MATTERS, YES.
ANYHOW, YOU ARE ALL WELCOME TO RELAX HERE, YES.
YOU HAVE BOUNTIES ON YOUR HEADS, YES. LEAVING WOULD BE DANGEROUS, YES.
BUT... I HAVE TO RESCUE THOSE TWO...
...AND CLAUDIA'S RESTAURANT. IT MUST HAVE BURNED TO THE GROUND BY NOW...
HOW... CAN I EVER MAKE IT UP TO THEM...?
IN REGARDS TO THAT, I HAVE SOME WISE ADVICE FOR YOU, ROSE-SAN, YES.

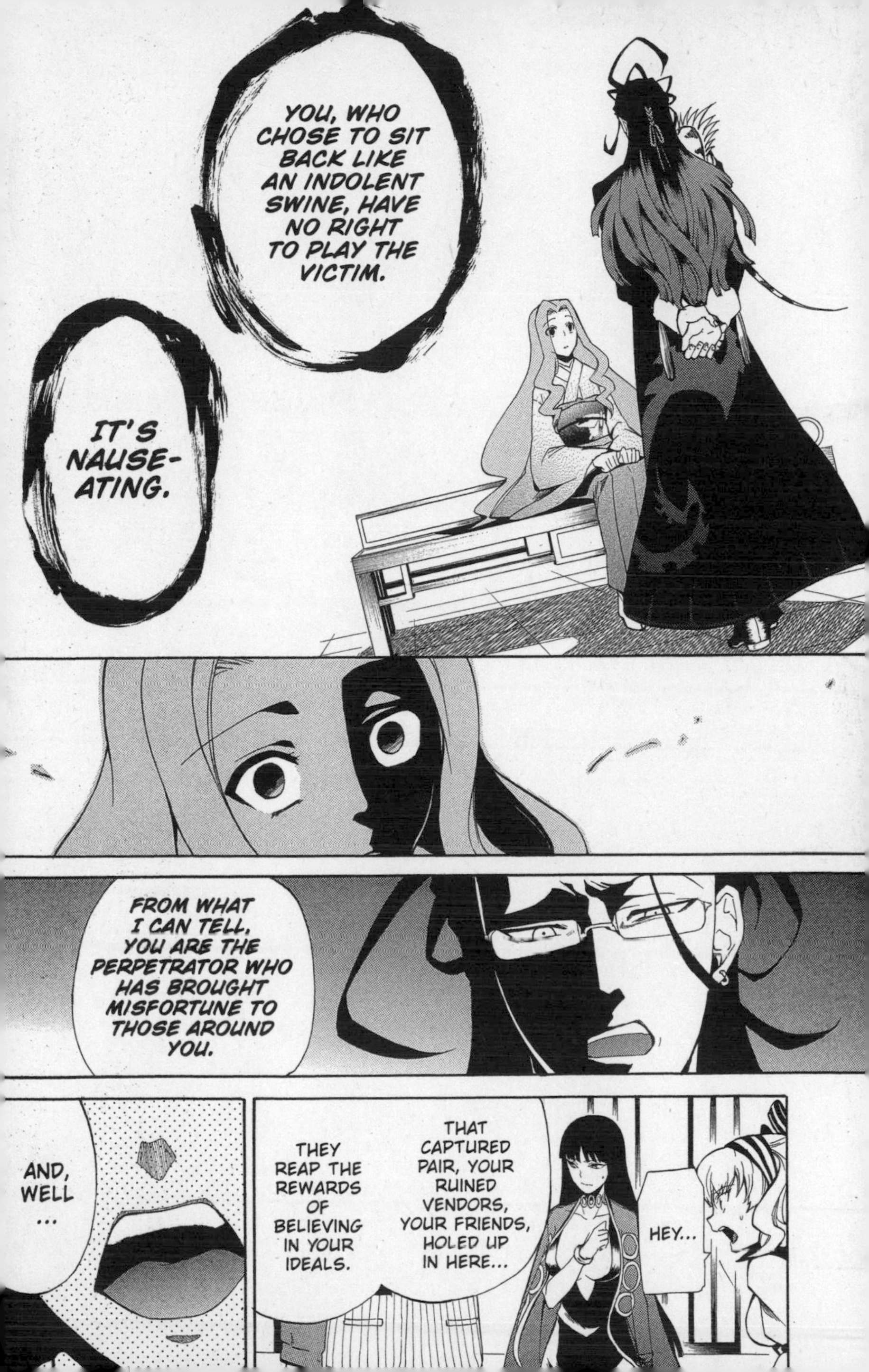
YOU, WHO CHOSE TO SIT BACK LIKE AN INDOLENT SWINE, HAVE NO RIGHT TO PLAY THE VICTIM.
IT'S NAUSE-ATING.
FROM WHAT I CAN TELL, YOU ARE THE PERPETRATOR WHO HAS BROUGHT MISFORTUNE TO THOSE AROUND YOU.
HEY...
THAT CAPTURED PAIR, YOUR RUINED VENDORS, YOUR FRIENDS, HOLED UP IN HERE...
THEY REAP THE REWARDS OF BELIEVING IN YOUR IDEALS.
AND, WELL ...

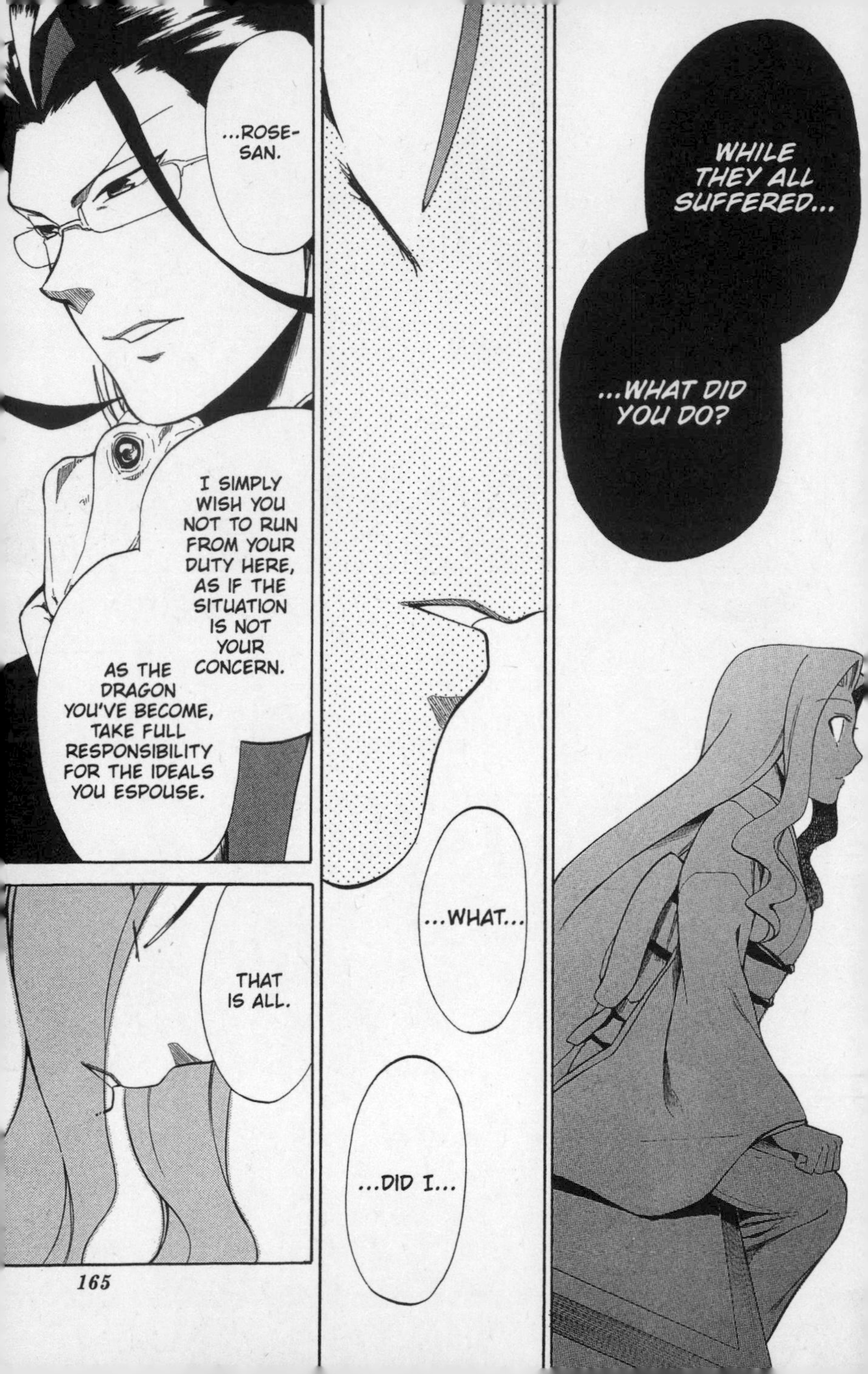
WHILE THEY ALL SUFFERED...
...WHAT DID YOU DO?
...WHAT...
...DID I...
...ROSE-SAN.
I SIMPLY WISH YOU NOT TO RUN FROM YOUR DUTY HERE, AS IF THE SITUATION IS NOT YOUR CONCERN.
AS THE DRAGON YOU'VE BECOME, TAKE FULL RESPONSIBILITY FOR THE IDEALS YOU ESPOUSE.
THAT IS ALL.

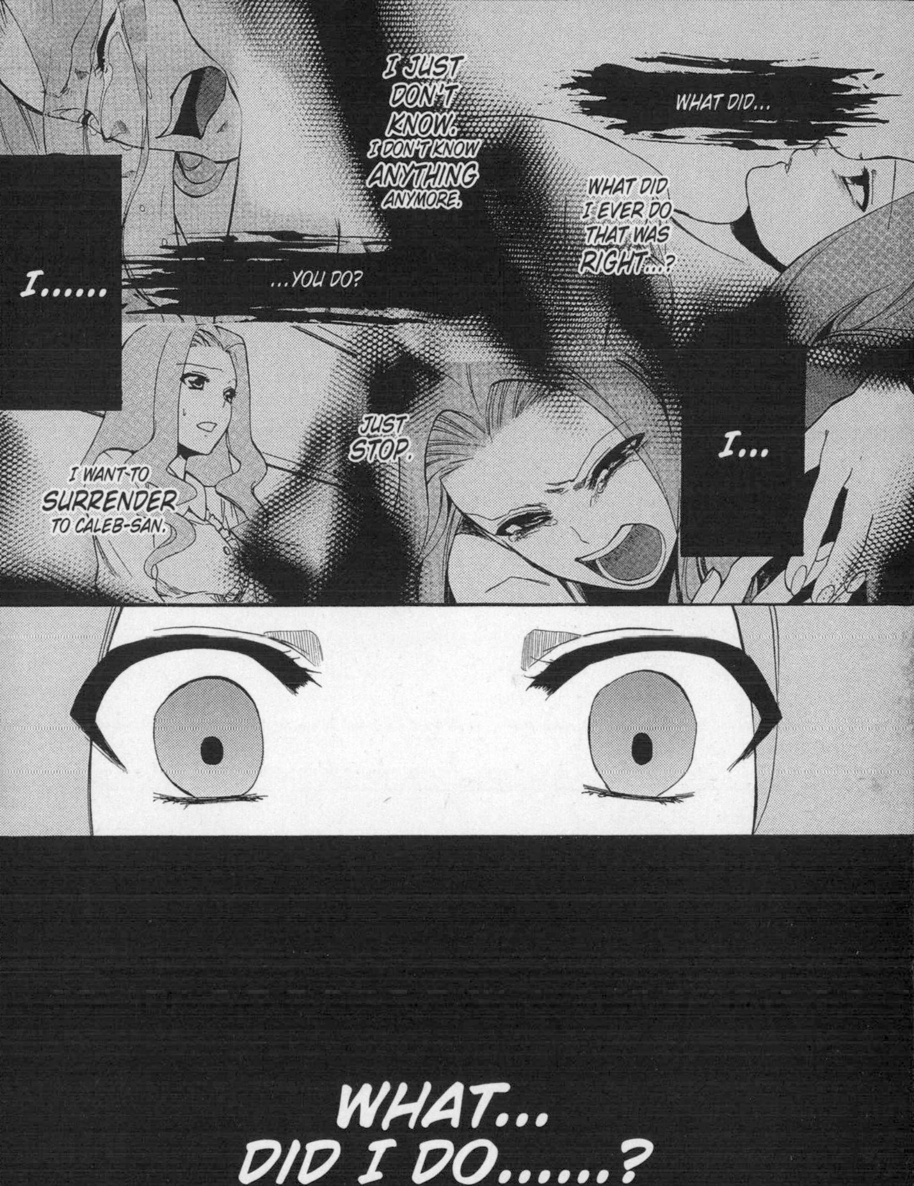
WHAT DID...
WHAT DID I EVER DO THAT WAS RIGHT...?
I JUST DON'T KNOW. I DON'T KNOW ANYTHING ANYMORE.
...YOU DO?
I......
I...
JUST STOP.
I WANT TO SURRENDER TO CALEB-SAN.
WHAT... DID I DO......?

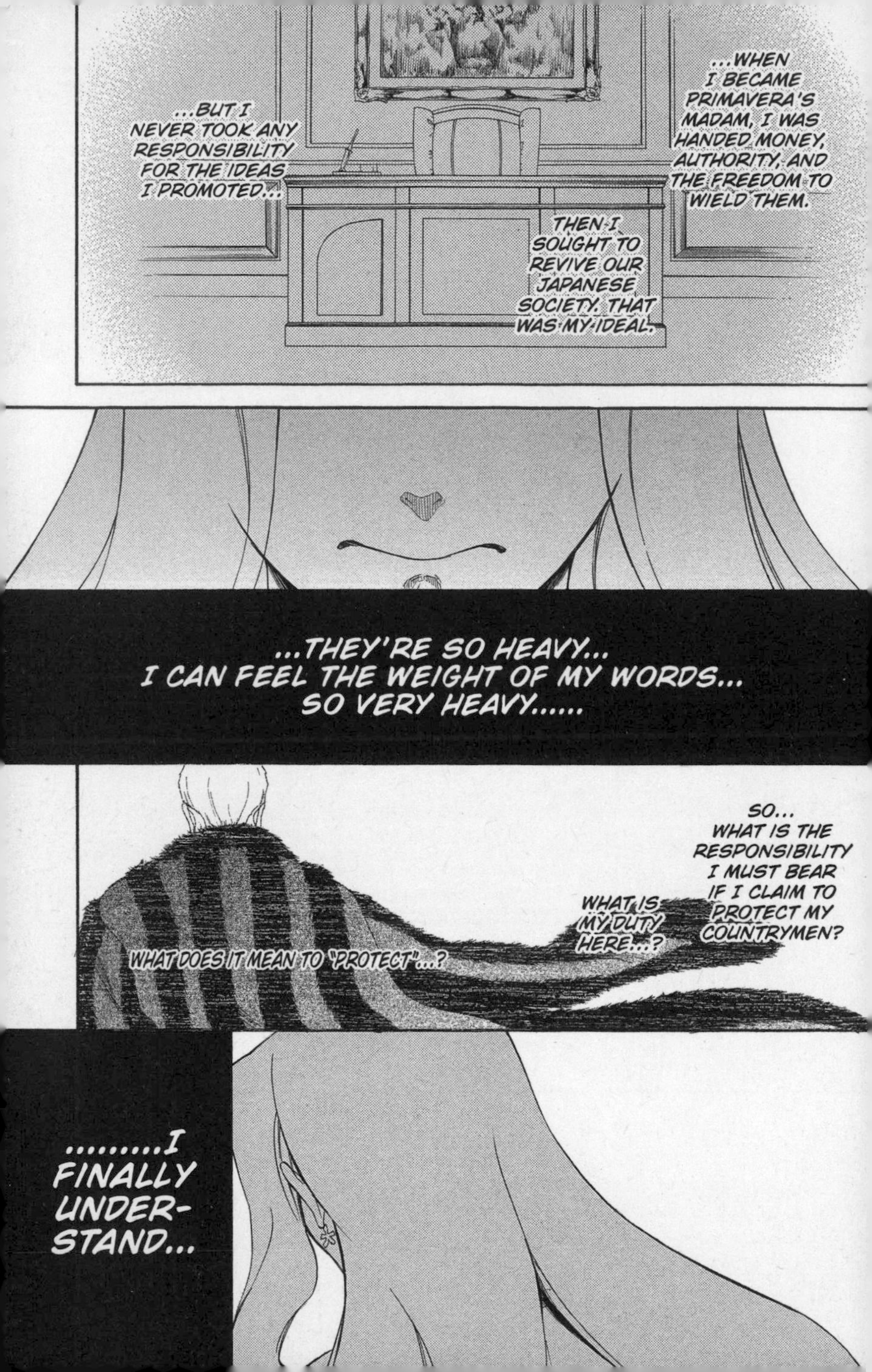
...WHEN I BECAME PRIMAVERA'S MADAM, I WAS HANDED MONEY, AUTHORITY, AND THE FREEDOM TO WIELD THEM.
THEN I SOUGHT TO REVIVE OUR JAPANESE SOCIETY. THAT WAS MY IDEAL.
...BUT I NEVER TOOK ANY RESPONSIBILITY FOR THE IDEAS I PROMOTED...
...THEY'RE SO HEAVY... I CAN FEEL THE WEIGHT OF MY WORDS... SO VERY HEAVY......
SO... WHAT IS THE RESPONSIBILITY I MUST BEAR IF I CLAIM TO PROTECT MY COUNTRYMEN?
WHAT IS MY DUTY HERE...?
WHAT DOES IT MEAN TO "PROTECT"...?
.........I FINALLY UNDER-STAND...

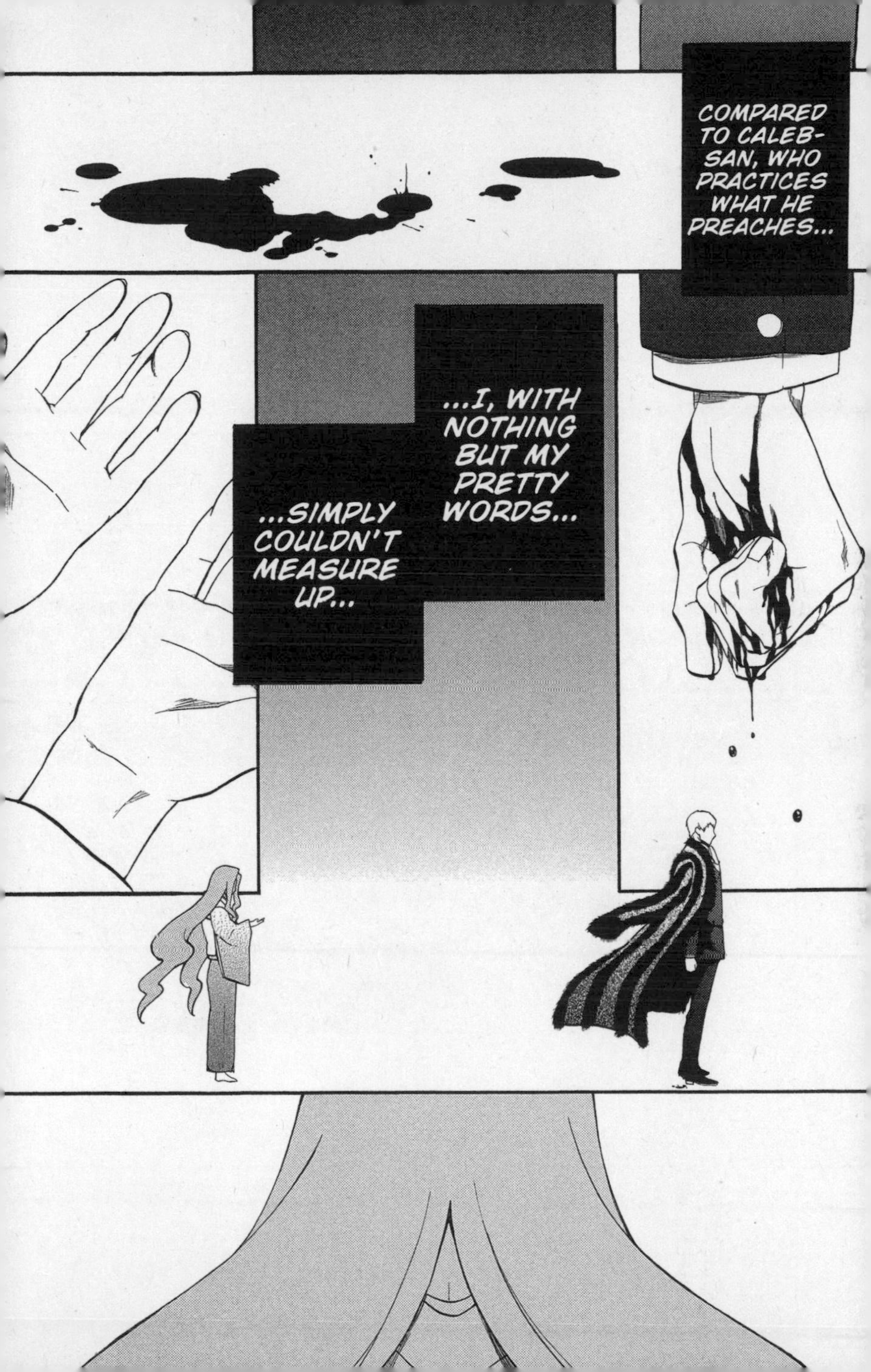
COMPARED TO CALEB-SAN, WHO PRACTICES WHAT HE PREACHES...
...I, WITH NOTHING BUT MY PRETTY WORDS...
...SIMPLY COULDN'T MEASURE UP...

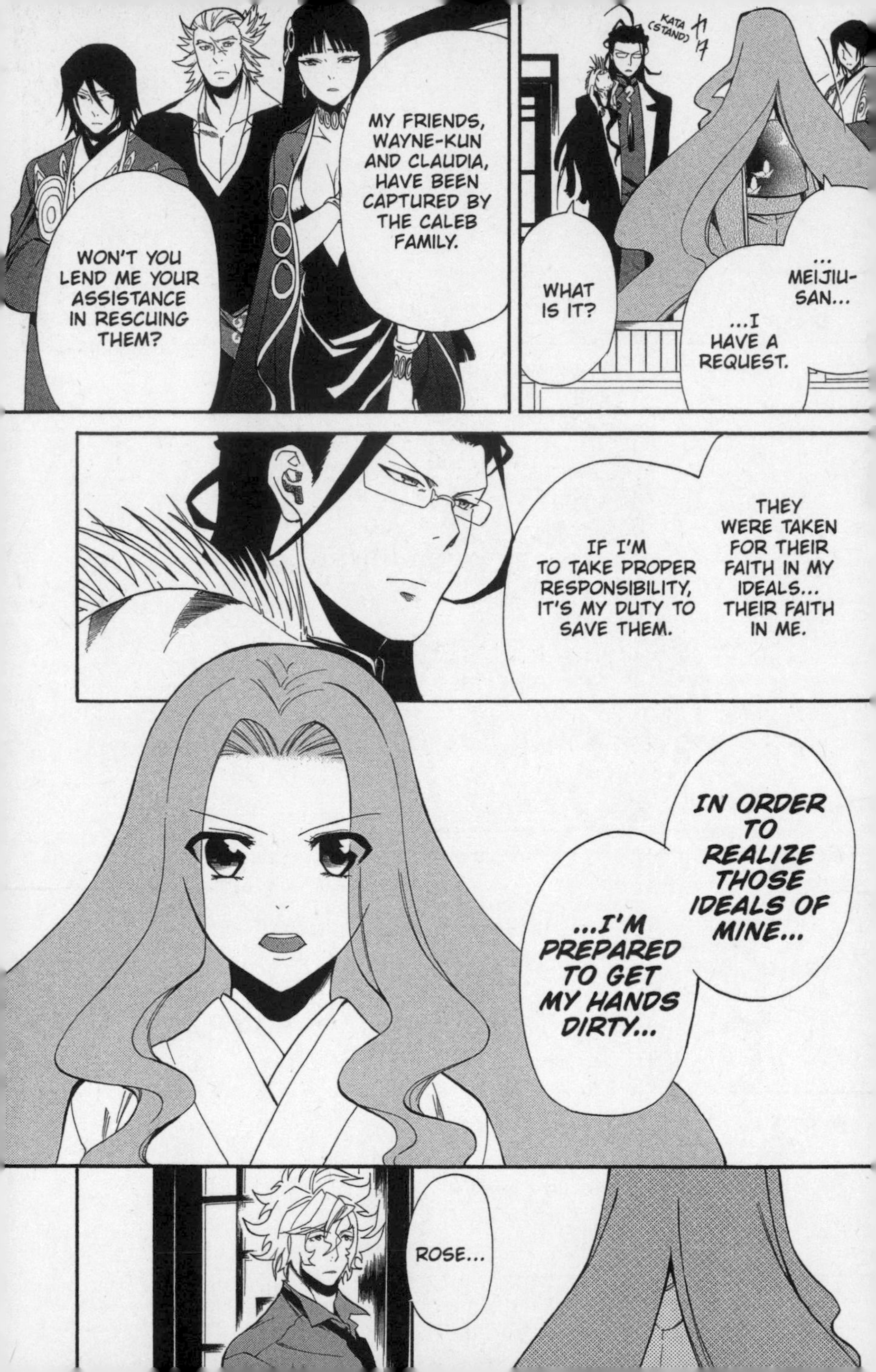
KATA (STAND)
...MEIJIU-SAN...
...I HAVE A REQUEST.
WHAT IS IT?
MY FRIENDS, WAYNE-KUN AND CLAUDIA, HAVE BEEN CAPTURED BY THE CALEB FAMILY.
WON'T YOU LEND ME YOUR ASSISTANCE IN RESCUING THEM?
THEY WERE TAKEN FOR THEIR FAITH IN MY IDEALS... THEIR FAITH IN ME.
IF I'M TO TAKE PROPER RESPONSIBILITY, IT'S MY DUTY TO SAVE THEM.
IN ORDER TO REALIZE THOSE IDEALS OF MINE...
...I'M PREPARED TO GET MY HANDS DIRTY...
ROSE...

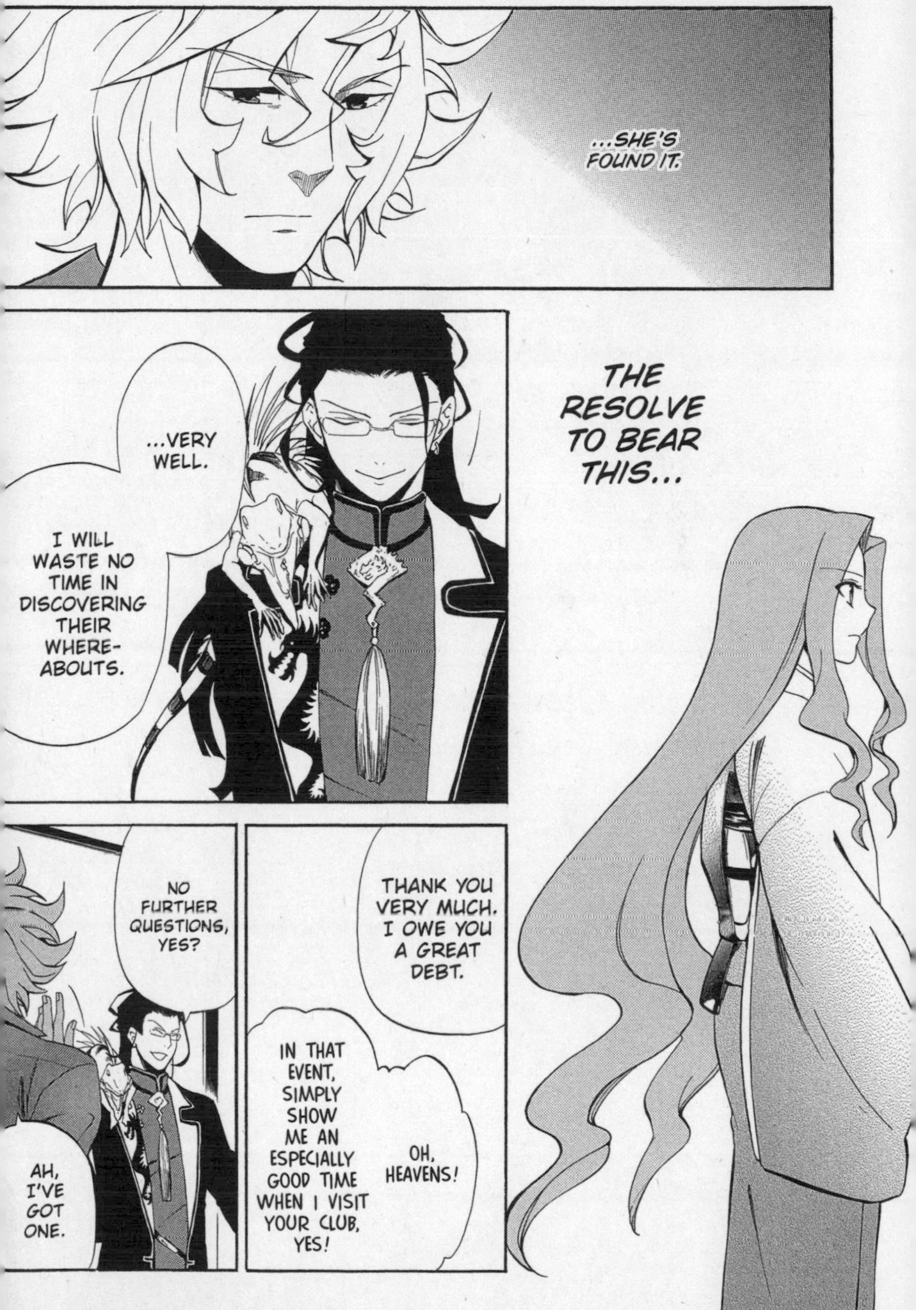
...SHE'S FOUND IT.
THE RESOLVE TO BEAR THIS...
...VERY WELL.
I WILL WASTE NO TIME IN DISCOVERING THEIR WHERE-ABOUTS.
THANK YOU VERY MUCH. I OWE YOU A GREAT DEBT.
OH, HEAVENS!
IN THAT EVENT, SIMPLY SHOW ME AN ESPECIALLY GOOD TIME WHEN I VISIT YOUR CLUB, YES!
NO FURTHER QUESTIONS, YES?
AH, I'VE GOT ONE.

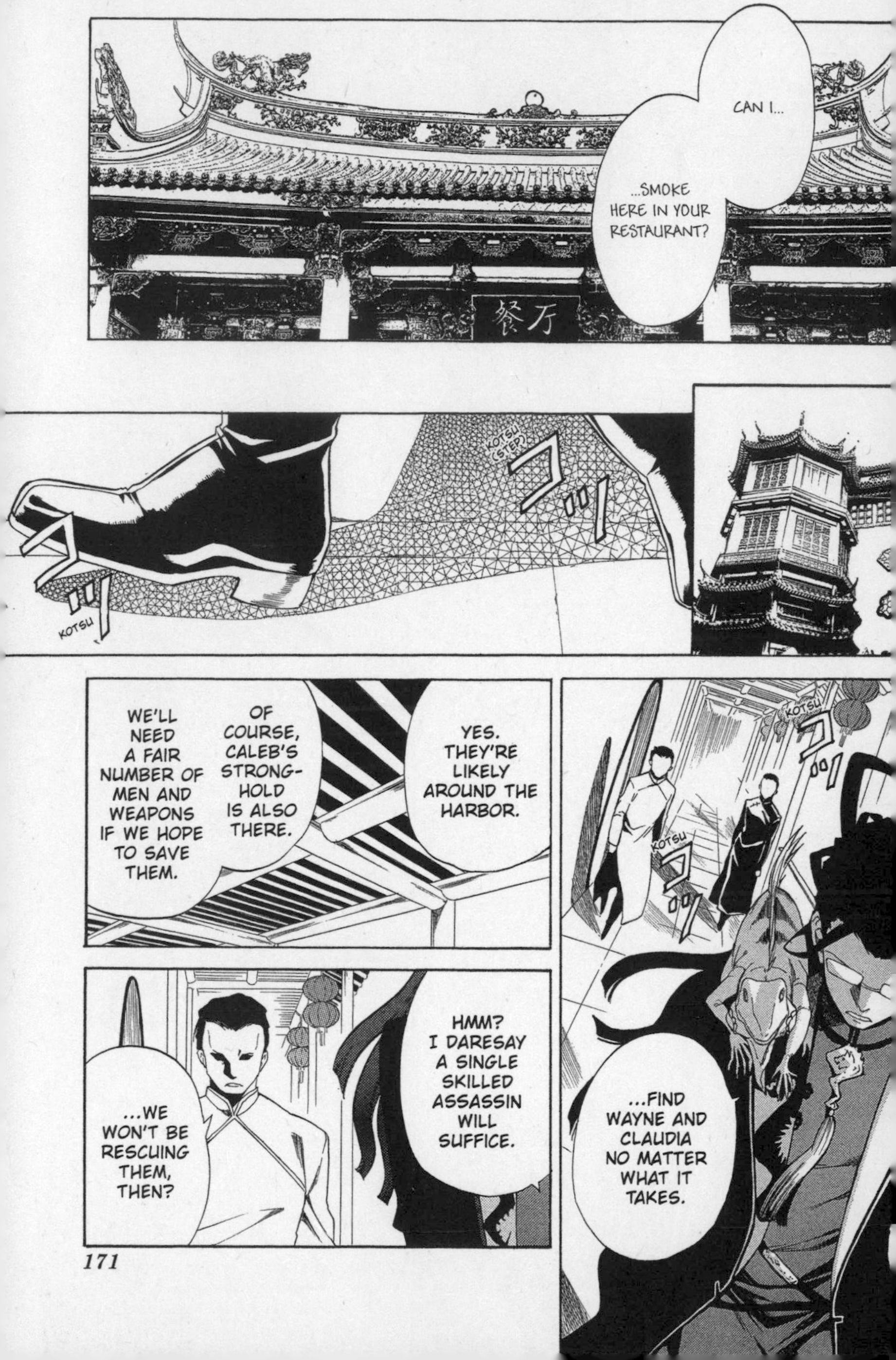
CAN I...
...SMOKE HERE IN YOUR RESTAURANT?
KOTSU (STEP)
KOTSU
KOTSU
KOTSU
...FIND WAYNE AND CLAUDIA NO MATTER WHAT IT TAKES.
YES. THEY'RE LIKELY AROUND THE HARBOR.
OF COURSE, CALEB'S STRONG-HOLD IS ALSO THERE.
WE'LL NEED A FAIR NUMBER OF MEN AND WEAPONS IF WE HOPE TO SAVE THEM.
HMM? I DARESAY A SINGLE SKILLED ASSASSIN WILL SUFFICE.
...WE WON'T BE RESCUING THEM, THEN?

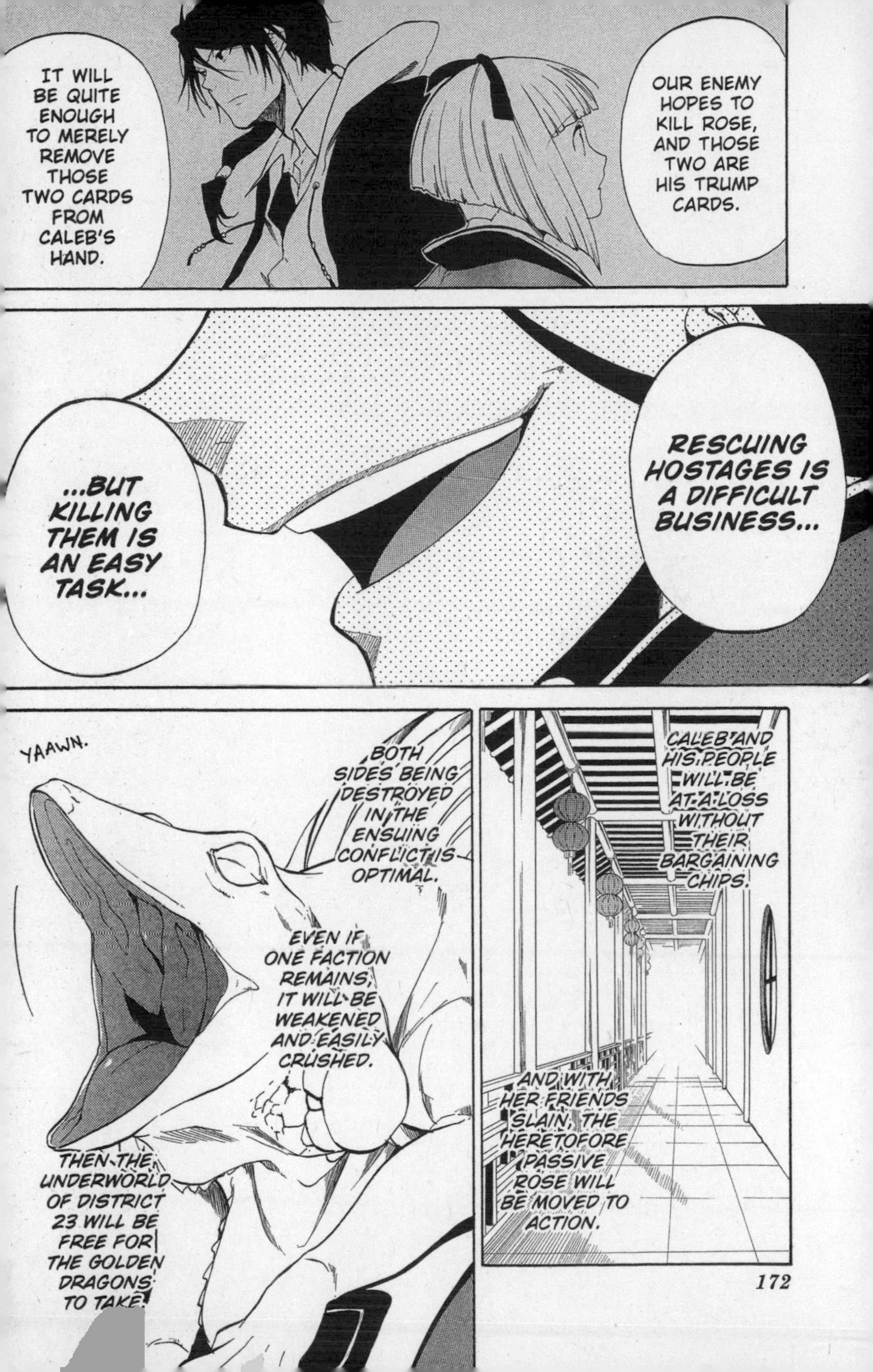
OUR ENEMY HOPES TO KILL ROSE, AND THOSE TWO ARE HIS TRUMP CARDS.
IT WILL BE QUITE ENOUGH TO MERELY REMOVE THOSE TWO CARDS FROM CALEB'S HAND.
RESCUING HOSTAGES IS A DIFFICULT BUSINESS...
...BUT KILLING THEM IS AN EASY TASK...
CALEB AND HIS PEOPLE WILL BE AT A LOSS WITHOUT THEIR BARGAINING CHIPS.
AND WITH HER FRIENDS SLAIN, THE HERETOFORE PASSIVE ROSE WILL BE MOVED TO ACTION.
BOTH SIDES BEING DESTROYED IN THE ENSUING CONFLICT IS OPTIMAL.
YAAWN.
EVEN IF ONE FACTION REMAINS, IT WILL BE WEAKENED AND EASILY CRUSHED.
THEN THE UNDERWORLD OF DISTRICT 23 WILL BE FREE FOR THE GOLDEN DRAGONS TO TAKE.

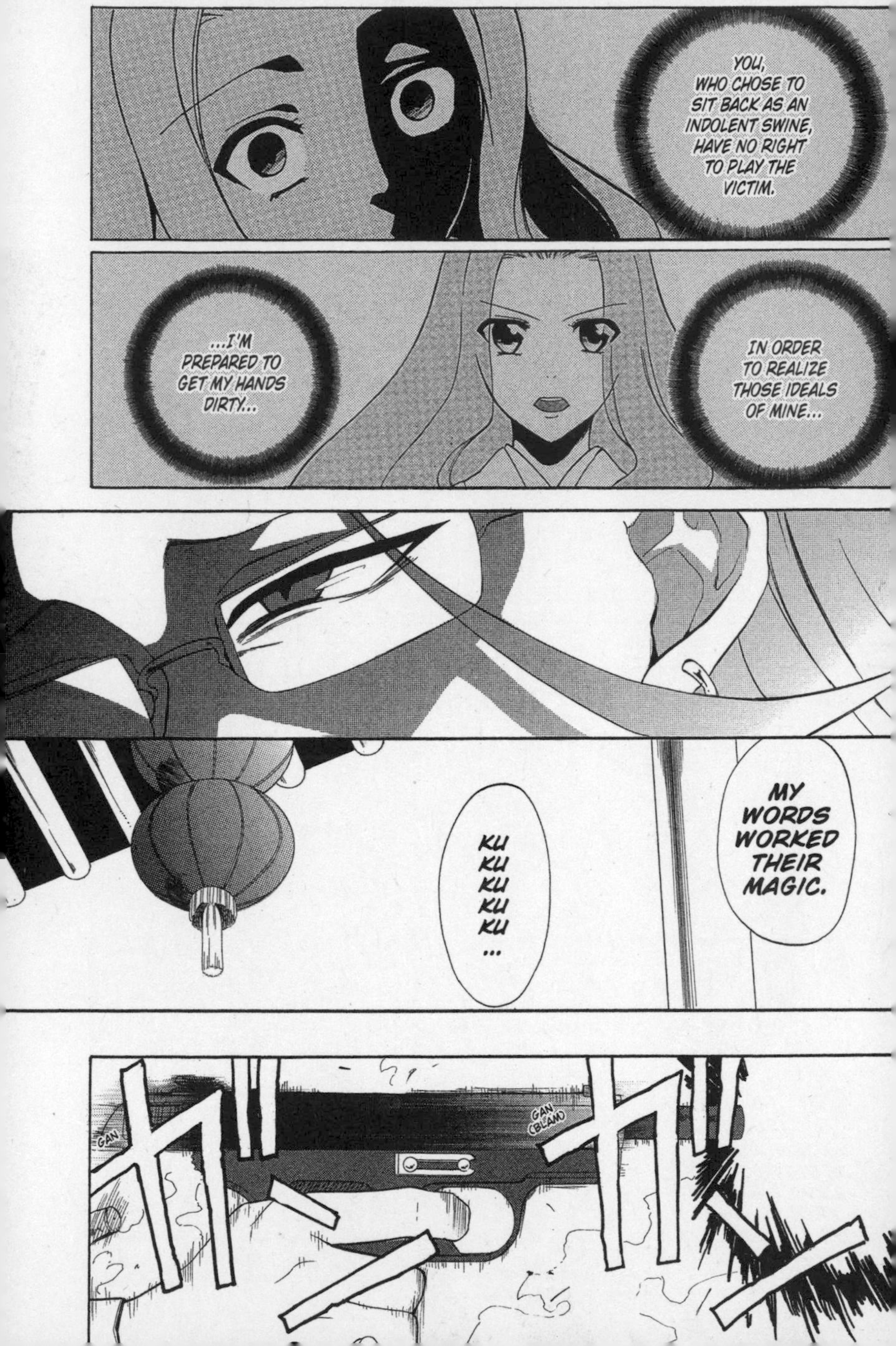
YOU, WHO CHOSE TO SIT BACK AS AN INDOLENT SWINE, HAVE NO RIGHT TO PLAY THE VICTIM.
IN ORDER TO REALIZE THOSE IDEALS OF MINE...
...I'M PREPARED TO GET MY HANDS DIRTY...
MY WORDS WORKED THEIR MAGIC.
KU KU KU KU KU...
GAN (BLAM)
GAN

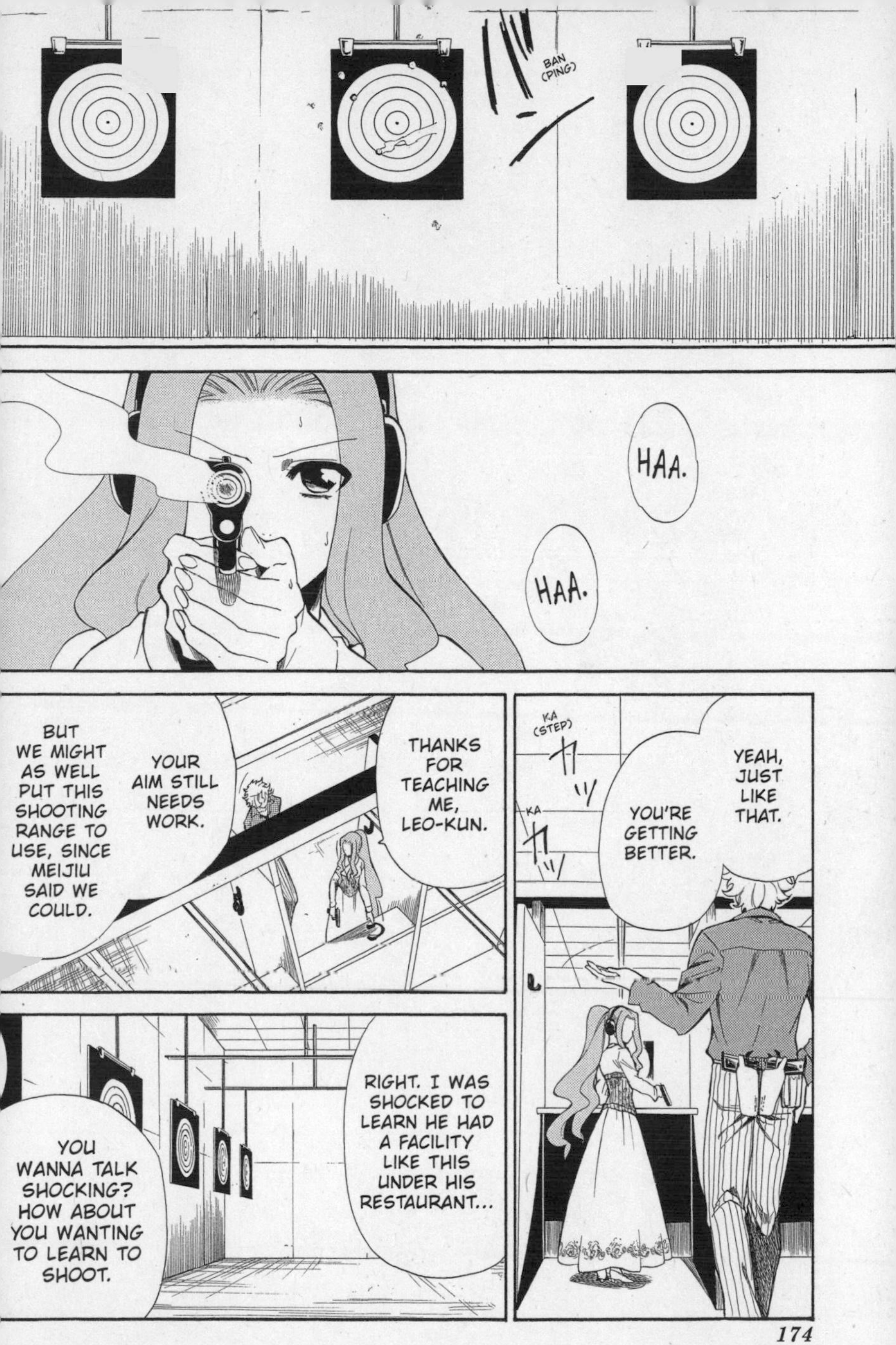
BAN (PING)
HAA.
HAA.
KA (STEP)
KA
YEAH, JUST LIKE THAT.
YOU'RE GETTING BETTER.
THANKS FOR TEACHING ME, LEO-KUN.
YOUR AIM STILL NEEDS WORK.
BUT WE MIGHT AS WELL PUT THIS SHOOTING RANGE TO USE, SINCE MEIJIU SAID WE COULD.
RIGHT. I WAS SHOCKED TO LEARN HE HAD A FACILITY LIKE THIS UNDER HIS RESTAURANT...
YOU WANNA TALK SHOCKING? HOW ABOUT YOU WANTING TO LEARN TO SHOOT.

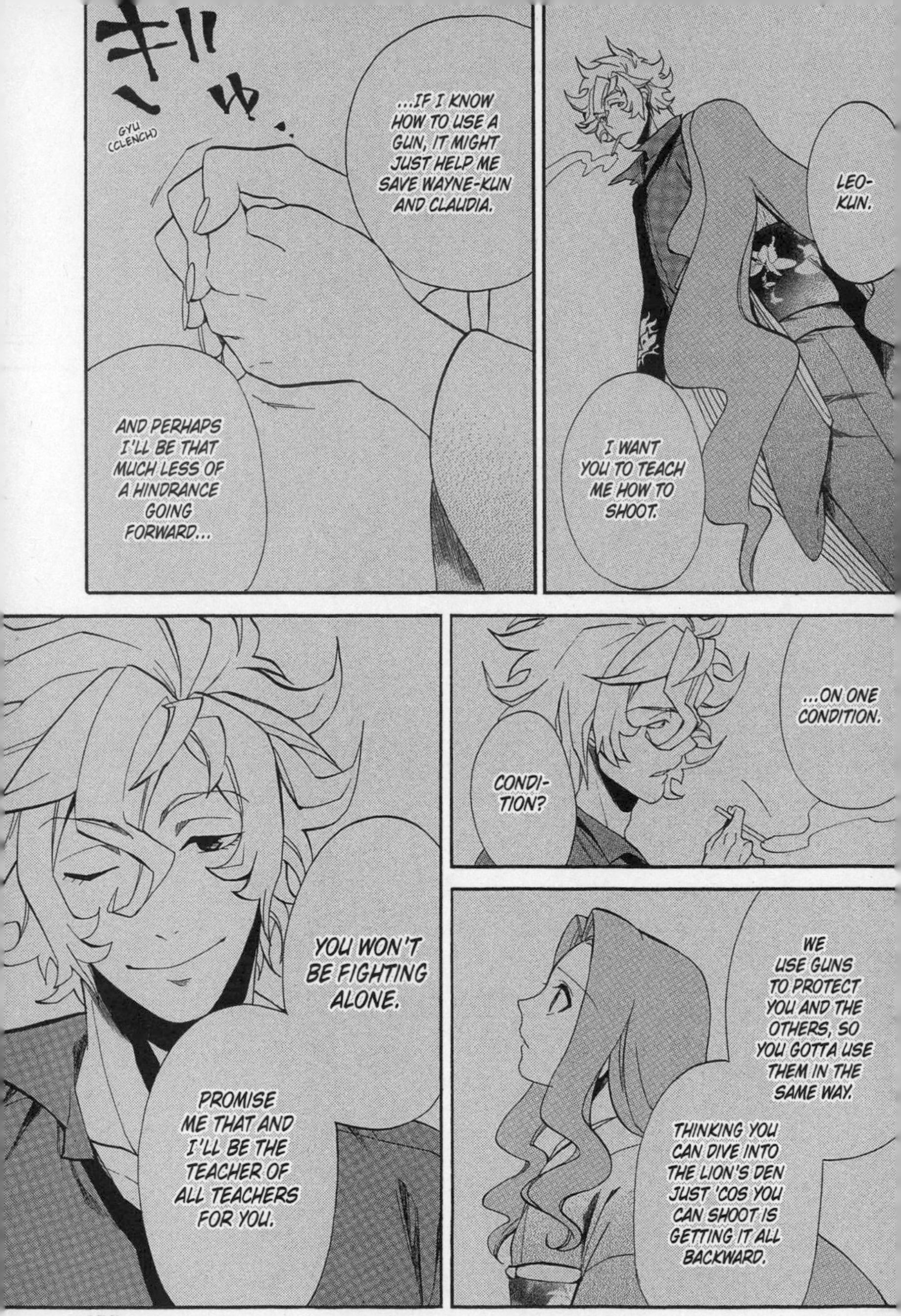
LEO-KUN.
I WANT YOU TO TEACH ME HOW TO SHOOT.
...IF I KNOW HOW TO USE A GUN, IT MIGHT JUST HELP ME SAVE WAYNE-KUN AND CLAUDIA.
キュ
GYU (CLENCH)
AND PERHAPS I'LL BE THAT MUCH LESS OF A HINDRANCE GOING FORWARD...
...ON ONE CONDITION.
CONDI-TION?
WE USE GUNS TO PROTECT YOU AND THE OTHERS, SO YOU GOTTA USE THEM IN THE SAME WAY.
THINKING YOU CAN DIVE INTO THE LION'S DEN JUST 'COS YOU CAN SHOOT IS GETTING IT ALL BACKWARD.
YOU WON'T BE FIGHTING ALONE.
PROMISE ME THAT AND I'LL BE THE TEACHER OF ALL TEACHERS FOR YOU.

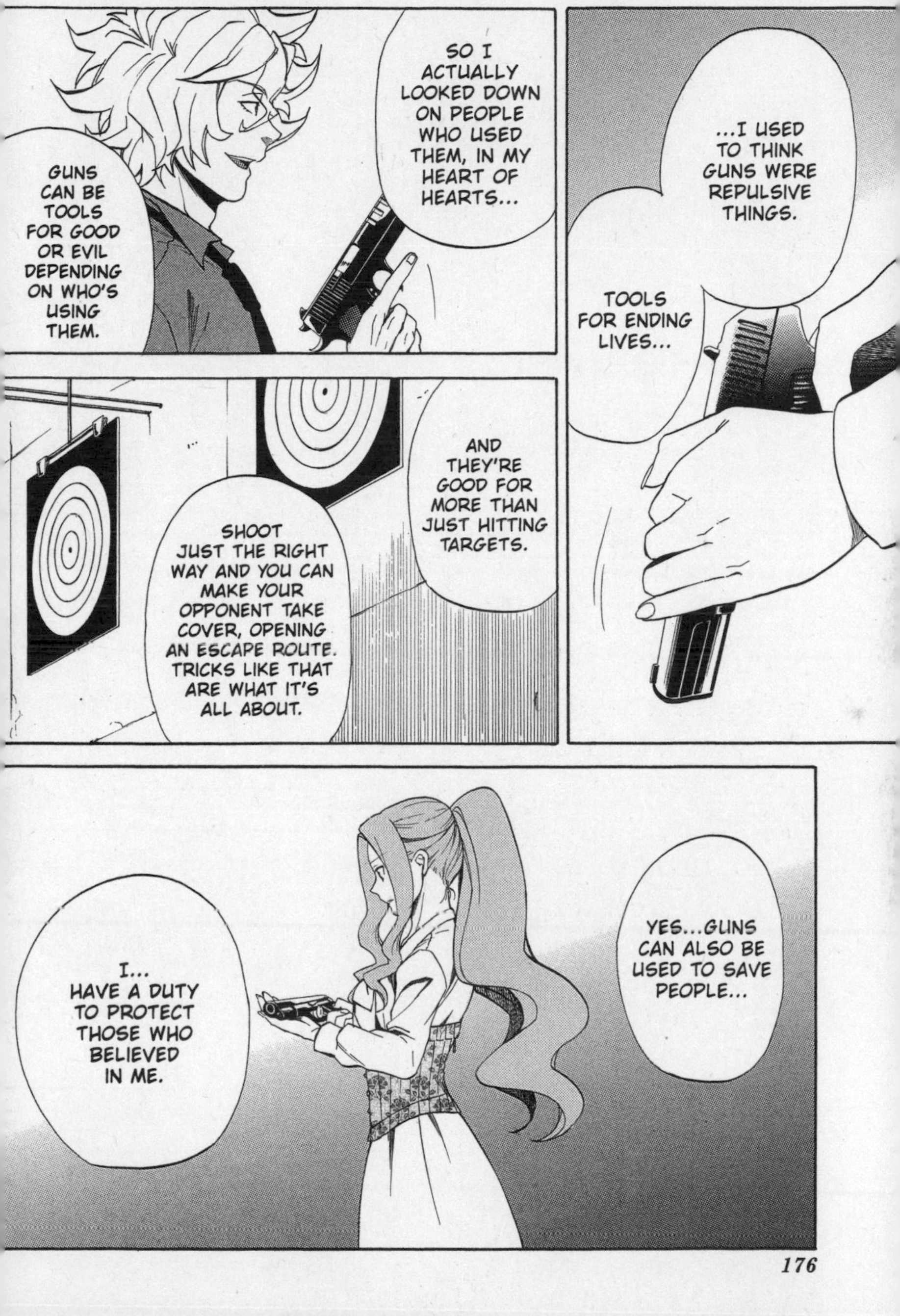
...I USED TO THINK GUNS WERE REPULSIVE THINGS.
TOOLS FOR ENDING LIVES...
SO I ACTUALLY LOOKED DOWN ON PEOPLE WHO USED THEM, IN MY HEART OF HEARTS...
GUNS CAN BE TOOLS FOR GOOD OR EVIL DEPENDING ON WHO'S USING THEM.
AND THEY'RE GOOD FOR MORE THAN JUST HITTING TARGETS.
...
SHOOT JUST THE RIGHT WAY AND YOU CAN MAKE YOUR OPPONENT TAKE COVER, OPENING AN ESCAPE ROUTE. TRICKS LIKE THAT ARE WHAT IT'S ALL ABOUT.
YES...GUNS CAN ALSO BE USED TO SAVE PEOPLE...
I... HAVE A DUTY TO PROTECT THOSE WHO BELIEVED IN ME.

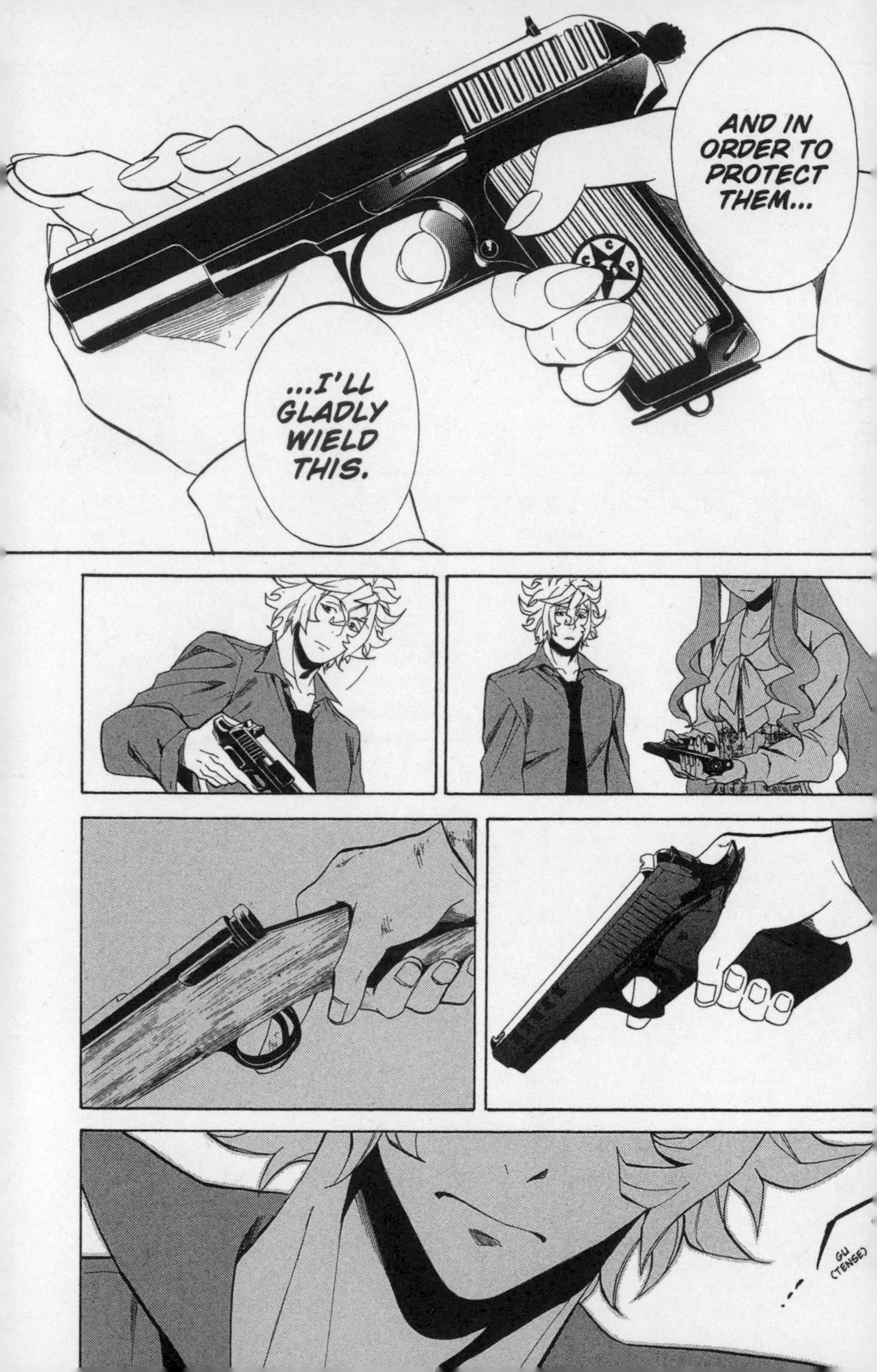
AND IN ORDER TO PROTECT THEM...
...I'LL GLADLY WIELD THIS.
GU (TENSE)

KATA
(GRAB)

...LEO-
KUN?

YOU'RE
A GOOD
GIRL,
ROSE.

IF ONLY...
I WERE AS
STRONG
AS YOU OR
CALEB...

HUH?

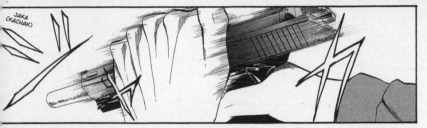

JAKA
(KACHAK)

...DURING
THE WAR,
I WAS AN
INSTRUCTOR
FOR NEW
RECRUITS
DOWN
SOUTH.

BAN
(BANG)

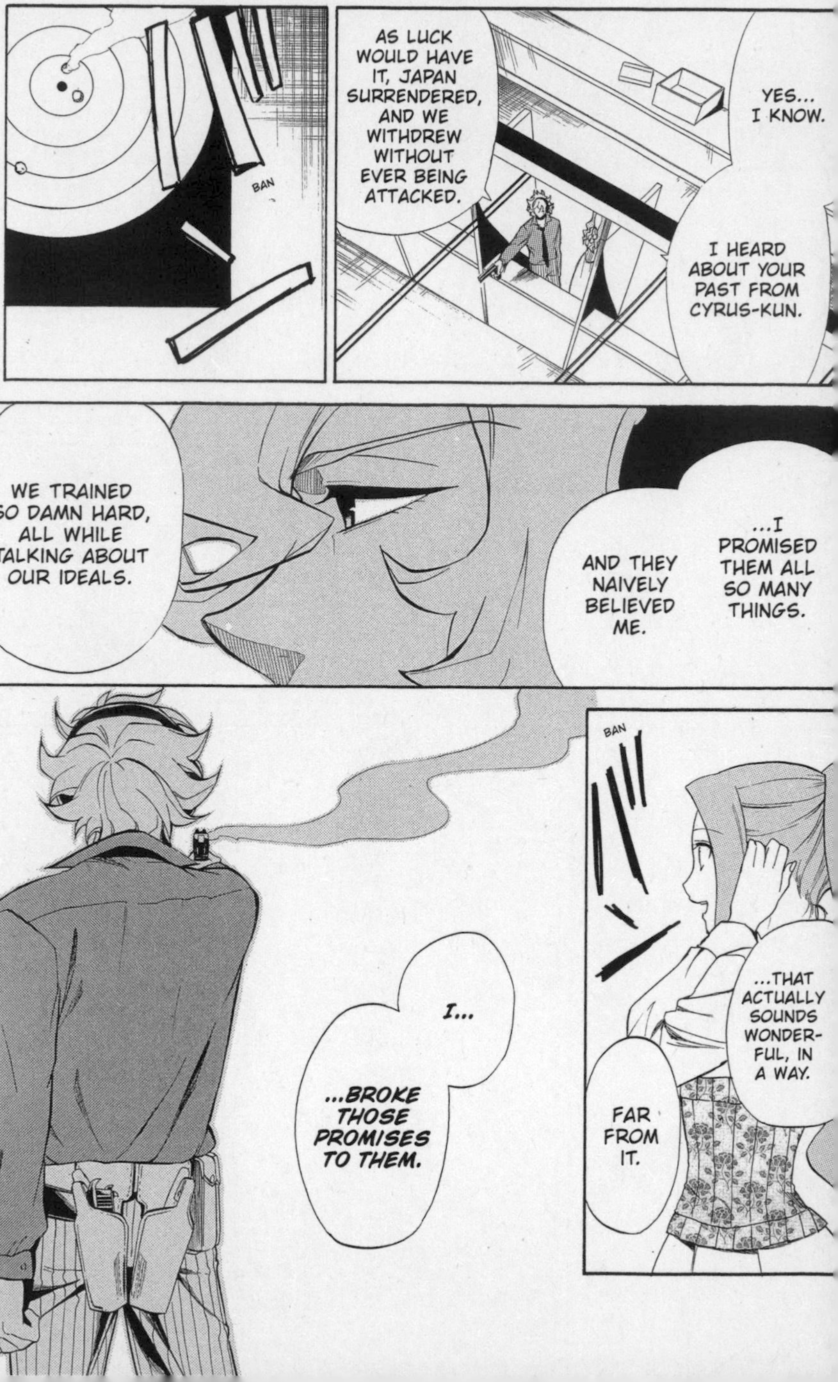
AS LUCK WOULD HAVE IT, JAPAN SURRENDERED, AND WE WITHDREW WITHOUT EVER BEING ATTACKED.
YES... I KNOW.
I HEARD ABOUT YOUR PAST FROM CYRUS-KUN.
BAN
...I PROMISED THEM ALL SO MANY THINGS.
AND THEY NAIVELY BELIEVED ME.
WE TRAINED SO DAMN HARD, ALL WHILE TALKING ABOUT OUR IDEALS.
BAN
...THAT ACTUALLY SOUNDS WONDER-FUL, IN A WAY.
FAR FROM IT.
I...
...BROKE THOSE PROMISES TO THEM.

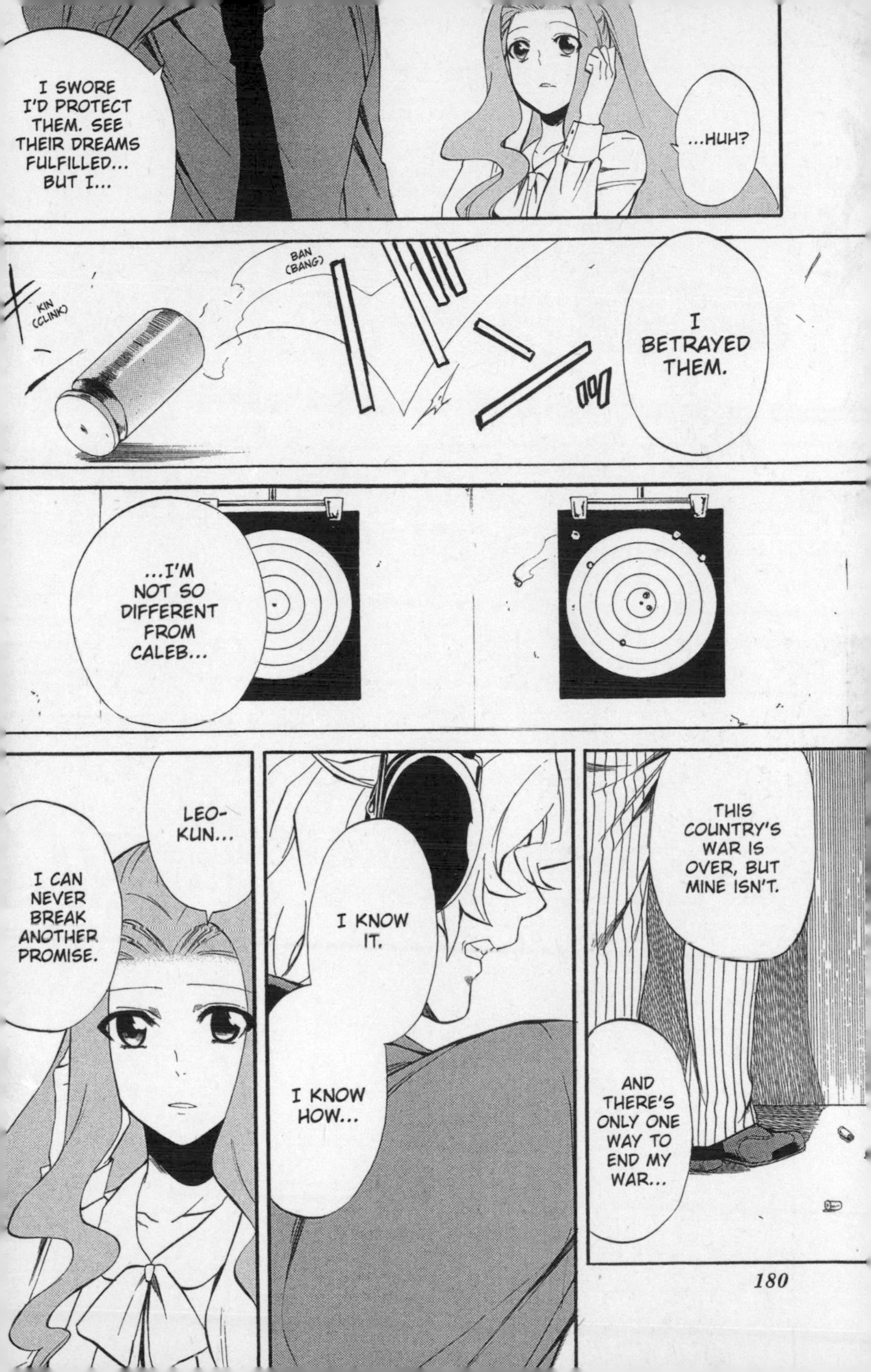
I SWORE I'D PROTECT THEM. SEE THEIR DREAMS FULFILLED... BUT I...
...HUH?
I BETRAYED THEM.
BAN (BANG)
KIN (CLINK)
...I'M NOT SO DIFFERENT FROM CALEB...
THIS COUNTRY'S WAR IS OVER, BUT MINE ISN'T.
AND THERE'S ONLY ONE WAY TO END MY WAR...
I KNOW IT.
I KNOW HOW...
LEO-KUN...
I CAN NEVER BREAK ANOTHER PROMISE.

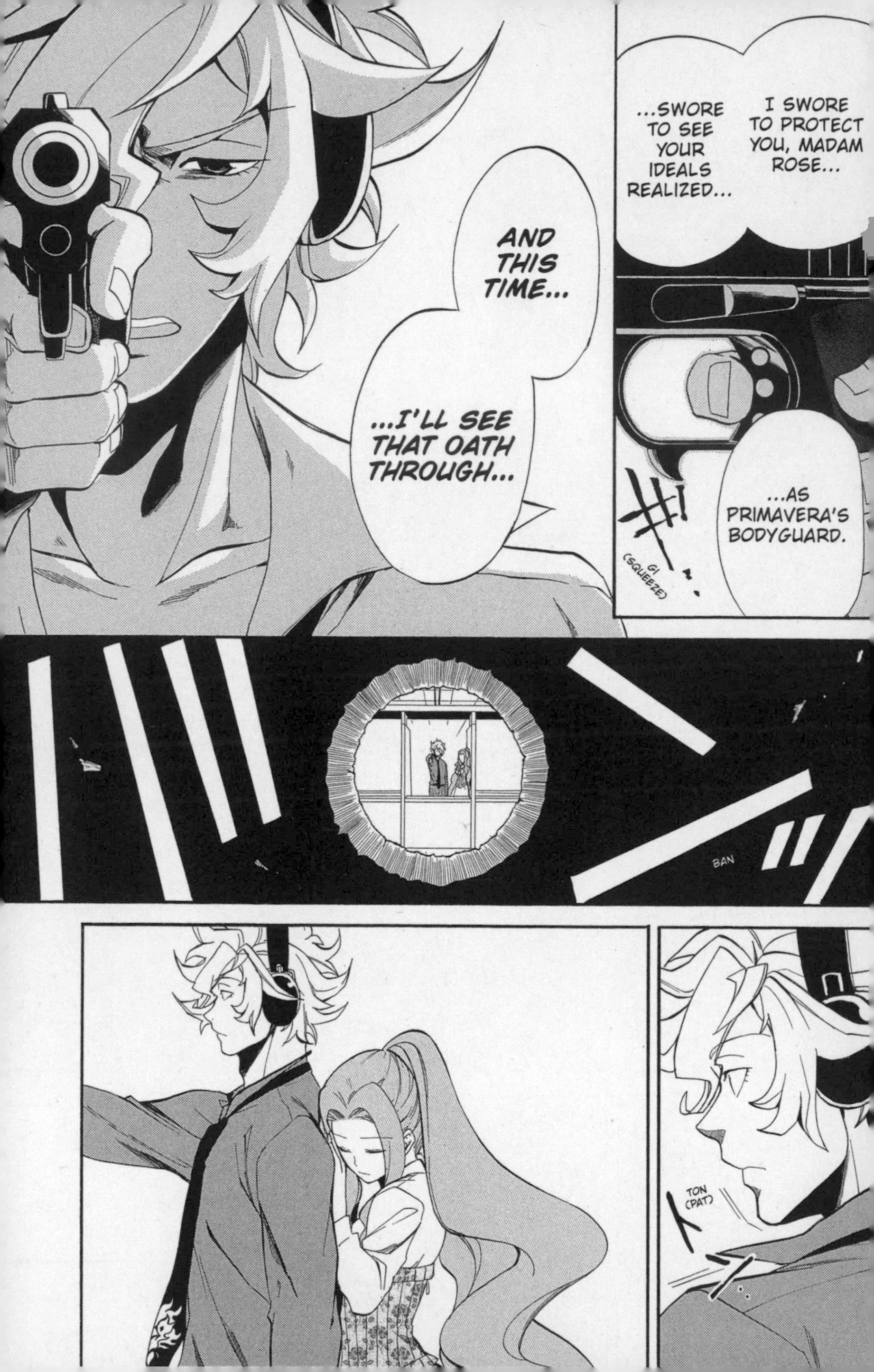
I SWORE TO PROTECT YOU, MADAM ROSE...
...SWORE TO SEE YOUR IDEALS REALIZED...
...AS PRIMAVERA'S BODYGUARD.
GI (SQUEEZE)
AND THIS TIME...
...I'LL SEE THAT OATH THROUGH...
BAN
TON (PAT)

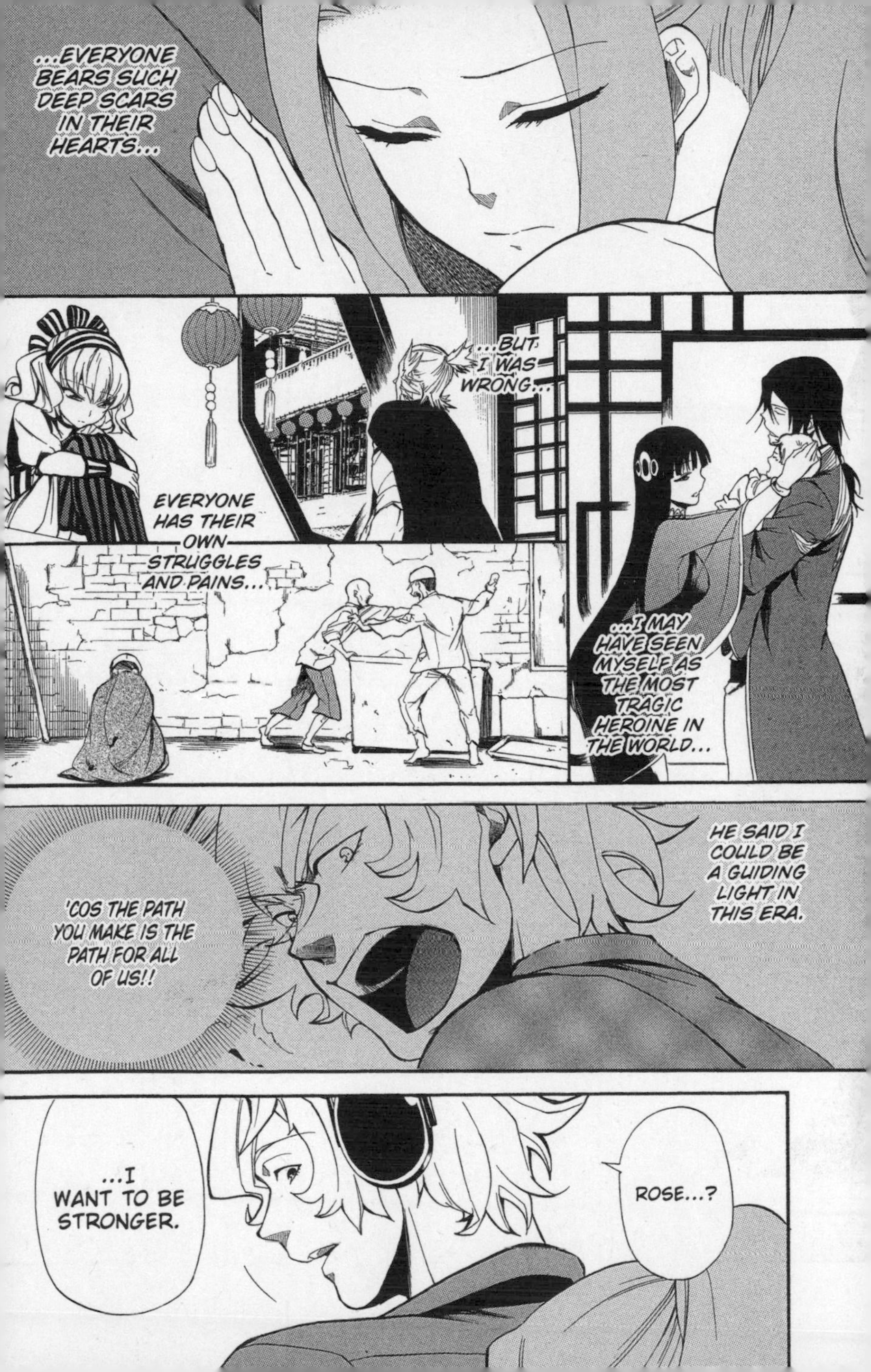
...EVERYONE BEARS SUCH DEEP SCARS IN THEIR HEARTS...
...I MAY HAVE SEEN MYSELF AS THE MOST TRAGIC HEROINE IN THE WORLD...
...BUT I WAS WRONG...
EVERYONE HAS THEIR OWN STRUGGLES AND PAINS...
HE SAID I COULD BE A GUIDING LIGHT IN THIS ERA.
'COS THE PATH YOU MAKE IS THE PATH FOR ALL OF US!!
ROSE...?
...I WANT TO BE STRONGER.

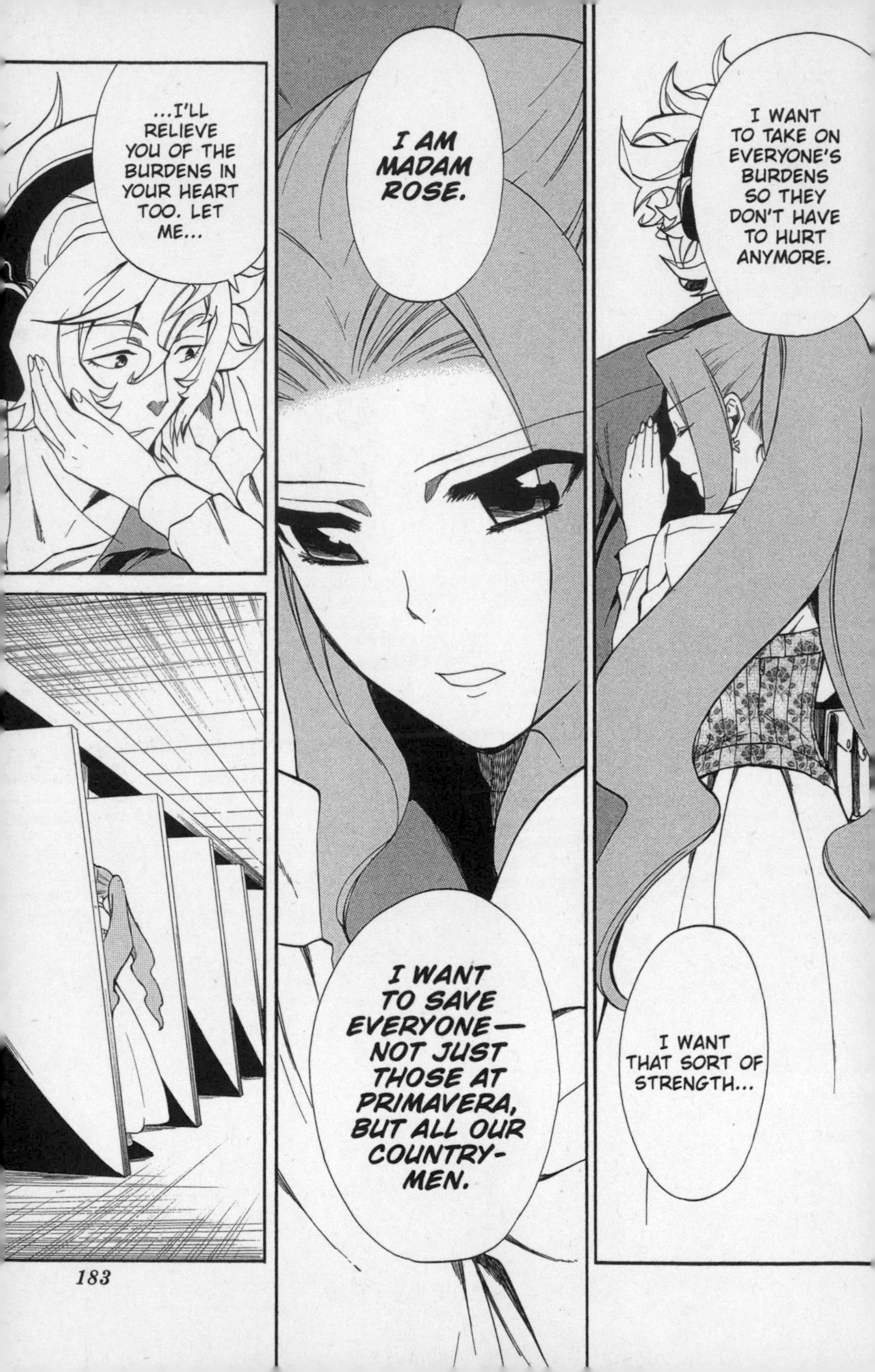
I WANT TO TAKE ON EVERYONE'S BURDENS SO THEY DON'T HAVE TO HURT ANYMORE.
I WANT THAT SORT OF STRENGTH...
I AM MADAM ROSE.
I WANT TO SAVE EVERYONE— NOT JUST THOSE AT PRIMAVERA, BUT ALL OUR COUNTRY-MEN.
...I'LL RELIEVE YOU OF THE BURDENS IN YOUR HEART TOO. LET ME...

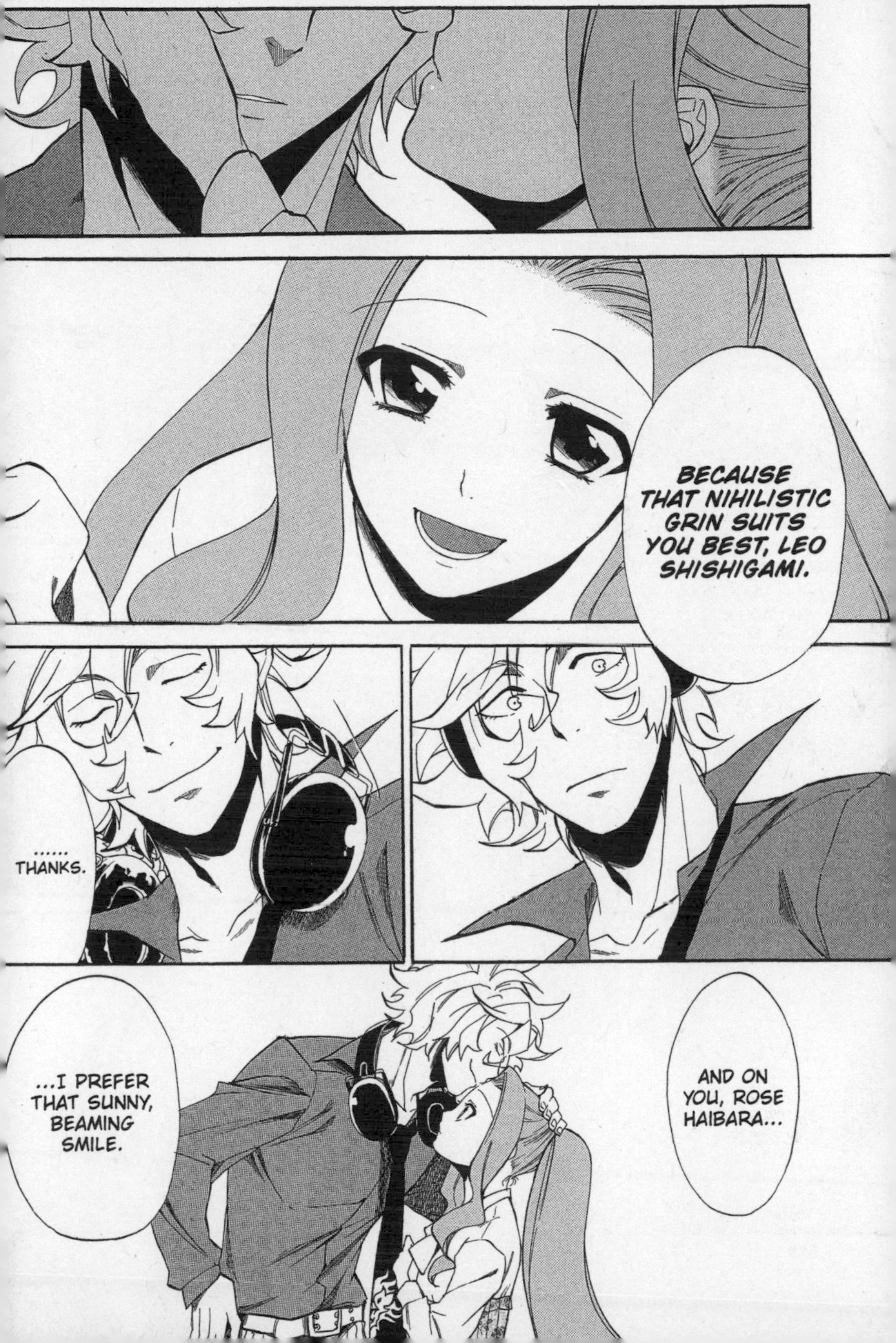
BECAUSE THAT NIHILISTIC GRIN SUITS YOU BEST, LEO SHISHIGAMI.
......THANKS.
AND ON YOU, ROSE HAIBARA...
...I PREFER THAT SUNNY, BEAMING SMILE.

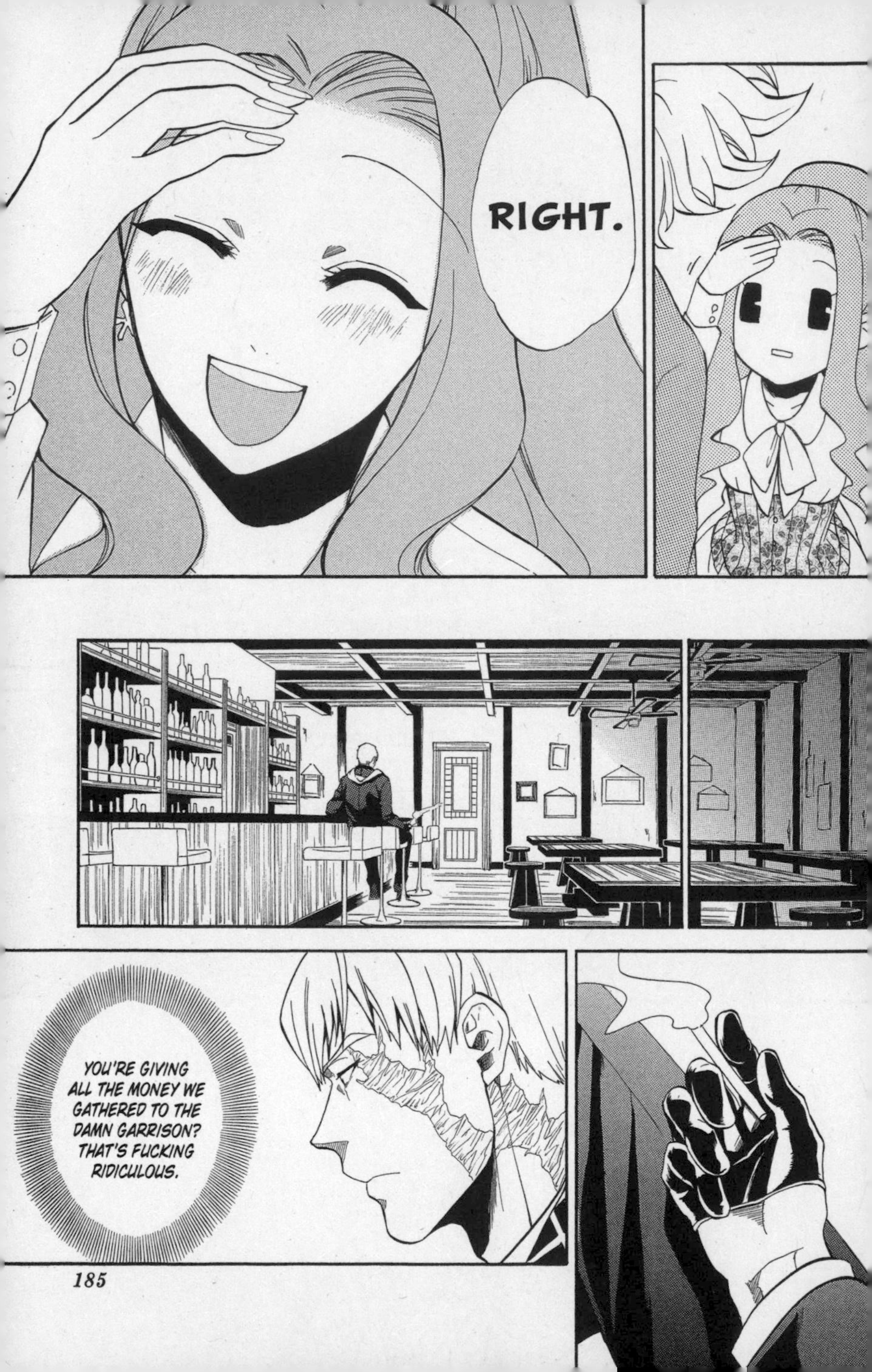
RIGHT.
YOU'RE GIVING ALL THE MONEY WE GATHERED TO THE DAMN GARRISON? THAT'S FUCKING RIDICULOUS.

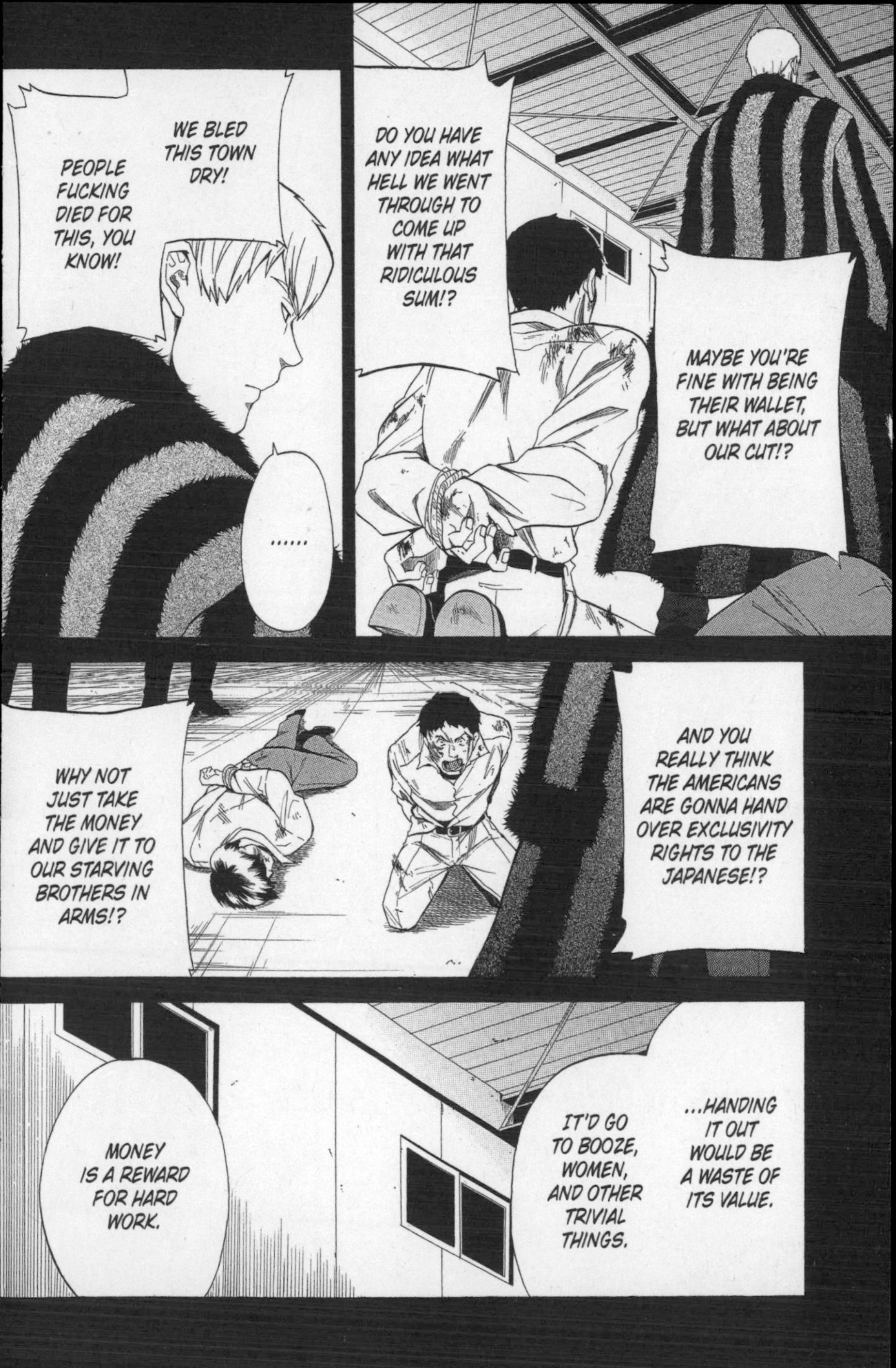
DO YOU HAVE ANY IDEA WHAT HELL WE WENT THROUGH TO COME UP WITH THAT RIDICULOUS SUM!?
MAYBE YOU'RE FINE WITH BEING THEIR WALLET, BUT WHAT ABOUT OUR CUT!?
WE BLED THIS TOWN DRY!
PEOPLE FUCKING DIED FOR THIS, YOU KNOW!
......
AND YOU REALLY THINK THE AMERICANS ARE GONNA HAND OVER EXCLUSIVITY RIGHTS TO THE JAPANESE!?
WHY NOT JUST TAKE THE MONEY AND GIVE IT TO OUR STARVING BROTHERS IN ARMS!?
...HANDING IT OUT WOULD BE A WASTE OF ITS VALUE.
IT'D GO TO BOOZE, WOMEN, AND OTHER TRIVIAL THINGS.
MONEY IS A REWARD FOR HARD WORK.

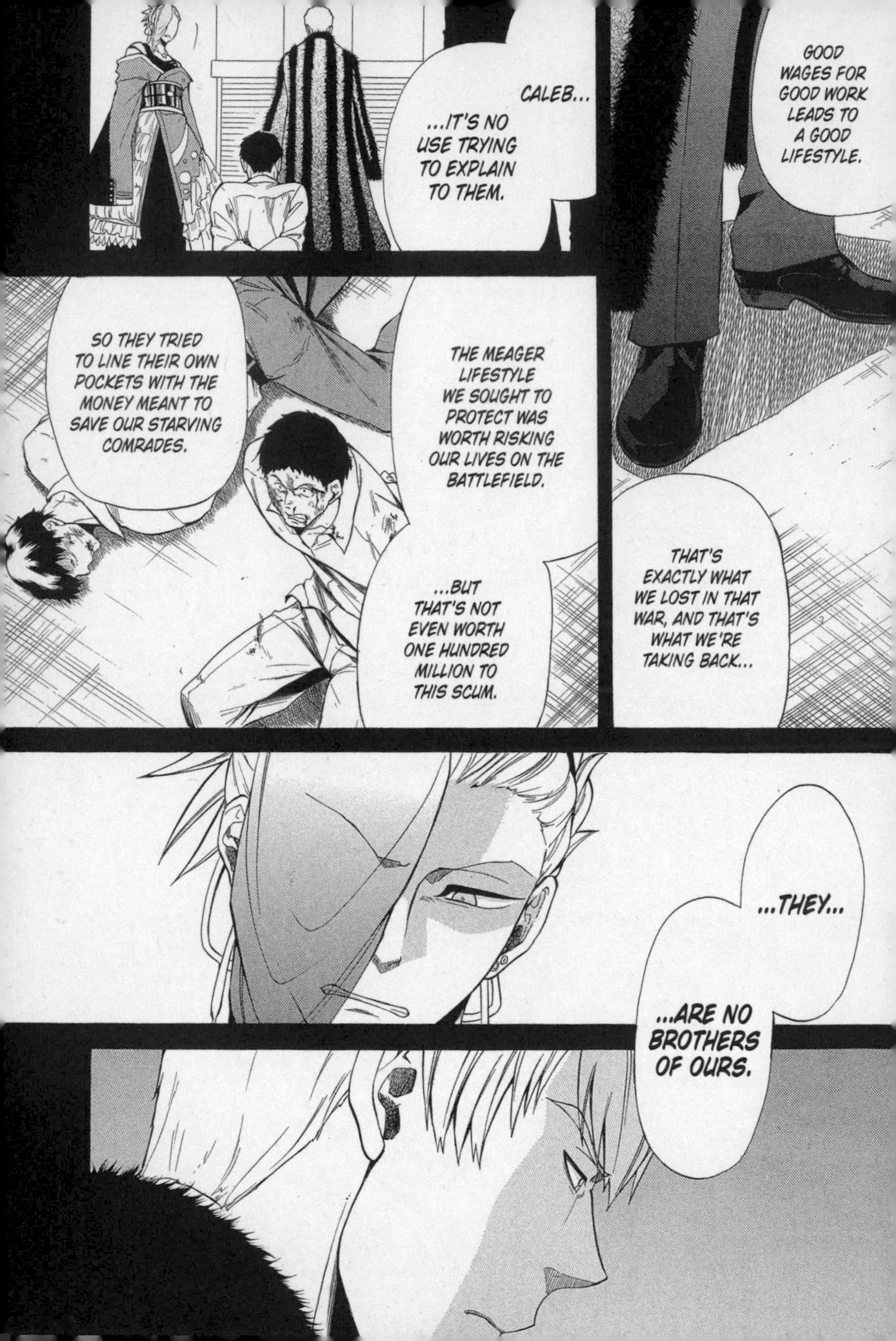
GOOD WAGES FOR GOOD WORK LEADS TO A GOOD LIFESTYLE.
THAT'S EXACTLY WHAT WE LOST IN THAT WAR, AND THAT'S WHAT WE'RE TAKING BACK...
CALEB...
...IT'S NO USE TRYING TO EXPLAIN TO THEM.
THE MEAGER LIFESTYLE WE SOUGHT TO PROTECT WAS WORTH RISKING OUR LIVES ON THE BATTLEFIELD.
SO THEY TRIED TO LINE THEIR OWN POCKETS WITH THE MONEY MEANT TO SAVE OUR STARVING COMRADES.
...BUT THAT'S NOT EVEN WORTH ONE HUNDRED MILLION TO THIS SCUM.
...THEY...
...ARE NO BROTHERS OF OURS.

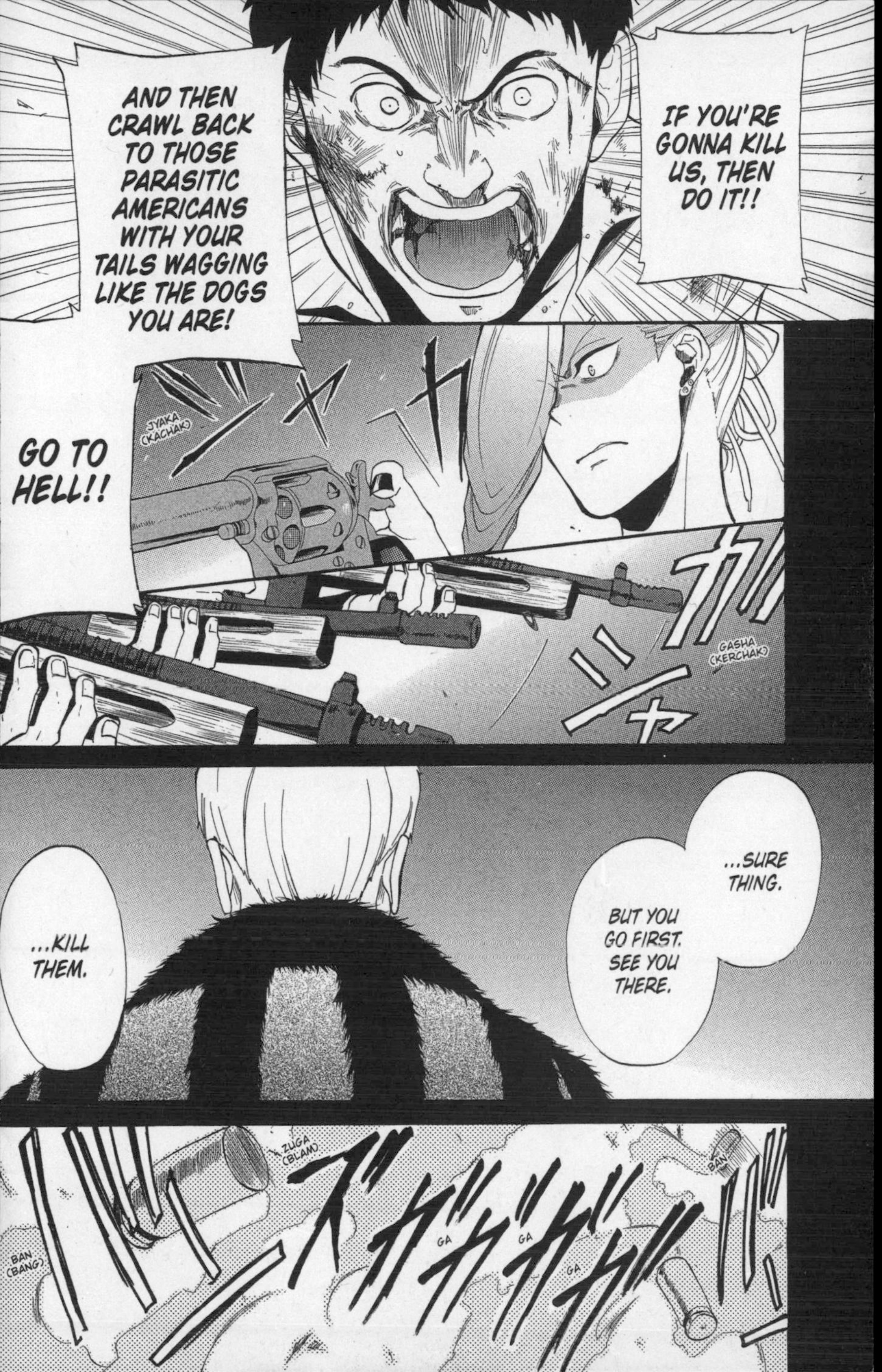
IF YOU'RE GONNA KILL US, THEN DO IT!!
AND THEN CRAWL BACK TO THOSE PARASITIC AMERICANS WITH YOUR TAILS WAGGING LIKE THE DOGS YOU ARE!
GO TO HELL!!
JYAKA (KACHAK)
GASHA (KERCHAK)
...SURE THING.
BUT YOU GO FIRST. SEE YOU THERE.
...KILL THEM.
BAN
ZUGA (BLAM)
GA
GA
GA
BAN (BANG)

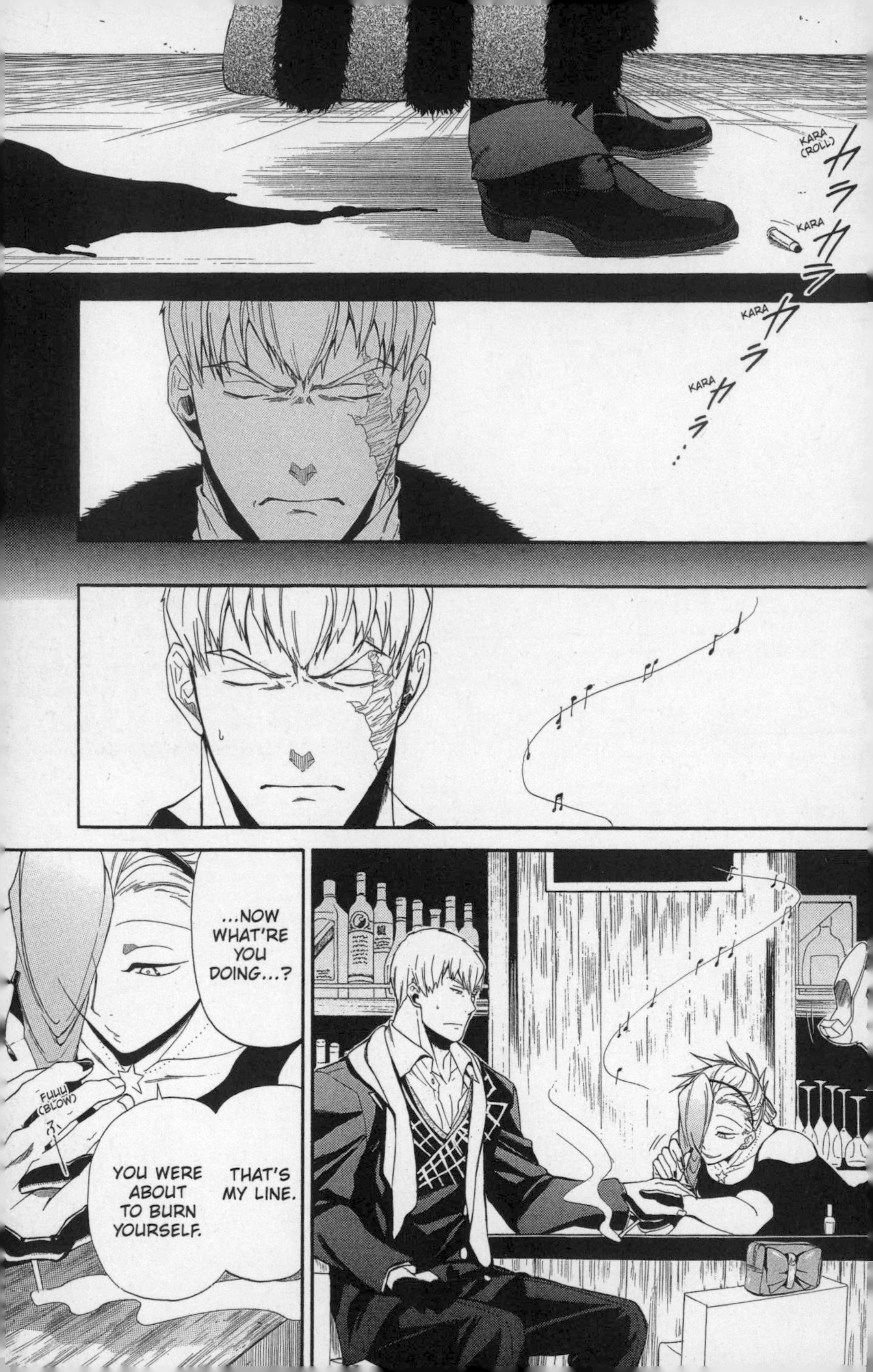
KARA (ROLL)
KARA
KARA
KARA
...NOW WHAT'RE YOU DOING...?
FUUU (BLOW)
THAT'S MY LINE.
YOU WERE ABOUT TO BURN YOURSELF.

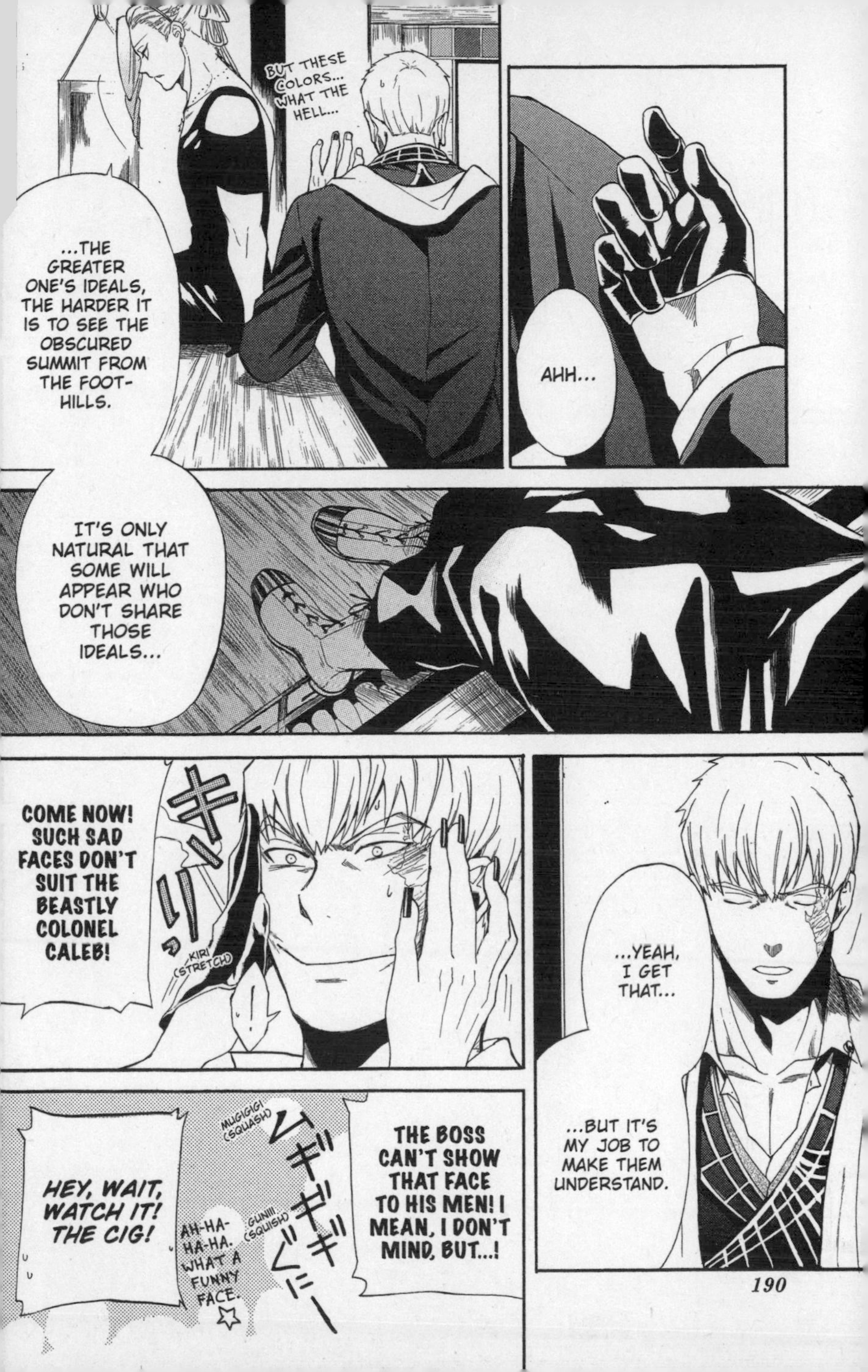
AHH...
BUT THESE COLORS... WHAT THE HELL...
...THE GREATER ONE'S IDEALS, THE HARDER IT IS TO SEE THE OBSCURED SUMMIT FROM THE FOOT-HILLS.
IT'S ONLY NATURAL THAT SOME WILL APPEAR WHO DON'T SHARE THOSE IDEALS...
...YEAH, I GET THAT...
...BUT IT'S MY JOB TO MAKE THEM UNDERSTAND.
COME NOW! SUCH SAD FACES DON'T SUIT THE BEASTLY COLONEL CALEB!
KIRI (STRETCH)
THE BOSS CAN'T SHOW THAT FACE TO HIS MEN! I MEAN, I DON'T MIND, BUT...!
MUGIGIGI (SQUASH)
GUNIII (SQUISH)
AH-HA-HA-HA. WHAT A FUNNY FACE.
HEY, WAIT, WATCH IT! THE CIG!

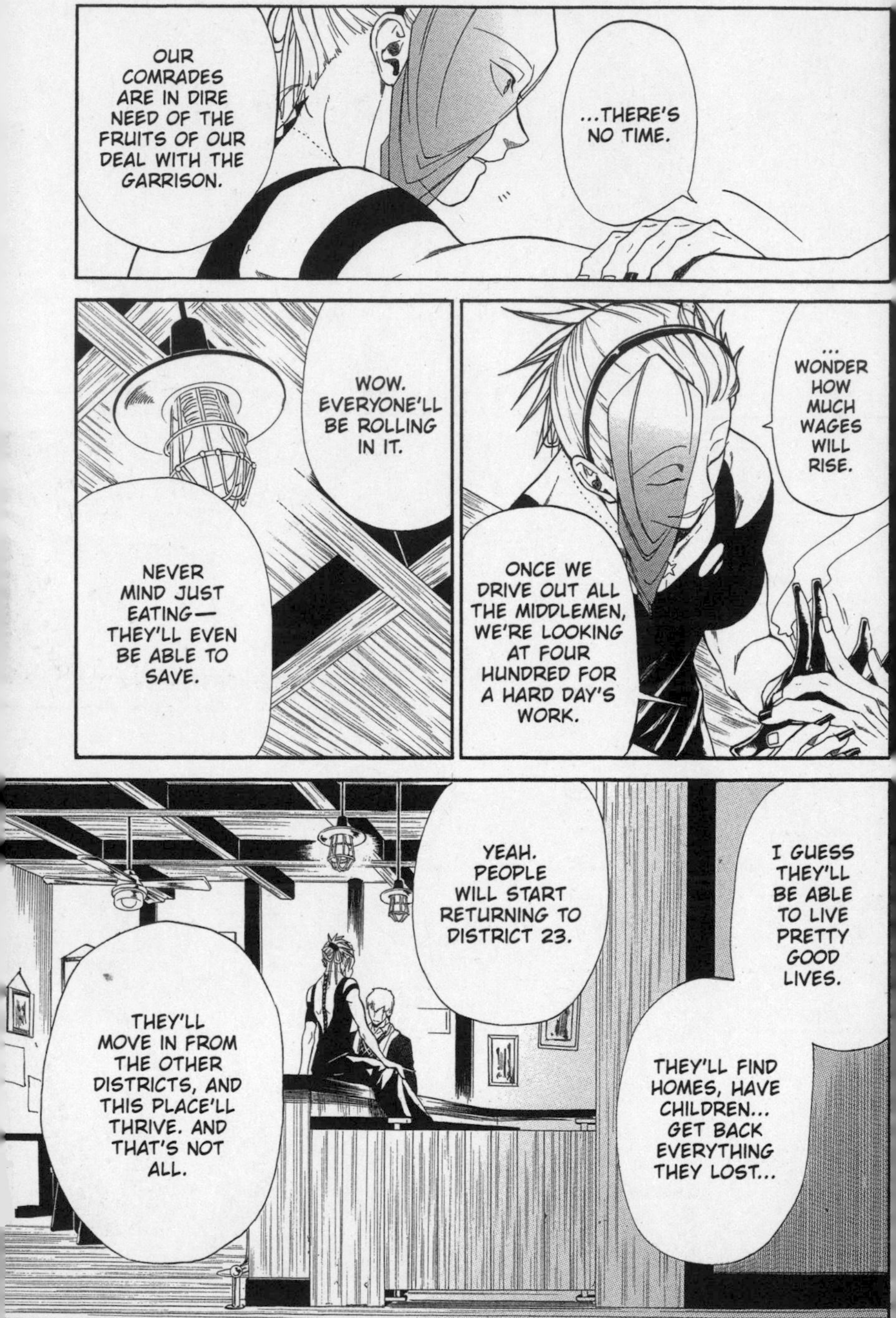
...THERE'S NO TIME.
OUR COMRADES ARE IN DIRE NEED OF THE FRUITS OF OUR DEAL WITH THE GARRISON.
... WONDER HOW MUCH WAGES WILL RISE.
ONCE WE DRIVE OUT ALL THE MIDDLEMEN, WE'RE LOOKING AT FOUR HUNDRED FOR A HARD DAY'S WORK.
WOW. EVERYONE'LL BE ROLLING IN IT.
NEVER MIND JUST EATING—THEY'LL EVEN BE ABLE TO SAVE.
I GUESS THEY'LL BE ABLE TO LIVE PRETTY GOOD LIVES.
YEAH. PEOPLE WILL START RETURNING TO DISTRICT 23.
THEY'LL FIND HOMES, HAVE CHILDREN... GET BACK EVERYTHING THEY LOST...
THEY'LL MOVE IN FROM THE OTHER DISTRICTS, AND THIS PLACE'LL THRIVE. AND THAT'S NOT ALL.

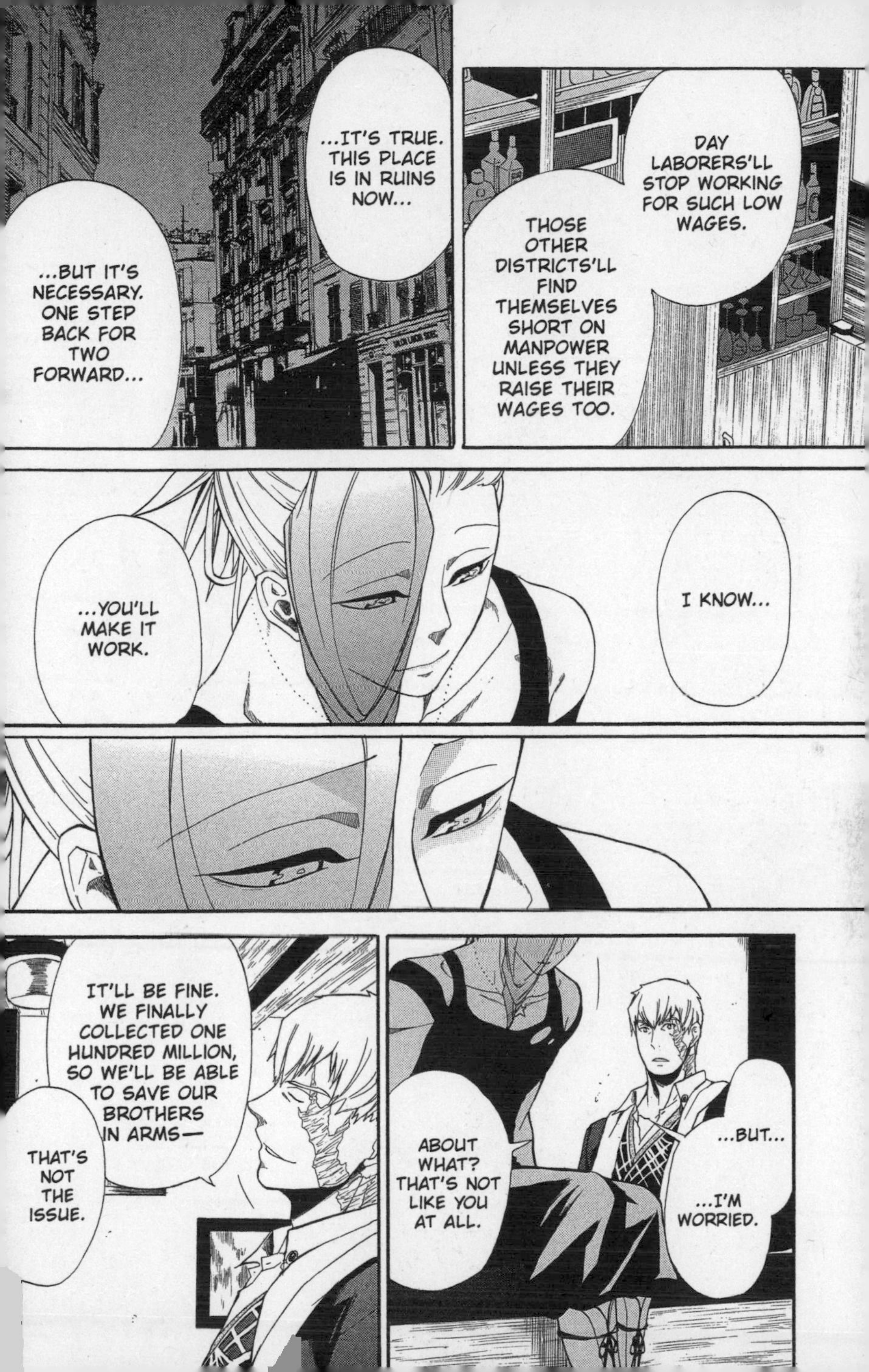
DAY LABORERS'LL STOP WORKING FOR SUCH LOW WAGES.
THOSE OTHER DISTRICTS'LL FIND THEMSELVES SHORT ON MANPOWER UNLESS THEY RAISE THEIR WAGES TOO.
...IT'S TRUE. THIS PLACE IS IN RUINS NOW...
...BUT IT'S NECESSARY. ONE STEP BACK FOR TWO FORWARD...
I KNOW...
...YOU'LL MAKE IT WORK.
...BUT...
...I'M WORRIED.
ABOUT WHAT? THAT'S NOT LIKE YOU AT ALL.
IT'LL BE FINE. WE FINALLY COLLECTED ONE HUNDRED MILLION, SO WE'LL BE ABLE TO SAVE OUR BROTHERS IN ARMS—
THAT'S NOT THE ISSUE.

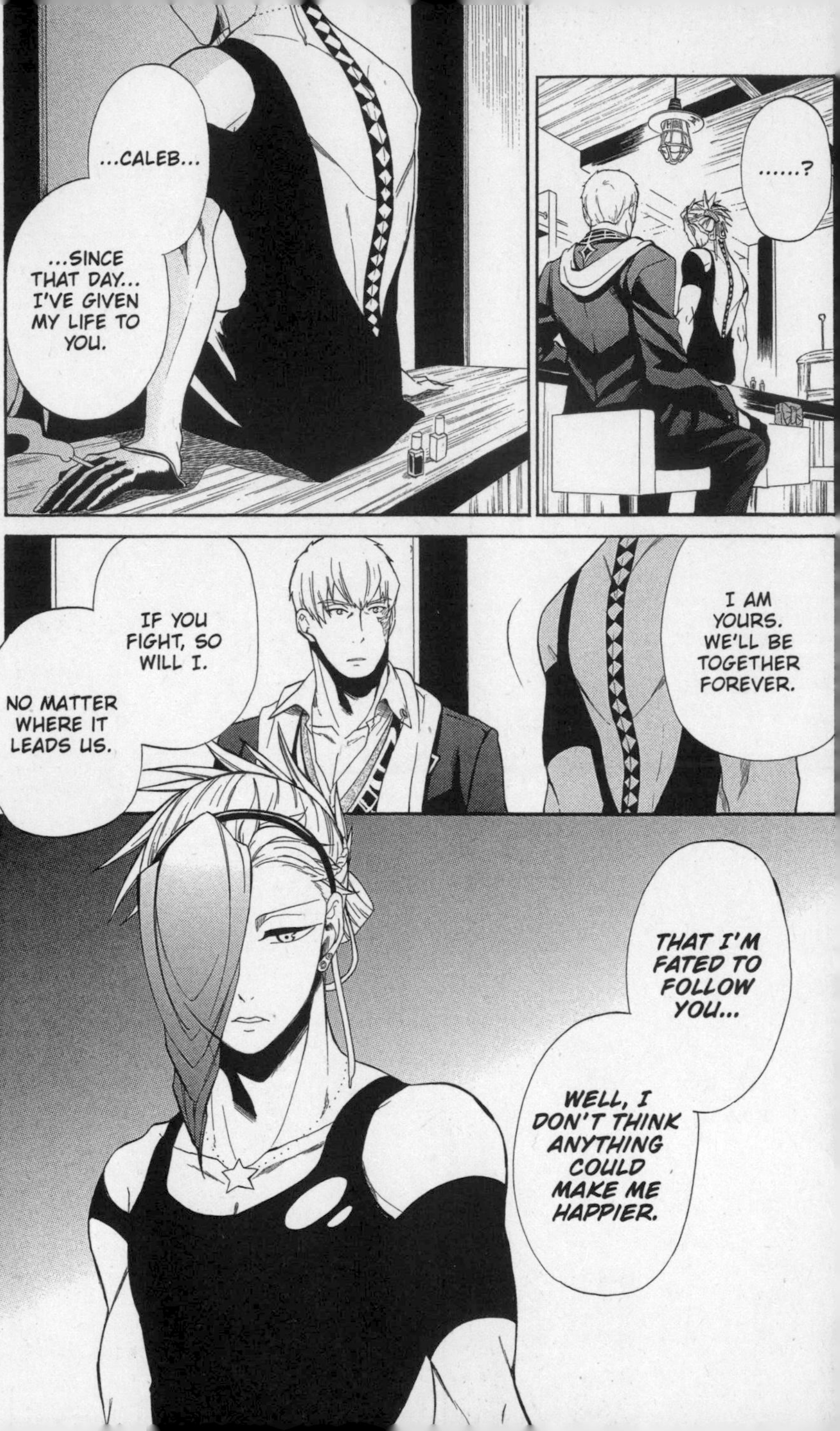
......?
...CALEB...
...SINCE THAT DAY... I'VE GIVEN MY LIFE TO YOU.
I AM YOURS. WE'LL BE TOGETHER FOREVER.
IF YOU FIGHT, SO WILL I.
NO MATTER WHERE IT LEADS US.
THAT I'M FATED TO FOLLOW YOU...
WELL, I DON'T THINK ANYTHING COULD MAKE ME HAPPIER.

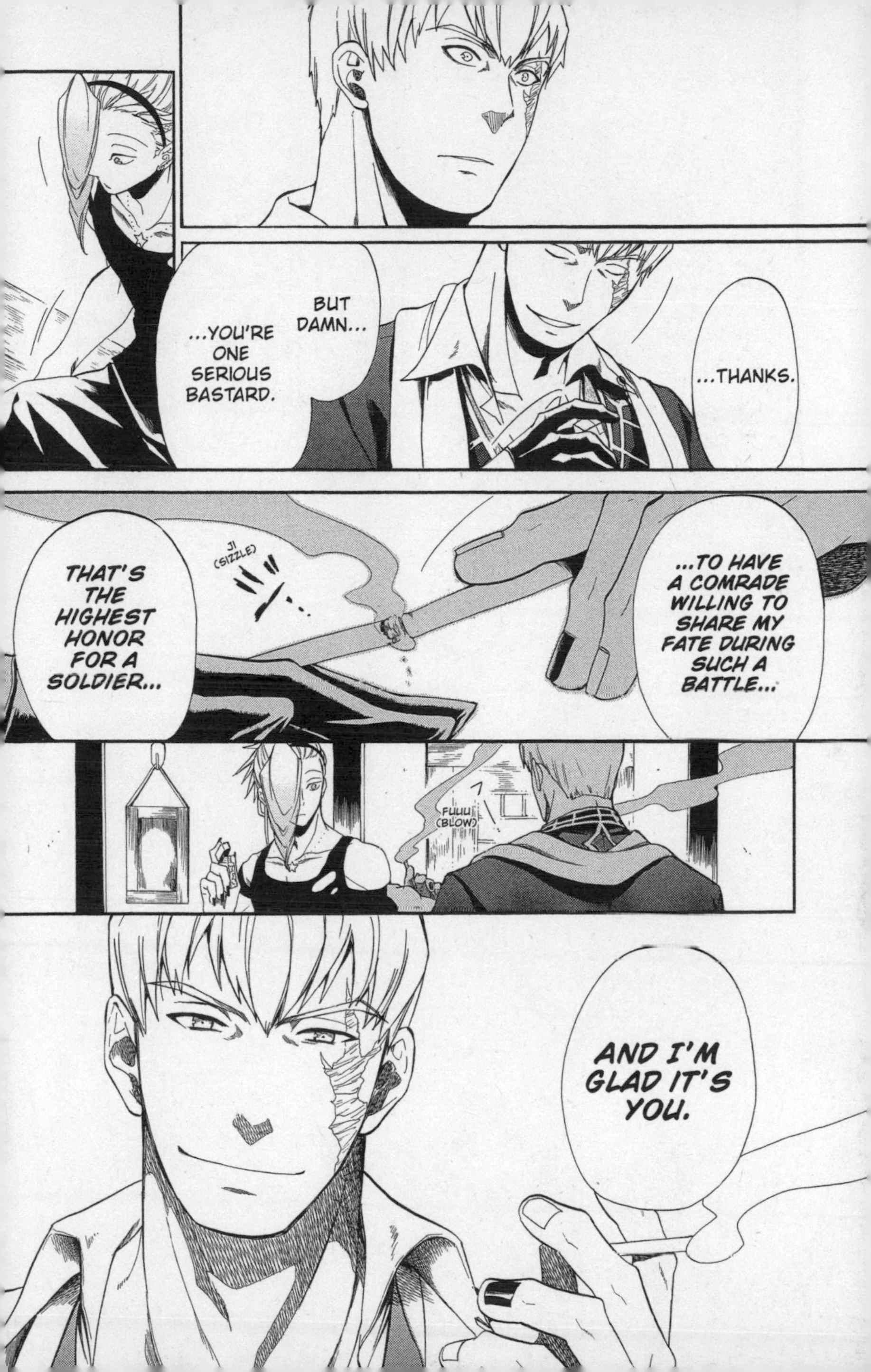
BUT DAMN...
...YOU'RE ONE SERIOUS BASTARD.
...THANKS.
JI (SIZZLE)
THAT'S THE HIGHEST HONOR FOR A SOLDIER...
...TO HAVE A COMRADE WILLING TO SHARE MY FATE DURING SUCH A BATTLE...
FUUU (BLOW)
AND I'M GLAD IT'S YOU.

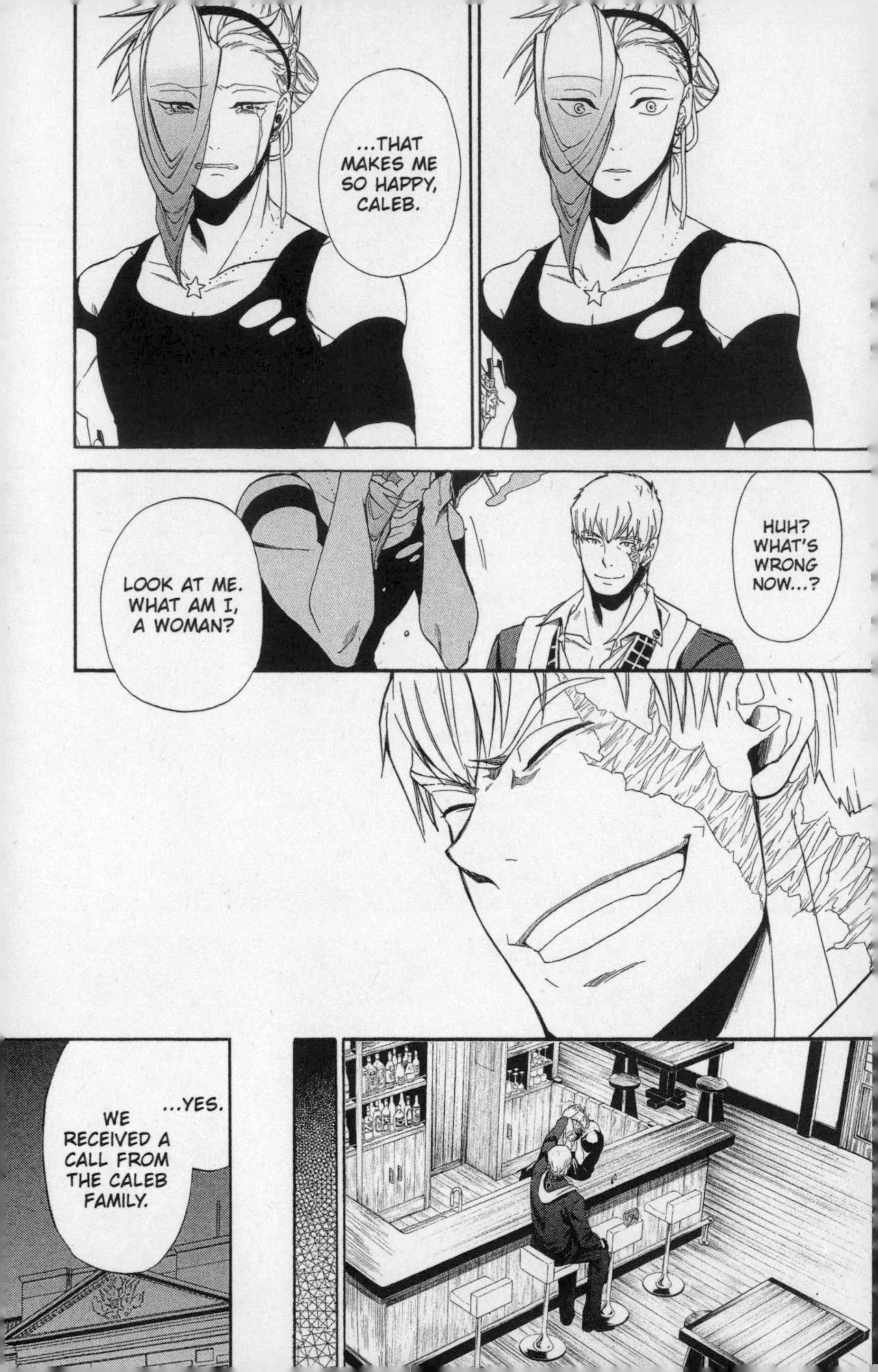
...THAT MAKES ME SO HAPPY, CALEB.
HUH? WHAT'S WRONG NOW...?
LOOK AT ME. WHAT AM I, A WOMAN?
...YES.
WE RECEIVED A CALL FROM THE CALEB FAMILY.

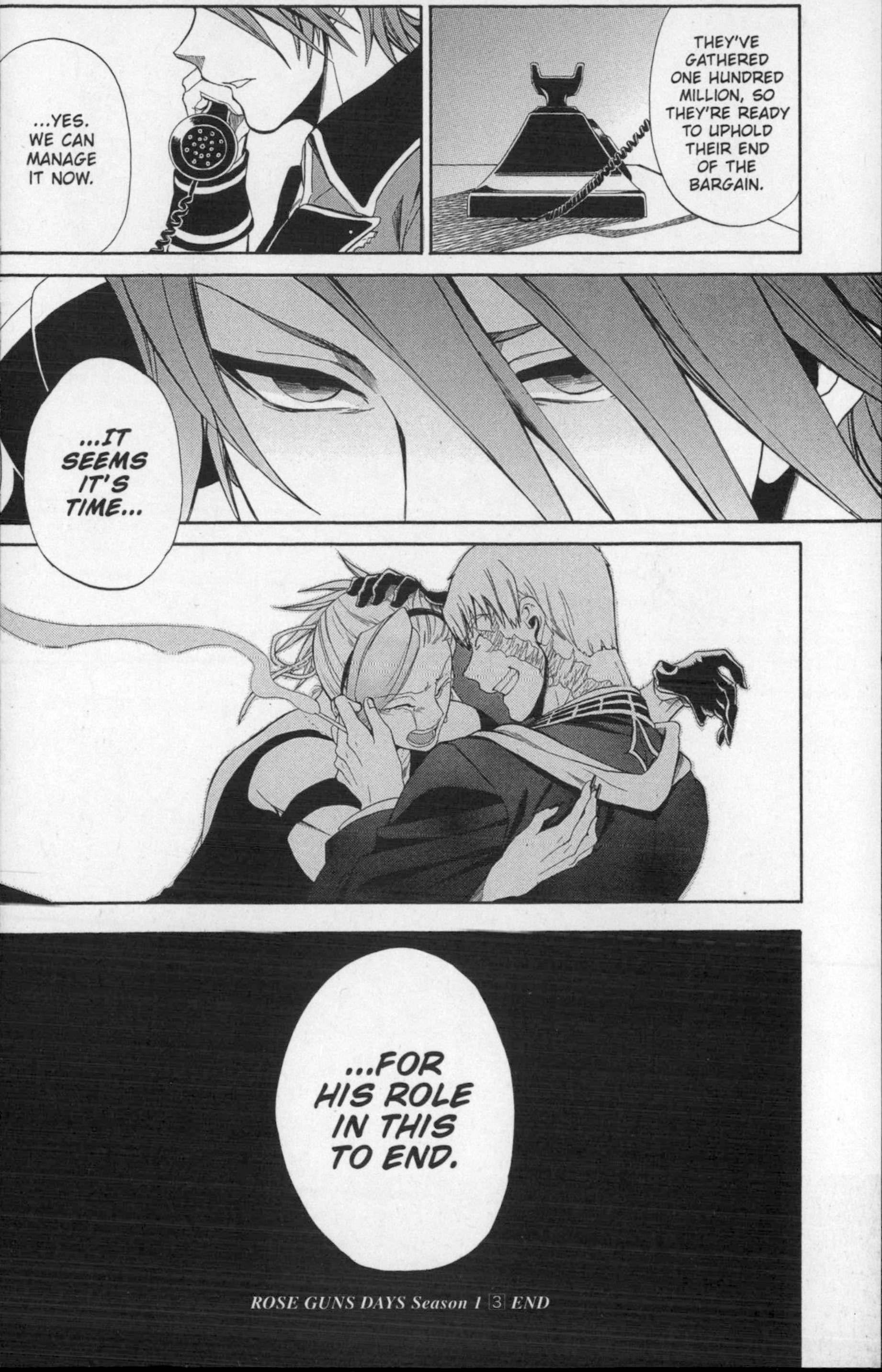
THEY'VE GATHERED ONE HUNDRED MILLION, SO THEY'RE READY TO UPHOLD THEIR END OF THE BARGAIN.
...YES. WE CAN MANAGE IT NOW.
...IT SEEMS IT'S TIME...
...FOR HIS ROLE IN THIS TO END.
ROSE GUNS DAYS Season 1 3 END

BONUS

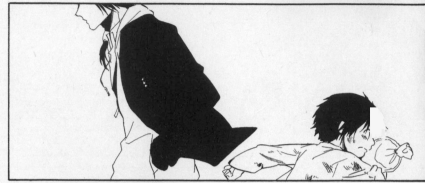

SHOW ME YOU CAN SURVIVE.

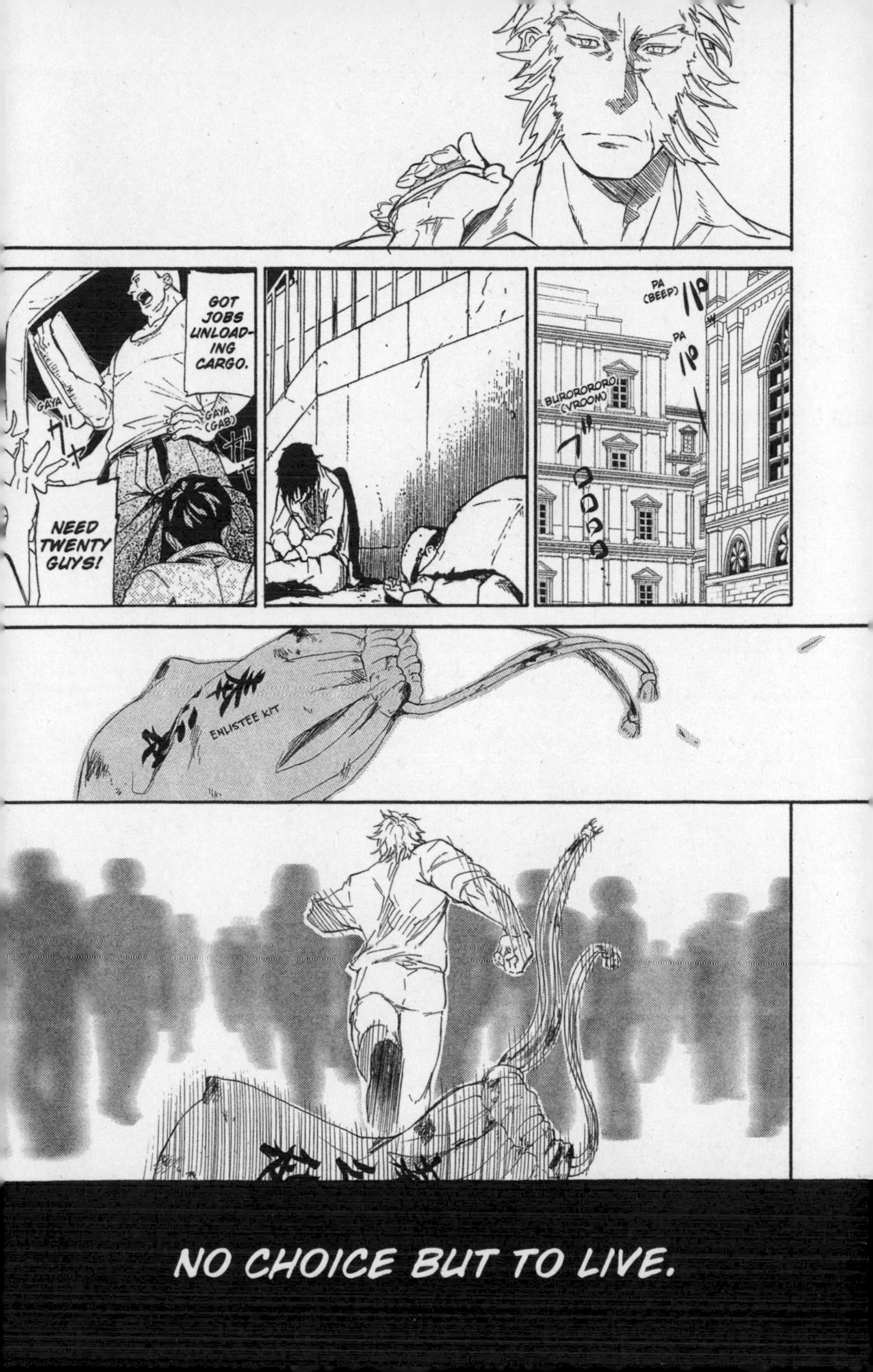
PA (BEEP)
PA
BURORORORO (VROOM)
GOT JOBS UNLOADING CARGO.
GAYA
GAYA (GAB)
NEED TWENTY GUYS!
ENLISTEE KIT
NO CHOICE BUT TO LIVE.

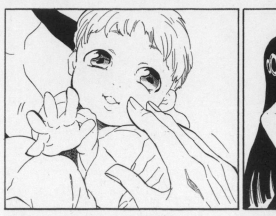

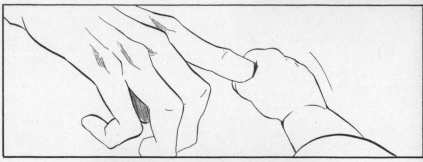

WE NEED TO LIVE.

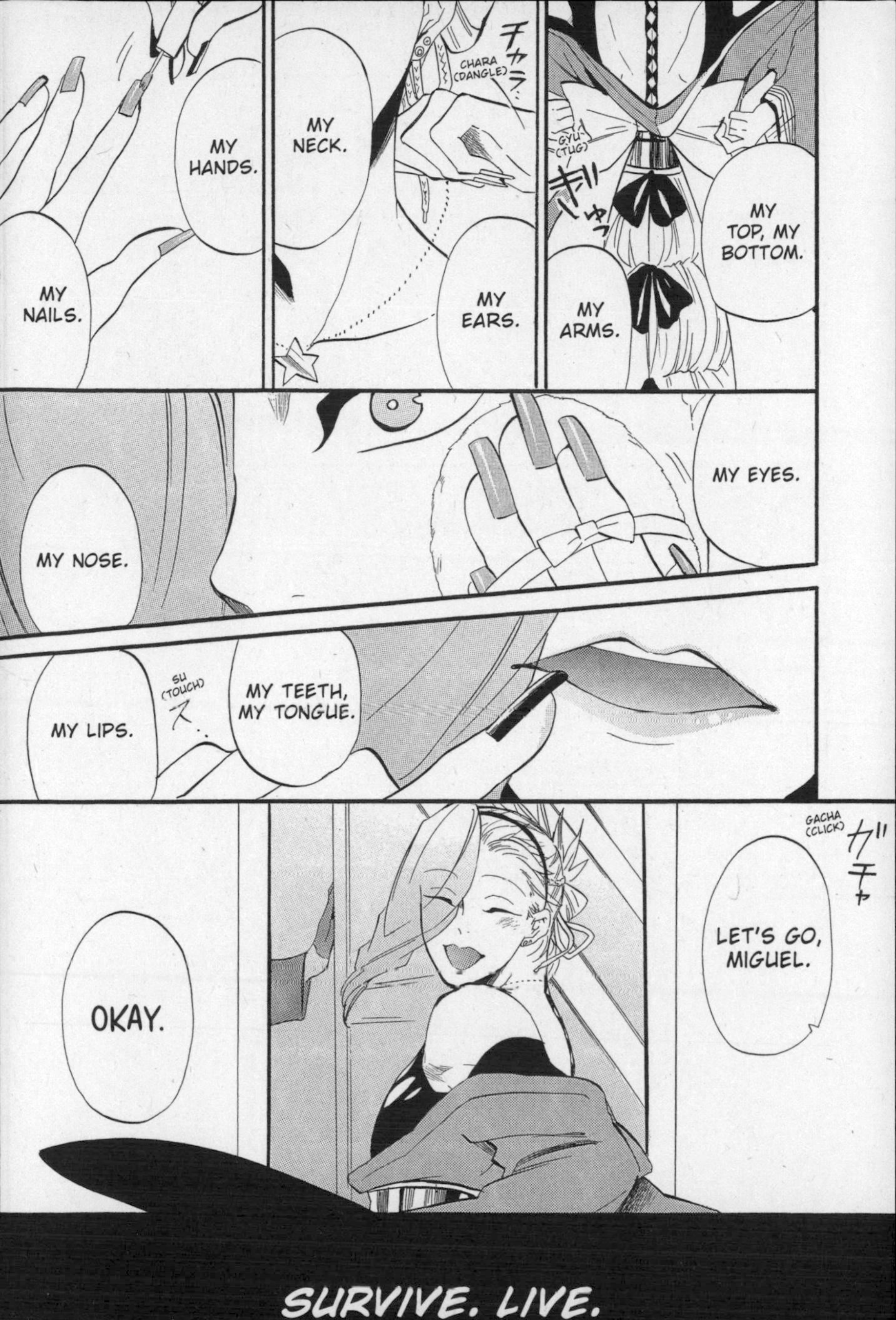
GYU (TUG)
ぎゅっ
MY TOP, MY BOTTOM.
MY ARMS.
CHARA (DANGLE)
チャラ
MY NECK.
MY EARS.
MY HANDS.
MY NAILS.
MY EYES.
MY NOSE.
MY TEETH, MY TONGUE.
SU (TOUCH)
ス
MY LIPS.
GACHA (CLICK)
ガチャ
LET'S GO, MIGUEL.
OKAY.
SURVIVE. LIVE.

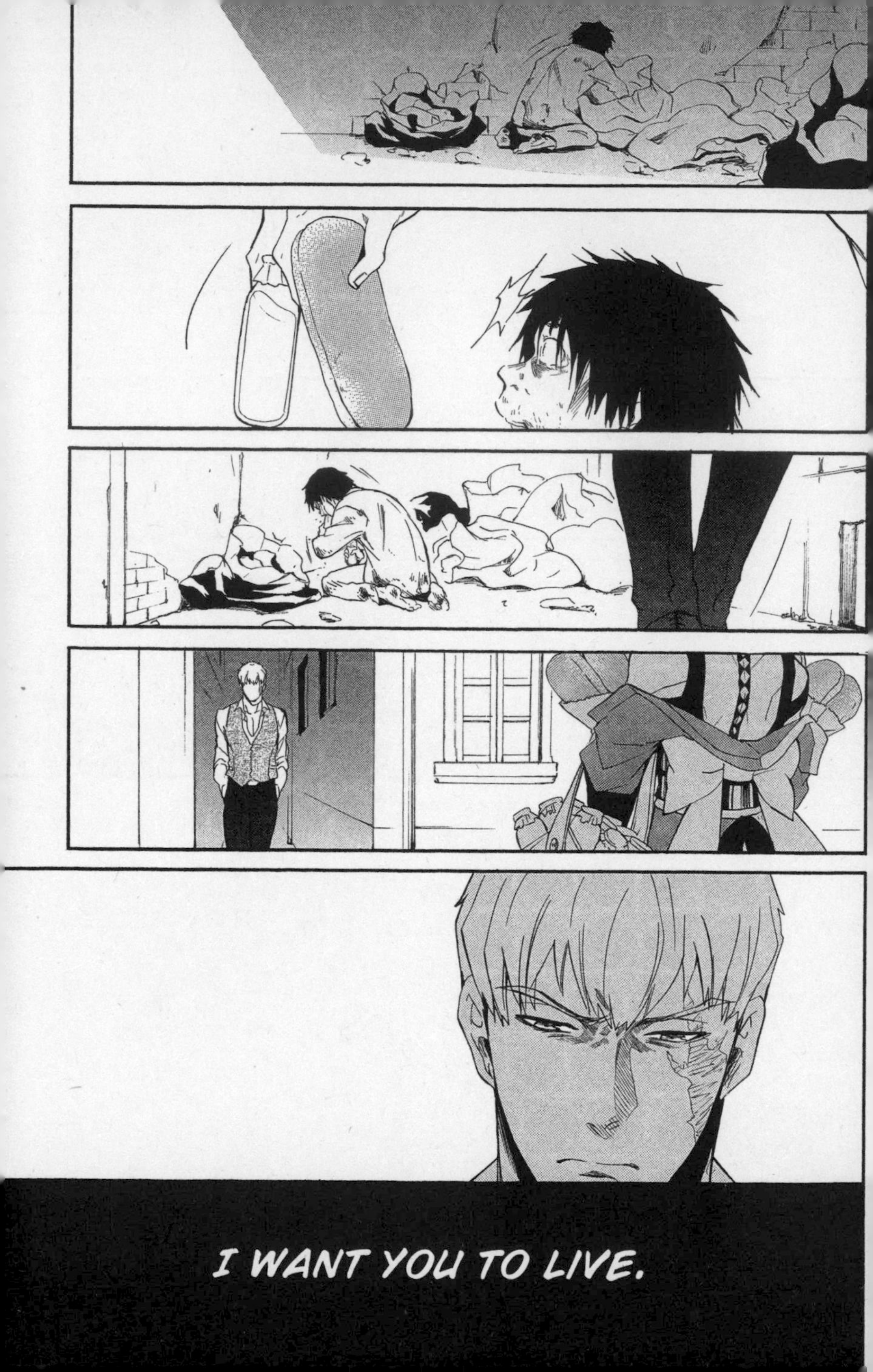
I WANT YOU TO LIVE.

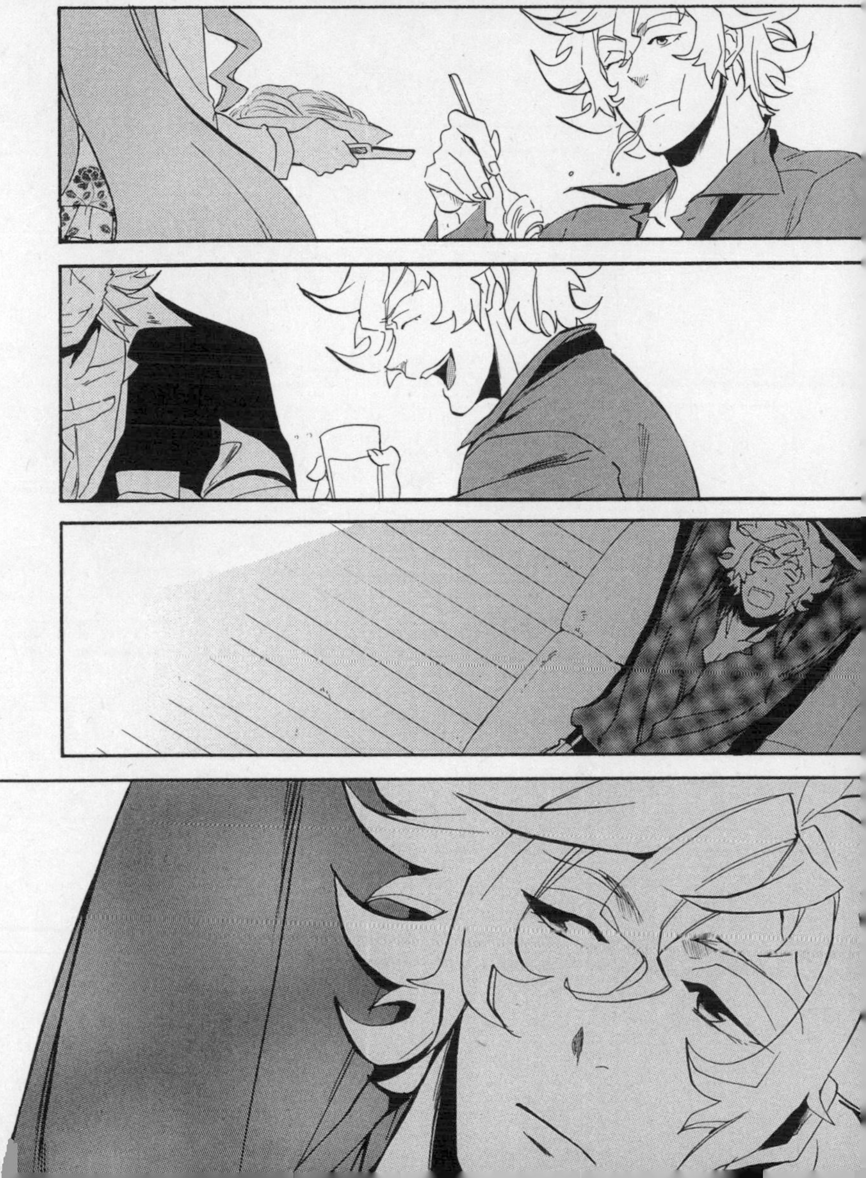

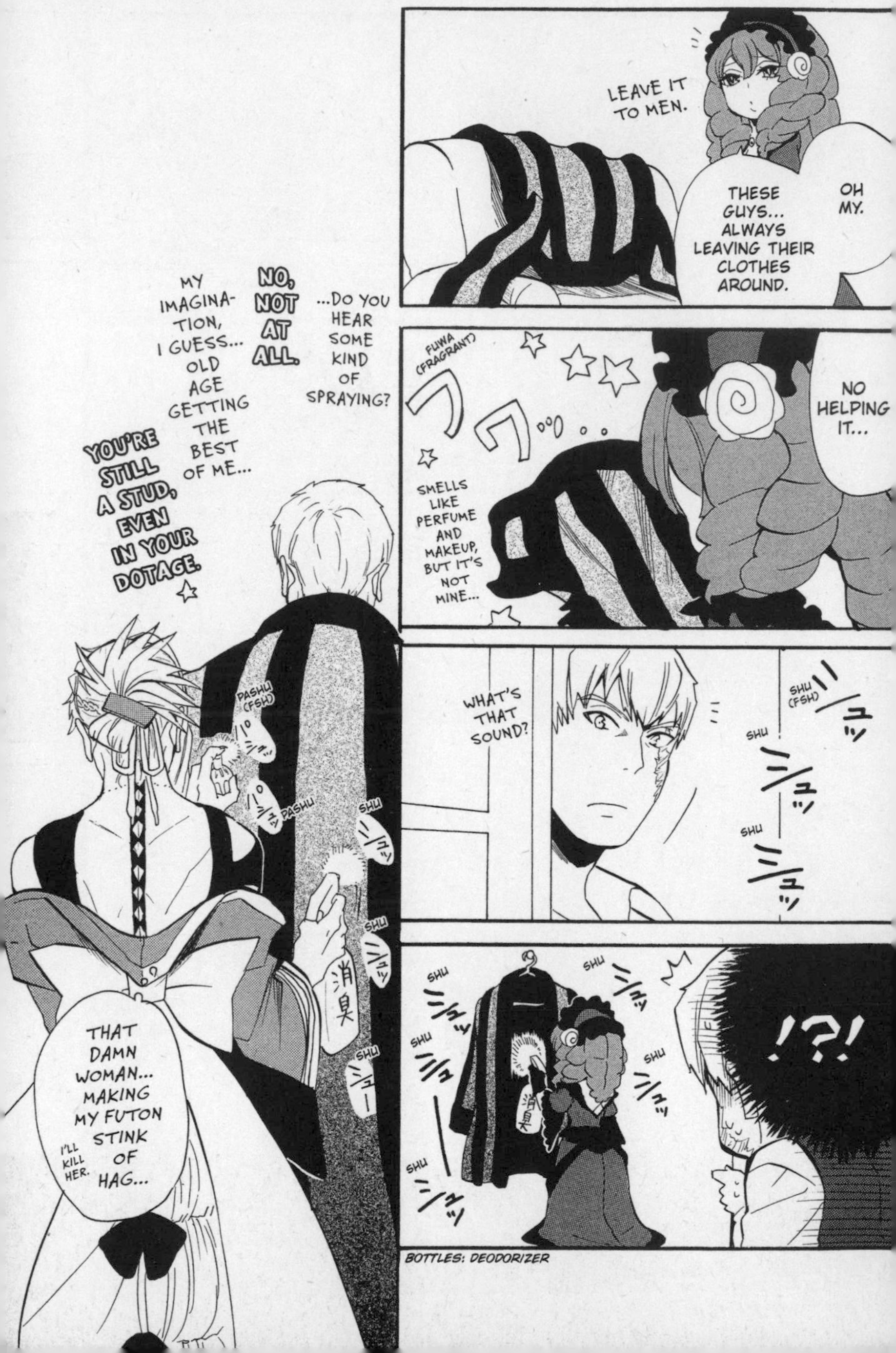
OH MY.
THESE GUYS... ALWAYS LEAVING THEIR CLOTHES AROUND.
LEAVE IT TO MEN.
NO HELPING IT...
FUWA (FRAGRANT)
SMELLS LIKE PERFUME AND MAKEUP, BUT IT'S NOT MINE...
SHU (FSH)
SHU
SHU
WHAT'S THAT SOUND?
SHU
SHU
SHU
SHU
!?!
...DO YOU HEAR SOME KIND OF SPRAYING?
NO, NOT AT ALL.
MY IMAGINATION, I GUESS... OLD AGE GETTING THE BEST OF ME...
YOU'RE STILL A STUD, EVEN IN YOUR DOTAGE.
PASHU (FSH)
PASHU
SHU
SHU
SHU
THAT DAMN WOMAN... MAKING MY FUTON STINK OF HAG...
I'LL KILL HER.

BOTTLES: DEODORIZER

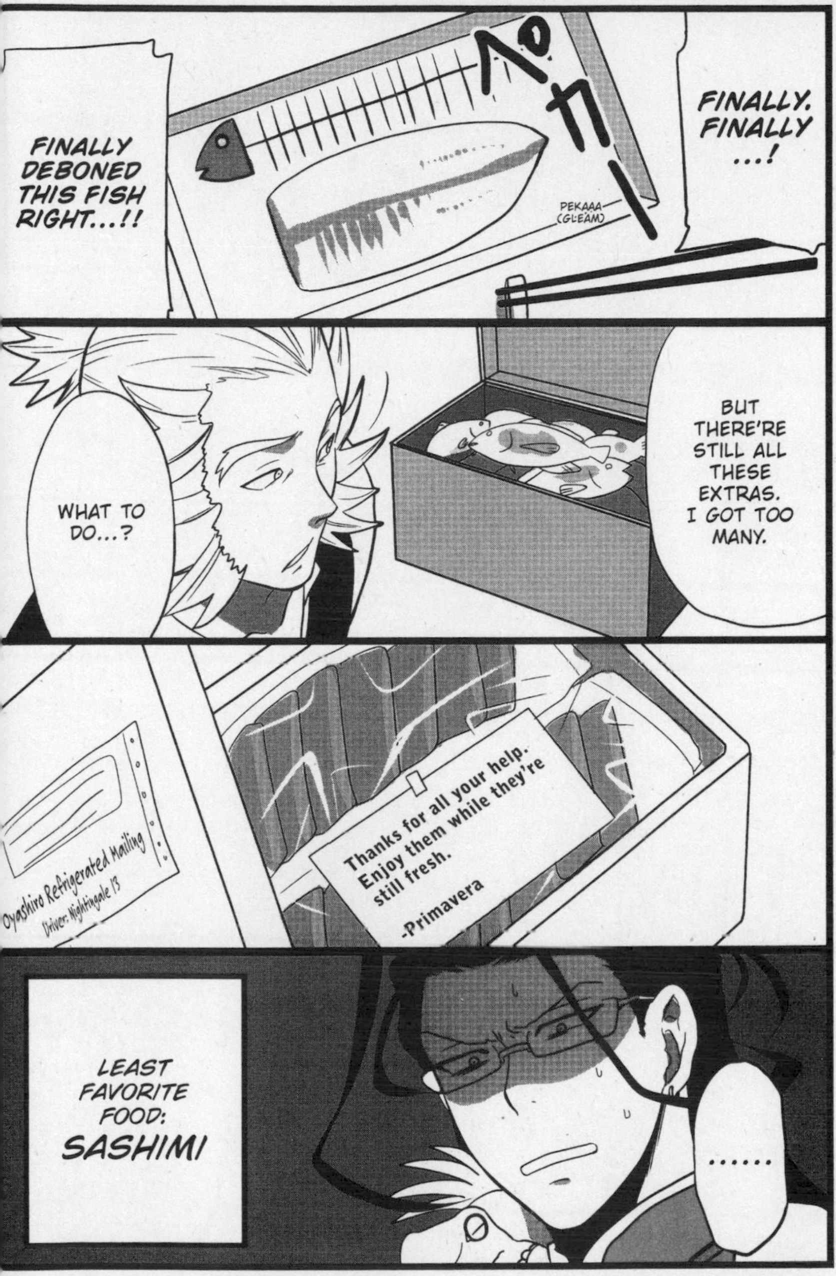
FINALLY. FINALLY ...!
PEKAAA (GLEAM)
FINALLY DEBONED THIS FISH RIGHT...!!
BUT THERE'RE STILL ALL THESE EXTRAS. I GOT TOO MANY.
WHAT TO DO...?
Thanks for all your help. Enjoy them while they're still fresh.
-Primavera
Oyashiro Refrigerated Mailing
Driver: Nightingale 13
......
LEAST FAVORITE FOOD: SASHIMI

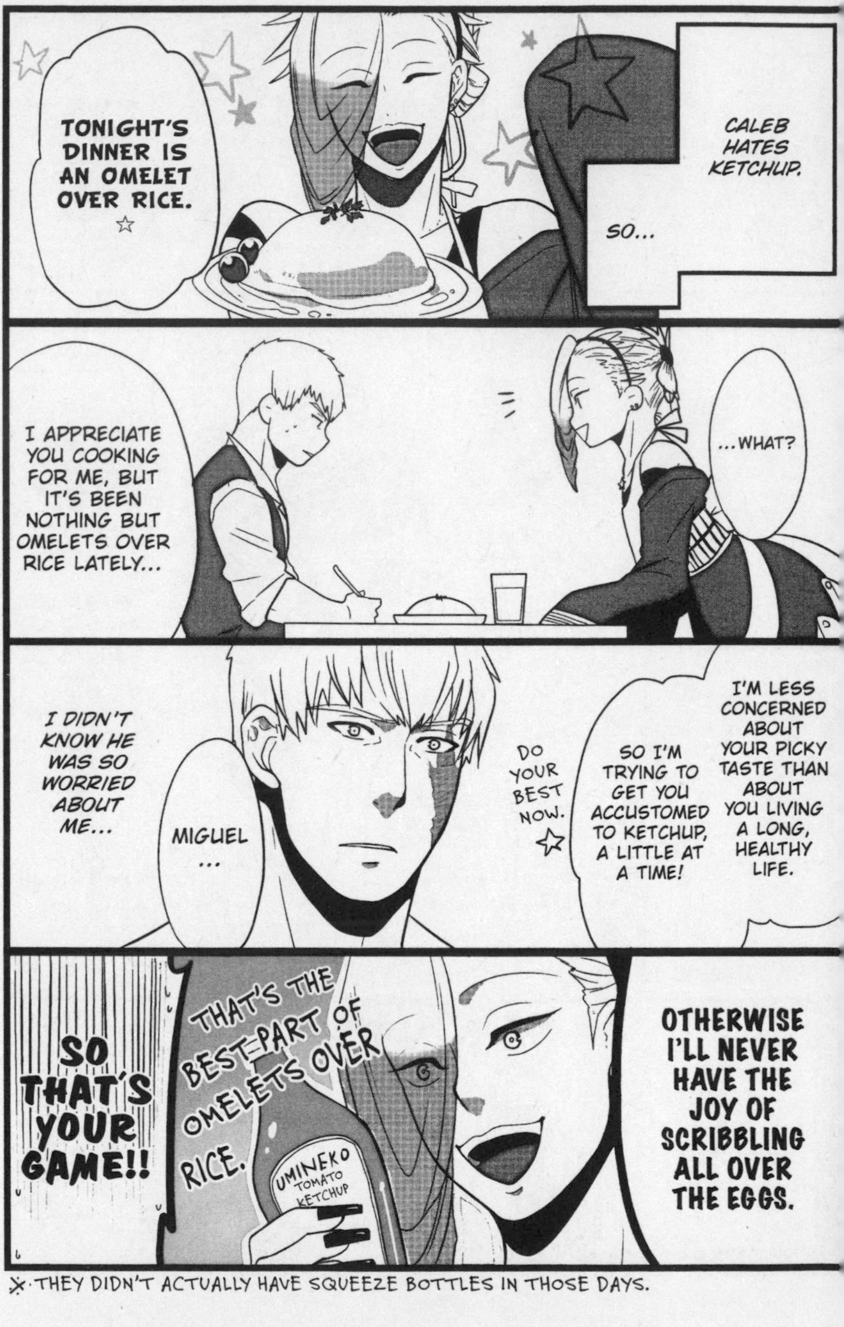
CALEB HATES KETCHUP.
SO...
TONIGHT'S DINNER IS AN OMELET OVER RICE. ☆
...WHAT?
I APPRECIATE YOU COOKING FOR ME, BUT IT'S BEEN NOTHING BUT OMELETS OVER RICE LATELY...
I'M LESS CONCERNED ABOUT YOUR PICKY TASTE THAN ABOUT YOU LIVING A LONG, HEALTHY LIFE.
SO I'M TRYING TO GET YOU ACCUSTOMED TO KETCHUP, A LITTLE AT A TIME!
DO YOUR BEST NOW. ☆
MIGUEL...
I DIDN'T KNOW HE WAS SO WORRIED ABOUT ME...
OTHERWISE I'LL NEVER HAVE THE JOY OF SCRIBBLING ALL OVER THE EGGS.
THAT'S THE BEST PART OF OMELETS OVER RICE.
UMINEKO TOMATO KETCHUP
SO THAT'S YOUR GAME!!

※: THEY DIDN'T ACTUALLY HAVE SQUEEZE BOTTLES IN THOSE DAYS.

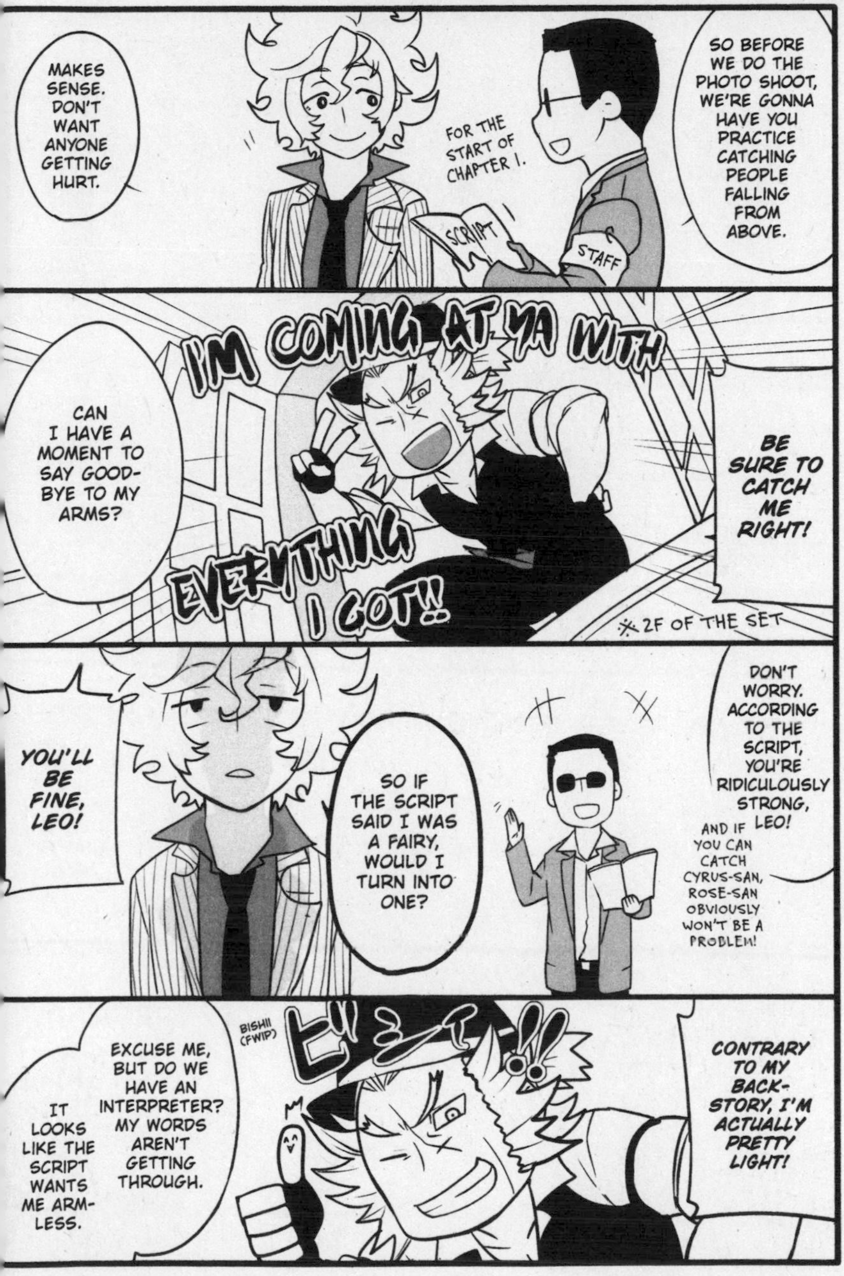
SO BEFORE WE DO THE PHOTO SHOOT, WE'RE GONNA HAVE YOU PRACTICE CATCHING PEOPLE FALLING FROM ABOVE.
FOR THE START OF CHAPTER 1.
SCRIPT
STAFF
MAKES SENSE. DON'T WANT ANYONE GETTING HURT.
BE SURE TO CATCH ME RIGHT!
I'M COMING AT YA WITH EVERYTHING I GOT!!
※2F OF THE SET
CAN I HAVE A MOMENT TO SAY GOOD-BYE TO MY ARMS?
DON'T WORRY. ACCORDING TO THE SCRIPT, YOU'RE RIDICULOUSLY STRONG, LEO!
AND IF YOU CAN CATCH CYRUS-SAN, ROSE-SAN OBVIOUSLY WON'T BE A PROBLEM!
SO IF THE SCRIPT SAID I WAS A FAIRY, WOULD I TURN INTO ONE?
YOU'LL BE FINE, LEO!
CONTRARY TO MY BACK-STORY, I'M ACTUALLY PRETTY LIGHT!
BISHII (FWIP)
EXCUSE ME, BUT DO WE HAVE AN INTERPRETER? MY WORDS AREN'T GETTING THROUGH.
IT LOOKS LIKE THE SCRIPT WANTS ME ARM-LESS.

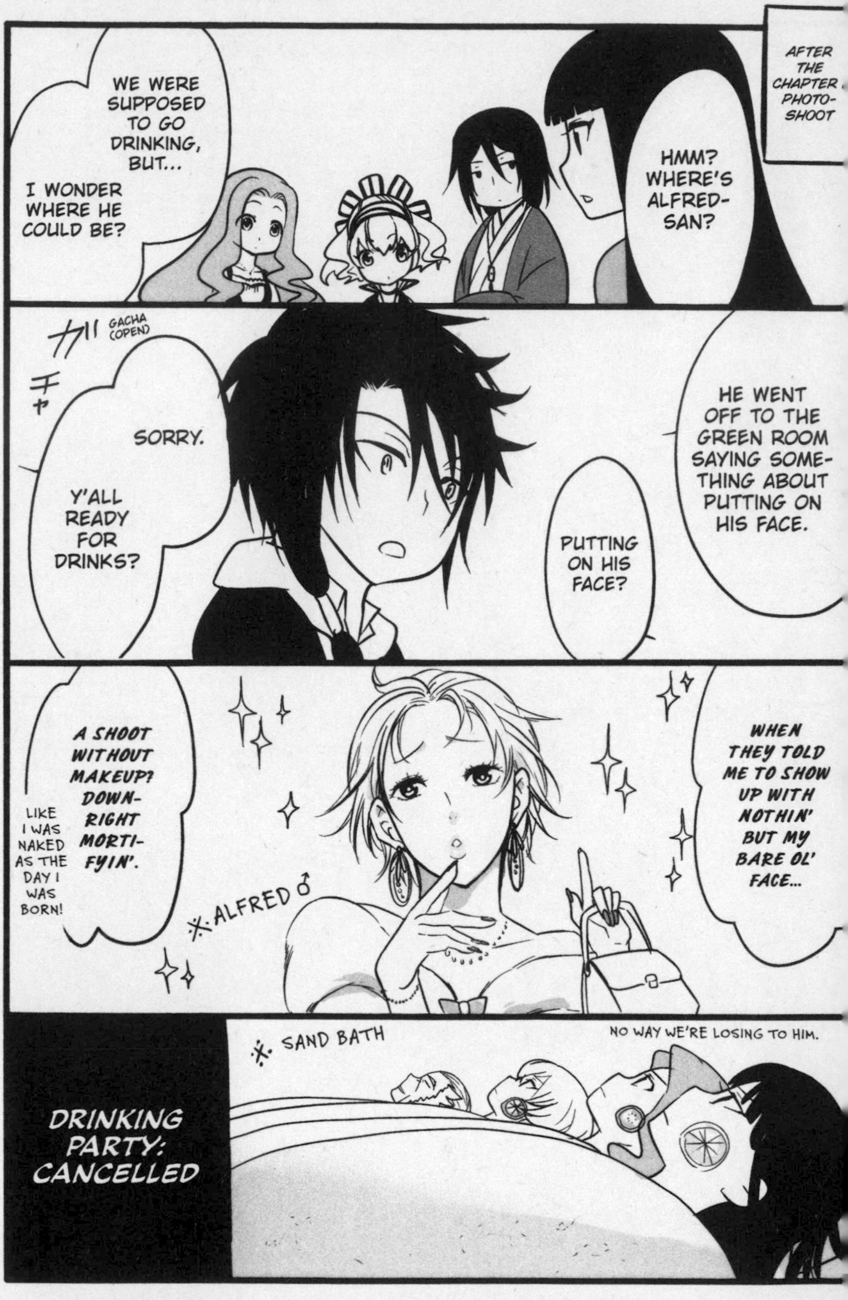
AFTER THE CHAPTER PHOTO-SHOOT
HMM? WHERE'S ALFRED-SAN?
WE WERE SUPPOSED TO GO DRINKING, BUT...
I WONDER WHERE HE COULD BE?
HE WENT OFF TO THE GREEN ROOM SAYING SOMETHING ABOUT PUTTING ON HIS FACE.
PUTTING ON HIS FACE?
ガチャ GACHA (OPEN)
SORRY.
Y'ALL READY FOR DRINKS?
WHEN THEY TOLD ME TO SHOW UP WITH NOTHIN' BUT MY BARE OL' FACE...
※ALFRED ♂
A SHOOT WITHOUT MAKEUP? DOWNRIGHT MORTIFYIN'.
LIKE I WAS NAKED AS THE DAY I WAS BORN!
NO WAY WE'RE LOSING TO HIM.
※ SAND BATH
DRINKING PARTY: CANCELLED

TRANSLATION NOTES

COMMON HONORIFICS

no honorific: Indicates familiarity or closeness; if used without permission or reason, addressing someone in this manner would constitute an insult.

-*san*: The Japanese equivalent of Mr./Mrs./Miss. If a situation calls for politeness, this is the fail-safe honorific.

-*sama*: Conveys great respect; may also indicate that the social status of the speaker is lower than that of the addressee.

-*kun*: Used most often when referring to boys, this indicates affection or familiarity. Occasionally used by older men among their peers, but it may also be used by anyone referring to a person of lower standing.

-*chan*: An affectionate honorific indicating familiarity used mostly in reference to girls; also used in reference to cute persons or animals of either gender.

-*senpai*: A suffix used to address upperclassmen or more experienced coworkers.

PAGE 4

Shogi is a Japanese board game similar to chess. Caleb is likening the entire war to a game manipulated by the true powers of the world.

PAGE 52

The **"exclusivity rights"** discussed by Caleb and Butler are essentially zoning, labor, and trade permits granted by the occupying military that give their holder priority when it comes to business in the area. The exchange of these rights for cash amounts to unofficially state-sponsored corruption. Caleb's goal is to acquire the rights and, in doing so, cut out the middlemen and eliminate the outsourcing of labor that Miguel explained in Volume 2.

PAGE 74

The name of Claudia's restaurant, **Kuroimo**, literally means "black potato."

PAGE 123

Ancient Chinese legend tells of a **koi** that, after swimming against the current of the Yellow River, reached a waterfall. It then swam its way up the waterfall and, upon reaching the top, was transformed into a dragon by the gods in recognition of its perseverance and determination. Lee likens the upstart Caleb to that legendary koi and himself to a natural-born dragon.

ROSE GUNS DAYS

ROSE GUNS DAYS SEASON 1 ③

RYUKISHI07
SOICHIRO

Translation: Caleb D. Cook

Lettering: Katie Blakeslee, Lys Blakeslee

ROSE GUNS DAYS Season 1 vol. 3
© RYUKISHI07 / 07th Expansion
© 2013 Soichiro / SQUARE ENIX CO., LTD.
First published in Japan in 2013 by SQUARE ENIX CO., LTD.
English translation rights arranged with SQUARE ENIX CO., LTD.
and Hachette Book Group through Tuttle-Mori Agency, Inc.

Translation © 2016 by SQUARE ENIX CO., LTD.

Yen Press
Hachette Book Group
1290 Avenue of the Americas
New York, NY 10104

www.hachettebookgroup.com
www.yenpress.com

Yen Press is an imprint of Hachette Book Group, Inc.
The Yen Press name and logo are trademarks of Hachette Book Group, Inc.

The publisher is not responsible for websites (or their content)
that are not owned by the publisher.

Library of Congress Control Number: 2015956854

First Yen Press Edition: March 2016

ISBN: 978-0-316-39151-1

10 9 8 7 6 5 4 3 2 1

BVG

Printed in the United States of America